The Psychoanalytic Study
of the Child

VOLUME XII

The Psychoanalytic Study

of the Child

VOLUME XII

INTERNATIONAL UNIVERSITIES PRESS, INC.
New York   New York

CONTENTS

Applied Psychoanalysis

Volume XIII of The Psychoanalytic Study of the Child, to be published November, 1958, will be dedicated to the memory of Ernst Kris, one of the founders of this annual publication.

The Editors

ERNST KRIS
(1900-1957)

Ernst Kris died at the age of fifty-six of a coronary thrombosis on February 27, 1957. He had recovered from an earlier attack seven years before to an extent that allowed him fully to resume the broad spectrum of his activities. Neither the vigor, the intensity of his work nor the enjoyment it gave him seemed significantly impaired and one could hope that this extraordinary capacity for creativeness and active participation in a great variety of interests and plans for the future were a reflection also of his state of health. When death occurred, it was sudden and came unexpected. Thinking of him, there is comfort in knowing that death came to him in this way; but it was cruel to his family and his friends.

Ernst Kris was a man of wide and genuine interests, far beyond the limits of his chosen field. In his contacts with people he was intensely alive, brilliantly imaginative and intuitive, and responded with rare subtlety and understanding to individual nuances in the people he met. Even those who knew nothing of his work recognized in him the distinct and strong personality. His talk was as interesting as his writing, and though he was certainly one of our best public speakers, one may well say that he was even more creative in talking to small groups. Thus conversations with Ernst Kris belong to our dearest memories. He was a kind and generous person, always gracious in social contacts of any kind. Still, his judgment on people and their work could be severe: he was intolerant of and impatient with cheapness. His ready enthusiasm was counterbalanced by a highly developed critical capacity. But you all know that Ernst Kris was an extremely complex human being, and even after many years of close contact with him, one could still be surprised by a new and admirable finesse or elegance of his feeling or thought.

In speaking to you today, it cannot be my purpose to give you a detailed and coherent picture of the man Ernst Kris was—nor of his work. His position in the history of psychoanalytic thought certainly calls for such evaluation, and will no doubt obtain it. My present and far more limited task is to evoke for you, many of whom were familiar with him, some significant features of his thinking and of his way as a scientist.

Ernst Kris was an important figure in the history of art long before he turned to analysis. The acuteness of his mind and thorough knowledge in a great many fields had attracted the attention of teachers of the University of Vienna at a time when he was still in high school. The precocity of his intellectual maturity and achievements fortunately proved, in his case, no handicap to further development; it just meant starting out on a higher plane than is given to most men, and led to natural and uninterrupted growth till the end. The work he did not long before his untimely death still pointed to new reaches of investigation, beyond his earlier achievements. Of the books and papers of his younger years, his preanalytic work, I am, of course, not a competent judge. But I know that they are held in high esteem and greatly admired by those who are. Two things are immediately apparent: the broad range of his interests, and that here speaks a thinker in his own right and a man backed by tremendous scholarship and fully at home in the problems and methods of the humanities. And, then, some basic traits of his, which were to develop fully after his contact with analysis, are already discernible in the early work: the abundance of suggestive ideas, his unfailing acuteness of mind, deep curiosity, tenacity of purpose, and beyond this, a very personal style of thought and expression, hard to describe but easy to recognize. Even then he was already what we all knew him to be at a later period in his life: a teacher who fascinated his audiences.

After having become a psychoanalyst and a member of the Psychoanalytic Society of Vienna in 1928, Ernst Kris still continued for some time to publish papers on art in line with his earlier historical interests and also retained till he left Vienna ten years later his position at the Kunsthistorisches Museum. The extensive studies of those years included also the attendance of some medical courses. But besides these activities which in themselves would have been sufficient to occupy the mind of a lesser man, there starts in the beginning of the thirties something strikingly new in his development—something new also, I think, in the history of analysis. I am speaking of papers like "A Psychotic Sculptor of the Eighteenth Century," "The Psychology of Caricature," "A Psychological Study of the Role of Tradition in Ancient Biographies," "Ego Development and the Comic," "Laughter as an Expressive Process," and others, all written around that time. With these works Ernst Kris had come into his own. One senses that, brilliant as the first fruits of his scientfic interests had been, there was something in him that could not be fully satisfied by the conventional methods of dealing with art and its history, and that it was analysis that released in him the ardent desire and the capacity to try a new approach. He who knew Ernst Kris before his encounter with analysis and after realizes that only in this field the rare and complex combination of his gifts could come to full fruition. The fact that in these papers and those that followed he could speak with the authority of an expert and with the sure judgment that his comprehensive professional education as an art historian had given him, is one reason why they represent something novel also in the development of applied psychoanalysis. And then, Ernst Kris was also the first to gear it to the new ideas in analytic psychology which were, at the time, in the making. These papers set a new standard for so-called applied analysis, too, because they were the expression of a highly complex, multidimensional thinking, and also more fastidious as to scentfic methodology than much previous work in this chapter of analysis had been. Their influence on psychoanalytic thinking and literature was and is considerable.

The interest in and writing on problems of art has remained one of the main trends in Kris's work, sometimes broken, but only temporarily, never interrupted in its essential lines. Five years ago he published his *Psychoanalytic Explorations in Art,* which is one of the truly important psychoanalytic works of our time and has a secure place in the history of analysis. In this book we find a series of his earlier papers, but it is interesting—because it is significant of his style of work—to note what changes some of them (especially those in the first part of the work) have undergone in this publication. His early psychoanalytic articles were written in a period of marked changes in psychoanalytic theory; Freud's reformulation of ego psychology, published not long before and difficult to assimilate for many, came naturally to Kris's way of thinking. Kris's whole work is safely grounded in a thorough assimilation of these theories— though there was, of course, in his case no fixation on just one phase of Freud's findings and ideas. But he recognized that in this approach lay rich and still unexhausted possibilities for an under- standing of the problems which were upmost in his mind; on the other hand, he was continuously on the outlook for contributions which the study of art and of creative processes could make toward a fruitful development of pyschoanalytic psychology. Thus every progress in the gradual unfolding of both clinical and theoretical insight in analysis is clearly reflected in the development of his work—which then, conversely, became an essential factor in this unfolding process.

In much of Ernst Kris's essays, a close integration of fact with hypothesis, a fruitful balance between individual observation and theoretical thinking is evident. In developing a theory, he tried, wherever feasible, to keep explicitly or implicitly clinical observa- tion in mind; and, on the other side, he did not use clinical material unless to make a point, test a guess, develop or verify a hypothesis. This approach has, in analysis, a noble ancestry; it goes back directly to Freud. Freud's style of thinking was familiar to Ernst Kris, not only through his writings. It is obvious that for a man of Kris's ready receptivity the personal contact with Freud must have been a de- cisive factor in his development. He was close to Freud both as an analyst and as a scholarly connoisseur of art and, of course, also through his marriage to Marianne Rie whose family had for a long time been associated with Freud and his family. This association was continued in London after both Freud and Kris had emigrated there. It was also Freud who made Ernst Kris an editor of *Imago* and thus introduced him to another field in which he proved his easy skill, as he later did as editor of *The Psychoanalytic Study of the Child*.

At the beginning of the last war, first in London and then in this country, he turned to the study of mass communication, working in close contact with the B.B.C. and other Government agencies in London, in Canada, and here. As a result of this he wrote, together with H. Speier, a detailed and impressive volume on *German Radio Propaganda* in 1944. Some papers on related topics written in the same years show, despite the changed subject matter and perspective, an amazing continuity in his endeavor to secure a conceptual framework which would best allow to bring psychoanalytic insight to bear on neighboring disciplines.

The following years show even more clearly his interest in the basic conceptual tools of analysis. There are a number of papers on "pure" theory and also on methodology. They were to give the reliable tools he later needed in his last venture: psychoanalytic child psychology. In the same years Kris also became an instructor at this Institute. Again, it was like the release of a long dammed-up life spring. I can say without overstatement that among the very many teachers of psychoanalysis in many countries I know, he had very few rivals. I may remind you, too, in this connection of his sometimes extraordinary discussions in this Society: they were, indeed, often contributions to a postgraduate training.

During the last years of his life, during the time of his activity at the Yale Child Study Center, the focus of his writings moved to psychoanalytic child psychology. Not that papers on other aspects of analysis are lacking in this period: as was his wont, he concurrently worked at other problems too—I have only to mention his enthusiastic interest in technical problems, also in problems of memory (see, e.g., "On Some Vicissitudes of Insight in Psychoanalysis" [1956], and "The Recovery of Childhood Memories in Psychoanalysis" [1956]), and in the history of psychoanalysis. His introduction to Freud's letters to W. Fliess deserves a particular mention too, because this is one of the most lucid essays on the prehistory of analysis. Still, his interest in the direct observation of children, in the formulation of expectations and their checking in individual cases, in the potentialities of analysis in interpreting his material was clearly in the ascendancy. The publication of *The Psychoanalytic Study of the Child,* in which many of his essays were printed, was an idea of Ernst Kris. At the Child Study Center he inspired a group of younger people who will, one hopes, continue his work. Among his articles on child psychology written during that period are those on "Psychoanalytic Child Psychology" (1950), on "Early Autoerotic Activities" (1951), on "Variations of Early

Parental Attitudes" (1953, written with Coleman and Provence), and some others—up to the last one which he had to leave unfinished. Looking back on the history of his thinking, we may state: the fact that Ernst Kris became more and more impressed by the potentialities for psychoanalytic psychology of direct child observation and in his later years turned to this field of investigation, is a natural outcome of the work of a lifetime; this turn is a necessary step also in the development of psychoanalysis in general, which is so clearly reflected in his work.

I have tried to present to you—and I am aware how little justice my presentation could do to it—some trends in the development of his scientific work. One might also try to speak of what were the constant elements which dominated his personal style of scientific thinking. Having shared much with Ernst Kris, in our life and work, in common scientific work often together with R. Loewenstein, and, through many years, in never long-interrupted discussions of psychoanalysis and of many other fields of common interest, the picture in my mind of his thinking is vivid and detailed. Here, I regret, I cannot give you more than a dry and summarizing sketch of what was a very much alive and impressive experience.

Though his knowledge and interests went far beyond the limits of our profession—as Freud wished it to be in the analyst—it was, with the exception of his first years as a historian of art, psychoanalytic thinking that provided the models for his approach whatever the field he dealt with, and in which the comprehensive and beautiful Gestalt of his intellectual world was safely anchored. His identification with it was total; and it was precisely the strong and secure feeling of this possession that allowed him a considerable degree of flexibility in developing it freely. His knowledge of psychoanalytic literature was, of course, comprehensive; but he also understood the implications of the work of Freud and others that had not yet been explicitly stated, that is those which are still beyond universally accessible knowledge—and this is a much rarer quality and equally important. Thus he acquired a sure judgment of what is compatible with the main body of analytic thinking and what is not; and which are the fruitful avenues and what are dead ends in psychoanalytic theorizing. He had, then, fully explored the potentialities of the analytic method. Also, he realized its limitations, as is particularly clear in his work on aesthetics.

There was something unusual in the forceful and precise way in which he delineated problems. His grasp of new ideas brought to his attention was immediate and his reaction to them always elucidating. In wrestling with a problem he never failed to be aware of its many facets—he did not fall prey to simplifications that sacrifice the whole to a detail, however suggestive or appealing. That is, he had the integrating strength to keep all the levels of a problem in mind, and was able to pass, whenever necessary, with ease and elegance from one level of abstraction to another. He was very observant and conscientious in the rendering of clinical details; and the gift of acute clinical perception was paired with an equal finesse in verbalizing his observations. While his verbal facility might have been even greater in talk than in writing, the felicitous expression was equally frequent in both. In the step from the observational data to theory, he did not lack freedom and courage of imagination. There was also scientific conscience and discipline to keep it in check. A great seriousness and much deliberate and repetitive working through went into his theoretical thinking—of which, however, in its final formulation no trace of heaviness was left.

The words of praise and of reminiscence are also words of parting and of mourning. His written work will survive and, in his colleagues and his students, the stimulating power of his thought and his personality. But nobody will fill the very distinct and very individual place in analysis he has left. And, beyond this, it is also true of him that it is in his most personal relationships that a man is most strictly speaking irreplaceable.

HEINZ HARTMANN, M.D. (New York)*

* Read at the Meeting of the New York Psychoanalytic Society on May 28, 1957.

CONTRIBUTIONS TO PSYCHOANALYTIC THEORY

THE NATURE AND DEVELOPMENT OF THE CONCEPT OF REPRESSION IN FREUD'S WRITINGS

CHARLES BRENNER, M.D. (New York)

The aim of the present paper is an exposition of Freud's concept of repression. Freud introduced the term "repression" at the very beginning of his psychoanalytic writings and from the start it was one of the fundamentals of psychoanalytic theory. There can be no doubt, therefore, of the importance of the topic and of the fact that it warrants careful study. In studying it, however, one must bear in mind that the concept of repression was not a static one that was first enunciated in final and finished form, but that it was rather one that changed and developed during the course of many years. These changes were the result of two mutually related factors: first, the availability of new data of observation which required extensions or modifications of the concept of repression, and second, changes in Freud's theories of mental functioning in general, theories of which the concept of repression formed a part and with the other elements of which it had to be consistent.

For the sake of convenience one may say that there were four principal stages at which Freud made important innovations in the concept of repression or significant additions to it: first, the stage of introduction of the concept, in 1894-1896; second, the period 1900-1906; third, the period 1911-1915; and fourth, the period 1923-1939. Accordingly the present paper has been divided into four sections which correspond approximately with these periods.

I

In any field of scientific endeavor new data may become available in either of two ways: by the application of existing methods of

investigation to new situations, whether the situations be ones of
experiment or observation, or by the development of new methods
of investigation. It was in the second of these ways that Freud
acquired the data on which he originally based the concept of repression (1895a). When he gave up the use of hypnosis as a means of
recapturing the unconscious pathogenic memories of his neurotic
patients and the affects which accompanied those memories, he first
substituted Bernheim's method of insisting that the patient remember what it was she claimed not to know, as, for example, when the
symptom in question had first appeared, what had happened at that
time that was painful or unpleasant, etc. This was the beginning of
the development of the psychoanalytic method as we know it today,
and crude as this beginning was by our present standards, it promptly
made something clear that had not been apparent as long as questioning under hypnosis had been the method of treatment: the
patients struggled against or *resisted* remembering the memories
which they were urged and commanded to reproduce. Freud himself
remarked that it was then a simple step to the assumption that these
memories had been actively put out of consciousness either when they
had occurred or soon afterward. In order to distinguish such active
suppression of a memory, usually a painful or distressing one, from
what was considered to be ordinary, unmotivated forgetting, Freud
proposed that it be called repression. Looking back on what he called
a simple step, one may, as a historian, take the liberty of disputing
Freud's modest characterization of this momentous hypothesis since
in fact it introduced into psychopathology the fundamental theoretical concept that *intrapsychic conflict* and its consequences were of
essential significance in the formation of neurotic symptoms.

Fresh data kept pouring in on Freud as he applied his new
method of investigation and treatment to more and more cases and
as he refined it by substituting for his initial insistence that the
patient remember, the various technical modifications that led to
what we call today the fundamental rule: that the patient relinquish
conscious control of his thoughts and say without exception and without reservation whatever may come to his mind.[1] Our major interest
at present, however, has to do not so much with technique as with
the consequences of its development and application. These yielded

[1] For the steps which led to this final technical formula, see Freud (1895a).

many new insights into the psychology of mental illness which are partly contained in the *Studies on Hysteria* (1895a) and partly in the "Further Remarks on the Defence Neuro-Psychoses" (1896). These new insights and formulations necessitated further additions to the concept of repression as well as restrictions and refinements of it.

Thus, for example, Freud's new data indicated that in the defense neuropsychoses (hysteria, certain phobias, obsessional neurosis, and some paranoias) the pathogenic, repressed memories of adult life, which were, to be sure, the immediate precursors and precipitating causes of the neurotic symptoms, regularly led back to still earlier experiences whose memory and painful affect had also been repressed, and eventually to one or more sexual experiences in childhood before the age of eight or ten years. Freud consequently altered his theory of the pathogenesis of these conditions and developed the familiar formula that apart from the important though unknown constitutional factors the basically pathogenic or predisposing factor for hysteria was a sexual experience in childhood in which the patient was the passive participant, while the analogous factor for obsessional neurosis was a similar experience in which the patient had taken the active role. This led Freud to postulate a specific precondition for repression which, as we shall see, later furnished the basis for the concept of primal repression: " 'Repression' of the memory of a distressing sexual experience of more mature years can be accomplished only in those persons in whom this experience can activate the memory trace of a childhood trauma." In addition it had become clear to Freud that repression was not necessarily, indeed not usually, a consciously initiated process so that he referred to it, in parentheses, as "the psychic mechanism of (unconscious) defense" or warding off (1896).

Still another consequence for the concept of repression of the newly discovered connection between the sexual life of childhood and the neurotic symptoms of adult life was a qualification of the idea that only the memories of painful or distressing events were repressed. This was still true of the events of mature years that were repressed, but clearly the sexual experiences of childhood which were repressed had been pleasurable *at the time when they had occurred*. It was only *later* that they had aroused the distressing emotions of guilt, shame, or disgust.

A final consequence of Freud's new knowledge for the concept of repression was the development of the two ideas of a return of the repressed from repression and of certain psychoneurotic symptoms as compromises between the previously repressed memory or memories on the one hand and the repressing forces of the personality on the other. At the time he wrote the 1896 paper Freud considered these ideas to be valid for obsessional neurosis, but he did not yet apply them to hysteria. The pathogenesis of hysterical symptoms was still formulated somewhat differently, as one can see from the following summary of Freud's views on the pathogenesis of the two neuroses.

In the case of obsessional neurosis he believed that there were the following, typical stages or periods: (1) the period of childish immorality, i.e., pleasurable, sexual seduction of another child or children; (2) with sexual maturity, the stage of what he called the primary defense symptom, e.g., guilt or shame resulting from self-reproaches for the sexual behavior of the first period; (3) the period of successful defense, during which the memories of the first and second periods remained unconscious and without any disturbing effect on the individual's psychic functioning; (4) the period of the return of the repressed memories, i.e., failure of defense, which constituted the illness proper, since *"obsessional ideas* are invariably *reproaches* which are transformed and are returning from *repression* and which have always to do with a *sexual* act from *childhood* which was carried out with pleasure" (italics in original).

It was in the same paper (1896) that Freud maintained that obsessional ideas and affects are compromise formations between what was returning from repression and the repressing forces of the mind. The latter forces "we propose to ascribe to the 'ego.'" In this connection we must be careful to remember that the word "ego" as Freud used it in 1896 came much closer to what we should today refer to as the conscious self than it did to the meaning which it eventually assumed in 1923 with the formulation of the structural hypothesis of the psychic apparatus.

In the case of hysteria Freud (1895a) believed that "hysteria arises as a result of the repression of an intolerable idea; that the repression is intended as a defense; that the repressed idea continues to exist as a weak (less intense) memory trace; and that the affect which has

been detached from the repressed idea is used for somatic innervation, a process called conversion of psychic excitation. We consequently believe that it is due to repression that the idea becomes the
cause of symptoms of illness, in other words, becomes pathogenic."
In another place in the same work Freud expressed the formulation
that the process or mechanism of conversion deprived the intolerable
idea (memory) of so much affect charge that the idea became weak
and could therefore be readily repressed. Here and in the paper of
1894 were the beginnings of the concept of psychic energy and its
economy which later became such a characteristic and essential part
of psychoanalytic theory and which were brought into particularly
close connection with the formulation of the theory of instincts. It
may be added parenthetically that Freud soon (1900) revised his
theories of the mechanism of hysterical symptom formation to include the concepts of compromise formation and of the return of the
repressed. The formulation just given appears to be a relic of the
hypnotic period that survived that era by a few years.

One may summarize Freud's views on repression during this first
stage (1894-1896) about as follows. He defined repression as the active
suppression of a memory and at first considered it to be a conscious,
voluntary act, though he soon recognized that it took place unconsciously rather than consciously. Memories which were repressed in
adult life were invariably painful ones, but the process of repression
in adult life was only possible in individuals who had had a sexual
experience in childhood, an experience which, though pleasurable
at the time it occurred, had been later considered bad or shameful
and whose memory had consequently been repressed. Repression was
a pathological mental process which was characteristic of the so-called
defense neuropsychoses. In particular, obsessional symptoms were
compromise formations and represented a return of the repressed
from repression.

II

Between the time of writing the second paper on the defense
neuropsychoses (1896) and the paper on the role of sexuality in the
etiology of the neuroses (1906), Freud was confronted by new data
which caused a revolution in his scientific theories. It was inevitable
that this swift development and rapid change in Freud's understand-

ing of psychic processes in general should bring with its changes in the concept of repression as well.

The new data referred to came from two sources: further psychoanalytic work with neurotic patients and Freud's self-analysis. The former made clear to Freud that what he had believed to be repressed memories of sexual experiences in childhood were often the repressed memories of sexual fantasies instead. This, together with what he had learned of his own psychosexual development by self-analysis, led him to the conclusion that sexual desires were a normal and regular feature of psychic life from early childhood on, rather than being unusual and per se pathogenic if they occurred before the age of eight years, as he had previously believed to be the case. These views were finally formulated in the famous monograph, *Three Essays on Sexuality* (1905), and were made the basis of the psychoanalytic theory of the instinctual drives which was first proposed in that work. Before its publication, however, Freud was occupied with three other books (1900, 1901, 1905a) which had as one of their principal aims a demonstration of the fact that the psychic functioning which was responsible for hysterical and obsessional symptoms in mentally ill patients differed relatively little from the psychic functioning responsible for various normal phenomena in healthy persons: dreams, jokes, and the slips and errors of everyday life.

As part of this momentous addition to psychoanalytic theory there was a corresponding revision in the concept of repression. Repression was no longer considered to be a pathological response in adult life on the part of an individual who had been predisposed by a childhood sexual experience, the memory of which was active though unconscious. On the contrary, repression was now recognized to be as much a part of the psychic functioning of persons who were normal as it was of those who were neurotic. Thus, for example, in the book on wit (1905a) we find the view expressed that repression occurred in healthy as well as in neurotic persons; that it was largely the result of cultural influences, though perhaps constitutionally prepared for;[2] and that one of its consequences was that what were once sources of

[2] It may be explained that the idea of a constitutional factor in repression was a reference to the phenomenon of latency which was assumed to be constitutionally determined (cf. p. 15).

pleasure to us, that is in early childhood, ceased to be pleasurable in later life.

In fact in the *Three Essays* (1905) and in the paper entitled "My Views on the Part Played by Sexuality in the Aetiology of the Neuroses" (1906) Freud emphasized the role played by repression in determining whether an individual would eventually become either normal, perverse, or neurotic. In other words, repression was now not only considered nonpathological, it was considered to be a decisive factor in determining or establishing normality. His formulation was that normal sexual function in adult life resulted from the repression of certain infantile components with organization of the remaining ones under the primacy of the genitals; that perverse sexual function resulted from an excessive development of a particular infantile component that should have been repressed; and that a neurosis resulted from the excessive repression of libidinal strivings. Here is the first statement of the proposition that is so familiar to us today, that the differences between the normal and the neurotic are differences of degree rather than of kind.

The formulation of the theory of the instinctual drives had its influence on the concept of repression in another way also. Previously the idea had been that repression was directed against the memories of certain experiences—sexual ones, as it turned out. Subsequently the formula was that repression was directed chiefly against the psychic manifestations of the sexual or libidinal instinctual drive, that is, against the sexual drive derivatives, as they would be called today.

On the basis of his recognition of the similarities between normal and neurotic psychic functioning Freud ventured to formulate some general theories on the subject. The first published version of these theories was contained in the Seventh Chapter of *The Interpretation of Dreams* (1900). As we now know, he had made at least one earlier attempt which he had abandoned as unsatisfactory (1895b).

The hypotheses concerning psychic functioning which Freud advanced in 1900 were not finished, definite, polished theoretical statements. As he himself emphasized, they were on the contrary preliminary and tentative, with many details left either vague or wholly undecided. Much that was then put forward retained its importance in Freud's theoretical ideas throughout his life, but much else was discarded or was considered less important than had first been thought to be the case. Conversely, Chapter VII contains the germs of nearly all of Freud's important theories, even ones that were not fully developed until fifteen or twenty years later. To summarize this chapter is therefore hardly feasible. It really requires a commentary, not a summary. For the present purpose it must suffice merely to mention the important theoretical concepts of the chapter which are pertinent to the topic of repression. These are (1) the concept of a psychic apparatus composed of functionally separable systems, called respectively the unconscious (ucs.), preconscious (pcs.), and conscious (cs.), or perceptual-conscious (pcpt.-cs.); (2) the concepts of psychic energy and cathexis; (3) the concepts of the primary and secondary processes of mental functioning, of which the former was characteristic of the system unconscious, while the latter was characteristic of the systems preconscious and conscious; and (4) the pleasure principle.

Within the framework of these theoretical concepts Freud gave the following account of repression in Chapter VII, an account which he explicitly characterized as cursory and incomplete. He spoke first about the repression of infantile experiences, a phenomenon which he later (1911) called "primal repression." The experiences in question, he said, preceded the development of the system preconscious (pcs.). This was in accordance with two elements of his current theories of psychic functioning: first, that the primary process was the mode of psychic functioning which was characteristic of the system unconscious (ucs.) and was limited to it, while the secondary process was similarly identified with the system preconscious (pcs.), and second, that "primary processes are present in the apparatus from the beginning, while the secondary processes only take shape gradually during the course of life." He went on to say of primal repression that when the system pcs. developed, its aims[3] were at variance with those of some of the infantile wishes and their associated memories of gratification, so that the activation of those wishes and memories, once pleasurable, would now produce unpleasure. (He remarked in passing that this transformation of the affective reaction connected with a wish or memory from pleasurable to unpleasurable formed

---

[3] This term meant approximately the moral and behavioral standards of the conscious part of the personality in later childhood and in adult life.

the essence of repression.) Hence, Freud continued, in accordance with the pleasure principle, the pcs. turned away from such wishes and memories. He conceived that in this way there resulted a store of infantile memories and wishes which never had been and never would be accessible to the system pcs. and which constituted the infantile core of what he later called "the repressed." This formulation was in accord with Freud's experience that infantile memories and wishes were not recoverable or rememberable as such in later years and that their existence had to be *inferred* from their effects on mental life, notably in dreams and in neurotic symptoms.

Moreover, this store of inaccessible memories was considered to be the precondition of all later instances of repression, inasmuch as the pleasure principle also required that the system pcs. turn away from any later preconscious derivatives of such infantile memories. The barring from consciousness of such preconscious derivatives Freud later called repression proper. He explained it, in accordance with the theories of mental functioning which he had in 1900, as consisting in the withdrawal of cathexis from these derivatives by the system pcs. Since the derivatives no longer had a preconscious cathexis, they were no longer part of or accessible to the system pcs., but were instead relegated to the system ucs.

To continue our summary of Freud's exposition of repression in Chapter VII, in the later course of events the repressions we have described might remain stable (successful repressions). However, if the unconscious, repressed wishes were reinforced organically (presumably Freud here referred to such phenomena as those accompanying puberty) and if they transmitted this reinforcement or increase of cathexis, as we might say now, to their derivatives, the latter would press for discharge despite the fact that they had been decathected by the pcs. There would then ensue a defensive struggle: the pcs. would intensify its way of opposing the repressed ideas, i.e., its countercathexes, which it had previously erected, but eventually the repressed ideas would force their way through to consciousness in some way or other either as those compromise formations called symptoms or as dreams, jokes, or slips. Freud added that the theory of neuroses maintained that it was only *sexual* impulses which could thus give rise to *neurotic symptoms*.

On reading Freud's exposition of his views on repression in 1900 one is impressed by their close approximation in most important respects to our present views on intrapsychic conflict and symptom formation. That Freud was able to divine so much so quickly about the functioning of the mind is one measure of his genius. It is impossible not to experience some feeling of awe at the sight of such giant strides being made by a man with little more than a decade of experience in psychoanalytic practice, without the benefit of a personal analysis except for the analysis of his own dreams, and with none to lead him or even to advise, with no footsteps to follow save his own. If this is not a unique incident in the history of science, it is at least an extraordinary one.

If one puts aside for the moment such feelings of admiration and awe and turns instead to a more prosaic, historical appraisal of the differences between Freud's views on repression in 1900 and those which he formulated later, one sees that in 1900 he attributed the repression of infantile sexual wishes and memories to certain maturational sequences in the development of psychic functioning (secondary process and the system pcs.) rather than attributing it to intrapsychic conflict, which he had already recognized as the basis, or at least as an inevitable part of later repression. As will be seen, Freud continued to believe that infantile repression was different in cause and mechanism from all later repressions for many years (see pp. 31-32); he did so, indeed, until the publication of *The Problem of Anxiety* (1926) and of the *New Introductory Lectures* (1932) (see p. 42 below).

We see therefore that until 1926 Freud supported the view that infantile repression occurred independently of experiential factors. For convenience's sake it seems appropriate at this point to mention other nonexperiential factors which Freud believed to be significant in repression, even though this will involve some slight departure from the chronological sequence of our exposition. Freud generally referred to the factors in question by the term "organic" (1905b, 1909b, 1925, 1930, 1933). The meaning of "organic" in this context was essentially that of "constitutional" or "hereditary," as is indicated by the following quotation concerning the development of shame, disgust, and aesthetic and moral ideals during the latency period (Freud, 1905b): ". . . this development is organically determined and fixed by heredity, and [though education has much to do with it] it can occasionally occur quite independently of educational influences."

In "A Case of Obsessional Neurosis" (1909b) Freud referred to a specific instance of "organic" repression, the repression of the sense of smell: ". . . the atrophy of the sense of smell, which was the inevitable result of man's assumption of an erect posture, and the consequent organic repression of his pleasure in smell. . . ." The most extensive elaboration of this particular idea is to be found in two long footnotes to Section IV of *Civilization and Its Discontents* (1930), where Freud advanced a fascinating speculation concerning the consequences for man's sexual life of his "organically" determined loss of pleasure in certain smells and his increased dependence on visual stimuli for sexual excitation. Similarly in his letter to Einstein Freud (1933) made reference to "organic reasons for the changes that have taken place in our ethical and esthetic ideals."

However, it must be noted that in his later writings Freud was cautious about the hypothesis of "organic" repression. Thus he concluded the second of the two footnotes referred to above (1930) with the warning that such ideas were still unconfirmed and might require revision since, for example, some inhabitants of Central Europe still used the odor of genital secretions as aphrodisiacs, i.e., still got conscious pleasure from such odors, a fact which would appear to contradict the hypothesis of "organic" repression, according to which man was constitutionally displeased or repelled by such odors in adult life rather than pleased and attracted by them. Similarly in a footnote to his *Autobiography* (1925) which was dated 1935 Freud qualified his previously held view concerning the role of constitutional factors in latency as follows: "The period of latency is a physiological phenomenon. It can, however, only give rise to a complete interruption of sexual life in cultural organizations which have made the suppression of infantile sexuality a part of their system. This is not the case with the majority of primitive peoples."

One more organic factor should be mentioned which Freud conceived to be important in the phenomenon of latency, although this is a factor which is only indirectly involved in repression. According to Freud (1905b), changes in the size and activity of the endocrine glands were responsible for the fact that the strength of the erotic drive was less during the latency period (six to twelve years) than during the preceding oedipal phase (two to five years) or during puberty (after twelve years). Thus he felt that the repressing forces of the personality had an easier task in subduing erotic drive derivatives in latency and were more successful in doing so.

The contributions to the theory of repression of this second period (1900-1906) may be briefly summarized as follows. First, the recognition that repression occurred in normal as well as in neurotic individuals. Second, the hypothesis that infantile repression was caused by sequences in the maturation of the psychic apparatus and that it was the precondition of later repression. Third, the hypothesis of organic factors in repression.

III

Incomplete though it was, the discussion of repression in the Seventh Chapter of *The Interpretation of Dreams* (1900) remained the most thorough exposition of the subject for more than a decade. It was not superseded until the publication of the Schreber case (1911) and of the two papers entitled "Repression" (1915a) and "The Unconscious" (1915b). Before proceeding to a consideration of these papers, however, it seems appropriate to glance at a few notions on the subject which were presented in a less systematic form in earlier papers. In "My Views on the Part Played by Sexuality in the Aetiology of the Neuroses" (1906), Freud noted parenthetically that he had begun to use the word "repression" to refer to the concept which he had previously called "defense." For a further discussion of the relation between the meanings of these two words as Freud used them, see below, p. 32 and pp. 35-36.

In the beautiful monograph entitled "Dream and Delusion in W. Jensen's 'Gradiva'" (1907), Freud also made some pertinent remarks concerning repression. In discussing the phenomenon of return of the repressed, he remarked that "the very means that were used to accomplish repression become the vehicle for its return." In the case in point the hero's childhood sexual attachment to a playmate had been sublimated in his interest in archeological relics, an interest which became resexualized in adult life when his neurosis broke out.

Later in the same monograph Freud says, ". . . 'repression' is a dynamic term that takes account of the interplay of forces in the psyche and that makes a twofold assertion: first, that there is an active tendency to express all psychic effects, including the effect of becoming conscious; second, that there is also a counter-force, a resistance, which can hinder a part of these psychic effects, again including becoming conscious. The hallmark of the repressed is precisely that it cannot become conscious despite its intensity," that is, despite its direct and indirect influence on thoughts, feelings, and behavior, among which would be included both dreams and neurotic symptoms. The explicit emphasis in this formulation on the tendency of psychic phenomena to press toward discharge and consciousness unless hindered by a repressive counterforce is a familiar part of all subsequent psychoanalytic thinking and is related to the theory of the instinctual drives which Freud had proposed in 1905.

In the Schreber case (1911) the difference between infantile and later repression, about which we have already remarked several times, was still further elaborated. The former was now considered to deserve a special name: primal repression, as opposed to the repression of later years, which was now called repression proper. As elaborated in the two metapsychological papers, "Repression" (1915a) and "The Unconscious" (1915b), primal repression was, if not synonymous with fixation, intimately connected with it and directly responsible for it. In primal repression the psychic representative of a drive or infantile wish was supposed to be barred from the system pcs. by the establishment of a countercathexis without ever having been cathected by the system pcs. in the first place (see pp. 26-27). Freud in 1915 retained the idea that such repressed constituents of the psychic life of infancy were a necessary precondition for all later repression. In the papers now under consideration he referred to this idea by speaking of the attraction which the repressed exerted on preconscious and conscious elements. Thus his formulation in these papers was that repression proper (later repression) was a process which was due in part to the fact that the system pcs. actively decathected certain elements and pushed them out (Nachdrängen) of the pcs. into the ucs. for moral and similar reasons, and in part to the fact that these elements were dragged down into the ucs. from the pcs. by the attractive power of the repressed.

Indeed, although there was no clear statement to this effect, the reader of these papers has the impression that at least in some cases the attraction exerted by the repressed might be the more important factor.

If one leaves the subject of primal repression and turns to the subject of repression in general, one may say that in 1915 as in 1900 Freud considered that repression could most easily be formulated as the withdrawal or withholding of cathexis from a psychic element. In his various discussions of the process in 1915 he was particularly interested in the *mechanisms* by which this was accomplished and in its *consequences* as observed in subsequent psychic functioning. He made it explicit that he considered both the consequences and the mechanisms to be different in normal and in neurotic individuals, but in his discussion of these topics he paid considerably more attention to their neurotic than to their normal manifestations. One may presume that this was for two reasons: first, that pathological cases were more familiar (better studied); and second, that they were of greater practical importance to him and to his colleagues in their analytic work. Thus more than half of the paper on repression (1915a) and a similar proportion of the section on repression in the paper on the unconscious (1915b) are concerned with a consideration of repression, substitute formation, and symptom formation in the transference neuroses: anxiety hysteria, conversion hysteria, and obsessional neurosis. In reading these discussions one may be misled into thinking that Freud wished to apply the term "repression" to the entire defensive struggle that leads to symptom formation unless one is careful to bear in mind his statement (1915a) that "it is not repression itself that produces substitute formations and symptoms, but that these phenomena are indications of a *return of the repressed* and arise from processes quite different from that of repression."

As to the consequences of repression itself, as distinguished from those of the return of the repressed (failure of repression), it "has as its consequence not only the barring [of a drive derivative] from consciousness, but also the prevention of the development of affect and of the initiation of (voluntary) muscular activity" which would be associated with the drive discharge in question (1915b). As Freud pointed out, this is a great deal, enough to give us considerable respect for the value of repression. All of these consequences of repression Freud explained by the hypothesis that the system cs.-pcs. normally controlled not only access to consciousness but also the development of affect, and the activity of the skeletal musculature. Since in repression preconscious cathexis was withdrawn or withheld, what had been repressed could not become conscious, could not give rise to affect, and could not lead to voluntary muscular activity.

However, Freud emphasized (1915a) that repressed drive derivatives were not annihilated; it was only their relation to the system pcs. that was interfered with. They continued to exist in the system ucs. and to organize, that is, to form further derivatives and connections. Indeed, they might almost be said to "luxuriate in the darkness" of the unconscious for two reasons: first, that fantasy formation in the ucs. was unchecked by any influence of reality; and second, that repression prevented satisfaction or discharge of the repressed drive derivative. Moreover, Freud (1915a) reiterated what he had previously stated (1900), namely that derivatives of the repressed found their way into consciousness and into emotional life in a variety of ways which ranged all the way from such normal phenomena as jokes and dreams to neurotic symptoms.

To continue with the topic of the consequences of repression, Freud (1911, 1915b) also suggested that there was a difference between repression in the transference neuroses and in the psychoses. However, a statement of his views on this subject must be prefaced by a sentence of explanation concerning his theories at that time of the nature of preconscious and unconscious cathexes. His idea was that the *preconscious* cathexis of the psychic representative of an object or drive derivative was attached to its expression in *words;* in the system *ucs.* on the other hand it was the *nonverbal* representation of the object or drive derivative that was cathected.

What Freud suggested about repression in neurosis and in psychosis was that in the former it was the pcs. cathexis that was withdrawn from the psychic representative of the drive derivative, while in the latter both pcs. and ucs. cathexes were withdrawn. Thus in the neuroses it was the word representations that were decathected. In other words, in neuroses repression prevented the translation of the repressed elements into words, while the nonverbal or "thing" cathexes, that is, their cathexes by the system ucs., remained unaffected by repression. In the narcissistic neuroses (psychoses), on the other hand, Freud considered that the process of repression involved the decathexis of both word and thing representations, that is, the withdrawal of cathexis by both the system pcs. and the system ucs. Later on, in the phase of restitution which Freud described for the narcissistic neuroses, the word representations might be recathected, but the thing representations remained decathected. The end result would consequently be that in the narcissistic neuroses there would be an absence of ucs. cathexes (cathexes of thing representations) although the cs.-pcs. cathexes were present (cathexes of word representations), whereas in the transference neuroses there would be an absence of cs.-pcs. cathexes, while the ucs. cathexes were maintained.

As for the *mechanism* of repression as he conceived it in 1915, Freud pointed out that the variations in the strength of repression which were observable in such phenomena as dreams and jokes indicated that the mechanism of the process was one which permitted a continuous though variable pressure or counterforce to be exerted against the repressed elements which in their turn were conceived of as continually pressing toward conscious representation and satisfaction or discharge (see pp. 30-31). In other words, he conceived of repression as involving an equilibrium between the repressed and the repressing forces whose end point and stability were both variable. The repressed was kept at bay, as it were, by what he proposed to call countercathexes.

If repression was successful, the countercathexes ensured against the emergence of the repressed altogether, or at least against its emergence in any save the most distant or disguised derivatives. If repression was unsuccessful (return of the repressed), the countercathexes prevented or militated against the emergence of the repressed in undisguised form.

In his 1915 papers Freud gave but one example of countercathexis in successful repression. This was that in the stage of successful repression prior to the outbreak of clinical symptoms in an obsessional neurosis, the countercathexis against the repressed sadistic impulses was the reaction formation of kindness and gentleness. It should be noted that his concept at that time was *not* that reaction formation was evidence of a countercathexis, or a manifestation of a countercathexis, but rather that it *was* the countercathexis. The same idea had been mentioned a decade before in the Dora case (Freud, 1905c), near the end of the first section: ". . . repression is often achieved by means of an excessive reinforcement of the thought contrary to the one which is to be repressed." In that instance, to be sure, Freud was discussing hysteria rather than obsessional neurosis, but the thought concerning the mechanism of repression is clearly the same as that which he later elaborated.

As for unsuccessful repression, Freud stated that in anxiety hysteria it was the substitute formation (e.g., the wolf in the case of the Wolf Man, or the horse in the case of little Hans) that functioned as the countercathexis, while in conversion hysteria the countercathexis was the psychic activity which determined "on which part of the drive representative the whole cathexis of the drive should be concentrated." To conclude this exposition of Freud's ideas about countercathexis one may add that he made the suggestion that it was the energy of the withdrawn, preconscious cathexis that was used for the establishment and maintenance of the counter-cathexis. It may be of interest to note that it was in connection with this speculation that Freud introduced and defined the word "meta-psychology" in his published writings (see, however, Freud, 1895b, p. 157).

In view of the later development of his theories one may profit-ably ask at this point what Freud's ideas were in 1915 on the rela-tionship between repression and defense. Did he consider that the two were synonymous, as he implied in 1906, or, if he did not, what did he consider the relationship between the two to be?

In the paper entitled "Repression" (1915a) he said that repression was not "a defense mechanism that had been present from the beginning of life." On the contrary, as he had pointed out earlier (1900), a precondition for repression was that a part of the per-sonality had developed which reacted to a particular instinctual gratification with unpleasure, and indeed that this unpleasure was greater than the pleasure associated with the instinctual gratification in question. He went on to say that repression "cannot arise before a sharp differentiation has been established between conscious and unconscious psychic activity, and that *the essence of repression con-sists merely in a barring from consciousness.* This concept of repression would be supplemented by the assumption that before such a stage of psychic organization the task of defense against drive impulses is under the domination of the other instinctual vicissitudes such as changing into the opposite and turning against the self."

It is clear, therefore, that Freud in 1915 no longer considered "defense" and "repression" to be synonymous. On the contrary, repression was considered to be one among several instinctual vicissitudes which might serve the purposes of defense. However, it would seem fair to say that he considered it to be the defense *par excellence* once psychic development had reached the stage specified in the preceding paragraph. Thus reaction formation, which today we should list among the defense mechanisms along with repression, was then conceived of as the countercathexis in certain cases of repression (see pp. 34-35). Presumably the same would have been true of defensive projection or identification: the projection or identification would have been considered to be the means (i.e., the countercathexis) by which the drive derivative in question was kept repressed (1896).

However, although Freud, as we have just seen, considered that repression could not occur in the earliest stages of mental life, he nevertheless conceived of it as a characteristic of immaturity in psychic functioning. The more mature psychic apparatus could dispose of unwelcome or inappropriate instinctual demands by a process of judgmental repudiation *(Verurteilung)* (1915a): "Repression is a predecessor of repudiation, something intermediate between repudiation and flight." Such a formulation was necessitated by the facts of psychoanalytic therapy: when the patient in analysis became aware of wishes (drive derivatives) which he had dealt with in childhood by repression, he could as an adult deal with them by the mechanism of conscious repudiation without having to repress them.

IV

In the interval between the metapsychological papers of 1915 and the publication of *The Ego and the Id* (1923), in which the structural hypothesis of the psychic apparatus was proposed, Freud made two references to the topic of repression which are worth noting.

In the "Metapsychological Supplement to the Theory of Dreams" (1917) he attempted to distinguish among various normal and pathological psychic states on the basis, as he expressed it, of which part of the psychic apparatus was decathected by repression in each. "In the dream," he said, "the decathexis, which is the equivalent of a withdrawal of libido or interest, affects all of the psychic systems equally, in the transference neuroses it is the cathexis of the system pcs. which is withdrawn, in schizophrenia the cathexis of the system ucs., and in hallucinatory amentia the cathexis of the system cs." Like many other formulations of this period, this one was to be superseded by the structural hypothesis and its corrollaries.

In "A Child Is Being Beaten" (1919a) Freud went to some pains to refute ideas concerning repression which had been advanced by W. Fliess and Adler. He reiterated that repression was due to conflict between an unacceptable drive derivative on the one hand and the psychic representatives of the outer world on the other (in later terms, between the id on the one hand and ego and superego on the other), and that it was *not* due to a conflict between one set of drive derivatives and another, whether between masculine and feminine wishes, as Fliess had suggested, or between aggressive and passive ones, as Adler had proposed.

At the beginning of the third decade of this century Freud was led to reformulate his theory of the psychic apparatus into the form usually known as the structural hypothesis (1923). The previous theory, according to which the psychic apparatus was divided into the systems cs., pcs., and ucs. was replaced by a new theory which divided the psychic apparatus differently, that is, into ego, id, and superego. It is important to note that the three divisions of the apparatus in the new theory were not in any way identical with those in the old. The new divisions were either wholly or largely new theoretical concepts.

According to Freud this basic theoretical revision, which involved a regrouping of the psychic functions and a reappraisal of many aspects of their interrelationships, was urged upon him by a consideration of certain of the phenomena of repression. In turn the theoretical revision led to changes in the concept of repression itself.

In *The Ego and the Id* (1923) Freud pointed out the readily observable clinical fact that resistances against drive derivatives might themselves be quite unconscious in their operation and might require the expenditure of effort in order to become conscious to the patient. It will be remembered that it was the observation that an expenditure of effort was needed to make something conscious which first led Freud to formulate the concept of repression and which served as an indicator that a particular psychic element belonged to the system ucs. From this it would follow that at least in some cases both the repressed and the repressing mental trends must be attributed to the system ucs. On the other hand it had been clear even in 1900 that the repressing trends bore a more intimate relation to the system pcs. than did the repressed trends. It was clear that the old theory could not be kept unchanged, therefore, since it would not make sense to attribute the repressing trends both to the system ucs. and the system pcs. A new theory was accordingly proposed. This took as its point of departure the consequences for psychic function and development of the mutual interaction of the inner world of the drives on the one hand and of the external world of the senses on the other, instead of being based, as the old theory had been, on the contrast conscious-unconscious. The new theory readily explained the clinical facts: like the system pcs. the ego was the repressing agency and normally controlled access to consciousness, the initiation of muscular activity, and the development of affect. Unlike the system pcs., however, a part of the ego functions, as Freud said, "God knows how large a part," was unconscious in the sense previously attributed to the system ucs.

Such basic changes in the theory of the psychic apparatus, however, could not fail to require some changes in the concept of repression itself. The most immediate and best known of these changes concerned the relationship between repression and anxiety. Until 1926, when *The Problem of Anxiety* was published, it had been believed that in successful repression there was no question of *anxiety*, though there may have been *conflict*. In unsuccessful repression, that is, in return of the repressed as for example in a psychoneurosis, it was thought that the libido which could not be adequately discharged because of repression was converted into anxiety. Neurotic anxiety was thus sharply distinguished from real fear by its origin. The former was transformed libido, the latter was the consequence of the perception of danger. As is well known, Freud largely dispensed with this distinction in *The Problem of Anxiety* (1926). Instead he advanced the view which has since been generally accepted by analysts that anxiety is the predecessor and motive for repression rather than its consequence. In addition he asserted that anxiety might arise from the operation of the drives in either of two ways: because the psychic stimuli arising from the drives were too intense to be adequately mastered or discharged, in which case the economic factors in the situation created anxiety anew; or because the ego anticipated danger in connection with the wishes arising from the drives in question. The latter of these two types of anxiety he called signal anxiety. Like so-called "real fear," it resulted from the perception or anticipation of danger, so that the old distinction between real and neurotic fear was largely abolished.

The other major revision in the theory of repression that Freud proposed in 1926 lay in the reintroduction of the term "defense." Like the first revision, it stemmed from the same fundamental change in orientation that underlay the new structural hypothesis, that is, the substitution of the antithesis: outer world of the senses (ego-superego) vs. inner world of the drives (id) for the old contrast between conscious and unconscious. Prior to the formulation of the structural hypothesis the contrast between conscious and unconscious had been, as it were, *the* guiding beacon to Freud in his attempts to explore the dark, unknown reaches of the mind and his various theoretical concepts had tended to be oriented toward this guide in one way or another. This was conspicuously true of his theory of the psychic apparatus and it was true as well for his views on the struggle against the instinctual drives, at least after the development of the system pcs. (see p. 35). Once his basic theoretical orientation had changed, however, the question of whether or not something was conscious or accessible to consciousness was no longer as fundamentally important as it had been, though obviously it was still of great significance. Once it was recognized that even the forces of that part of the personality which mediated between the drives and the environment and which on occasion opposed the drives, that is, the forces of the ego itself could be as inaccessible to consciousness as the repressed drive derivatives, it became easier, as we shall see, to conceive of the struggle against the drives in broader terms than had previously been possible and without viewing it as exclusively from the angle of accessibility to consciousness, as had previously been done.

Thus in *The Problem of Anxiety* (1926) Freud noted that some of the methods used by the ego to control or deflect the drives, like undoing, for example, had so little in common with the repression observable in conversion hysteria that it seemed preferable not to use the same term for them. In addition, he remarked that defenses against the drives were probably present and operative before the psychic apparatus had differentiated sufficiently to permit repression to occur (see p. 35).

These considerations influenced Freud to reintroduce the term "defense" which he had first used in 1894. Any method used by the ego to control or deflect a drive derivative which it judged to be dangerous or which was so intense as to produce anxiety for economic (quantitative) reasons was to be called a defense. The term "repression" was to be reserved for a particular defense. Perhaps, as Freud remarked (1926), it would turn out that different defenses were characteristic of different neuroses: repression of hysteria; undoing, isolation, and reaction formation of obsessional neurosis, and so on. The distinction between "repression" and "defense" was not greatly elaborated by Freud in *The Problem of Anxiety* (1926), but it was generally accepted in psychoanalytic theory and was the basis for the classic work on the subject which appeared some years later: Anna Freud's *The Ego and the Mechanisms of Defense* (1936).

The last systematic statement on repression in Freud's own writings was in the *New Introductory Lectures* (1932). Though neither detailed nor complete, this statement concerning the process and consequences of repression is worth reviewing. In it Freud summarized the steps leading to repression in the following schematic way: as the ego becomes aware of a nascent instinctual impulse, it first fantasies the satisfaction of the impulse and then remembers, with some degree of anxiety, the danger situation associated with that satisfaction. Thereupon repression, or some other defense, ensues to suppress, to remove, or to make powerless the instinctual cathexis of the nascent impulse.

Freud believed that this happened differently in normal and in abnormal cases: ". . . the ego succeeds in this task if it is strong, and if it has assimilated the impulse in question into its organization. [Presumably this would be an example of judgmental repudiation, see p. 36.] In the case of repression, however, the impulse is still a part of the id, and the ego feels weak . . . The more the development of anxiety can be restricted to a mere signal, the more the ego can make use of defensive acts which amount to a mental binding of the repressed and the more the process approximates to the standard of a normal modification of the impulse, without of course ever reaching it."

It must be understood that the word "normal" in this context does not mean "average" or "usual," but rather "without pathological consequences," since Freud had long since recognized the ubiquity of repression in childhood. What he referred to in the passage just quoted was the idea that if a drive became assimilated into the ego (subject to secondary process), it could no longer produce neurotic symptoms, even if it was denied gratification or discharge; while if it was excluded from the ego, it continued to pursue an autonomous existence, to press for discharge, and to threaten to appear as a symptom whenever the ego's countercathexis should be inadequate to its task of thoroughly holding it in check. References to "the pathogenic nature of repression" in this sense are to be found in several places in Freud's later writings (1924a, 1924b, 1937) in addition to the one just cited. Indeed in the article which he wrote for the *Encyclopaedia Britannica* (1924a), he included the pathogenic nature of repression among the *essentials* of psychoanalytic theory. This is understandable, since this idea expresses in theoretical terms the whole rationale of psychoanalytic therapy. Thus, in "A Disturbance of Memory on the Acropolis" (1936), he referred to "the normal method of warding off what is painful or unbearable, by means of recognizing it, considering it, making a judgment upon it and taking appropriate action about it . . ."

To return to the discussion of repression in the *New Introductory Lectures* (1932), Freud described the consequences of repression for the instinctual life as follows. First, the drive might keep its cathexis and persist in the id, though continuously opposed by a countercathexis of the ego; second, the drive might be completely abrogated or decathected and its cathexis be wholly diverted into other channels, as normally happened for example in the case of the oedipus complex (Freud, 1924b); and third, a libidinal regression might occur, as is conspicuously the case in obsessional neurosis.

In the case of the third of these possibilities it is clear that Freud did not bother to distinguish clearly between the concept of defense in general and that of repression in particular (see p. 40), since he referred to regression as a consequence of repression rather than as one of the defense mechanisms which might operate in addition to the mechanism of repression. The same lack of a clear distinction is probably present in the statement of the second of the possible consequences of repression as well, since the total decathexis of the oedipus complex was thought to be the consequence of the extensive and complicated processes of identification and reaction formation that normally resulted in the establishment of the superego (Freud, 1924b).

The topic of primal repression also came up for brief discussion in both *The Problem of Anxiety* (1926) and the *New Introductory Lectures* (1932). In the former work he still referred to the phenomena in question as "primal repressions," but in the latter he simply called them "the earliest and most fundamental repressions." In accordance with his new theories of anxiety and mental functioning, he attributed such repressions to the effect of excessively strong instinctual impulses on the immature ego. These automatically produced anxiety on an economic or quantitative basis, anxiety which impelled the ego to react with repression or some similar defense mechanism: "the earliest and most fundamental repressions arise directly from traumatic factors, where the ego comes into contact with an excessive libidinal demand; these traumatic factors create their own anxiety anew . . ." (1932). Thus, Freud's eventual view about infantile or primal repression was that its cause and mechanism were not essentially different from those of repression in later life. However, anxiety, the motive for repression, was considered to be (or likely to be) different at the two times: in infancy anxiety was typically produced on an economic or quantitative basis, while in later life anxiety was typically of the signal variety.

In Freud's last complete work, *Moses and Monotheism* (1939), there is a statement concerning conditions for a return of the repressed which is of interest. According to this statement the three conditions for a return of the repressed are: (1) a weakening of the ego, as happens for example with physical illness or in sleep; (2) a strengthening of the drives, as for example in puberty; and (3) the advent of current impressions or experiences which are so similar to the repressed in content that they awaken it. As Freud expressed the last of these conditions, "The repressed becomes operative behind what is current and with its help."

The reason for paying attention to this statement of Freud's is that the third of the conditions given represented something new in Freud's statements on pathogenesis. Prior to that time he had considered only the first two conditions. See for example the discussion of precipitating pathogenic factors in the Schreber case (1911), where the emphasis was exclusively on libidinal frustration and not at all on the similarity between Schreber's real success and his repressed oedipal wishes. See also the discussion of pathogenesis in "Some Character Types Met With in Psychoanalytic Work" (1916), where the pathogenic effect of success in vulnerable individuals (those wrecked by success) was attributed to frustration and the consequent uncontrollable increase in the strength of repressed libidinal wishes. It is interesting to note that the later idea that current experiences might awaken the repressed because of their similarity to it, although not explicitly stated until 1939, was hinted at in the paper on "The Uncanny" (1919b), the basic idea of which had to do essentially with this mechanism: ". . . complexes which have been repressed are once more revived by some impression . . ."

Despite the lack of a full statement by Freud himself, it would seem possible to summarize his latest, or, if one prefers, his final views on repression as follows. Repression is one of several defense mechanisms which the ego may employ against an instinctual drive which is the source of anxiety. Thus the *occasion* or *motive* for repression is anxiety, usually anxiety aroused by a derivative of an instinctual drive. The *target* of repression is ordinarily a libidinal drive, but it is possible that repression may also be employed on occasion against an aggressive or destructive drive (Freud, 1930) and it certainly may be so employed against a superego demand (Freud, 1923).

The *mechanism* of repression consists in the establishment of a countercathexis by the ego. Repression is thus possible only after a substantial degree of ego development has taken place. The mechanism of the earliest, infantile repressions is the same as that of later ones, i.e., the establishment of a countercathexis by the ego. However, the infantile repressions are the basic ones. Later repressions are by and large repetitions or consequences of the infantile ones. The adult ego represses something only to the extent that, and only in those areas where it is still infantile as a consequence of infantile repression, or other similar, infantile defenses. With these exceptions it can deal with instinctual demands and with external stimuli in other ways, e.g., in the case of the former by judgmental repudiation, in the case of the latter by adaptive behavior of some kind.

The source of the energy of the countercathexis in repression is uncertain. Perhaps it comes from the pool of neutralized libidinal energy which is generally at the disposal of the ego for the purpose of carrying out its various functions (1923). In any case an equilibrium is established between the repressed drive and the countercathexis of the ego which is relatively stable, but which may shift in one direction or another under circumstances to be described below.

The *effects* of repression are twofold. In the first place, the drive and its derivatives are excluded from the ego and are consigned to the id, which means that as long as the repression is maintained the repressed drive has no access to consciousness, produces no emotional consequences, and does not give rise to any motor activity aimed at gratification of the drive. However, the repressed drive persists in the id and exerts a persistent pressure in the direction of emergence into consciousness and of gratification. Consequently, there is a tendency for derivatives of the repressed drive to intrude into the functions of the ego and to reach consciousness in dreams, jokes, fantasies, slips, neurotic symptoms, and other similar psychic manifestations which in general may be described as compromise formations.

Such compromise formations are referred to as instances of a *return of the repressed*. The return of the repressed implies a failure of repression, a failure which may be either temporary or prolonged, either so direct as to be unmistakable or so disguised as to be hardly perceptible, and either of such slight practical importance in the life of the individual as to pass quite unnoticed or of such great importance as to be decisive for the whole future course of his life. There are three general conditions under which a return of the repressed may occur: (1) a weakening of the defenses of the ego, as by illness or sleep; (2) a strengthening of the drives, as in puberty or as the result of long continued frustration; (3) a correspondence between the content of current experience and of the repressed drive. To these should be added the influence of current seduction, which presumably corresponds in part to each of the three conditions just mentioned.

Repression is thus seen to be a potentially pathogenic method of defense. It produces a crippling of the instinctual life, but also by the same token a constriction of the sphere of influence of the ego and a continuing drain on the ego's store of available psychic energy. A repression which has once been established may occasionally be abrogated spontaneously and the hitherto repressed drive assimilated into the organization of the ego (1923). More often, however, such a favorable result can only be brought about by analytic therapy.

BIBLIOGRAPHY

Freud, A. (1936), *The Ego and the Mechanisms of Defense*. New York: International Universities Press, 1946.

Freud, S. (1894), The Defence Neuro-Psychoses. *Collected Papers*, I. London: Hogarth Press, 1924.

—— (1895a), Studies on Hysteria. *Standard Edition*, II. London: Hogarth Press, 1955.

—— (1895b), Project for a Scientific Psychology. In: *The Origins of Psychoanalysis. Letters to Wilhelm Fliess, Drafts and Notes: 1887-1902*. New York: Basic Books, 1954.

—— (1896), Further Remarks on the Defence Neuro-Psychoses. *Collected Papers*, II. London: Hogarth Press, 1924.

—— (1900), The Interpretation of Dreams. *Standard Edition*, IV, V. London: Hogarth Press, 1953.

—— (1901), The Psychopathology of Everyday Life. *The Basic Writings of Sigmund Freud*. New York: Random House, 1938.

—— (1905a), Wit and Its Relation to the Unconscious. *The Basic Writings of Sigmund Freud*. New York: Random House, 1938.

—— (1905b), Three Essays on Sexuality. *Standard Edition*, VII. London: Hogarth Press, 1953.

—— (1905c), Fragment of the Analysis of a Case of Hysteria. *Standard Edition*, VII. London: Hogarth Press, 1953.

—— (1906), My Views on the Part Played by Sexuality in the Aetiology of the Neuroses. *Standard Edition*, VII. London: Hogarth Press, 1953.

—— (1907), *Delusion and Dream* [in Jensen's *Gradiva*]. London: Allen & Unwin, 1921.

—— (1909a), Analysis of a Phobia in a Five-Year-Old Boy. *Standard Edition*, X. London: Hogarth Press, 1955.

—— (1909b), Notes upon a Case of Obsessional Neurosis. *Standard Edition*, X. London: Hogarth Press, 1955.

—— (1911), Psychoanalytic Notes on an Autobiographical Account of a Case of Paranoia (Dementia Paranoides). *Collected Papers*, III. London: Hogarth Press, 1925.

—— (1915a), Repression. *Collected Papers*, IV. London: Hogarth Press, 1925.

—— (1915b), The Unconscious. *Collected Papers*, IV. London: Hogarth Press, 1925.

—— (1916), Some Character-Types Met with in Psychoanalytic Work. *Collected Papers*, IV. London: Hogarth Press, 1925.

—— (1917), A Metapsychological Supplement to the Theory of Dreams. *Collected Papers*, IV. London: Hogarth Press, 1925.

—— (1919a), "A Child Is Being Beaten." *Standard Edition*, XVII. London: Hogarth Press, 1955.

—— (1919b), The "Uncanny." *Standard Edition*, XVII. London: Hogarth Press, 1955.

—— (1923), *The Ego and the Id*. London: Hogarth Press, 1927.

—— (1924a), A Short Outline of Psychoanalysis. *Encyclopaedia Britannica*, II.

—— (1924b), The Passing of the Oedipus Complex. *Collected Papers*, II. London: Hogarth Press.

—— (1925), *Autobiography*. New York: W. W. Norton, 1935.

—— (1930), *Civilization and Its Discontents*..London: Hogarth Press.

—— (1932), *New Introductory Lectures on Psychoanalysis*. New York: W. W. Norton, 1933.

—— (1933), *Why War?* London: Hogarth Press, 1939.

—— (1936), A Disturbance of Memory on the Acropolis. *Collected Papers*, V. London: Hogarth Press, 1950.

—— (1937), Analysis Terminable and Interminable. *Collected Papers*, V. London: Hogarth Press, 1950.

—— (1939), *Moses and Monotheism*. New York: Knopf.

THE CHILDHOOD OF THE ARTIST[1]
Libidinal Phase Development and Giftedness

PHYLLIS GREENACRE, M.D. (New York)[2]

This presentation may be somewhat premature. The subject is
one about which one thinks slowly and hesitantly, perhaps because
genius is always somewhat dazzling and mysterious. Whether the
term "giftedness," "creativity," or "marked talent" is used, still the
idea of genius is close at hand. The differences in definition as well as
nuances in their usage reflect somewhat various ideas of the nature of
genius. To my way of thinking, creativity is a special capacity which
may or may not be associated with great ability; but it is usually only
of general significance when it is part of a constellation of special
abilities and drives—which make for the creative individual. Creativity does not seem to have a great deal to do with superior intelligence
in terms of quotients, even though excellent intelligence may contribute to the productions of the creative person. In this paper I
shall use the term the *artist* as a generic one referring to those
possessing unusual creative productivity in any field. My presentation is both schematic and hypothetical, without full documentation
and supporting evidence even for some fundamental parts of it,
except in so far as occasional illustrations may tend to be of this
nature. Neither am I reviewing the work of others who have contributed to this subject. There has been a great deal written that I
have not yet had a chance even to read, valuable though it is; nor to
reread some articles which I am sure have contributed to my ideas.
It has been my intention to use the present formulations as a kind of
work sheet, or blueprint of what is to be further investigated and
correlated with the work of others.

[1]Adapted from a paper read as part of a panel discussion at the meeting of the
American Psychoanalytic Association, in New York, December 1956.

[2] From the Department of Psychiatry of the New York Hospital and Cornell University Medical College, New York.

There is a suspicion that I have been led into this too early presentation by my excursion last year into the field of pathography in the investigation of Swift and Carroll (1955)—and that this led like the path of the inebriate into deeper draughts. Before going into the main topic of this paper, I would first like to present a few aspects of the uses and limitations of biography and autobiography in the study of genius. In a naive way it might seem that the study of autobiography supplemented by biography would be the method *par excellence* of understanding the individual genius. What could be more first-hand and authentic than what a man writes about himself? It is, as it were, from the horse's mouth.

This is of course an illusion. Every analyst knows that the account of his life which a patient insistently gives at the beginning of his treatment, "for the record" as it were, is not only imprecise but often filled with gross distortions and characterized by startling omissions. It is not only that the patient is not onto himself and aware of his deeper motivations, but that the individual memory is a great remaker of events, modeling and remodeling them throughout life with an extraordinary plasticity to make the cloak of remembrance do duty for one occasion after another, to meet both needs and fashions—with all of the skill and less noise than a good tailor.

A rather striking example of this was the case of a patient who had been through more than one period of analysis without revealing the nature or even the fact of having been involved in a tragic family catastrophe early in childhood. The original stunning pain together with the distress that followed and the neurotic guilt investing it had caused it to be left behind in an unused pocket of memory. It was not forgotten and could not be since it involved the sudden death of more than one member of the immediate family. But the ever-changing and increasing complexity of his life focused vision of himself in a series of changing forms more suitable for the *here* and *now,* and practically by-passed memory of this early tragedy. Nor is this patient's autobiographical statement much more distorted than that of most others. Nicholson (1947) in the *Development of Creative Biography* remarks, "Creative Biography necessitates something more than diagnosis, it necessitates a scientific autopsy; and this sense of a vigorous post-mortem is just what the autobiographist has always found it impossible to convey" (p. 15).

It must be recognized that autobiography, whether given verbally in the course of treatment or written for publication, is always produced for an audience, and often for an occasion. The audience always consists of at least two sections: the self and "the others"—whoever they may be. These three factors (occasion, self-estimate, and impression on others) combine to make pressures here, expansions there, possible explanations at one time which in further editions are treated as facts; and so it goes. What is true of the autobiography is also true, perhaps often to a lesser extent, of journals and diaries. But here again, journals which are kept very fully generally have, somehow, phantom figures looking over the shoulders of the writers. Otherwise they tend to deteriorate into becoming mere memoranda. Then there are the letters which famous people have written throughout their lifetimes. They certainly are intensely valuable if they are accessible. They too often partake of the journal quality if they are written after the gifted one has attained some recognition or at least after he has recognized his own abilities. They generally have the advantage of being addressed individually to the audience and so present varied and sometimes extreme rather than consistent self-moldings. Further there is often more spontaneity and immediacy in their writing. But those seemingly insignificant letters and jottings dealing with unimportant affairs are often most fruitful and revealing and yet are frequently lost or edited out of collections. For example, in the earlier publications of Swift's *Journal to Stella* much of Swift's "little language" was omitted as unbefitting a man of fame even though it gave an understanding of some of the most humanly poignant needs of the great satirist. Consequently in studying any given artist (no matter what his medium), one must draw on all these sources if they are available, and more too.

From my limited experience in studying the lives of artists and saints, I would think that all this is of but limited value unless pondered carefully and correlated with the products of the lifework of the creative person. Here we generally find the less clearly censored dreams of the artist. They too are cut, edited, trimmed down to a beautiful economy if the artist is a good one, and they too are produced for an audience, the collective one of the world at large or even of future generations. But in their emergence they show irrevocably the changing preoccupations, needs for externalization and the searchings for harmony from the artist's own changing and developing life situations. The true artist may be more faithful with deeper inner integrity in his relation to his collective audience than he is with his personal connections.

If all memory, as we ordinarily use the term, would seem to be but a cloak constantly in process of renovation, sometimes with gross additions of new material—in other words, if all memory has a screening function, how else shall we understand the man within it? Certainly we must examine the cloak and know that it reveals much of the man within and is genuinely a part of him, but neither mistake it for the man within, nor discard it as of no value because it is not he. There are many critics of psychoanalysis and many psychoanalytic patients who protest, "But why should she (or he) put much stock in all this, when there is no clear memory of these things." There is often a note of triumph in such protests. Or, if our work has been able to go a bit deeper, there may be the addition, "I only feel as though this might have been so, but how can I tell." If this attitude persists greatly, it has in itself to be analyzed. It generally indicates a rather special need of the patient to see himself as some kind of formal figure on the stage of life, rather than to feel himself as the growing, working, changing individual he is and has been. In my experience, reconstructions, if they are done painstakingly and with an almost sacred regard for the endless forms in which old experiences are emerging, become a working part of the individual, which under optimum conditions are assimilated and used without so much self-awareness. But reconstructions which are forced insistently represent the analyst's image of his patient or of himself, and are worn with increasing distress or discarded by the patient according to the degree of misfit. In studying the psychic life of the artist, it is probably necessary to use the methods of reconstruction of the analyst, in which the artist's production takes the place of many analytic hours. But there are limitations and temptations, for the artist analysand cannot talk back. If all memory is a screening process, so may this be true of official history.

I am indebted to Dr. Ernst Kris for directing me to Misch's *History of Autobiography in Antiquity* (1951) and to Dr. David Beres for Nicolson's *Development of English Biography* (1947). But especially invaluable is Dr. Kris's own book, *Psychoanalytic Explorations in Art* (1952). It is impossible for me to determine how much I have taken over from him in my own terms, for it is not the sort of situation in which I can quote specifically this and that passage but rather, like a good analysis, it has worked upon me against my own considerable resistances, in ways that I have assimilated without being clearly aware of how and when. In the chapter on "The Image of the Artist —A Study of the Role of Tradition in Ancient Biographies," Kris presents in a much more specific and detailed form the story of the distortions of biographies of Italian Renaissance painters, to fit a family romance pattern in which the artist is biographized as a shepherd boy whose talent is accidentally discovered by an older already renowned artist, who becomes his genius father and patron. Kris points out that this was given a specific form in commentators on Dante's *Divine Comedy* who made the construction from a scant reference of Dante's and gave rise to the tradition that Giotto was a shepherd boy who was so discovered by Cimabue, the then established master, whom Giotto subsequently surpassed. Kris points out that there is little factual evidence for this story, but that it was the crystallization of a tradition which became fixed for some time as the appropriate biographical account of painters of genius. Its connection with the Christ story is obvious. It seems, however, that the family romance problem is inherent in unusually deep imprint in the lives of artists. We no longer demand that the official biography shall be literally cast along these lines. But reading the lives of various writers has led me to think that the family romance constellation has an intrinsically strong place in their psychology and probably in that of the creative person in any field.

Before deserting the subject of the biography or even autobiography of the artist, we might emphasize certain changes in what might be called "biographical perspective" in the fairly recent past. I am not a sufficiently serious student of history, history of literature, or history of the development of science to present this in any accurate detail. It is apparent to the naked eye, such as mine, however, that a change in the accepted demand of biography appeared in English literature after the first World War and was clearly announced in the biographies of Lytton Strachey in the early 20's. This began to be called, in this country at any rate, the debunking method of biography. It sometimes became as fanciful and as faulty as the bad historical novel has become, and represented the hauling down of heroes. It sometimes contained, however, a new growing respect for life as it is, and not as it is glorified to appear. Something similar had already been appearing in a gradual way in changes in English literature. Only in the first half of the nineteenth century could a heroine in an English novel be homely—a feat scarcely yet achieved by the American cinema. It is conspicuous that since the beginning of the twentieth century there has been an increase in interest in the childhood of great people. This interest is reflected in many fields and is certainly apparent in changes in education, in literature, in social legislation as well as in many other ways. In my own mind I always think of the possible influence in this country as well as in England of the novels of Charles Dickens nearly half a century before such interest crept definitely into biography and autobiography. Certainly this interest in childhood antedated psychoanalysis, which gave it, however, new depths and perspectives with an enormous interest in artistic productions as well as in the artist's estimate of himself. Having recently read such autobiographical accounts of present-day writers as Sean O'Casey (1956), Herbert Read (1940), Richard Church (1956), Osbert Sitwell (1952), Stephen Spender (1951), C. S. Lewis (1955), Christopher Isherwood (1947), and a few others, I have been impressed with the willingness of many writers of today to reveal much of their early emotional life and problems, and in a few instances to view themselves self-consciously much in terms of analytic patients or as they conceive analytic patients to be. All this deserves more than this extremely hasty account, but will have to wait for more careful study in the future.

II

This second section of the paper consists of a series of tentative formulations and questions regarding the effect of marked talent or potential talent or giftedness on the early childhood of the artist. I have used the term "talent" rather than the more exalted one of "genius," although I believe that the same questions and problems would be true in both conditions, which may differ only in degree. I am aware again that some would consider talent and genius of quite different quality and that talent is often used to mean simple unusual brightness or special skill, without regard for the element of originality. In this present paper, however, I shall not differentiate talent from genius except in the matter of degree. *Talent* is defined by the Oxford Dictionary as "Mental endowment, natural ability," from the parable of the talents (Matt. XXV, 14-30), and further as "Power or ability of mind or body viewed as something divinely entrusted to a person for use and improvement"; while the term genius has much more the connotation of spirit or the visitation of the God-power himself, alternately described as extraordinary capacity for imaginative creation, original thought, invention or discovery. In the sense in which I am using the term talent, it is necessary to differentiate it from brightness or appearance of brightness whose development is the result largely of enforced practice or drill.

What then are the basic characteristics of creative talent? Are they inborn? Both questions seem difficult to answer. From the subjective accounts of creatively talented people writing of their own work and lives, and especially from some descriptions of the creative process itself by those gifted ones who were experiencing it (Ghiselin, 1955), it seems possible to describe the basic characteristics under four headings: first, greater sensitivity to sensory stimulation; second, unusual capacity for awareness of relations between various stimuli; third, predisposition to an empathy of wider range and deeper vibration than usual; and fourth, intactness of sufficient sensorimotor equipment to allow the building up of projective motor discharges for expressive functions. The unusual capacity for awareness of relations between various stimuli must involve sensibility of subtle similarities and differences, an earlier and greater reactivity to form and rhythm—thus a greater sense of actual or potential organization, perhaps a greater sense of the gestalt. It has been said that the creatively talented person sees three dots at once, not as three separate points, but as constituting different line and triangle forms (Gerard, 1946). The increased empathy associated with creative talent would seemingly depend on the sensory responsiveness to the individual's own body state as well as to the external object, and appears as a peculiar degree of empathic animation of inanimate objects as well as a heightened responsiveness and anthropomorphisizing of living objects. The difference between empathy and sympathy is here especially conspicuous. Such animation of the inanimate and anthropomorphisizing ordinarily is lost after early childhood, but in gifted individuals remains active either in its own right or appears in the form of the ease and wealth of symbolization.

Next as to the question of whether talents are inborn, this may be further subdivided into questions whether they are inherited according to definite biological laws, or whether they are otherwise congenital, i.e., potentially present at birth but due rather to a sport appearance. Obviously genius or marked talent has, through the ages, been thought to be the gift of the Gods, as the very definition of the word implies. Galton's early study of *Hereditary Genius,* first published in 1869 and revised in 1892, strongly supported the idea of inherited genius. When one reads this today, however, it is singularly unconvincing in certain respects. There is doubtless much to be learned from biologists on this point. But I know of no decisive study.

It is also apparent that it is difficult if not impossible to differentiate potentially talented infants from less gifted ones. Not only is there the problem of how much any difference is already operative to a degree to show in behavioral responses in infancy, but further that temporary variations of general bodily conditions or of external environmental ones may obscure or heighten the degree of responsiveness of a more ordinarily endowed infant, as well as that of the gifted one at a time when inherent differences are not yet decisively projected in performance. Especially may it be true that a potentially gifted infant with oversensitivity in sensory responsiveness, either in general or in some special sense, may be at first more than usually overwhelmed by the onrush of stimulation and in the extreme react less rather than more. In all of this, it seems one must be aware of the limitations of direct observation even though study of such observations as part of the development of life studies may ultimately lead to the most valuable results.

There are also dangers of overemphasizing heredity. Identification plays a very important role in the selection and zeal for a field of development of talent. Particularly is one aware of the complete disregard of or ignorance of such possibilities in a study like Galton's, important as that was for its time. The problem of identification simulating inheritance is probably as great in the development of talent as it is in the appearance of certain neuroses in successive generations. In the latter case it may appear as though the neurosis were inherited when more thorough scrutiny shows clearly that it is passed on by contact, direct and indirect, through subtle processes of identification. (The influence of identification even with legendary parental figures is seen strikingly in the case of the tragic poet, Thomas Chatterton, who wrote phenomenally good poetry when under the influence of identification with a fifteenth-century "father," but otherwise, under his own aegis, showed much less talent.) It is also particularly tempting to ascribe genius to heredity when it appears in a member of a family possessing other members who are unusually bright. Undoubtedly intellectual brightness, e.g., involving excellent memory and quickness of response, is a help to greater productiveness and enhances creative imagination but cannot substitute for it. Observation of many of the "quiz" shows of current television programs is sufficient to indicate the striking difference between the accomplishments of unusual memory (piling up impressive stores of factual information, possibly of neurotic defense value) and the flowering of really creative imagination.

Further it may be useful here to consider certain questions regarding the development of the child prodigy and even those extraordinary cases of pseudo-prodigy or skill development against a background of generally undistinguished or even inferior intelligence— the peculiar prodigy known as the idiot savant. This condition sometimes occurs in childhood, less frequently in adult life. There are some people of genius who have shown a prodigious development early and whose mature genius appears as a fairly continuous outgrowth from the promises of childhood. There are also a number of others whose genius does not become evident until adolescence or young manhood; and still an appreciable few whose genius only flowers in middle age or later. Conversely it is true that some spectacular prodigies peter out and develop into humdrum, rather undifferentiated individuals doing routine work. Others become bright and effective individuals but not seemingly possessed of remarkable talent or genius.

It appears that child prodigies may be divided into three groups. *First* are those in whom the precocious development appears as a spontaneous, rapid unfolding of the inner demanding pressure for unusual growth in some way inherent in the child himself. *Second* are those in whom the prodigy performance is mainly the result of demands of adults, usually the parents who push the child, using him as an extension of themselves in an attempt to realize some expansive ambitions in which they have felt themselves frustrated. One sees this not uncommonly in the field of athletic prowess and physical skill as well as in intellectual and artistic endeavors. A very restrained but moving account of the problems engendered or accentuated in such a child is given in the autobiographical account of Norbert Wiener (1953), indubitably an extraordinarily brilliant boy but so pushed by an ambitious father as to limit his spontaneity and his confidence in spite of his considerable attainment. *Third* are those in whom the remarkable performance is the result of neurotic conflict with the development of special achievement usually on a somewhat compulsive basis as part of an effort to overcome or counteract a masturbation addiction which is heavily charged with anal problems. From a recent review of some of the clinical reports on lightening calculators as this condition developed in imbecilic as well as in well-endowed individuals, it seemed rather indicated that the apparent facility at calculation resulted from an extension of counting compulsions. This is of some interest since the propulsive force of fantasies first associated with and then detached from masturbation appears to be of considerable importance in gifted individuals as well as in these retarded ones. But skill on a compulsive basis as a substitute for masturbation is limited by the span of the memory and the continuation of practice; whereas skill in a gifted individual is but part of the unfolding of the imagination which may originally gain impetus in connection with masturbatory activity but becomes liberated from it.

It is striking that some of these skilled but untalented individuals appear to be sensitive to gestalt configurations of numbers. Further scrutiny of the accounts of their performances suggests, however, that such awareness of patterned relationship of figures and groups of figures is not flexible or general, but restricted to a set of ritualistic performances, possibly derived from some elements in the situation in which the counting calculation was originally developed. It partakes rather of a rigid and empty, though superficially spectacular mnemonic scheme of narrow applicability.

In discussing the relationship between potential talent and libidinal phase development, I would wish to make clear that while recognizing the difficulties in making direct observations on infants and in determining the presence of potential genius at birth, I am myself largely convinced that genius is a "gift of the gods," and is already laid down at birth, probably as a sport development which finds especially favorable soil for its evolution in families where there is also a good inheritance of intellect and a favorable background for identification.

If we think then of the potentially gifted infant as possessing a conspicuously greater than average sensitivity to sensory stimulation, this might mean both an intensification of the experience and also a widening of it to include not only the primary object which is focused on but more peripheral objects which are related in some degree or fashion to the primary one in their ability to arouse somewhat similar sensory responses. To illustrate this with a hypothetical example: we might conceive that the potentially gifted infant would react to the mother's breast with an intensity of the impression of warmth, smell, moisture, the feel of the texture of the skin and the vision of the roundness of form, according to the time and situation of the experience—but more than might be true in the less potentially gifted infant. Such an infant would react also more widely and more intensely to any similar smells, touch or taste sensations or visions of rounded form which might come its way. Thus we can conceive of the fact that for the potentially gifted infant the primary object which stimulates certain sensory responses to it is invested with a greater field of related experiences than would be true for the infant of lesser endowment. As part of this reaction, too, there would inevitably be a greater vibration and need for harmonizing the inner object relationships (as the perception of the object reacts on and combines with other body sensations) and the world of sensory impingement. In an effort to clarify this in my mind, I have adopted the phrase "collective alternates" to describe this range of extended experience which may surround or become attached to the main focus of object relationships. I am not sure that this is a good term, but I have not been able to think of a better one and for the sake of economy shall continue to use it in the present discussion.

In this connection it seems to me that this may be the beginning of the love affair with the world which seems to be an obligatory condition in the development of great talent or genius. From the study of lives of artists and from such analytic experience as I have had with them, it seems that the artist invariably has some kind of genuine collective love affair. "Writing is an act of love" says an epigrammist, "If it isn't that, it is handwriting" (Cocteau, 1956). I believe that this collective love affair has been too often considered largely as the narcissism of the artist, whereas it partakes more of an object relationship, though a collective one, than has been considered. It seems unlikely that the artistic performance or creative product is ever undertaken purely for the gratification of the self, but rather that there is always some fantasy of a collective audience or recipient, whether this is a real audience, as for the stage, or the un, seen audience of the writer or painter; whether this be contemporary or extend into the limitless future. The artistic product has rather universally the character of a love gift, to be brought as near perfection as possible and to be presented with pride and misgiving.

Such love affairs with the world occupy varying relationships with individual love relationships, sometimes one being at the expense of the other; at other times, or in other individuals appearing as quite separate or as complementary attachments. But generally the more powerfully demanding one is that of the world. Further it is possible that in the libidinal phases of development of the infantile years, the presence of such collective alternate relationships permits diminution of the effect of critical situations involving the individual object relationships—critical situations which would otherwise tend to limit or temper the dominance of any given phase in the process of or at the height of maturing. Again to illustrate this with a hypothetical example: such a gifted child, on being forced to exert control of his bowels, may the more readily turn to play with mud or fecal substitutes, which he begins to fashion according to his current imaginative play wishes toward his own bowel movements. He will do this more readily and more extensively than the less gifted child, and will submit to bowel training, which at the same time may have less meaning to him than it would to the more average child. This has some bearing on problems of sublimation.

Especially is this true in the oedipal phase which may normally, in the male child at least, end relatively abruptly—to be reinvoked in a new version at puberty and thereafter. In the gifted one, however, the individual object may be only apparently relinquished, to appear rather in a glorified collective form which becomes the object of the love for a time. The ideals seem to be extended even more than the prohibitive conscience is developed, as the oedipal wishes are expanded, apparently desexualized by their deflection from a personal genital aim, but not renounced. The castration fears remain active and may invade the functioning toward the collective alternates, but their force is usually somewhat less focused. It is usually intensely strong and vivid, however, in the individual object relationship, where it does not produce an abandonment of the oedipal object but only a by-passing of this in favor of the larger collective, more powerful one. It seems that gifted children may solve their oedipal problems less decisively than more average children do. The apparent desexualization of the love object may be due as much in the postoedipal phase to the biological lessening of sexual pressure at this time as to the reaction of the castration fear which is further overcome by heightened identification too with collective power.

Indeed the conditions of the latency period generally appear as a paradigm of the development of talent. It is conspicuous then that under the lessening of sexual pressure and the relinquishment of the oedipal aims, a period of actual heightened physical growth sets in normally in which aggressive drives are used much in the service of mastery, of learning, exploring and experimenting. Even in non-gifted children the latency period may be a time of great artistic interest and development. Especially if the incomplete closure of the oedipal phase has permitted the extension of some sexual interest, the explorations and drives toward creative productions seem propelled and colored by the conflict. Under such circumstances there may be the appearance of seeming talent, and the expectation arises in others that the child will mature as an artist. Commonly, however, except in the presence of inherent gift, this flowering of the latency period goes into eclipse with the onset of puberty and reappears scantily, if at all, as "interests" and hobbies thereafter. In such latency development of artistic interest, the content of the productions is sometimes discernible as derivatives of masturbation fantasies, either extended from or detached from masturbation itself and presented in projected and disguised forms.

In the libidinal phase development of the child of potentially great talent or genius, there is then an even less decisive than ordinary progression of the phases which overlap and communicate with one another in a way which more closely resembles the libidinal organization of the perverse individual than that of the neurotic. At the same time it is coupled with an intensity of all experience which may be disconcerting as it is revived in later life. Talented people are not immune from neurotic and psychotic developments under all conditions, but neither is there an intrinsic connection between talent and neurosis, except in so far as this kind of incomplete organization of libidinal structure may predispose to intense episodes of dissociation, which are, however, of less ominous prognostic significance than would be true in the less gifted person.

In the perverse individual the overlapping, fusion, or at best too great communication between different phase drives, results in too easy substitution of one for another or sometimes in chaotic disorganization. Problems resulting from these states are frequently played out on the own body. In the talented person or one of genius such confusion may be obviated by the discharge through channels of developed or developing talent. In this situation there may be a full play at different times of the different preoedipal drives, continued even with or accessory to an oedipal re-enactment in the formation of the love gift of the creative product. In studying the creative process, however, as it is described by various people of genius, one is struck by the imprint of the pregenital patterns.

The question of the choice of form of creativity—the area of expression of talent—also demands consideration: the problem of *why* there is the universal genius such as Leonardo or the more frequent development of talent is one or at most two directions. Indeed in slightly gifted people the stimulation to work in more than one direction sometimes seems to produce distraction and limitation of development. It is possible that the universal genius may have been more frequent in past centuries and during times when the mass of technical knowledge was not so great. Certainly too the direction of development of creativity may conceivably be influenced by the needs of the surrounding world and the way in which this is indirectly transmitted to the developing child. It is also conceivable that the direction of expression of genius may be determined by special gifts, transmitted by inheritance or in some way determined before birth in which some sensorimotor functional constellation is especially superior and becomes the dominant channel of reception and production. In general, however, we are more impressed with the probability that a potential genius has polymorphous possibilities, some of which may be inhibited by special circumstances of early development; but more conspicuously that direction of development of geniuses or talent is largely determined by identifications.

The experience of awe in childhood, the forerunner of the mystical experience, is described with special intensity by creatively gifted ones. That this belongs to the two periods of special sensations of exhilaration and upsurges of intense animation, characteristic of the latter part of the second year and to the fourth-fifth year (the phallic phase), has seemed to me evident in many clinical studies of less gifted individuals, as well as in the autobiographical statements of artists (Greenacre, 1956). It may be that the identification then with a father—or with a specially powerful god-like father—begins at this time and is felt rather regularly due to the combination of the sharpness of the body sensation with the intensity of the sensory sensitivity to the outer world. Whether this image of the father is then retained as a God or put in other terms, remains largely determined by the tradition of the time and place. Kris (1952), in discussing this same problem (in "The Image of the Artist"), remarks, "A young sculptor in whose life the idea of being 'discovered' could play a considerable role, associated the fantasy of the sudden unfolding of his talent with the idea, disclosed in his dreams, of being given a real, i.e., a fully grown penis by the father image of his discoverer. The matrix from which this fantasy evolved was the old competition with the patient's real father who had been successful in the same branch of art."

It would appear to me that this description takes very much into account the phenomenon which I have described as penis awe, dependent in most individuals on the actual seeing of the adult tumescent penis at a time when the child himself is in a particularly sensitive state. It is possible that in children of potential genius this inner state of awareness of tumescent feeling may be especially strongly pervasive. Combining with the sensitive perception of external objects, it may give rise to sensations of invigoration, inspiration and awe. These depend not so much on the actual sight of the penis as on a communion with outer forms which reflect inner feelings in a way which I have tried to describe under the title *collective alternates*. It seems to me also that under such conditions the development of the family romance in especially strong form is inevitable. Such a child must develop an early attitude of glorification of the parents in accordance with the peculiar vibrancy and capacity for near ecstasy derived from his own body states. Fortunate is such a child if the own father fulfills the need for the model with which then to identify. It is my suspicion, however, that in some instances where this is not true, the child carries the ideal with him as though it were the real father, and that subsequent identification may be made and the development of direction of talent determined in part at least by the chance encounter with some individual or even some experience which strikes a decisive harmonizing note with a part of the hidden image of the father, belonging to the original experience of infantile inspiration. I am not sure that with children of potential genius the contact with an actual individual may be required for the crystallization of the identification with the idealized image.

Certainly the family romance in exaggerated form is present in many writers, and may be ubiquitous in artists of all sorts. It is readily decipherable in many of the *nom de plumes* of writers as well as in the search for and expectation of finding the patron, which seems part of the apparent naive dependency and unworldliness of many gifted people.

All of this leads to questions of the relation of creativity to the process of sublimation and allied problems in less talented people. I see these questions in slightly different perspectives than those recently presented (Hartmann, 1955; Kris, 1955). I would not limit the term aggression to hostile aggression—certainly not to the expression of a force always hostile in its aims. An army which enters a territory to improve it and make new constructions is still an aggressive force and its energy may be turned with varying degrees of rapidity from benevolent to hostile aims. Hostility seems further to have some implication of motivation. I would think of the aggressions of life as shows of force in whatever direction. The expansive aggression of growth of one organism may be destructive to another without being hostile.

During the first months of life there is not a clear differentiation of the sexual drives from the general energetic aggressive ones. This condition gradually changes during the first two to three years. A great deal of the energy endowment of the young infant is still used in the process of growth—in the actual increase in the size of the infant and in the unfolding of its functioning. This utilization in growth has been even more extreme in the prenatal period when the increase in size and organization from a single fertilized cell to the fantastically complicated and developed infant at birth is a demonstration of a force which would really overwhelm the universe very shortly if it were not slowed down. Such slowing down in rate of physical development does occur progressively until mature body size is reached in late adolescence. That the process of growth involves aggressive force was brought vividly home to me by the remark of my friend, Dr. Susanna Haigh, who said: "When I see the crocuses and the snowdrops pushing their way through the frozen earth at the end of winter, I am appalled at the fierceness of the tender shoots. It would take a swing of a pick-axe to do as good a job." Incidentally, the use of the word "shoots" for these early growths is a significant recognition of their force. This is the fierceness of expanding development and not of hostility. It is in this process of growth and its slowing down lest it explode the organism that I would see the basis of the death instinct; granted that this evolution from the beginning of life to death is at a different level than we conceive of instincts biologically. It more nearly approaches a cosmic rhythm, which affects inanimate as well as animate organizations. Personally I can no more conceive of life without an intrinsic movement toward death—the death instinct, so-called—than I can conceive of perpetual motion.

But to get back to the human species, the baby of five to six months extending its legs and pushing with its feet against the lap of the mother does so from the aggression of developmental force, not from the aggression of hostility. Later on, however, derivatives of this same force may be used in hostile attacks against the mother or others who stand in his way or interfere with the attainment of some goal or desire. Hostile aggression implies a sufficient degree of individuation for there to be a sense of the self and the other(s) against whom activity is directed.

Further in this early little differentiated stage of the drive development, the libidinal aspects of activity must consist in the state of gratification and comfort (or lack of it) achieved in the course of any activity, whether this is accomplished as a result of the patterned inherited instinctual pressure or in a more diffuse pleasure when performance itself fulfills the needs of expanding growth. To attempt an illustration: the gratification to the infant in nursing may not only be the attainment of a sufficient supply of warm milk for the satisfaction of hunger (and so indirectly for the further growth of the body), nor the passive comfort of warmth of contact with the mother's body, but it probably contains also the satisfaction of the use of the special neuromuscular equipment engaged in sucking, i.e., the satisfaction of the discharge of a developmental tension.

I would understand the unfolding growth pressures as they become organized, partly through maturation and partly through experience, and are increasingly capable of working in some sort of relative harmony as forming the somatic nucleus of the beginning development of the primary autonomous ego. There follows then a further development of libidinal (sexual) drives and the capacity of hostile aggressive ones in the service of self-defense or positive attack. The maturing of the central nervous system means the development of the psychophysical equipment for the more economical control and direction of the forces of the body. I would conceive of there being possible a considerable interchange between the expression of aggression in autonomous growth and that which is object- or goal-directed in necessary cooperation with growth processes, but acts directly and sometimes destructively on the environment for the satisfaction of its own needs.

This may be of some importance in understanding special conditions of early ego development and of sublimation in creative people. These may in turn contribute something to the understanding of sublimation in more ordinarily endowed ones. It is also possible that in very gifted people a process comparable to sublimation in those of more average endowment does not occur, inasmuch as they possess much more mobility of libidinal energy, and change of aim and object is achieved with greater flexibility, although often accompanied by outer displays of disturbance. I want to make clear, however, that I am not here attempting any comprehensive statement but only making a few tentative suggestions regarding some problems which need much more careful study.

If the conception of libidinal phase development (under condition of potential creative giftedness) which has been presented, has any merit, it may be considered further that this early sensory oversensitivity together with the greater reactivity to rhythm and gestalt relationships of form would bring the infant into a wider range of awareness of his own body and of the surroundings as well. How early and in what way this might operate would of course depend on other early circumstances as well, including special birth conditions, the presence of any defects in development, and the nature and immediacy of the relationship to the mother. It may also be that such an intensification and extension of the field of reactivity would form the anlage for the development of a greater richness of capacity for symbolization, which is so characteristic of creative people, and for the continued exigent demands of the primary process later in life.

Under most conditions such an infant would probably develop an intense and demanding relationship to the mother and to other early personal objects. The reactivity to the peripheral field might at first be largely extensions of these. Subsequently (I would conceive it roughly as from the latter half of the first year on) a powerful libidinal investment in the areas of the collective alternates, either in general or in some chosen part, might arise coexistent with that to the personal objects. The relationship between the forces of the individual personal object cathexes and those of the collective alternate ones would appear to exist in varying balances depending on a complexity of factors which cannot now be gone into.

What I would want to emphasize, however, is that this balance would influence very much the outline and organization of the incipient ego development; especially the growth of any self-image or self-representation; and even of perceptions of the self. It is conceivable that under what are generally considered favorable conditions of infancy, the primary (personal) self-representation would be at first the dominant and might always remain the firmer or more solid one. But in the course of time there may precipitate some rival or accessory self-image, again partly determined by the contact with some accessory adult idealized figure, who condenses and consolidates some area of the collective alternates through furnishing special sources of identification. Fortunate is that creative child or youth who has available within his own family individuals suitable for these identifications and reinforcements of his own creative needs.

Indeed, I do not believe that this is a mere whimsy of mine. It is evident in studying the lives of markedly creative people that such splits in the self-presentation, going over into even a split in the sense of identity, do occur and relatively frequently—sometimes developing along parallel lines and sometimes alternating, one emerging from cover of the other. This division into the two or more selves may be experienced in childhood with some distress and with the wish to deny the creative self in favor of the social stereotype, which exerts so much constricting pressure during the school years. The creative self is then felt as freakish, abnormal and to be fought. Under many circumstances, this struggle continues into adult life, when the more conventional self may be more or less guardian or enemy of the creative self. In the latter instance one may see the literal escape from one to the other. All this, it would appear, must also contribute to the ubiquitous and specially strong family romance among creative people.

Under conditions of frustration and disappointment in the personal object the creative individual may turn to the collective one(s); or the movement may be in the opposite direction. Under still other circumstances frustration in one area may lead to reciprocal inhibition in the other. Clinical illustrations may be developed in some later paper. These are matters determined by—among other factors —the degree and fashion in which the collectively determined creative function has been used too much in the service of the personal defense mechanisms, i.e., has been subjected to the burden of displacements, the effect of which depends on the amount, form, and location of the libidinization. In the extremely gifted individual, however, there may be a sufficient margin in the development of the artist-self to overcome all but the most sweeping displacements of this kind. It also means that among some creative people, the rhythm of personal disappointment giving rise to renewed efforts of realization through artistic endeavors has become established early and sets a pattern which causes them to fear even the illusion of a well-developed personal life, lest it deprive them of the impetus for creative production.

At this point I would want to make clear that my own conviction is that creative activity is highly libidinized and that without this libidinal charge it could come to naught. I would even suspect that it may carry the whole gamut of mixed libidinal phase pressures, genital and pregenital, more diffused and with wider and deeper range than is true in the less gifted person, but discernible in the form and nature of the creative process and in the artist's relation to his own creative product. It may be that the capacity to turn emotional drive to artistic creation is determined not only by the amount of gift endowment, but as part of this by the ease, mobility and plasticity of the communication between the individual (personal) emotional interests and those of general outer world, or collective significance. Further, the creative activity of the artist seems to me also highly aggressive, but with aggression allocated to special growth developments, to extents probably much greater but not wholly different from the situation of sublimation in those of lesser talent. The problem of ego-syntonicity in the artist is further complicated by the degree of acceptance or denial of the creative talent by the total individual and not merely by some competent part of the self.

What I have said here crudely and in first draft may not differ greatly in some essentials from others' views, even though terms may have been used somewhat differently. My formulation indicates, however, why I find the term *neutralization* so difficult in this connection. To me *neutralization,* borrowed presumably from chemistry, has the natural connotation of something which has been rendered inert, or at least temporarily ineffective. I would think of the need for a specific process to produce neutralization and a somewhat similar but reversed one again to produce deneutralization before a new direction of force or activity might arise. It is not that borrowing a chemical term is in itself objectionable. "Sublimation" itself and "valence" are such borrowed terms. But sublimation seems a more apt and condensed metaphor for it implies change in physical form —through diffusion as a gas and reprecipitation as a solid—without change of chemical structure. This is, however, accomplished by changes in temperature. Sublimation also has the connotation inevitably—though without chemical foundation—of conversion into a higher form. With "neutralization" the comparison fits less well. If by neutralization one meant a stage of busy and productive peace such as neutral nations are supposed to have, then the metaphor would seem more appropriate. Parenthetically I have thought the limitation of the term "aggression" to mean "hostility" may have been reinforced in recent years by the emphasis on the culpability of the aggressor nations.

There is one way, however, in which the energy passing from individual to the collective objects might seem to me to approach something like a neutral state. That is in relation to specific masculine or feminine differentiated direction. In other words, I would think of some degree of loss or diminution of sexual polarity; love of mankind, fervid but both diffuse and intense, expressed very much in the creative love gift, may take the place of or be in communication with the love of a man or of a woman. Perhaps this is the more possible in those gifted ones, the artists, who by the very nature of their early libidinal phase development must have not only a higher capacity for bisexuality, but a greater fluidity in changes of emphasis between the various libidinal phase drives. The reaction of the artist to the collective object(s) also involves utilization of the most primitive but acute empathic responses to an extent greater than is true in relation to the personal object. It is the force of the amalgamation of this dominant primitive empathy with the summation of experiences of the total span of life, which acts then in a depolarized sexual way in the struggle for harmony of which the creative product, the love gift, is the outcome. This struggle for harmony takes the place of some (much or little) of what might otherwise go into the personal love relationships of a polarized sexual nature. When the polarity of the personal sexual investment is not appreciably diminished and displacement has occurred too massively, then the collective love affair also assumes (by this direct displacement or by the rigidity of reaction formation) too much of the personal conflict. It is then subject to the same hazards, usually derived from the castration conflict, which have existed in the personal sphere. The site and nature of the displacement will further determine the character of the symptomatic invasion of the creative activity.

One may examine these matters sometimes in the situations of slightly or only moderately gifted people in whom, through early overtraumatization, a sensitivity and flux of libidinal phase development has occurred. Here one sees a much simpler situation, complex though it is. Though the analysis of such patients is extremely difficult and arduous, one sees the gradual liberation of the bound energy to produce a greater possibility of dominantly genital-sexual love, but the constitution remains susceptible and the personal sexual love relationship may be sustained only in so far as it may be supplemented by libidinized interests of a nonpolarized type. That such a person may not become a good creative artist depends rather on the mediocrity or at least lack of superiority of the basic endowment; and on the fact that his sensitivity, the result of unfortunate early conditions rather than of special gifts of nature, has not had the same range of reactivity, nor produced the same compelling need for seeking harmony. I must reiterate, however, that I have not carried these ideas into repeated and carefully checked extensive application to clinical cases, nor tested them out in the study of famous people. In any event, they may need both correction and refinement.

Some few rather less important observations may be discussed before closing this paper, certain special problems and difficulties of people of marked talent. If the talent is very great, there is indeed a sense of pressure, an obligatory quality to the expansion of development. If, while this is still in a state of potentiality, for any reason channels of outlet are blocked, states of frustration and blind frenzy with very slight provocation may arise. The best description I know of this is in Helen Keller's autobiography, in which she gives a picture of her inner explosiveness before her need to communicate could be channeled expressively after the illness which cut off both sight and hearing.

It was probably an intuitive awareness of this obligatory creative pressure as well as his enthusiasm for a biological genetic classification of people that led Galton to conclude that genius always asserts itself: that it will not remain hidden. Indeed, the compelling drive of creativeness, sometimes contrary to the conscious wishes of its possessor, may give the creative activity the semblance of a special kind of addiction for which there is no cure. Galton considered that three qualities of "ability—combined with zeal, and the capacity for hard labor" are essential to genius and are inherited. Again he says, "If a man is gifted with vast intellectual ability, eagerness to work, and the power of working, I cannot comprehend how such a man should be repressed." Once more he took an emphatic stand, "People seem to have an idea that the way to eminence is one of great self-denial from which there are hourly temptations to diverge: in which a man can be kept in his boyhood only by a schoolmaster's severity or a parent's incessant watchfulness and in after life by the attractions of fortunate friendships and favorable circumstances. This is true enough of the great majority of men, but it is simply not true of the generality of those who have gained great reputations. Such men— biographies show to have been haunted and driven by an incessant craving for intellectual work. If forcibly withdrawn from the path that leads toward eminence, they will find their way back to it as surely as the lover finds his mistress. They do not work for the sake of eminence, but to satisfy a natural craving for brain work, just as athletes can not endure repose on account of their muscular irritability, which insists upon exercise. It is very unlikely that any conjunction of circumstances should supply a stimulation to brain work commensurate with what these men carry in their own constitutions ... [The natural disposition of genius] keeps a man ever employed,— now wrestling with his difficulties, now brooding over his immature ideas, and renders him a quick and eager listener to innumerable almost inaudible teachings, that others less keenly on the watch, are sure to miss."

Thus Galton makes quite clear his appreciation of the difference between superior skill attained through demanded practice and that achievement which derives chiefly from the inner pressure of essential endowment. While his insistence on the constitutional elements in genius, or as he sometimes refers to it as "great eminence," led him to emphasize inheritance in ways which we might now question, he brings out some interesting peripheral observations and assumptions. In accordance with his belief in the inheritance of genius and its appearance, he may rather have ignored the instances in which genius became manifest and obligatory late in life. From the analyst's angle, the study of such men would be most illuminating.

I would interpolate a few of Galton's observations—aside from his emphasis on inheritance—because they are interesting and because they show that, in spite of his conscious focusing on inheritance and insistence that it alone was responsible for the appearance of genius, he inevitably came upon other determining factors. Although he concluded generally that the "female influence is inferior to that of the male in conveying ability," he realized that this might not be entirely due to hereditary factors, and added cautiously at a later time, "I think there is reason to believe the influence of females but little inferior to that of males in transmitting judicial ability," and that such influence might not be wholly due to inheritance is tacitly admitted in his discussion of men of science. Here he states that the fathers of the ablest men in science have frequently been unscientific; and elsewhere states, "It therefore appears very important to success in science that a man should have an able mother. I believe the reason to be that a child so circumstanced has the good fortune to be delivered from the ordinary narrowing, partisan influence of home education . . ." and again indicates that the sons of the most gifted men in science have only become themselves distinguished in science if they have also truth-loving mothers.

Another interesting conclusion arrived at by Galton was that in general men of genius were more often of good physical constitution than otherwise and added, "I do not deny that many men of extraordinary mental gifts have had wretched constitutions, but deny them to be an essential or even a usual accompaniment." From studying the mortality of his men of genius, he concluded "that among the gifted men, there is a small group who have weak and excitable constitutions, who are destined to early death, but that the remainder consists of men likely to enjoy a vigorous old age." This was true in the group of artists and distinctly so in that of poets, but it came out in most startling definition in the cases of men noted for their remarkable precocity. The mortality curve was only normal in those who did not appear to have been eminently precocious. Scientific men lived the longest and the number of early deaths among them was decidedly less than in any other groups. All this is interesting and provocative and deserves much more careful study. I have quoted Galton's work, for though first published nearly a century ago, it was one of the most comprehensive studies of men of genius ever attempted. Incidentally, in my hesitation to psychoanalyze the dead artist, I found some amused comfort in the discovery that in recent years the psychologist, Terman (1917), did post-mortem tests on Galton and decided that in his childhood his I.Q. had been 200.

32

PHYLLIS GREENACRE

BIBLIOGRAPHY

Church, R. (1956), *Over the Bridge. An Autobiography.* New York: E. P. Dutton.
Cocteau, J. (1956), *The Journals of Jean Cocteau.* New York: Criterion.
Galton, F. (1869), *Hereditary Genius. An Inquiry into Its Laws and Consequences.* London: Macmillan, 1925.
Gerard, R. (1946), The Biological Basis of Imagination. *Sci. Monthly,* LXXIV.
Ghiselin, B. (ed.) (1955), *The Creative Process.* Berkeley: University of California Press.
Greenacre, P. (1955), *Swift and Carroll. A Psychoanalytic Study of Two Lives.* New York: International Universities Press.
—— (1956), Experiences of Awe in Childhood. *This Annual,* XI.
Hartmann, H. (1955), Notes on the Theory of Sublimation. *This Annual,* X.
Isherwood, C. (1947), *Lions and Shadows. An Education in the Twenties.* Norfolk, Conn.: New Directions.
Kris, E. (1952), *Psychoanalytic Explorations in Art.* New York: International Universities Press.
—— (1955), Neutralization and Sublimation. *This Annual,* X.
Lewis, C. S. (1955), *Surprised by Joy. The Shape of My Early Life.* London: Geoffrey Bles.
Misch, G. (1951), *History of Autobiography in Antiquity,* 2 Vols. Cambridge, Mass.: Harvard University Press.
Nicholson, H. (1947), *Development of English Biography.* London: Hogarth Press.
O'Casey, S. (1956), *I Knock at the Door. Swift Glances Back at Things That Made Me.* New York: Macmillan.
Read, H. (1940), *Annals of Innocence and Experience.* London: Faber & Faber.
Sitwell, O. (1952), *Left Hand, Right Hand. The Autobiography of Sir Osbert Sitwell,* Vol. I. London: Macmillan.
Spender, S. (1951), *World within Worlds. An Autobiography.* New York: Harcourt, Brace.
Terman, L. M. (1917), The I.Q. of Francis Galton in Childhood. *Am. J. Psychol.,* XXVIII.
Wiener, N. (1953), *Ex-Prodigy. My Childhood and Youth.* New York: Simon and Schuster.

NORMAL AND PATHOLOGICAL MOODS: THEIR NATURE AND FUNCTIONS

EDITH JACOBSON, M.D. (New York)

PART I

THE GENERAL NATURE AND CHARACTERISTICS OF MOODS, AND THE PROCESSES LEADING TO MOOD MANIFESTATIONS

The psychoanalytic study of emotions is still predominantly concerned with the problem of anxiety, the affect whose role in the defensive struggle of the ego and in the development of neurosis is certainly unique. Lately, however, our increasing preoccupation with the psychoses appears to have veered our interest to a broader area of affective manifestations. In mental disorders, affective and mood disturbances are indeed such a prominent and characteristic symptomatic feature that they even lent their name to the manic-depressive group. Thus, the time seems to have come for further inquiries into the nature and functions of affects and affective states in general.

The following presentation will be concerned with the moods and mood conditions, such as can be observed in the realm of normal and pathological experience. It is intended as a continuation of ideas expressed in some previous papers (1953a; 1954b) dealing with the psychoanalytic theory of affects and with their infantile development in the course of ego-superego formation.

As a point of departure for our study we may resort to a practical, commonplace example showing mood vacillations within a normal range in a young man, named John.

John had fallen in love with a girl, Anne. His emotional situation resulted in experiences which evoked conspicuous mood conditions. John had spent a very pleasurable evening with Anne who had shown most favorable responses to his courtship. Having left her in a very happy mood, he had fallen asleep with marvelous daydreams and

woke up in high spirits. He devoted himself eagerly to his daily
work, in expectance of the next evening which he planned to spend
again with his sweetheart. His happy, elated mood lasted all day. But
in the late afternoon he called her up for a confirmation of their date
and was shocked to learn that she had decided not to see him for the
next three days. No reasons given! The level of his mood dropped
sharply. For the next days he tried in vain to persuade her over the
phone to change her mind or to give him at least a plausible explanation for her behavior. Her responses alternated between kind, or
even loving, and cool, detached, or even hostile attitudes. She appeared to be in a conflict whose motivations were unknown to the
unfortunate lover. Dependent on her attitudes, he vacillated during
these days between periods of rather good, expectant mood and of
either angry and irritable or sad and hopeless or dejected and depressed mood. While in a good mood, he anticipated gratification
from all the world around him; he slept well, he got out of bed early,
he disregarded the rainy weather, the disagreeable attitude of his
boss, the negligence of his typist. In so far as his attention was not
diverted by thoughts about Anne, he could think and act more
quickly and imaginatively than usual and cope easily with the manifold difficulties in his job and everyday life. While his mood was bad
and angry, he reacted with irritation to his superior, with temper
outbursts toward his secretary, and got into a row with another car
driver. As sadness would overcome him, he would feel like weeping,
remembering sad events in the past and present. When he became
discouraged and depressed, he felt inert and indecisive; he was, indeed, not in a mood to work or to be active at all. His moods affected
even his characterological peculiarities, e.g., his reaction formations.
In general John was a kindly man, predisposed to intensive reactions
of pity in view of suffering. However, while in a happy and elated
mood, the successful lover tended to ignore the gloomy aspects of
life around him altogether; and while he was in an alternately hopeless, dejected or furious mood, the sight of suffering made him feel
either sorry for himself or angry and disgusted at the world around
him. John's rapid and intensive emotional vacillations disclosed, besides, his (constitutional or acquired) propensity to react with strong
though not pathological mood fluctuations to either pleasurable or
painful experiences.

From our description of the various familiar mental phenomena
which John displayed, we may draw some basic inferences regarding
the nature of moods in contradistinction to affective states of a different order. When we described John as being in love, for instance, we
also referred to an enduring feeling state, but to one that is certainly

not a mood. A variety of pleasure and unpleasure experiences arose, with the different vicissitudes of his love, as expression of alternating, specific libidinous and also aggressive discharge patterns. They reflected either John's sexual and emotional neediness, his expectation of relief, his gratification, or his frustration, his disappointment, his dissatisfaction. Even these different emotional reactions do not represent moods, but they induced a series of mood conditions.

These changing moods found expression in particular qualities of his feelings as well as of his thought processes and his performances during the whole day, no matter what their object had been. They affected his emotional responses, his attitudes and his behavior, with regard not only to his girl friend but also to his work and to the whole surrounding object world, and influenced the choice and the course of all his activities.

In fact, moods seem to represent, as it were, a cross-section through the entire state of the ego, lending a particular, uniform coloring to all its manifestations for a longer or shorter period of time. Since they do not relate to a specific content or object but find expression in specific qualities attached to all feelings, thoughts and actions, they may indeed be called a barometer of the ego state.

The ubiquity and uniform coloring of a mood, its distinct and pervasive nature, and the obvious connections between its various manifestations are responsible for its conspicuity. Indeed, we can easily guess a person's mood from his facial expression and behavior, even if he is not fully aware of it, without knowing the whole complex gamut of this person's feelings and thoughts at a particular time. Since mood manifestations represent actually a unit, the separate investigation of the feeling aspects of a particular mood, even if it be in the foreground, is of course inadequate without concomitant scrutiny of the associated phenomena in the realm of thoughts, attitudes and actions.

Our statements are in keeping with Webster's brief definition of mood, which expressly designates mood not as an affective state but as "a particular state of mind, especially as affected by emotion, as to be in a mood to work." This definition refers to the further fact that moods, as in our example, are induced by significant emotional experiences expressive of one or more focal discharge processes. Such an experience may be stimulated from within (through physiological or purely psychological processes) or without and need not come to full emotional awareness. It may be significant either in terms of the current reality or because it is associated with significant conscious or unconscious memories. But whatever the part of past or current events in the provocative experience, the ensuing mood manifests the spreading influence of the focal discharge process, of which this experience is expressive, on all other discharge patterns. Hence the moods must reflect resultant common qualities and characteristic deviations in the speed course and rhythm of the sum total of drive-discharge processes developing over a certain limited span of time. They may be designated as a temporary fixation of generalized discharge modifications. Once a mood has established itself, it affects all patterns of responses to stimuli or objects of the most different kind, including, as in our example, typical, individually acquired emotional responses to specific stimuli; e.g., reaction formations, such as shame or pity, individual preferences or dislikes, and so on.

This brushing off of particular qualities and modifications of focal discharge patterns on all others distinguishes the nature of moods sharply from that of affective states, such as love or hate and their manifold derivates, which develop from specific though possibly complex tensions and relate to definite ideational representations. The nature of such states is determined not only by the specific drive quality and by the stability and intensity of the cathexes, but—in contrast to the moods—by the specific objects in which the feelings are vested.

It is noteworthy that these object-directed emotional states as such are not even characterized by pleasure-unpleasure qualities. Feelings of pleasure or unpleasure only arise with gratification or frustration of the underlying strivings, under the influence of ego and superego which help to mold the various discharge patterns. Moreover, such feeling states and the discharge reactions which develop with their varying vicissitudes may become moods as they spread out and predominate in the whole field of the ego for a certain span of time. Thus, anger at somebody or something may turn into an angry mood, love or hate into a kind or hostile mood, anxiety into an anxious mood, as soon as they have ceased to relate only to special, selected objects or notions.

When scanning our common vocabulary for moods, we detect

that it covers a very broad field of mental states. The mood attributes refer by no means only to pleasure-unpleasure qualities, or to a high or low level of mood. They are not even restricted to feeling qualities, but may point to ideational or also to such functional and behavioral aspects as predominate in the mood manifestations. For example, we may be either in a dull, an uninspired, in an alert, a creative, or in a contemplative, thoughtful, philosophical mood.

In addition, as mentioned by Webster, we speak of being or not being in the mood to do this or that, such as feeling or not feeling this morning in the proper mood to work, in the evening to turn to our preferred hobby and at night to have fun or to rest.

Evidently a particular mood, though asserting itself indiscriminately in relation to any kind of object, may also stimulate a special type of pursuit. In this case we describe the mood quality according to a different category than in the case of a good or bad, a sweet or angry mood. We refer to an awareness or an impulse indicating that our discharge patterns, at the time being, are especially well suited for certain aims, pursuits or objects. In a state of gaiety, for instance, a person will be in a mood to joke or listen to jokes. Such moods may originate in an initial experience of a special quality, whose repetition or avoidance appears desirable. Gratifying work may keep us in a mood to work, or even encourage continued absorption by the same subject; being fed up with the special kind of activity may, by evoking unconscious or conscious wishful fantasies, result in a mood to do the opposite, such as to seek pleasure instead of work; and so on.

Evidently, it is hardly possible to classify moods, except according to quite different categories which overlap each other. E.g., moods may be popularly classified as good or bad moods, a distinction that refers primarily to pleasure-unpleasure qualities but hints at a general prevalence of libidinous versus aggressive drive discharge: both the angry and the depressed mood must be considered "bad" moods. But someone might be in a triumphant mood which is felt to be good and pleasurable, though based mainly on aggressive discharge. On the other hand, sadness, which must be regarded as "bad" mood, appears to involve special libidinous discharge patterns. Moods may also be distinguished from the perspective of the speed of discharge, according to the high or low mood levels which do not quite correspond to good or bad mood qualities. One may be keyed up or excited in a pleasurable or unpleasurable way, with prevalence of either libidinous or aggressive discharge phenomena. Or a person may be in a quiet, either happy or gloomy mood. Moreover, moods might be distinguished according to the conspicuous prevalence of mood phenomena in the area of feelings, thoughts or actions, such as a happy or an unhappy mood, a thoughtful or dull mood, an enterprising or lazy mood. This only goes to show that attempts at mood classifications are neither very promising nor very constructive. But the attempt to classify them according to qualities makes us aware that, in whatever category, we commonly conceive of moods in a dualistic way; i.e., in terms of good or bad, happy or unhappy, high or low, active or passive, kind or angry, etc. This reflects, of course, the unmistakable dualism in all psychobiological happenings: the drive dualism, the biological vacillations between tension and relief, and the inevitable changes between pleasure and unpleasure enforced by reality.

So far moods had been defined as a temporary fixation of generalized discharge modifications, induced by a significant experience whose discharge pattern lends its qualities to all discharge patterns. But precisely how can characteristics of a focal discharge process impose themselves on all discharge processes?

To produce a mood, the provocative experience must certainly be of a particular intensity and cause unusually high energetic tensions which cannot be immediately and sufficiently relieved by a focal discharge process only. In this case, the memories of the provocative experience will remain strongly hypercathected; thus they may attain the power to influence the energetic and cathectic conditions in the whole realm of the ego.

In John's case, for example, his happy experience with Anne had not only left an intensely vested memory of his initial success and gratification. Its stimulating effect had been such that it replenished him for a certain period with libidinous surplus energy sufficient to raise the narcissistic and object cathexes in all areas of his ego by virtue of general cathectic displacements. Thus during that delightful day the libidinous resources at John's disposal were richer in general, whereas the aggressive forces had been reduced. Consequently his self-esteem rose not only as a lover, but with regard to his abilities in all fields. He likewise showed increased libidinous investments not only in Anne, but in the whole world around him. At this point the significant factor of anticipation had been called into play. Drawing general inferences from his initial success, John from now on anticipated happy and gratifying experiences modeled after the first one; not only with Anne, but with all other objects around him.

This inner situation can be described in a different manner. The replenishment and the redistribution of the libidinous forces through generalized cathectic shifts had evidently resulted in temporary, qualitative modifications of the concepts of the self *in toto* and of the entire object world. These concepts had assumed a special coloring whose optimistic quality differed from the usual one. Generalized complementary notions had been fixated in John: he thought of himself as an active, successful, happy-go-lucky fellow, and accordingly of the world around him as a gratifying, benevolent, pleasurable world. With regard to the object world, these notions represented a generalized transference of certain hypercathected, pleasurable attributes from Anne to all objects; with regard to himself, the generalization and temporary fixation of a momentary, hypercathected, correspondingly pleasurable aspect of the self. Evidently the hypercathexis of such special notions can be sustained only through hypocathexis of all contradictory inferences derived from past experiences; i.e., by way of a temporary denial of unsuitable memories.[1] By calling the respective notions "complementary," I wish to convey that they always reflect a definite aspect of the inter-relationship between self and object world. In a particular mood we might indeed consciously feel: today I am a different person and have a different relation to the world; and the world, in turn, looks different in relation to me.

In John's case, his pleasantly modified optimistic notions then became the carrier of correspondingly hopeful fantasies inducing

[1] I mentioned the tendency to generalization in a previous paper, on "Denial and Repression" (1957). There I discussed the primitive nature of this tendency in connection with the concretization of psychic manifestations and showed that both are involved in the mechanism of denial. Moreover, I pointed to the role of generalization in the development of moods.

further pleasurable reactions and successful, gratifying actions.[2] Since our moods affect our attitudes and behavior patterns, the responses we get as a result of our actions will commonly do their best to confirm and promote, in turn, the notions on which our mood is based, until reality interferes sufficiently to bring about changes of these concepts and consequently of our mood. John's good mood, for instance, lasted as long as the hypercathexis of his happy memories and of the concepts based on them could be maintained in the face of reality. The influence of reality on the moods will be discussed in greater detail below.

To repeat: it appears that an experience causes a change of our mood only if it can bring about qualitative changes in the representations of the self and of the object world *in toto*. It stands to reason that the temporary fixation of such drastic qualitative modifications can then, in its turn, exercise a generalized uniform influence on the qualities of all discharge patterns.

Our description is of clinical value inasmuch as it bears reference to familiar phenomena observed in pathological mood conditions. We know that in depressed and elated states the whole self is felt to be "different," either bad and inferior or good and superior, and the entire object world correspondingly appears unpleasantly or pleasantly transformed. But we must realize that not only in pathological but in any type of mood variations, our self- and object-representations undergo such qualitative modifications.[3]

---

[2] Had John had a striking success in a competitive business transaction, he would also have felt elated. But in this case his experience might have favored a triumphant mood expressive of increased aggressive investments in all kinds of objects and pursuits; this would have given impetus to further aggressive reactions and actions. This only goes to show the extent to which the proportion between libido and aggression, and their distribution in the cathexes of the self and the object world, influence the mood qualities and the whole ego state.

[3] Certain shades within the normal range of moods, which bear little reference to the mood level or to special pleasure-unpleasure qualities, arise from very subtle modifications of the object- and self-representations. These are moods whose attributes point not to emotional or functional characteristics, but to ideational trends, as the contemplative, thoughtful, philosophical moods previously referred to.

PART II

THE ECONOMIC FUNCTION OF MOODS; EARLY MOOD
PREDISPOSITIONS AND THEIR DEVELOPMENT

We are indebted to Freud for his remarks on the constructive
economical function of the mourning process which accomplishes the
gradual return of libido to current, realistic aims and gratifications.
Freud concluded that pathologic depressive processes seemed to have
the same economical effect. However, our previous scrutiny of the
processes underlying mood conditions in general permits us to extend
Freud's economic considerations even further.

If it is characteristic of all moods that they allow a repetitive
affective discharge on a great number and variety of objects, such a
prolonged discharge in small quantities, combined with reality testing, must liberate psychic energy from fixated positions and reopen
the gate to new investments. This gradual discharge process certainly
tends to protect the ego from the dangers of too explosive, overwhelming discharge, even though moods do not preclude and may
induce repeated, sudden, dramatic discharge reactions, such as outbursts of sobbing or laughter or anger. Thus, moods in general appear
to serve a definitely useful, though primitive, economic function.
However, the ultimate economic success will depend largely on the
extent to which this prolonged discharge process permits a true reality
testing. In this respect we find decisive differences between normal
and anomalous mood conditions, which will be discussed below in
the comparative study of normal and pathological moods.

In view of the primitive nature and function of moods, it is not
surprising that we find a propensity to moodiness, to offensive moods,
or to conspicuous or prolonged swings of mood in individuals who
are characterized by their particular inability to tolerate tensions, to
accept loss as a frustration; persons whose ego operates predominantly
on a primary-process level with high quantities of deneutralized
psychic energy which threaten to be suddenly discharged.

We must assume that such persons call on this primitive type of
economic regulation so continuously and conspicuously because they
are in need of it. Evidently their ego lacks the capacity for subtle,

"secondary-process" modes of economic functioning and affective defense; it does not have a sufficient number or variety of discharge
channels and of differentiated discharge patterns at its disposal. Since
this is indicative of either an arrested or a regressively archaic ego
and superego structure, we are not surprised to find that the mood
pathology is so prominent in psychotic disorders. But even though
psychotics and to some extent also neurotics display an economical
need and hence a propensity for conspicuous mood deviations and
pathological mood qualities, we must emphasize that the normal ego,
too, preserves the use of this primitive economic modality.

In John, for instance, we described a sequence of rather normal
mood phenomena developing from his experiences with Anne. To be
sure, John showed a definite proclivity to strong and rapid mood
vacillations. Evidently his ability to keep his narcissistic and object-
libidinous cathexes *in toto* on an even keel, notwithstanding outside
influences, was not too well developed. Although his mood qualities
remained within the common affective range, we might regard his
mood instability as marginal or, at least, as expressive of a particular
mood predisposition.

In persons with definite mood predispositions we find a conspicuously frequent recurrence of special, temporarily fixated modifications regarding the concepts of the self and the world, based on
generalized inferences and transferences from the past. In people
with chronic mood deviations, such as chronic pessimists or chronic
optimists, these concepts and the resulting discharge patterns become
enduringly fixated.[4]

Within the frame of general affective predispositions we can, in
fact, observe individual predispositions to certain prevailing or recurring mood conditions already in earliest childhood; e.g., to even
or uneven, to good or bad moods, or to definite mood vacillations.
Of course, little children display noisier and more intense affective
manifestations in general, because of still insufficient ego-superego
control. Their moods are commonly of brief duration and change

---

[4] The special meaning of "fixation" in this frame of reference, versus fixation in
the common analytic usage of the term, is self-evident. By (infantile) fixation we mean
either the tendency to respond to certain stimuli with preferred discharge patterns
modeled at earlier developmental stages, or else the enduring hypercathexis of a special
conscious or unconscious object-representation. In this connection we may express the
suspicion that the lasting infantile fixation to a love object always goes along with
the fixation of corresponding infantile features of the self-representations.

rapidly. Their inability to sustain moods, especially painful moods, for a long time, is due to the relative instability of object cathexes, their tension and pain intolerance, their readiness to accept substitute objects and gratifications. The affective scale of children is more limited because of lack of ego differentiation. As a result of constitutional and environmental influences, of instinctual maturation, of ego and superego formation, early infantile affective and mood predispositions will thus naturally undergo many changes. But at any developmental stage they represent an outstanding characteristic of the total personality.

An individual's general affective predisposition reveals his inherent preference for special affectomotor reactions. The mood predisposition, on the other hand, reflects his greater or lesser tendency to fixate, for longer or briefer periods, special concepts of the self and the world, and, consequently, special affectomotor discharge patterns, with but scant regard to the varying external stimuli.

Regarding the early infantile influences on the development of pathological mood predispositions, we can easily visualize the impact of repetitive or prolonged exposure to the same type of experiences, such as of overgratification or deprivation. Their influence on the mood development will be especially harmful at a stage when the need-gratifying object is still the main representative of the object world, and when the child, as yet unable to discriminate between different objects, has a natural tendency to easy cathectic displacements from one to all objects. In such a child the primitive tendency to generalize his experiences will be maintained and become the carrier of a definite, anomalous mood predisposition.

From the psychoanalytic study of manic-depressive states, which show a severe pathology of the superego functions, we know that superego formation has a singular influence on the development of affective and mood control, and thus of mood predisposition. I touched upon this problem in my paper on "The Self and the Object World" (1954b) where I discussed the complex control system arising with the constitution of the superego. Suffice it to repeat that superego formation has a modulating effect on emotional expression in general; that the rises and falls of self-esteem become specialized indicators and regulators of the self- and object-directed cathexes in the total ego, and of the resulting discharge processes.

However, we must realize that the main function of the superego in normal adults is a selective one. In fact, only as long as guilt feelings remain localized and refer to specific—conscious or unconscious —forbidden strivings, can they serve as an effective warning and directive signal. Then they do not induce a mood, but set the defensive activity of the ego in motion. But the presence or absence of generalized superego pressure tends to inhibit or stimulate ego activity in general by slowing up or hastening the speed course of object-directed discharge, irrespective of special aims and objects, in a uniform manner. In this case, superego approval or disapproval will no longer relate to special, unacceptable instinctual strivings; it will refer to opposite notions of the total self in terms of black and white, of "being good, expecting reward" or "being bad, expecting punishment." Such generalized notions may also develop in normal persons and cause mood vacillations within a limited range. The ego will then make temporary use of a more primitive economic modality, at the expense of superego function at a higher level. But defective superego structure or superego regression may lead to a permanent loss of the signal function of the superego, which will then be replaced by the tendency either to conspicuous rapid or extreme pathological mood swings, or to a more or less fixated lowering or rising of the mood level.

No doubt, the role of the superego and of superego formation in the establishment of general affective and mood control is most significant. However, I may repeat that long before superego formation, some children may show impressive mood stability, whereas others may very early suffer from unusual moodiness or even from infantile types of mood pathology.

The conspicuousness of such early infantile affective and mood predispositions shows the extent to which they are determined by such factors as the child's inherent drive intensity, the depth and intensity of his object cathexes, his inherent tendency to respond to frustration, hurt, or deprivation with lesser or greater, rapidly passing or more enduring ambivalence. Thus we must not overrate the influence of the superego and of superego formation on the moods and the level of mood. Moreover, with complete maturation during the period of adolescence, the superego's rigid controlling grip becomes relaxed, permitting the ego greater affective freedom and flexibility.

Its influence then extends mainly to the regulation of the mood level and to the toning down and modulation of moods and affects in general. But the manifold and rich affective colors reflect the ego's structure and the freedom of its responses. Thus the contributions made by the superego to keep the moods and the affects on a comparatively even level do not justify the inference that normal persons manifest less variety of mood phenomena.

Quite the contrary: comparing normal and pathological mood manifestations, we are impressed by the fact that people with pathological and conspicuous mood qualities or mood swings appear to lack all the subtle shades and nuances that we find in normal persons. This may be caused by ego defects as well as by an archaic or defective superego structure. Consequently, qualities and vacillations of mood are good indicators not only of a person's current conflictual or conflict-free situation, but also of the pathology of ego and superego. They assume particular symptomatic and diagnostic significance in psychotic disorders. The loss of differentiated mood shades manifests itself especially clearly in cases where the mood remains fixated at a high or low level for a longer period. The dark shades of low and the sharp lights of high spirits appear to absorb and outdo the delicate mood shadings. The monotony of their mood is one reason why not only chronically depressed but also chronically hypomanic people get on our nerves.

This is valid, of course, with regard not only to moods but to affective phenomena in general. The severer the affective and mood pathology, the more restricted and less varied become the affective scale and the emotional tones. At first sight this statement does not sound true with respect to the hysterics, whose affects and moods frequently show such sparkling lustre. But although their affects are overintense and dramatic, they are not really modulated. Their range of emotional colorings is limited due to the lack of subtle, subdued emotional and mood shadings. The affective iridescence of schizoids is even more deceptive in this respect. Their affects and moods are sometimes fascinating because of their unfamiliar, strange, uncanny nature; but they are not rich, warm, and vibrant, they have a cold and brittle quality. Mentioning them calls to our mind, of course, that the pathology of affects manifests itself not only in hyper- or hypointensity of affects and moods, in anomalous mood vacillations

and in the pathological reduction of finer emotional shadings in
favor of limited but offensive or strange affective and mood colors,
but also in the striking differences between warm and cold affect
qualities which I briefly discussed in the aforementioned paper.

To summarize the essential points I have tried to bring out so
far: Moods are ego states characterized by generalized discharge modifications which temporarily influence the qualities of all feelings,
thoughts and actions. They are evoked by intense experiences which
cause high energetic tensions leading to an overflow and spreading
of energy throughout the ego by virtue of cathectic shifts. These
processes go along with generalized transference phenomena, a point
that emphasizes the differences between moods and object-directed
feeling states. The latter are characterized by libidinous or aggressive investments in specific objects. But the moods transfer the qualities of the provocative experience to all objects and experiences; thus
they impart a special coloring to the whole world and hence also to
the self. Since they permit gradual, repetitive discharge with reality
testing on many objects, they must be regarded as a primitive economic modality of the ego.

The states of sadness and grief, of gaiety and cheerful elation,
lend themselves especially well to illustration and further elaboration
of these points. I have therefore selected these two opposite types of
normal moods for a more extended study and re-examination from
our present vantage point.

<h2 style="text-align:center">PART III</h2>

Two Normal Types of Mood Variations: The Nature of Sadness
and Grief, of Gaiety and Cheerful Elation

In "Mourning and Melancholia" Freud (1917) pointed out that
grieving persons tend to dwell on their memories of the happy past.
But this seems to contradict my contention that the overinvestment
of the provocative experience—which in grief would be the tragic
event of loss—is what induces the mood. Evidently, my foregoing
statements call for further scrutiny of the process of mood development.

Since the term "grief" singles out but a particular prolonged and profound state of sadness caused by the loss of a love object, I prefer not to restrict our study to the state of grief but to extend it to sadness in general. Let us first examine the nature of sadness and the types of experiences that induce this affective condition.

To be sure, sadness is an emotional response of the ego to suffering. The suffering may arise from realistic external or from inner, conscious or unconscious, sources; it may develop from identification with the suffering of others. The suffering that promotes sadness seems to be always caused by experiences—or fantasies—of loss or deprivation, such as by loss of gratification either previously gained or expected, by loss of love, by separation, or in the case of mourning, by loss of a love object. But it may also have physical sources, although sadness does not seem to be directly evoked by physical hurt or pain. During sickness, especially prolonged illness, sadness may develop from the concomitant emotional suffering caused by the loss of instinctual and emotional gratifications. Even though sadness develops from experiences of loss and deprivation, which tend to provoke aggression, its qualities hint at the involvement of predominantly libidinous elements in the processes causing this state. In fact, it seems that sadness presupposes the presence of sufficient object-libidinous cathexes. Angry and sad mood, e.g., commonly exclude each other, although it frequently happens that aggression is used as defense against a painful experience of sadness.

In other words, unlike depression, sadness as such does not involve an aggressive conflict, either with external reality or endopsychically. It certainly does not arise from inner tension between ego and ego ideal, but seems to be induced by tensions within the ego, which must be carefully studied. Practically, of course, states of sadness frequently show depressive features, and in depressed states feelings of sadness may prevail. But clinical observations suggest that sadness predominates in depression only as long as the libidinous investment in the object world can be maintained by the veering away of aggression to the self.

During treatment, severely depressive patients who have withdrawn their libido from the object world may indeed display an intense longing for sadness. They may even consciously realize that could they only be sad and weep, they would "feel for the world" again. And actually a relieving "sweet sadness" may break through at the moment when they are achieving a libidinous recathexis of their lost love objects and of pleasant memories relating to them.

Quite in contrast to depressive states of this type, we find in grief and in normal sadness of any kind a preoccupation with the happy experiences of the past—or the expected gratifications which could not be attained—combined with painful desires to gain or regain them. Above I pointed to the seeming discrepancy between this undeniable overinvestment of grieving persons in their happy past, and the supposed hypercathexis of the sad events which induced the grief.

The example of a recently widowed woman in deep mourning will help us to clarify this point. In an interview with this woman I could easily observe how she would talk, for some time, about her past happy life with her husband; then, turning to the painful period of his sickness and death, burst into tears; only to go back to her wonderful memories, and return to the tragic events and her painful current situation with another eruption of grief.

This vacillating attitude seems to be characteristic of the processes underlying states of sadness and grief. Apparently, the painful experience of loss leads to an inner dichotomy. On the one hand, the emotional pain—like physical pain—seems to regenerate and mobilize libidinous forces which, flooding back to memories of the happy past, stir up those highly charged longings to regain the lost gratifications. On the other hand, the highly vested memory of the tragic event has become the carrier of sad anticipations. Both wishful fantasies and painful anticipations spread out and tend to be attached to all objects to which the deprived person tries to relate. Especially those associated with the lost objects or pleasures seem to invite this nostalgic search for happiness lost. Confronting the deprived person with what he cannot attain or regain, reality, in its turn, confirms the sad anticipations and fixates a tragically altered picture of the self and the world. However, while reactivating and recharging the sad memories, the repetition of the experience of loss on many objects lends itself to innumerable painful but relieving discharge processes. At the same time, these very repetitions revive the happy memories and wishful fantasies again. Thus, reality promotes a circular process which continues, with corresponding affective discharge manifestations in ever-diminishing quantities, as long as the mood lasts. Even-

NORMAL AND PATHOLOGICAL MOODS

tually, prolonged reality testing achieves a gradual renunciation of the wishful fantasies and liberates libido for new pursuits.

Hence, states of sadness or grief appear to develop as a contrast effect induced by the discrepancy and vacillation between equally overinvested, opposing memories and fantasies. Highlighting the contrast to the happy past, and painting the inviting and then depriving reality in dark colors, the frustrated search for happiness lost makes the world depriving and empty, the self deprived and poor.

Yet, is it true that sadness and grief lead not only to to impoverishment of the world, but also of the self (ego)? In his comparison of grief and depression, Freud (1917) stressed the lowering of the ego feeling, the ego impoverishment in melancholia, in contrast to the grieving person. "In grief," he said, "the world becomes poor and empty; in melancholia it is the ego itself." But any commonplace example will confirm that sadness, too, affects the self, though in a significantly different manner than depression. This is the decisive point. Freud's remarks refer to the waning of self-esteem in depression, the criticism regarding the world and the self, which is not characteristic of states of sadness and grief. Inasmuch as the sad person cherishes his past, he will feel deprived but not bad and worthless or empty. In other words: the libidinous cathexis of his self in its current situation is reduced, but not in favor of aggression; the libidinous object cathexes are likewise maintained, though they may also be reduced. An increase of aggression in the cathexes of the self and the world, that would lead to either angry or depressed mood, is prevented by the precious memories of a happy past and of a previously rich self. We shall return to this point and, in particular, to the different attitudes toward the past in the discussion of depression.

Inasmuch as the stability of his self-esteem and his object relations is essentially unshaken, a grieving person may be able to sustain his normal relationships, interests and activities. But the gratifications which they may otherwise grant, though consumed, cannot be properly enjoyed, since any pleasure, if permitted to develop at all, is tinged with pain because of what is searched for and missed. We can observe, for instance, that a sad person listening to a beautiful concert may be profoundly moved by it and even enjoy it, but at the same time respond with painful waves of sadness and with an outburst of tears. In profound mourning, of course, we frequently see that persons will restrict their object relations because of their absorption in the memories of lost happiness and their hopelessness regarding the future. Some refuse to have experiences which cannot be associated with the love object; others shrink back from anything that points too painfully to their loss. But even though the object world of grieving persons is temporarily narrowed and all experiences bear the touch of sadness, the object relations, in so far as they are maintained, are not changed with regard to their libidinous quality. Inasmuch as they are, sadness is mingled with hostility or depression.

Since full satisfaction of the self cannot be gained as long as sadness prevails, object relations and ego activities acquire a subdued quality. They lack the audible pulse of cheerful activity, those noticeable, recurring waves of increasing narcissistic and object cathexes which result from full gratifications and prepare renewed pleasurable experiences and actions. The oppressive nature of "silent sadness" has evidently much to do with a general restriction of free affecto-motor discharge, caused by reduced transference on reality; a transference which is either too painful to bear or in hopeless grief not even needed. But the affective inhibition of grief manifestations may also point to an underlying ambivalence problem; in this case the sadness will have depressive features. At any rate, the more strongly and persistently the longing is attached to and confronted with reality, the more intense and uninhibited will be the discharge by weeping, crying, sobbing. This may turn sadness into a relieving and even a rich experience. Though painful, these repetitive dramatic discharge eruptions will lead to an all the more drastic relief, the more they involve not only secretory (quiet weeping) but full affecto-motor discharge (sobbing). For this reason we may feel even greater sympathy for the unrelieved, "quietly sad" person.[5]

Some remarks may be added on self-pity, which is often inter-

[5] Here I may refer to Bibring's paper on depression (1953). First of all, I am doubtful whether a mood condition, i.e., an ego state, can be regarded as a primary ego response comparable to anxiety. While I would not object to describing sad or even depressive reactions as such primary responses, I believe and have tried to show that the development of a depressed state involves a more complex cathectic process. Moreover, the situation of helplessness and hopelessness resulting from an inability to change the situation is certainly also present in states of grief without depressive features.

mingled with sadness. Self-pity introduces a special gratifying narcissistic element into sadness, by hypercathexis less of the gratifications lost than of the "poor, deprived self that needs love and sympathy." The unpleasant effect on the observer has to do with his justified suspicion that this poor self has gained much more importance than the lost object.

States of gaiety or normal, cheerful elation are the pleasurable counterpart of sadness. Like sadness they are founded on libidinous processes which in their case, however, lead to pleasurable discharges. When opposing the state of sadness and grief to joyful, happy mood conditions, we encounter an interesting question. Are such pleasurable moods, too, evoked by an inner "contrast" situation? Or do they simply develop whenever happy anticipation aroused by an uncommonly pleasurable wish fulfillment imposes itself on all other experiences? To be sure, in order to induce a cheerful, gay, happy mood the provocative experience must have a certain momentum, something that makes it unusual or extraordinary. This suggests at least a certain "contrast" to the uneventful past. Practically, moreover, joyfulness develops very frequently from a happy event following a previous state of worry or sadness; e.g., when a person expects or experiences the return of a love object whose absence had previously saddened him. In this case the present wish fulfillment, as opposed to the painful past, provokes abundant cheerful anticipations which paint the world and the self in glamorous "contrast" colors.

Analogous to sadness, joyfulness also arises from a discrepancy, though from an opposite one: between a world unpleasant as it was and might continue to be, and pleasant as it turned out and is now expected to be. We recall that in "Mourning and Melancholia" Freud mentioned this contrast as the motivating experience for normal elation. However, not by any means do gay, joyful, elated moods always develop subsequent to conditions of strain or worry or sadness. They certainly cannot be regarded only as expressions of relief from trouble. Nor can we agree that pathological states of elation, as has been suggested, are mere reactions of relief from a previous depression. Nevertheless, we must remember that the gain of pleasure is always a "regaining" which must inevitably conjure up memories of previous loss or deprivation or suffering in general; all the more so, the more intense and the more unexpected the wish fulfillment.

In this connection we may recall what we know about the psychology of laughter, the most dramatic expression of gaiety, comparable to the weeping in sadness. A most significant factor in this affective reaction is the suspense effect evoked by the building up of high tension followed by sudden, unexpected, drastic pleasurable relief. Here, too, we find the idea of a "contrast." The building up of high tension would be unpleasant and provoke disagreeable anticipations, but for the gay emotional atmosphere which creates "opposite" expectations of cheerful relief. It is the suddenness of this relief that sets off the eruption of laughter.

In view of this we may well suspect that the "contrast effect," as achieved by the factor of "unexpectedness," plays a significant role in all states of cheerfulness, gaiety and pleasurable elation. To be cautious, we may assume that cheerful moods are evoked by pleasure experiences of unexpected intensity which are in sharp contrast to a previous indifferent or unpleasant situation. In either case, the embellishment of the world must originate in the fact that reality, by contradicting or surpassing anticipations derived from the past, grants unexpectedly high pleasure. When in a cheerful mood, we can indeed frequently observe a strange undertone of surprise or wonder that life can really be as enjoyable as this. We can assume that the factor of unexpectedness in the provocative experience is also operative in the development of sad mood conditions. The occurrence of very good or very bad events seems to be forever "unexpected." For this reason we observe in cases of prolonged fatal illness that the relatives during the period of preparation for the worst have worked through their grief and are no longer mourning, or even are relieved, when death actually comes.

Some remarks may be added concerning the undeniable closeness between sadness and joy, between weeping and laughter. I am not referring to the fact that explosive laughter can also lead to secretory discharge; i.e., evoke tears. What I mean is the strangely scintillating state "between laughter and tears," the "tragicomical" category. We can easily understand such midway or mixed conditions and the rapid transition from the one to the opposite state, if we remember that these opposite moods both arise from a contrast between happy and unhappy, good and bad notions. In normal moods it is reality that confirms either the one or the other notion, that swings the mood scale to the good or bad side. It is comprehensible that reality can create situations which may very easily shift this scale from the one to the other side. Tragicomical situations may well concomitantly or alternately point to the darker or brighter aspects of life, thus inducing a mixed or vacillating, iridescent, sad-humorous mood condition.

PART IV

A COMPARATIVE STUDY OF NORMAL, NEUROTIC, AND PSYCHOTIC MOOD DEVIATIONS

If we could not rely on the total symptomatic and psychodynamic picture in whose frame the affective states commonly appear, at first sight we would frequently be at a loss to distinguish, from the phenomenological point of view alone, between normal mood deviations and those which arise from pathologic desires or from neurotic conflicts. In this case, not the mood itself is pathological in nature but its motivations. And in cases where the symptom formation exhausts itself in the development of a mood condition, such as a depressed state, we find ourselves occasionally in serious differential-diagnostic doubts regarding the neurotic or psychotic nature of the condition.

The reason for these difficulties is that moods, with either normal or pathological qualities or motivations, are in any case an economic modality of the ego, which temporarily reinstates a "primary-process" type of mental functioning.

To be sure, inasmuch as moods involve transference phenomena of a generalized nature, they always lead to a temporary impairment of critical judgment and discrimination with regard to our own self and the object world. They produce a primitive, "subjective," prejudicial or even illusional type of feeling, thinking and behavior, which tends to resist reality testing. To the extent to which this reality testing can assert itself, the mood condition will subside. In so far as moods, normal or anomalous, color or at least overstate one aspect of reality and understate or blot out differing or opposing aspects, they always involve, to some extent, mechanisms of denial and distortion of reality. But the nature of this denial is quite different in normal and in pathologically motivated mood conditions, and provides us with significant differential-diagnostic criteria.

To begin with, in normal moods the denial does not extend to the provocative external event or to its immediate emotional impact which evokes the mood. If a person mourns the death of his wife or is jubilant on the return of his son, the motivations for such moods are realistic and mostly conscious. But even more: if Freud stated that in grief the whole world has become empty, this is correct, at least from the subjective standpoint of the grieving person. The gloomy color which the world assumes for him is the result of what we may call a normal denial: the denial of potential substitute gratifications which life might be able to grant him if he could only accept them. In this case, as in any other normal mood condition, the mood has certainly a realistic basis. There is commonly also a distinct, sometimes painful awareness that the mood is "subjective" in nature; that the world and the self as such have not changed; that they only "appear" different because "we are in such and such a mood." The blotting out of notions contradicting the mood is not complete, and the qualitative modifications remain in normal bounds. Thus moods will be within the normal range and appropriate in quality as long as they are compatible with our momentary external and internal reality and can be recognized as temporary ego states due to conscious reactions to realistic events. They will yield to reality testing and consequently be controllable and of limited duration. The less conscious the sources from which the moods arise, the less easily can the psychic situation be mastered and the more inappropriate will be the mood qualities. The duration of a mood depends, of course, also on the impact of the provocative experience. In grief, for instance, it may be so severe that the economic process requires an extended period to achieve its purpose. Grief certainly demonstrates particularly well that the duration of a mood is not as such a criterion for its normal or pathological character. The rapid passing of grief or other moods may well be an expression of defective or shallow object relations. And a very prolonged mourning period may either be caused by the severity of the loss, or by an inability to resolve unconscious conflicts with the lost object.

From the fact that even psychotic depressive states tend to pass spontaneously, as it were, Freud concluded that the economic process in such states must be essentially the same as in grief. But this cannot be wholly correct. In fact, as soon as unconscious conflicts participate in the development of the mood, they preclude an ultimate economic success. I have already referred to the limited economic function of pathologically motivated moods. The economic failure rests on the fact that infantile fixations prevent a reality testing sufficient to guarantee a true liberation of psychic energy from its original fixated position. What happens is essentially the same as in the case of a repressed infantile traumatic experience which a person unconsciously tries to overcome by repetitions of the trauma. Each time, this will result in relieving, affective discharge reactions. However, since repression precludes a reality testing leading to mastery of the traumatic situation, the repetitions will continue unless the repressed experience is brought to consciousness. Similarly, moods arising from unconscious sources permit only a sort of spurious reality testing, causing repetitive discharge reactions which are economically useful inasmuch as they finally lead to a temporary subsiding of the mood. But the hypercathexis of the pathogenic, repressed memories survives the mood and tends to turn reality into a constant source of renewed provocations, thus re-establishing the disturbed (anxious or hostile or depressed) affective state. If the mood deviation arises from a pathological narcissistic conflict, reality testing becomes even less effective or, in psychotic mood conditions, impossible.

Moods induced by narcissitic conflicts permit in general less reality testing than moods evoked by conflicts with the external world. Although the latter affect the self too (as we pointed out in the case of grief), they require predominantly a testing of external reality.

But in case of narcissistic conflicts the mood disturbance arises from the discrepancy between the self-representations and the ego ideal (superego) or the wishful image of the self, respectively. Hence it requires predominantly a testing of inner reality. External reality can be used only as a medium on which the self can assert its value. Unfortunately the self-critical agents, which test our inner reality, are deeply rooted in the unconscious and therefore highly arbitrary.

Moreover, our self-representations are in general even less realistic than our object-representations; consequently self-awareness is
not too well developed even in normal persons. Thus, our chances
for correct self-evaluation are, at best, limited. Indeed, those introspective capacities which are a prerequisite for constructive reality
testing appear to be a rather exceptional gift.

The difficulties of reality testing manifest themselves even in
moods evoked by a narcissistic conflict which has a realistic basis.
Let us consider the simple case of a man who is depressed because
he is doing badly in his job. His depression will arise from the discrepancy between his own narcissistic expectations and his realistic
failure which makes him temporarily feel that he is altogether an
inadequate person. The disapproval of his superiors will, of course,
influence and probably confirm this picture of himself. But the more
reasonable his expectations, and the more his self-evaluation is
founded on correct, rational judgment, the more likely is his self-
esteem to be restored by increasing self-assertion in his job. Yet, even
though he tests his ego functions on the medium of external reality,
i.e., on his work, it is the critical part of his ego—or, in moral conflicts, the superego—that has the last word and determines the good
or bad quality of his self and consequently his mood.

Hence, with regard to such moods we must modify our previous
statement that moods involve a generalized, temporary transference
from one object to the whole object world. In moods caused by
narcissistic conflicts, not longings for objects but narcissistic desires
are attached to the world or are expected to be satisfied through the
medium of the world. The higher and more illusory the narcissistic
expectations and the less realistic the self-representations are to begin
with, the more pathological will be the conflict and thus the resulting
mood.

A woman who unconsciously believes she is castrated and has a
phallic image of herself is bound to find in any little failure evidence
for her inferiority and to react to it with depression.

The infantile origin and the demonic power of the superego
make moods evoked by unconscious superego conflicts especially resistant to reality testing. The latter becomes impossible when the
superego has replaced the object world and, independent of its

standards and judgment, condemns and punishes the self or, the opposite, renounces its critical functions.[6]

Let us examine the different kinds of denial and distortion in neurotic and psychotic states, with some brief examples. Assuming a person were to get into a bad (irritable or angry or depressed) mood because his breakfast was ten minutes late, we should certainly suspect him of being neurotic. His mood exaggerates the importance of the provocative external event; it definitely distorts his own situation in the world and is, if not inappropriate, at least irrationally motivated. But if a public speaker were to develop a profound depression after a successful speech, he would be seriously sick. In this case his reaction to success and the resulting mood would be inappropriate; i.e., paradoxical. The drop of his self-esteem and of the mood level, which might be isolated from a full, conscious, intellectual awareness of his success, would deny its meaning as a result of unconscious conflicts of a masochistic type. And finally, in case a devoted husband who had just lost his wife were to respond with an elated mood manifesting itself in hectic pleasure-seeking, the state would be severely pathological. If such a mood were induced by a denial of the factual events, it would be definitely psychotic: his fantasies would not distort, but completely replace reality. If he were only denying the tragic impact of reality (cf. Lewin, 1950), the denial would be less severe and not necessarily psychotic. In such a case we commonly speak of a denial of the underlying sadness, but this it not quite correct. The denial of a mood condition looks different. Not rarely we find, for example, that persons whose facial expression, attitude, behavior betrays their bad mood, remain unaware of their condition or even pretend to be in good spirits. Many patients with objective signs of a depression consult the physician for physical reasons and cannot accept the correct diagnosis of their state. In these cases the mood awareness[7] is affected and an existing mood denied.

6 It is noteworthy that in true depressives, the longings for love and approval are not rooted in happy memories of the past, as is the case in grief. They are reactive in nature and, even if attached to the world, are removed from past and current reality. For example, a woman who had responded to the loss of her husband with a severe paranoid-depressive state, in which she complained about her disillusionment with the world and the senselessness of her life, said, when reminded of other widows in worse situations, "They have at least happy memories in which to live."

7 Mood awareness, which is mainly feeling awareness, develops as part of the self-representations and hence is a narcissistic phenomenon, whereas the affects and the moods as such are ego experiences involving both the objects and the self.

Our brief examples prove that we must make a distinction not only between many types, but also between varying degrees of denial and distortion which can be involved in mood development. In general, denial affects both the self and the object world; but it may lead to more conspicuous distortions of one or the other. It may be directed against the provocative event itself, against its impact or its meaning. Moreover, the denial may operate directly against external reality, or affect primarily the inner imagery and only secondarily—by way of projection—external objects and facts. And finally, there may be a secondary, defensive denial of an existing— appropriate or inappropriate—mood condition, i.e., a disturbance of the mood awareness.

The foregoing considerations regarding the different types of denial in normal and anomalous moods, and the limitations of reality testing in the latter, will be of value for the following brief comparative discussion of some special mood conditions and their pathological counterparts. This discussion will be restricted to our present frame of reference.

Comparative studies have been a legitimate approach since Freud's (1917) and Abraham's (1911; 1924) papers on mourning and depression. In certain respects this traditional comparison between grief and depression has been misleading. It suggested, by implication at least, that depressive states are always pathological, as opposed to the normal nature of grief. Moreover, in one way or another, the pioneering papers of Abraham (1911; 1924) and Rado (1928), Klein's work (1948), and even Lewin's illuminating studies on depression and related states (1950) have laid greatest emphasis on the role of early infantile response patterns in the modeling of such conditions. Hence our notions tend to link them up with the idea of introjective and projective mechanisms and of severe ambivalence conflicts causing regression to narcissistic, oral and anal positions. Thus, we easily lose sight of the fact that depressed as well as elated states may well develop in the range of normal mood conditions.[8]

This was shown in the example of John, who reacted to his varying experiences with Anne with alternating states of happy elation, of sadness, of anger, and of depression. All these responses had sufficiently realistic roots to lead to appropriate mood conditions which

8 In "Mourning and Melancholia" Freud discussed states of normal elation.

NORMAL AND PATHOLOGICAL MOODS 99

remained quantitatively and qualitatively within normal limits. Further evidence of their normal nature was the successful effect of reality testing. Not only did his mood easily yield to changes in Anne's attitudes; when Anne, after some weeks of a troubled relationship, actually gave him up, he went through an emotionally stormy period. But then he succeeded in re-establishing his affective and mood equilibrium, and some months later formed a satisfactory new attachment to another girl.

Our example certainly shows that the different qualities of sadness and depression as such are not expressive of the normal nature of sadness and of the pathological nature of depression. However, inasmuch as these differences arise from a prevalence of libidinous or aggressive forces in the whole realm of the ego, they point to the dangers inherent in depressed as well as in hostile mood conditions. Whereas the libidinous nature of sadness and grief (without depressive features) is indicative of an absence of conflict, hostile and depressed states always develop from aggressive tensions and hence are the expression of a conflict situation—either neurotic or psychotic, or one with reality. In other words, such conditions have a pathological potential that gains momentum to the extent to which the unconscious enters the conflict or—even worse—to which regressive processes are set in motion.

Moreover, the narcissistic disturbance, the affection of the self to which I referred already in our study of sadness, is more ominous even in normal depression than in mere sadness and more consequential with respect to the ego functions.

The aggressive, critical element is what lends value properties of quite a different order to the world or the self, respectively, in hostile or depressive moods than in sadness. The values whose loss or gain evokes sadness or happy elation are those of pleasure, of gratifications gained from the world. We may call them id values. But in depressed moods and states of hostility, of aggressive excitement, the world or the self, respectively, appears inadequate, faulty, bad, or injurious. They are derogated, criticized with regard to their strength, ability, superiority, or moral perfection; i.e., in terms of ego or superego values. Thus the core of the narcissistic disturbance in depression is always an experience of failure, though not necessarily of moral failure. The more the superego contributes to the conflict, the more will the self be conceived of as morally bad, expecting punishment from without or within. Frequently, though, the conscious feelings and ideas of inadequacy fend off hidden guilt conflicts.

Such qualitative changes in the relationship between the world and the self can be found even in the range of normal hostile and depressed mood conditions. But the particular modification or disturbance of this relationship will depend on the individual—either realistic or neurotic or psychotic—nature of the underlying conflict, and consequently on the vicissitudes of the instinctual forces in its development. We know that hostile and depressed moods can gain intensity through the "calling away" of aggression from the self to the world or vice versa. Thus, angry moods need not be primarily caused by hurt or disappointment. They may develop from narcissistic conflicts, e.g., from guilt conflicts or experiences of failure or faults when the self-directed aggression is secondarily turned toward the object world. They may then protect the person from a depressed condition. This tendency to blame the world rather than oneself is all too familiar even in normal persons.

Reversely, depressive states may be induced by a shift of aggression from the objects to the self. Since this vicissitude prevents a devaluation of the object world, it serves as an effective defense against ambivalence conflicts, especially when the latter involve the danger of loss of a significant love object. It may be stressed that these vicissitudes per se do not necessarily involve introjective and projective mechanisms. Depending on the degree to which such mechanisms are called upon, persons will then criticize themselves for the world's inadequacies or blame the world for their own faults. In the latter case the hostile states will assume paranoid qualities. We shall return to the problem of paranoid mood conditions further on.

At this point we shall rather study the modifications of the self and the world arising from these vicissitudes. We stated above that in mood conditions the self and the world assume "complementary" qualities. However, if the veering away of aggression to the self in depression is accompanied by a reactive libidinous hypercathexis of the world, they may acquire an opposite coloring. The world may then be inflated and appear glorified, idealized or even aggrandized at the expense of the bad, deflated self. Reversely, in hostile states the world may appear to be bad, inadequate or worthless, in favor of a good, superior, inflated self.

Such qualitative changes may still occur in the range of neurotic affective states, but they will certainly make us suspect the presence of underlying psychotic processes or at least of narcissistic conflicts at a regressive or archaic level.

In persons who relate to the object world only by way of narcissistic identifications, all conflicts, even those involving the object world, will be narcissistic in nature. Since in this case the boundaries between self- and object-representations are indistinct, any deflation of the self may communicate itself to the world, or the derogation of the world will be cast back upon the self. Should this happen, they are likely to assume identical qualities. This may be observed in such pleasurably hypomanic moods in which both world and self appear to be rich, wonderful, ideal, or again in those pessimistic, depressive conditions in which the world and the self are represented as equally bad, unpleasant, empty or worthless.

The point of departure for our last considerations were the shifts of aggression between the self and the world to be observed in hostile and in depressed conditions. However, it seems necessary to underline that depressive states do not always develop from attempts to resolve ambivalence conflicts by a veering away of aggression from the love object (the object world) to the self. They may well be directly evoked by a primary, narcissistic conflict.[9] But narcissistic conflicts which evoke depressed states are by no means always indicative of narcissistic regression leading to drive defusion. Such states may be intensified or influenced by infantile narcissistic conflicts, but they may also be caused directly by realistic experiences of failure, inadequacy or moral transgression.

We used, above, the example of a person doing badly in his job. Even if he is not a neurotic, he may well react to his failure with a depressed state and general feelings of inadequacy. If he is normal, these will subside to the extent to which his work is improving and he is able to assert himself. Should he feel tempted to commit or actually have committed a morally wrong or questionable act, we

9 Freud (1917) stressed this point in reference to melancholic depression and hinted in this connection at the possibility of a primary, endogenous ego impoverishment.

would not be surprised if he were to respond with remorse and depression.

For a study of the specific influences which different realistic or neurotic motivations or conflict situations can exert on the qualities of the resulting moods and, due to the differences in reality testing, on their course and vicissitudes, we may best resort to a few brief examples of sad, distressed, and hostile mood conditions.

Our first example concerns Miss A., an attractive, flirtatious, hysterical girl who is unconsciously in search of an incestuous love object and tends to develop striking and erratic mood variations. She suffers alternately from dramatic depressed and rather uncontrolled hostile states. According to the mood of the moment, she complains that either lack of chances or her own lack of charms prevent her from getting a husband. Her bad moods pass temporarily whenever she meets a man who shows some interest and looks like a suitable partner. But they return when nothing develops from such encounters. At last, she succeeded in forming a promising attachment to a nice young man who resembled her brother. However, since her object choice was determined by her incestuous desire, guilt feelings compelled her to relinquish this man. She managed to irritate him so much by her erratic behavior that finally he lost patience and gave her up. This rejection threw her into a serious, anxious depression with continuous outbursts of uncontrolled, copious weeping and sobbing. After recovery from this depression, the girl would probably have continued her frustrating search (and recurring reactive depressions and hostile states) had she not decided to undergo psychoanalytic treatment.

Our second example is one of normal grief with depressive features. Mrs. B., a middle-aged widow in a state of profound mourning after the loss of her husband, was not an analytic patient. She came to me only to discuss certain family problems, but these interviews gave a revealing picture of her emotional state. A woman with a very intense emotional life and vivid affective expression, she showed rather stormy mourning manifestations. Although controlled in the presence of other people, she would weep copiously when alone, dwelling on her memories of the beloved partner. She would feel the need again and again to visit the same places in the mountains whose beauty they had used to enjoy together. In her mourning state, the scenery would move her even more than before; but a beautiful view, a sunrise or sunset now evoked outbursts of weeping in association with her memories of the delight she had shared with her husband. Despite her dramatic reactions, however, she conscientiously stuck to her work, albeit with a lack of enthusiasm. She even found comfort and enjoyment in it, but these were mingled with her all-pervasive sadness. Though she had reduced her social activities, she felt a definite need for the company of those old friends who had also been close to her husband and would talk with her about him.

Mrs. B. reported that in the beginning of her grieving period, she had felt very depressed and remorseful for having failed her husband in so many ways. She particularly regretted that she had so often let him provoke her to angry outbursts. Since she wept while talking about this, her guilt reactions likewise seemed to be vivid, painful experiences accompanied by tears.

Mrs. B.'s grief reactions were strikingly different from those of her friend, Mrs. C., whom she sent to me some months later because she felt worried about her condition. Mrs. C. was also a widow, and one and a half years ago had lost her sister to whom she had been uncommonly attached. Since that time she had been in a chronic depressed state from which she could not recover.

In contrast to Mrs. B., Mrs. C. was an emotionally overrestrained, somewhat detached, obsessive-compulsive personality type. For Mrs. C. the beauties of nature had ceased to exist; she could not respond to them with any feeling. In general her emotional life seemed to have become empty. She could not take any serious interest in anything, not even in her work. At the same time she felt very restless. She avoided the company of her friends and preferred to spend her free time at parties or on visits with casual acquaintances. It turned out that these attitudes were in keeping with her basic defenses. By refusing to relate deeply to the outside world unless she was certain of being granted pleasure, she had always avoided being confronted with painful realities as much as she could. Both her detachment and her hunt for superficial pleasure saved her from the onslaught of those very painful emotions to which Mrs. B. submitted. The compulsive type of her affective defenses suggested the presence of much more intense ambivalence conflicts than in the case of Mrs. B. Mrs. C. spoke much of her guilt feelings about everyone and everything—except her late sister. Evidently, she had to deny and displace them because she could not bear to face the intensity of her conflict with the sister and of the hostility from which it arose.

Comparing the mood conditions in these three cases, we find that in Miss A. the central conflicts, causing hostile and anxious-depressed states, were definitely not problems of ambivalence but oedipal conflicts. Miss A. was not a girl who suffered from an inability to love. Her hostile behavior with men was only a defense against her incestuous impulses. Her anger at the world, which "did not offer her sufficient chances," was unconsciously directed at her oedipal rival, her mother. And her depressive complaints about her lack of charms referred likewise to her inability to compete with her mother. They covered up her unconscious need for punishment, caused by her incestuous guilt conflict. Her rationalizations concerning her mood disturbances resulted in a rapid passing of her hostile mood whenever she met a promising man, and her depression vanished as soon as she was able to gain his attention. This is what we meant by speaking of a spurious or pseudo reality testing. She could test reality only within the bounds of those motivations for her moods of which she was aware. Thus she was grieving about the loss of her lover, yet without knowing why she lost him and why she could not find or accept any man. Her unconscious oedipal conflicts were the reason for an acting out that led inevitably to a continuous recurrence of her mood disturbances.

In the case of Mrs. B., we can observe a rather normal mourning process that in many ways confirms and exemplifies my previous statements on sadness and grief. What lent a depressive coloring to her sadness was a conflict caused by hostility feelings toward her late husband, feelings of which she apparently had been and was fully aware. This awareness permitted the development of an introspective process, with a testing of her inner reality sufficient to help her fairly soon to overcome her remorse and the depression induced by it.

Quite in contrast to Mrs. B., Mrs. C. responded to the loss of her sister with grief turning into a chronic state of depression, which to my knowledge even now, after two years, has not essentially changed. A series of pathogenic features combined to produce this unduly prolonged disturbance. The central problem in her case is an ambivalence conflict of infantile origin. It had led to frank manifestations of hostility toward the sister, which after the latter's death Mrs. C. endeavored to forget and to deny. But even though she had also loved her sister very dearly, her grief could not find frank expression because she could not face the depth of her loss. She tried to evade the experience of sadness by running after superficial pleasures which left her empty. In other words, Mrs. C. escaped from a testing of the external as well as of her own inner reality. The unfortunate fact that she denied the impact of her loss, the nature of her past relationship with the sister and the true reasons for her guilt feelings, precluded a reality testing that might have resolved her conflict. It did not even permit relieving discharge reactions that might have gradually re-established a normal mood level.

When we compare the depressed states in these three persons with regard to their influence on their ego functions, we are again impressed by a significant difference. To be sure, in Miss A. the mood disturbances affected her activities, inasmuch as her constant preoccupations and her acting out with men and the resulting emotional vacillations undetermined her ability to concentrate on her work or on other pursuits. But there were no signs of a general depressive inhibition of thoughts and actions.

In Mrs. B.'s case, the grieving resulted in a preference for certain activities and relationships with concomitant limitation or exclusion of others. Mrs. C., however, suffered from depressive inhibitions of her thought processes and her work, inhibitions that were covered up by her restless pseudo activities.

This comparison suggests that the degree to which depressed states cause generalized inhibitions depends on the intensity and the nature of the underlying ambivalence conflicts, and the extent to which the depression aims to ward off hostility toward the world (the love object).

The inhibition of the ego functions in depressed states leads us to a further ego problem: the differences regarding the identifications in grief and in depression. In the case of Mrs. B. a conspicuous feature came to my notice. This woman talked about a grieving reaction which she had also experienced in the past after other object losses. It pertains to the identification with the love object which quite normally follows the loss of a beloved person. I had mentioned above that sadness may arise from identification with the suffering of others; this element plays a role also in grief. Mr. B.'s last illness had been brief but painful. His wife had shared his suffering with him, and after his death continued to feel and behave as though sharing with him the painful loss of life, in the same way as they had previously shared its manifold pleasures. Thus her fantasies encompassed not only the loss of her own gratifications, gained from and with the husband, but also the happiness he had enjoyed and of which he was deprived by his death. Although I have not found any references in the literature to this reaction, it is certainly a common mourning phenomenon given frequent expression in painful outbursts, such as "If only he—or she—were still alive and could have seen or experienced this or that happy event!" (It is characteristic that Mrs. C. did not seem to react in this manner.)

In the case described above, this magic fantasy of identification with the love object's loss of life's joys seemed to be the point of departure for certain superego and ego identifications which gradually developed in the course of the mourning period and led to lasting structural changes in the ego. In fact, I could observe that these especially painful thoughts had turned into an increased, constructive preoccupation with those interests and activities which her husband had particularly enjoyed or had liked her to pursue. She behaved as if by doubling her own efforts in those areas she could make up for what he had lost. When her mourning was over she remained, for instance, more attached to those beautiful mountains than she had been before; and in general she pursued more intensely those interests which her husband had shared with her. Besides, she developed ambitions particularly in those areas of her own work in which he had shown special interest and ambition for her (superego identifications). Years later she would respond to achievements in these areas with painful feelings of sadness at the idea how her husband would have enjoyed her success. Viewed in terms of her initial fantasy of identification with the husband's fate, her future realistic identifications replaced not only the lost husband and the gratifications he once had granted, but also his lost life and the gratifications he had gained from her and with her. This double aspect shows that identifications in grief are also in the service of preserving in memory the inner relation to the object now lost.

Here we observe that in grief the identifications develop as a constructive outcome of the grieving process. They may start—and possibly always start—at a magic fantasy level; but they gradually progress to the ego level and eventually bring about solid, selective ego alterations. Evidently the libido liberated in the mourning process cannot be immediately used for new personal object relationships which would replace the one lost. Instead, it is absorbed by the identifications and used for investments in new sublimations and ego functions. In fact, we frequently see that grieving persons, after the first stormy mourning period is over, begin to double their efforts in work or start new, absorbing activities founded on identifications with the lost object.

We know the extent to which ambivalence conflicts may interfere with the building up of such identifications during the mourning period. Mrs. C., for instance, escaped from her grief precisely into those superficial pleasures which her rather severe and sick sister had not been willing and able to share with her, which indeed she had frankly rejected and criticized. Thus, Mrs. C.'s activities seemed to originate in her rebellion against the older sister—a mother figure. On the other hand, we may suspect that her guilt feelings not only prevented her enjoyment, but were responsible for depressive reactions to those very pursuits.

In some patients I observed another interesting type of mourning reaction. They did develop identifications with the ambivalently loved lost object. But they would respond with depression when catching themselves, now, in the very attitudes or character traits which they had rejected in their love object. In other words, because they had loved the lost object, such patients identified with it. But inasmuch as they had hated it, they punished themselves for their hostility by first assuming the object's bad characteristics along with the good ones (masochistic identifications) and then hating themselves for this.

Thus the identification processes in grief may have many different vicissitudes; they may have constructive results or, under the influence of neurotic ambivalence conflicts, secondarily provoke depressive conditions and other pathological manifestations. But inasmuch as they bring about structural changes in the ego, they develop gradually as an outcome of the grieving process; whereas, in psychotic conditions, narcissistic identification processes introduce and mark the onset of a depressive period. Since these latter processes are founded on archaic incorporation fantasies, they cannot succeed in exerting a constructive influence on the ego but may lead to the development of delusional ideas.

This brings us to our last problem, the psychotic hostile or depressive mood conditions, which we shall discuss rather briefly and only from our present vantage point. I stated above that we do not always have sufficient criteria to distinguish at first sight between neurotic and psychotic mood conditions. However, if we can clinically observe them over a prolonged period and in addition have the opportunity to study the psychodynamic picture, we find characteristic differences in the nature and structure of neurotic and psychotic emotional states even when the latter do not lead to delusional symptom formation. What are the factors that determine their different qualities and their different course?

This is not the place to go into a general discussion of the psychoses. But we must call to mind that psychotic disorders are characterized by severely regressive processes involving all systems, and that these processes go along with drive deneutralization and drive defusion. Consequently there will be a tremendous surplus of deneutralized aggression which may invade all systems. Eradicating the superego functions, these aggressive forces may flood the ego and provoke it to destructive actions; or they may accumulate in the superego, thus smothering all ego functions, and possibly lead to self-destruction. As a result of the drive defusion and of ego and superego regression, the conflicts inducing mood conditions will be at a very primitive, narcissistic as well as sadomasochistic level; the mechanisms used for the purposes of defense and restitution will be archaic in nature.

This state of affairs has of course a paramount influence on the distortions of the self and the object world, and thus accounts for the ineffectiveness of reality testing in psychotic moods. Especially when delusions develop, the delusional ideas and the corresponding affective mood manifestations are, as we know, rigidly fixated and more or less inaccessible to external influences and events. They indicate a withdrawal from the object world, which has removed the mood from reality and reality testing.

We shall not discuss the special varieties of pathological modifications and delusional distortions which the self- and object-representations may undergo in the course of psychotic hostile or depressive mood development. We are sufficiently familiar with their clinical manifestations and with the specific mechanisms which bring them about.

I shall, however, briefly discuss the specific nature of those mechanisms of introjection and projection which may result in psychotic forms of identification.[10] Above I stressed that shifts of aggression

10 I discussed this issue at some length in previous papers (1953b; 1954a).

between the self- and object-representations need not always go along with introjective and projective processes. We may now point out that the latter are by no means always identical with the introjection of object-images into the self-images (or superego, respectively), or with the projection of self-images onto object-images. It is only these latter processes which are characteristic of psychotic conditions. They bring about different types of pathological identifications in different groups of psychoses, which will lend their particular psychotic qualities to the distortions of the self and the world.

I have dealt with psychotic identifications in one of the aforementioned papers (1954a), but did not discuss one essential point which belongs into our present context. When I stressed that in melancholic depression the patient "treats himself as if he were the love object," I indicated that his self-representations appear to have assumed those very qualities which he unconsciously ascribes to his love object. Inasmuch as such a type of identification leads to a fixated, possibly delusional, but only qualitative modification of his total self, it must evoke and be part of a mood condition.

Yet in schizophrenic delusional identifications the patient may "become" a different person. In this case his self is not qualitatively changed as a result of the identification. He may replace his own with the new, delusional identity. Such a process does not involve a mood development, although his new identity will of course influence his whole ego state. If a person believes he is Napoleon, he will certainly manifest grandiose attitudes and a corresponding behavior; but he may vacillate between a benevolent-friendly, a tyrannical-aggressive, and a paranoid-hostile state, all of which may be in harmony with his paranoic delusion.

What I said is, of course, equally valid with regard to the delusional changes of the object world. As long as they are qualitative, the world may appear to be rejecting, accusing, intentionally slighting. Spread-out paranoid delusional ideas will arise as part of a paranoid-hostile or a paranoid-depressive mood or a mixed condition. But truly paranoic delusions, where a new identity may be attached to previously well-known persons, do not appear in the frame of a mood. This is why patients with fixated and systematized delusions of persecution may appear quiet and inconspicuous on the surface, until they pick up a gun and shoot Mr. X because they know he is not their old lawyer or physician but a secret agent instigating a communist plot against them.

This difference between the two types of psychotic identification —between the one causing qualitative delusional changes of the self and the world, which evoke mood conditions, and the one that creates new identities—has clinical significance. It makes comprehensible why paranoic ideas of the latter type lend themselves to systematization. Since they do not involve generalized transference phenomena but remain localized and centered about definite single objects, they may leave whole areas of the ego unaffected. Within the area of the ego where the paranoic system develops they may of course spread out, may jump from one object to another, or may gradually extend to a number of persons who become associated to and part of the plot.

This restriction to a particular ego area, which may remain isolated, is especially characteristic of true paranoia. As we know, such patients may appear perfectly sane and emotionally undisturbed until something is touched upon that relates to the paranoic area; only then may their sickness become manifest. It is this localization which permits a gradual systematization of the delusion, such as is impossible in paranoid mood development.

In paranoid schizophrenics we can observe both: paranoid notions in the frame of paranoid mood conditions, and true paranoid delusions with or without systematization. From what I said it follows that in the case of paranoid mood conditions, especially those having a cyclic course, we may have great difficulties deciding whether they are the expression of a schizophrenic process or of a manic-depressive psychosis; only long-term observation enables us to make the correct differential diagnosis.

The problem just discussed leads us immediately to another question. Why and under what circumstances does this pathological process sometimes exhaust itself in the production of a psychotic mood condition without further symptom formation, as is the case in manic-depressive disorders; of a condition which may develop to a peak, then gradually and spontaneously subside, and leave the person practically restored until another period sets in? While I cannot answer this question, I may venture some tentative remarks.

Infantile environmental factors certainly may have a paramount pathogenic or predisposing influence on the development of psychoses, and disturbing current experiences may provoke the final psychotic break. But few psychiatrists doubt that psychoses are based on endogenous, as yet unknown, physiological processes. The more suddenly the pathological, psychophysiological psychotic process sets in, the more rapid will be the processes of regression and drive defusion. In this case the sudden surplus amount of destructive energy may be able to attack and overrun the whole ego. To put it differently: the ego, suddenly taken unawares, will be unable to do more than to call immediately on mood development as a safety valve for discharge. However, since moods are states involving the whole ego in the way described above, they are apt to interfere with special defensive operations of the kind that can be used for the solution of localized conflicts. This precludes the formation of symptoms other than those expressive and part of the mood condition. But we must not forget that psychotic mood conditions encompass a much wider range of symptoms than do neurotic mood conditions. We remember not only the physiological symptoms, such as insomnia and loss of weight and appetite, but also the variety of hypochondriacal manifestations. The objection may be raised that schizophrenic episodes and also periods of psychotic depression mostly have a forestage announcing the imminent onset of the acute illness, and that depressive or hypomanic periods often seem to develop gradually.

However, the onset of the actual episode is commonly sudden. Manic-depressive patients whose depression worsens gradually may nevertheless remember precisely the day when their depression began and often also the day when it was over, when they "woke up" and suddenly "felt different, healthy again." My suspicion that the sudden acute onset of the illness is the reason for an involvement of the whole ego, causing immediate mood development, appears to be further confirmed by the comparison of the prognostically more favorable type of schizophrenia which produces recurring episodes, with the symptomatology in the slowly developing schizophrenic process. The latter may affect first the one, then the other area, or else slowly expand, invade the whole personality and eventually lead to a general mental disintegration. Such patients may of course show a particular moodiness. They may tend to react with sudden, inappropriate affective outbursts and mood swings. They may impress us by the flat, cold qualities of their affects and the final loss of feeling

capacities. But in the course of such chronic or progressively developing disorders there is hardly a stage where characteristic, prolonged
mood conditions become predominant in the total clinical picture.

The question of the different influences of suddenly or slowly
developing physiological changes on the symptomatology leads us
back once more to the economic problem, with which we shall terminate this study.

We concluded that psychotic mood conditions which have led to
delusional development offer little chance for reality testing. But we
noted that the repetitive, prolonged discharge as such might be
economically effective enough to cause the mood eventually to subside, for some time at least. In those ominously quiet, paralyzing
types of depression in manic-depressive patients, however, and in
states of catatonic-depressive stupor, there is hardly an opportunity
left for affective discharge to the outside. The discharge is, as it were,
mute; it is centripetal. I mentioned this point in a previous paper
(1954b), where I stated that patients with melancholic forms of
depression who noisily attack themselves are better off, inasmuch as
they can at least discharge their self-directed aggression by way of
self-accusations.

How is it possible, under these circumstances, that depressive
conditions in which the tensions cannot be relieved by discharge to
the outside ever come to an end? And yet we observe that patients
who have spent months or even years in a catatonic stupor may get
up one day, begin to move and eat and talk, and within a brief period
may return to life.

Such observations make us suspect that psychotic depressive or
manic conditions are terminated, not by the economic process involved in the mood, but by physiological changes which may set in
suddenly or slowly. These processes might also change the proportion
between aggressive and libidinous forces in favor of the latter and
by promoting drive refusion, enable the patient again to vest libido
in the external world. From my clinical observation I gained the
impression that only at the moment when patients began to reinvest
psychic energy in the world and to discharge onto the outside world,
the mood reacquires a useful economic function whose value increases as the patients become accessible to treatment and capable of

reality testing. This is why psychotherapy in a psychotic-depressive period is most profitable during the final phase.

BIBLIOGRAPHY

Abraham, K. (1911), Notes on the Psycho-Analytic Investigation and Treatment of Manic-Depressive Insanity and Allied Conditions. In: *Selected Papers on Psycho-Analysis*. London: Hogarth Press, 1927.
—— (1924), A Short Study of the Development of the Libido. In: *Selected Papers on Psycho-Analysis*. London: Hogarth Press, 1927.
Bibring, E. (1953), The Mechanism of Depression. In: *Affective Disorders*, ed. P. Greenacre. New York: International Universities Press.
Freud, S. (1917), Mourning and Melancholia. *Collected Papers*, IV. London: Hogarth Press, 1925.
—— (1921), Group Psychology and the Analysis of the Ego. *Standard Edition*, XVIII. London: Hogarth Press, 1955.
Jacobson, E. (1953a), The Affects and Their Pleasure-Unpleasure Qualities in Relation to the Psychic Discharge Processes. In: *Drives, Affects, Behavior*, ed. R. M. Loewenstein. New York: International Universities Press.
—— (1953b), Contribution to the Metapsychology of Cyclothymic Depression. In: *Affective Disorders*, ed. P. Greenacre. New York: International Universities Press.
—— (1954a), Contribution to the Metapsychology of Psychotic Identifications. *J. Am. Psa. Assoc.*, II.
—— (1954b), The Self and the Object World: Vicissitudes of Their Infantile Cathexes and Their Influences on Ideational and Affective Development. *This Annual*, IX.
—— (1957), Denial and Repression. *J. Am. Psa. Assoc.*, V.
Klein, M. (1948), *Contributions to Psycho-Analysis, 1921-1945*. London: Hogarth Press.
Lewin, B. D. (1950), *The Psychoanalysis of Elation*. New York: Norton.
Rado, S. (1928), The Problem of Melancholia. *Int. J. Psa.*, IX.

ON DEFENSE AND DEVELOPMENT:
NORMAL AND PATHOLOGICAL

JEANNE LAMPL-DE GROOT, M.D. (Amsterdam)

In studying the concept of defense one is confronted with much confusion in psychoanalytic literature about a lot of problems. I name only a few of them:

1. Is "defense" in itself a pathological phenomenon or are we entitled to speak of "normal" defense mechanisms and defensive processes?

2. What is the relation of childhood neurosis to the defense mechanisms?

3. We may turn our attention to the chronology of defense mechanisms.

4. What is the role of defensive processes in the total ego organization?

5. We could examine the different analysts' views regarding the practical question of whether or not every defensive process has to be dissolved during analytic treatment.

More questions could be raised. In this communication I shall limit myself to the presentation of only a few ideas on some of the points. I begin with the first problem mentioned above.

Can we speak of "normal" defense, or does every defensive process belong in the realm of pathology? What conception of defense is most fruitful in analytic theory and practice? There is no doubt that Freud first made use of the term defense *(Abwehr)* in connection with psychopathology (1894, 1896). It seems that many authors tend to retain this early employment of the term and want to reserve it for neurotic and other forms of maldevelopment. They do so in spite of the fact that at later times, e.g., in *Inhibitions, Symptoms and Anxiety* (1926), Freud clearly showed the connection between "normal" and "pathological" defense mechanisms.

Speaking of the relation between "repression" and "defense," Freud (1915) recommends the rehabilitation of the latter term as "a general designation for all the techniques the ego makes use of in conflicts, which may lead to a neurosis." "Repression" is to be viewed as one special defense mechanism.

In his contribution to the Symposium on Defense Hoffer (1954) mentions this statement of Freud's, and further adds that many authors consider defense mechanisms to have "their own history and source." He continues: "They [the defense mechanisms] may be traced back to their origin in the primary processes, e.g., in displacement and to the genuine mechanisms which the growing ego successively develops from inborn patterns, that is to the autonomous ego functions; they are often highly developed, very complicated structures of the mind."

Hartmann (1939) has shown how important it is "to view mental processes not only in their interplay with mental conflict but also from the part they play in respect to adaptation." Hoffer cites a number of other authors, who point out that defense mechanisms may be used "regressively" or "progressively"; they may "protect" the ego or "destroy" it (Eissler, 1953).

Nevertheless one repeatedly encounters the idea that defense mechanisms are pathological phenomena. Fenichel (1945) considers only sublimation to be a normal one and regards all others as pathogenic.

Anna Freud, in her book *The Ego and the Mechanisms of Defense* (1936), describes different defensive attitudes of which she says that they can also be seen in normal reactions. She includes them, however, under the heading "Preliminary Stages of Defence."

We should like to find a way out of these confusions. With this purpose in mind, I propose to examine two well-known defense mechanisms encountered in severe psychic illness: projection and identification.

Projection may be used in paranoid psychosis, identification (based on the mechanism of introjection) may, e.g., lead to severe symptoms in a melancholic patient.

When we turn to observations of infants, however, all of us assume that processes of projection and introjection play a considerable role in every infant's normal growth. None of us would think of a severe pathological process in this context. Therefore it might be confusing when Melanie Klein and others use certain terms taken from clinical psychiatry—e.g., "depressive position" or "persecutory anxiety"—to describe early processes in normal infants.

When we turn our attention to the newborn's behavior we see a somewhat different picture. The newborn responds at first merely somatically to outer and inner stimuli. To the shortness of oxygen during birth the infant reacts with putting into motion the respiratory organs, in order to "incorporate" oxygen. When hunger and thirst stimuli arrive the newborn will drink; this means it incorporates fluid food by sucking the mother's breast. Incorporation of oxygen and food as well as egestion of carbonic acid and excrements are normal regulative reactions to the metabolic processes tending to maintain a physiological homeostasis.

In this connection, experimental psychologists and ethologists speak of mechanisms of regulation and adaptation. There are other adaptive processes in the human newborn (though fewer than in newborn animals), e.g., the adaptation of the skin capillaries to stimuli of cold and heat, the closing of the eyelids when too strong a light stimulus reaches the eye, etc.

We assume that the first primitive awareness that inner and outer world are separate entities arises in connection with the different bodily responses to inner and outer stimuli.

It still is difficult to decide at what point we are entitled to begin to speak of psychic phenomena in the infant, at what moment the body ego is enlarged with a mental ego. Among many factors the maturational state of the central nervous system apparently plays an important role. But we may take it for certain that the psychic life develops on the base of somatic reactions or, to put it more precisely: in interplay with them. This is one of the expressions of psychosomatic entity.

In a theoretical discussion in a small work group in Amsterdam, Bastiaans, referring to observations on psychosomatic patients, made the suggestion that every neurotic defense mechanism could be traced back to a normal somatic regulation or adaptation mechanism, and would represent quantitative variation of the latter.

There is one early definition of Freud's (1905) which points to what one could call a "psychosomatic" viewpoint. It runs: "The defensive processes are the psychic correlates of the flight-reflex and follow the task of guarding against the origination of pain from inner sources." It points to the correlation of body reactions to dangerous stimuli (flight) and mental reactions guarded by the pleasure-pain principle.

When a little child projects unpleasurable drive stimuli and sensations upon the outside world and simultaneously introjects images of need-satisfying objects, the mechanisms of projection and introjection are not used merely for "flight" (and "fight"), but at the same time as regulative and adaptive processes.

A physically healthy child growing up under favorable circumstances, with a loving, understanding and tolerant mother, presents itself as a friendly, gay, charming and harmonious little creature. We are naturally aware of the fact that every individual's growth proceeds on the basis of conflicts. But we should not overlook the fact that in these so-called "normal" children the conflicts resulted for the time being in a regulation of the emotional and instinctual needs and an adaptation to the outer world. I hasten to add that I am certainly not of opinion that thereby these well-balanced little children would be prevented from acquiring neuroses in later times. There are too many examples of harmonious children finally developing more or less severely disturbed personalities.

What I wanted to suggest, however, is that we view the neurotic defense mechanisms as pathologically exaggerated or distorted regulation and adaptation mechanisms, which in themselves belong to normal development. One might raise objections and say that this formulation is merely a terminological variation. I do not think that is correct. I believe that apart from decreasing some of the confusions mentioned above, my formulation has the advantage of stressing the connection (or the continuum) of physiological-biological and psychic processes, both in the normal and in the abnormal. Last but not least, it may prevent us from overlooking normal developmental processes in our children as well as in our patients. I absolutely agree with Brierley (1947) and Hoffer (1953) that "our closer association with mental disease . . . has often hampered our dealings with normality" and that "the personal integrity of the patient [may be] impaired by the omission of the normal aspect of the rôle of defence in mental functioning." For the "normal aspect of the rôle of defence" I should like to substitute "the role of adaptation and regulation in all processes that deal with mental conflicts."

I realize that one could justifiably reproach me for speaking loosely of "normal" and "pathological" and of "health" and "disease," without giving clearer definitions. I cannot solve this problem in its complexity, and will remind you of the well-known, though stale statement that "normality" and "health" as well as "disease" are merely practical conceptions which so far defy scientific definitions.

We may nevertheless try to throw some light upon one special function which is indispensable for a person's psychic health—the synthetic or integrative function—precisely by using the viewpoint of the psychosomatic entity. The infant uses the inborn and the learned regulation and adaptation mechanisms to establish physiological homeostasis in metabolism. The little child does the same to attain psychic equilibrium. We know that it is the task of the ego to develop a synthetic, integrative, harmonizing function.

The little child's growing, but still primitive and unstable ego organization has to learn with the mother's help how to regulate its drives and affects, its needs, etc., as we mentioned before. In the first years of life the mother is indispensable both for the normal *bodily* and mental growth. However, she remains so much longer for the mental development.

When the mother-child symbiosis succeeds in establishing and promoting a synthetic, regulative ego-function and when in addition the mother is able to further the child's independence in the successive development, the outcome may really be a well-balanced personality. Or, examined from the reverse side, we may say: since every normal infant's instinctual needs come into conflict with the outside world, which can offer only limited satisfaction and always has to demand restrictions, the regulative ego functions cannot develop in a harmonious way when one or both of the partners of that early mother-child bond fail in the cooperative interplay. Such a failure impairs the normal growth of the still weak ego organization and threatens the ego with being overwhelmed by the drives and affects; thus inner conflicts are added to the outer ones, signaled by anxiety.

When the mother is aware of the child's emergency situations, she may be able to furnish the necessary support for the child's ego growth and a new balance may come into existence. When she fails to do so, the way is open for more or less severe neurotic disturbances in the child. The same may happen when the other partner in the mother-child relationship, the little child itself, falls short of its task in the cooperation, either through an unfortunate instinctual disposition (e.g., tameless drives, too much ambivalence, too strong clashes between libido and aggression or active and passive strivings, etc.) or through a lack of indispensable inborn ego capacities.

I will choose the process of identification to illustrate the pathological use of mental mechanisms. In normal development identifications play an important role in learning. When identification is used to ward off danger situations, it may go so far as to overwhelm the child's total ego organization. The child's personality so to say "melts together" with the mother. The resulting loss of one's own identity is experienced with strong anxiety and may lead to a severe damage of further development. I shall come back to this point later on.

Now I should like to give an example of a favorable collaboration between mother and child in a relatively normal boy of age two years nine months. The boy was a lively, well-balanced child. Toilet training was accomplished in a quiet, natural way about the second year. After the birth of a new baby when the boy was two years two months old he wetted his bed only two or three times. About half a year later the bed wetting suddenly reappeared. At first his mother did not understand what had happened. Nothing extraordinary could be discovered in the family situation. Then, however, the mother became aware of the fact that the boy was masturbating and having erections, much more frequently than before.

On an appropriate occasion she spoke with her little son about his erections, apparently in a natural, reassuring way, with full acceptance of his masculinity and his right to pleasure and masculine pride. The next night everything was alright. After several weeks the enuresis came back, but only for a short time. Following this period it never recurred up to the present time. The boy is now three and a half years old.

In the meantime his ego development had advanced also in other respects, as I should like to demonstrate in an occurrence, the explanation of which I owe to Miss Anna Freud. When the boy was three years one month old he was taken on an excursion during which he traveled by car over a very long bridge. He admired it very much and was impressed by the many cars passing over it at the same time. Some hundred meters further alongside lies a second, a railway bridge. When the boy was told that trains were running over this second bridge, he said: "But *cars* are running over it, *too*." To the answer: "No, that one is only for trains," he replied with the utmost conviction: "But *formerly* there were cars running over that bridge, too."

I did not understand the meaning of this statement, but Anna Freud gave a fascinating explanation of the event. She thought the boy wanted to say: "Formerly all pleasureable experiences were allowed to be made everywhere." She is of the opinion that the boy's statement indicated his readiness to accept limitations. This acceptance and the distinction between former and present times represent an achievement of the ego's development. Some months later this explanation was confirmed by a second experience.

The boy is the owner of a number of small toy cars. He is especially fond and proud of a "Chevrolet." During another excursion the boy again traveled over the long bridge. This time a train was just passing over the railway bridge. He was happily excited and said: "*Formerly* when I was driving in my Chevrolet I was passing by that bridge like the train is doing now."

I would sum up the successive events in the following way. In the inner conflict, caused by an increase of masculine, genital sexuality, that for a moment had threatened his inner balance, the still weak ego had made use of the mechanism of regression to an earlier phase and produced the symptom of bed wetting. With the mother's support the ego succeeded immediately in discontinuing the regressive process. The boy returned to the former state of ego achievement in mastering again the excretory functions and in developing new ego capacities: the distinction between past and present and the acceptance of the different possibilities of satisfaction.

Such regressive phenomena occur very often during the period of the little child's ego growth, just as do other defensive attitudes in conflicts which provoke anxiety. Should we speak of a neurosis and of defense mechanisms in this connection? This question brings us to the second point I mentioned in the introduction of this paper: When do we have to speak of childhood neurosis and what processes have to be considered as normal developmental ones?

The answer apparently does *not* lie in the nature of the mental mechanisms used by the growing ego in its reactions to conflicts. We mentioned already that projection and identification are normal regulative and adaptive mechanisms. By making use of them the ego learns to distinguish between inner and outer world, to develop reality testing, etc. Especially identifications play a paramount role in learning processes, in acquiring different skills, in learning how to handle emotional and instinctual needs.

Regressions and anxiety never fail to appear in normal development. Isolation of past and present events furthers the orientation in time and so stimulates the phase-adequate development. I think the answer is better to be looked for in the examination of the *ways* the different mechanisms are made use of by the child's ego.

When, at first with the help of a kind of auxilliary ego borrowed from the mother, the ego succeeds in making use of the various mechanisms from the aspect of their regulative and adaptive side, the conflicts may be solved in a way that stimulates balance and growth. When, however, the ego has to fight too strongly against the drives, it has to use all available forces for the maintenance of its still weak, just established organization. In this case there is a greater opportunity for a lasting disturbance in balance and for an arrest in development.

This ideas gives rise to the question of what causes the child's ego to go the one or the other way. I think, among the many ego capacities necessary for a favorable solution of these conflicts, there is one of the utmost, perhaps decisive, importance. It is the ego's capacity to deal with the child's aggressive drives. Or, in other words, the child's capacity to neutralize (and sublimate) aggression. I remind you of Freud's suggestion to view mental conflict in regard to aggression. Every conflict, whether between child and environment or between ego and id, provokes free aggression. And it is precisely aggression that is least tolerated in free discharge, that is most dangerous for the developing ego organization when turned inside, and that in many cases is more unsuitable for neutralization than is libido. Even in conflicts in the sexual sphere it might be the fate of the simultaneously provoked free aggression that becomes decisive for the final outcome.

In the analysis of one of my adult patients it ultimately became clear that the aggressive, mocking and sneering way in which his mother had rejected the little boy's exhibitionistic genital wooing had provoked his own overwhelming aggressive response with the final result of a rigid standstill in his ego development.

Among other factors the switching off of the normal learning processes by means of identifications, of which I spoke before, played here a decisive role. The little boy's sexuality was reduced to a passive surrender toward the father. He identified with the passive mother image to such a degree that he lost his own identity. In his adult sexual life every approach to a woman meant a melting together with her. To escape the danger situation of losing his self he had to summon up nearly all his strength. The result was an inhibited personality with very restricted ego capacities.

Such observations point at the same time to the paramount importance of the mother's attitude toward the little child's aggression. In my patient every trial to master aggression was counteracted by the mother. A well-balanced mother, on the other hand, is a well-suited object for identification and may thus come to be of very great help to her child in the latter's effort to learn the controlling of aggression, to neutralize aggressive energy and to use this energy in the building up of the ego organization.

Returning to our question of what constitutes neurosis in childhood, I should like to summarize as follows. Mental mechanisms, which may later be used as neurotic defense mechanisms in adult neuroses, are normal developmental mechanisms in early childhood, as long as they serve and promote the ego's regulative and adaptive capacities.

I remind you here of Anna Freud's well-known statement (1945) that, in the assessment of childhood disturbances, we should make use of the criterion of an unimpaired advancement in ego development. In full agreement with this view, I should like to continue: regulative and adaptive functions of the so-called defense mechanisms are particularly endangered when the capacity for neutralization of aggression is not sufficiently present. Furthermore, we should speak of a real childhood neurosis only when the defensive function of the mechanisms outbalances the regulative function *and* holds up the continuation of ego growth.

Here a critical remark is in order. In every child's development there is one phase in which the first condition—the prevalence of the defensive aspect of a special mechanism—is a regular and normal occurrence. This is the oedipal phase, in which the mechanism of repression comes to the fore. In our culture every child has to repress his sexual and aggressive strivings inherent in the oedipus complex. However, after a more or less *"normal"* solution of this complex, the ego development receives a great impetus for further unfolding, and no neurosis develops. Precisely because the defensive function in repression of oedipal conflicts is indispensable, the preconditions for the coming into existence of a real neurosis become stronger in this phase. These considerations are in accord with Freud's very early view of the oedipus complex as the nucleus of the neuroses.

Perhaps we really could keep to this view for the average child. While preoedipal developmental disturbances may contribute to a particular unfortunate shaping of the oedipus complex, it is still the fate of the ego's development during and after the oedipal phase itself which decides whether a more or less fixed neurosis will orig- inate or not. Only in infants who from the very beginning show severe disturbances, either caused by inborn factors or by serious deprivations, we may observe fixed neurotic symptoms in the pre- oedipal phase. We could assume that in these cases either the ego was lacking every possibility for advancement in development or that it was exposed to a precocious and therefore heavily endangered devel- opment, so that a regulative and an adaptive use of the available mechanisms was eliminated from the beginning.

Be that as it may, in the preoedipal phase it is more often the mother's neurosis or other environmental circumstances that cause usually reversible disturbances in the little child. After the decline of the oedipal phase, when a preliminary shape of the child's person- ality and the establishment of his superego have taken place, the child's circumscribed neuroses take a certain fixed shape.

In this context I merely want to mention the fact that an obses- sional neurosis arises only in the latency period. When repression in latency and adulthood fails to be sufficient for defensive purposes, other mechanisms are used in the attempt to ward off the returning repressed contents; among them are mechanisms that formerly served regulation and adaptation, as for instance projection, identification, isolation, turning inside, etc. I will not name them all because they are well-known from Freud's and Anna Freud's works.

It would be fascinating, however, to pursue the vicissitudes of the different mechanisms, on the one hand from the viewpoint of their adaptive, regulative aspects, and on the other hand, their defensive aspects during the personality's development from birth to maturity. This brings us to our third point: the chronology of defense mechanisms. In following the chronology of specific mechanisms, we might really discover that all pathological defense mechanisms seen in the neuroses and psychoses of latency and adulthood are the very same mechanisms that served normal ego development in early childhood and that at a later stage may be used simultaneously in a distorted way to ward off the re-emergence of the insufficiently repressed strivings. It is possible that some mechanisms become fixed only after the superego has been established, as for instance the turning of aggression against the self. The regulative, constructive side of this process furthers the consolidation of social norms and ethical values, whereas its defensive function operates in a destructive way and may lead to severe pathological guilt feelings and self-damage. Usually this mechanism is not observable in infants, though there are cases described of self-injuries in early childhood. We might perhaps also discover that even those defense mechanisms which work in the service of the superego have their forerunners in relation to ego activities.

I leave this theme for further investigation and now turn to our fourth point: the place of the defensive processes in the total ego organization.

I speak here of defensive processes because in the course of development the ego, making use of different mechanisms, builds up a complicated defensive organization. From latency onward parts of this organization can be mobilized to ward off other parts of it. This may happen when the latter part proves to be endangered in new stages of development, in which additional demands are made upon the ego. I give one example instead of many.

In the preoedipal phase the little boy's passive strivings toward the mother may be countered by the growing ego through a specific regulative and defensive mechanism, namely, through activation of active tendencies. In the oedipal situation the normally increased masculine urges may become a danger in connection with rivalry with the father. The boy now remobilizes passive strivings as well as ego reactions to ward off his masculine fantasies. Whether the boy finds a normal solution to his oedipal conflict or not depends upon the ego's capacity to save his active strivings from repression (or from being warded off) and upon the degree to which the ego succeeds in neutralizing and sublimating these active strivings. In our neurotic patients this faculty of the ego proved to be too weak in relation to the instinctual urges, hence the result was a feminine sexual relationship to the father. In the course of further development such a father attachment can again be warded off and covered by a distorted, seemingly masculine behavior in life.

It is clear from the foregoing that the ego's defensive activity constitutes a very important part—yet, it is true, only one part of the total ego functions. Instead of examining in detail all ego activities and achievements, I will only stress once more the importance of considering the normal regulative-adaptive functions of the various mechanisms and processes, and their influence upon the development of other ego capacities, both on the intellectual and on the emotional level. I have illustrated this process in regard to the mechanism of identification.

Finally I want to mention again a specifically significant point. According to one of Freud's definitions, neuroses are disharmonies in the ego organization. Among the many factors that are responsible for those disharmonies, we have already referred to one of particular importance: the personality's capacity to neutralize aggressive energy. This capacity is dependent on the one hand upon the quality and intensity of the drives, and on the other hand upon very specific ego properties, but its development may be stimulated or counteracted by objects in the environment.

Turning to our fifth and last point, I think we can do away with a frequent misapprehension, expressed in the demand that psychoanalytic treatment should attempt to demolish the ego's defensive organization. For many of us it is self-evident that we should not, and even could not, succeed in our endeavors to live up to this "requirement." Nevertheless we often encounter pronouncements such as: "The patient's defense mechanisms have not disappeared, therefore he is not yet cured." Or: "You should aim at doing away with your patient's defenses," etc.

Keeping in mind that every defense has originally a regulative-adaptive function, we can correct these remarks. In analysis we should try to give the patient's ego the opportunity for abolishing the pathological, rigid employment of the mechanisms in the neurotic conflicts, and we should try to open ways for their regulative, constructive use in order to promote a harmonious afterdevelopment and unfolding of the total personality.

BIBLIOGRAPHY

Brierley, M. (1947), Psycho-Analysis and Integrative Living. In: *Trends in Psycho-Analysis*. London: Hogarth Press, 1951.
Eissler, K. R. (1953), The Effect of the Structure of the Ego on Psychoanalytic Technique. *J. Am. Psa. Assn.*, I.
Fenichel, O. (1945), *The Psychoanalytic Theory of Neurosis*. New York: W. W. Norton & Co.
Freud, A. (1936), *The Ego and the Mechanisms of Defense*. New York: International Universities Press, 1946.
—— (1945), Indications for Child Analysis. *This Annual*, I.
Freud, S. (1894), The Defence Neuro-Psychoses. *Collected Papers*, I. London: Hogarth Press, 1949.
—— (1896), Further Remarks on the Defence Neuro-Psychoses. *Collected Papers*, I. London: Hogarth Press, 1949.
—— (1905), *Wit and Its Relation to the Unconscious*. New York: Moffat, Yard, 1917.
—— (1915), Repression. *Collected Papers*, IV. London: Hogarth Press, 1949.
—— (1926), *Inhibitions, Symptoms and Anxiety*. London: Hogarth Press, 1936.
Hartmann, H. (1939), Psychoanalysis and the Concept of Health. *Int. J. Psa.*, XX.
Hoffer, W. (1954), Defensive Process and Defensive Organization: Their Place in Psycho-analytic Technique. *Int. J. Psa.*, XXXV.

SOME THOUGHTS ON INTERPRETATION IN THE THEORY AND PRACTICE OF PSYCHOANALYSIS[1]

RUDOLPH M. LOEWENSTEIN, M.D. (New York)

If one compares the psychiatry before Freud and its development since Freud's discoveries, one is struck by an essential difference. The symptoms of neurosis were formerly accounted for in purely descriptive terms, and the terms were no more than labels. The essential change which Freud introduced in the approach toward neurotic symptoms was that one could consider them explainable. They acquired a meaning; they were no longer regarded as foreign bodies within the mind, but as an intelligible part of the personality.

But they can be understood as part of the personality only after having been correctly interpreted. The neurotic symptom stands for the patient's memories, conflicting tendencies, thoughts, impulses, fears, which instead of appearing as such are disguised as a neurotic symptom. These tendencies as well as the disguising forces must be interpreted in order to understand and explain the meaning of a symptom.

As we know, at a later stage Freud was able to establish that the neurotic symptoms are determined by typical pathogenic conflicts and that the forces underlying them, the libidinal and aggressive drives, as well as the forces of defense against these drives, present particular developmental characteristics and can be described in a scientific way. This is why in reports published on the results of analytic investigations of individual neuroses, the symptoms are usually interpreted in terms that strike psychoanalysts as well as their critics as being relatively monotonous. When we interpret the meaning of a neurotic symptom, we explain it dynamically as an interplay of forces and genetically as a result of the interplay between

[1] The Brill Memorial Lecture of The New York Psychoanalytic Society, delivered at The New York Academy of Medicine, March 26, 1957.

developmental and environmental factors. Yet this apparent monotony stands in conspicuous contrast to the immense wealth of
data and information about human beings which our interpretative
work yields to us in each individual psychoanalysis.

Is the comparative monotony in our explanations of the neurotic
symptoms due to an insufficiency of our knowledge? Indeed, we find
that psychoanalytic explanations are more convincing when they
constitute a tracing back of neurotic symptoms to particular pathogenic conflicts than when we attempt the reverse: a synthesis, trying
to account for the particular development that ensued from a given
conflict.

But perhaps this relative monotony of our scientific explanation
of neurotic symptoms is not due only to these limitations of our
knowledge. The contrast, I believe, rather reflects the difference in
kind between interpretations we use when attempting to condense
the result of an individual analysis and to express the meaning of a
neurotic symptom in generalized scientific terms, and those we use
within the individual analysis when we aim to explain the meaning
of a dream, for instance, or to reconstruct a specific conflict that left
its imprint on the patient at a certain age.[2]

In his book *Die Grundlagen der Psychoanalyse* (1927), which
unfortunately has never been translated, Hartmann stressed a point
which characterizes the scientific position of psychoanalysis as opposed to other approaches to psychology and psychopathology.
Psychoanalysis offers explanatory concepts, theories and hypotheses,
as well as a great wealth of observational data. As in other natural
sciences, the concepts were derived to some extent from these observations; but they transcend them and, in their turn, permit organization of the data and often help to discover new facts.

Let me present a concrete example. A very severely obsessional
neurotic, who was referred to me after many years of unsuccessful
treatment with another analyst, puzzled me by the fact that at the end
of the hour she would usually ask me to repeat my interpretations
several times over. It occurred to me that Freud had described a
similar behavior in an obsessional patient as expressing an unconscious doubt, a disbelief in the words of the interlocutor. But the

---

[2] Devereux (1951) has rightly pointed out that one interprets something *to someone*,
i.e., to the person whose material is being interpreted.

differences between the two cases were great. My patient's need to
have interpretations repeated was limited to the analytic situations,
whereas in Freud's patient the symptom was more generalized.
Moreover, my patient's demand to hear the interpretation several
times was consciously motivated by the need to get the greatest
possible relief from it, which was not so in the case of Freud's
patient. Phenomenologically, i.e., on the level of conscious thought,
there were considerable divergencies. The analogy lay in the fact
that both patients were obsessional neurotics and that I was entitled
to suspect in mine the same type of unconscious ambivalence as
Freud could infer in his. Thus my reason for applying the knowledge derived from Freud's case to mine was based upon the use of
an explanatory concept; namely, that in both instances an underlying ambivalent attitude and a reaction formation against it might
have determined comparable behavior: the need to have the interlocutor's words repeated. As is characteristic of concrete interpretative work, these interpretations led my patient ultimately to discover
the very complicated, specific motives for this behavior. After prolonged analytic work she indeed became consciously aware of ironical
and mocking feelings toward the analyst.

We see here that the more general, explanatory concept common
to these cases was the unconscious ambivalence in the patients. A
more specific, individual meaning was that of unconscious, mocking
disbelief in the words of an analyst. This juxtaposition exemplifies
types of what in analysis we call interpretation. Thus the various
meanings attached to the term interpretation can be brought out by
approaching it from various points of view: (1) interpretations as
statements of general, explanatory concepts; (2) as statements about
the results of psychological investigation of a given person; (3) as
used in the individual therapeutic analysis. These three aspects overlap partly, but present sufficient divergent elements to be thus distinguished from each other.

To illustrate the differences one could say that my patient's wish
to have interpretations repeated was the result of disguised ambivalence. More particularly, it was the expression of a mocking disbelief. The psychological investigation, which aimed to uncover the
history and the motives of this disbelief, revealed that it referred

to a former analyst, to the analytic treatment as such and to the reasons for these repressed doubts and resentments. In the therapeutic procedure, the interpretative work encompassed not only all the preceding steps, but also the various means needed to enable the analyst as well as the patient to gain insight into this state of affairs and, finally, to enable the patient to deal with her resentments in a different way than by obsessional symptoms.

A discussion of interpretations from a methodological point of view, or rather from the point of view of their scientific logic, was undertaken by Bernfeld in his paper "Der Begriff der 'Deutung' in der Psychoanalyse" (1932). Without going into the details of this valuable study, I may briefly say that he draws a distinction between the structure of interpretation as a tool of psychological investigation and that of interpretation as a therapeutic tool, but without discussing the latter. Interpretations as tools of psychological investigation are classified by Bernfeld in the following categories: interpretation of the unconscious intention;[3] functional interpretations, disclosing the function of a given psychological phenomenon within the framework of the personality or a part of it; diagnostic interpretations; symbolic interpretation; and finally, most important in psychoanalysis, the genetic interpretation by which the genesis of a phenomenon is being reconstructed: "It is always," he states, "aimed at the reconstruction of a concrete, completed, psychic process. This aim is contingent on two essential premises. (1) The process to be reconstructed must have left traces behind it. (2) Some regular, consistent relation must exist betwen specific psychic, personal experiences and the traces they leave, permitting the former to be determined, inferred, 'interpreted' from the latter."

Bernfeld thus throws into relief the existence in psychoanalysis of what he calls a "Spurenwissenschaft": a "science of traces" left by past mental phenomena, which he compares to the analogous reconstructive processes in archeology.

Most psychoanalytic literature concerns either the results of this science of tracing (i.e., the reconstructions) or the description of such traces of past phenomena, while writings on psychoanalytic tech-

---

3 "Finale Deutung." He mentions, by the way, that this type of interpretation, however important it may be practically, is very often misused by analysts.

nique deal more specifically with the methods of obtaining those traces and of putting them to use for ultimate reconstructive processes. The question logically arises as to the criteria on which our interpretative work is based, or the way by which we arrive at the meaning of the patient's material. Two authors have particularly dealt with this problem: Robert Waelder and Susan Isaacs.

In his paper "Kriterien der Deutung" (1939), Waelder compares the work of psychoanalysis with that of other sciences: criminology, history and linguistics. According to him, it is based on inferences drawn from various clues.

Isaacs, in her paper "Criteria for Interpretation" (1939), not only mentions the inferences we draw from the patient's material, but also stresses the importance of what she terms "perception of the unconscious meaning of the patient's words and conduct as an objective process." Among examples used to explain analytic work to nonanalytic students, she cites the following: "a boy of five years of age, one day at a meal, addressing no one in particular, said in a very subdued voice, 'I don't like dreams: they are horrid things'; and then, after a pause, 'and another thing—I don't have any'." She found "that every hearer, save the most obtuse, appreciates perceptually that in his denial the boy actually makes a positive statement, namely, that his dreams are so horrid that he wishes he did not have any, and cannot bear to remember them. The ordinary hearer does not set out his awareness of this in conceptual terms, as analysts have learnt to do, using it as a means of generalizing the mechanism of denial; but everybody perceives the immediate concrete meaning." She adds that the difference between the ordinary hearer and the analyst resides in the degree of the latter's education.

One might wonder whether the unqualified use of the term "perception" here is correct, or whether this immediate grasp of the meaning of the child's words does not presuppose the existence of innumerable, preconscious inferences. We might agree with Isaacs that the analyst's understanding of his patient is sometimes based upon such immediate comprehension (highly improved by specific training in which his own personal analysis is not a small factor). But however direct or immediate such understanding of other human beings may be, it is usually combined with the countless preconscious inferences which everyone draws from both verbal and nonverbal expressions of an interlocutor.[4]

We touch here upon the complex problem of the understanding of one human being by another. There can be no doubt that the very young child perceives and understands the facial expressions of his mother in a way that may be called immediate or direct, and unconscious understanding of emotional states of the mother may exist even in older children (Burlingham, 1935). But the problem becomes more complicated as the child learns to understand and use speech, i.e., with the addition of verbal communication. From here on the understanding by way of clues and cues is superimposed on his direct perception of the mother's and other persons' emotional states, so that these two modes of comprehension become combined.

However interesting it might be at this point to discuss the ways in which human beings gain knowledge of the mental life of others, I am afraid this would lead us too far afield. While we may assume that such understanding can come about through inference, empathy or perception, it is important to add what Hartmann (1927) stressed; namely, that an additional and much more reliable way of knowing about other human beings is provided by the objective, scientific method of psychoanalytic investigation. I do not intend here to attempt a presentation of the psychoanalytic investigative method, but shall touch upon it only inasmuch as it directly concerns the problem of interpretation. Briefly, we may say that the psychoanalyst's means of obtaining observational data include all the ways by which one human being understands another. The psychoanalytic method employs also two steps that are unavailable to any other form of psychological investigation. The first of these is the method of free association, which provides the analyst with some additional data and prepares the way for the second step, the interpretation.[5] By means of interpretations the analyst is able to acquire further, otherwise inaccessible, data.

[4] Recently Dr. Leo A. Spiegel, in this Society, mentioned the work of Egon Brunswik on the role of cues in perception, which the latter also applied to the perception of social phenomena.

[5] For the sake of brevity, I neglect here all the intermediate or preparatory steps: interventions (Loewenstein, 1951a), confrontation (Devereux, 1951), clarification (E. Bibring, 1954), parameters (K. R. Eissler, 1953).

Freud originated the comparison between psychoanalytic investigations and those of archeology. It was an analogy he liked to use, but he also stressed the fundamental difference between archeological research and the uncovering of the remote past in an individual. In "Constructions in Analysis" (1937), he pointed out that we are not dealing with dead remains, but with living human beings. Save for a few exceptional finds, archeologists work with relics of objects destroyed once and for all, whose reconstruction at best can merely reach a certain degree of probability. But in the psychoanalyst's objects of research everything essential has somehow been preserved, although buried, and it is only a question of psychoanalytic technique whether it can be brought to light. He also emphasized other differences between them; namely, that he psychological object is incomparably more complex than the material one and also that we know so much less about it. And he adds that "our comparison between the two forms of work can go no further than this; for the main difference between them lies in the fact that for the archaeologist the reconstruction is the aim and end of his endeavours while for analysis the construction is only a preliminary labour."

If we apply the same comparison more specifically to our work of interpretation in psychoanalysis, we find other significant differences. First of all, even the best preserved relic of antiquity may remain unnoticed until the curiosity of some searcher uncovers it; only then can it become capable of influencing the present. By contrast, the buried remains of an individual's past may influence his present not only during but because of their concealment, and it is precisely due to this indirect influence they exert on the person's actual behavior that they become subject to investigation and thus can be uncovered at all. Another striking difference is that not only the buried psychic objects continue to live and to express themselves in the patient's present behavior, but also the agents of distortion, the defenses, persist and remain active as continuous, most stubborn obstacles to their unearthing. Every analyst knows that in the transference both the buried past and the repressive forces come singularly alive again and even may put an end to all investigation. But if properly dealt with, these transference phenomena become the analyst's and patient's best allies in uncovering the forgotten past.[6]

Bernfeld (1932) spoke of the difference between interpretation as an investigative procedure and as it is used in the therapeutic process. Indeed, in an investigation, any elements of the personality may become subject to scrutiny; in a therapeutic analysis, not all can be investigated but some must be.

An investigation may be satisfied with the psychoanalytic exploration of a dream, for instance, or a type of dream. But it is obvious that for the analytic investigation of more complicated aspects of the human personality an actual psychoanalysis is necessary, whether this process leads to a therapeutic result or not. The therapeutic analysis, in its turn, is essentially based upon a process of investigation, but of a very particular type. Thus the therapeutic and investigative procedures, although different as to intention, yet are identical inasmuch as the former hinges on the latter. Furthermore, the analytic inquiry becomes a therapy if it is an investigation not alone for the investigator but for the patient as well.

In archeological research, the work of investigation culminates in the achievement of reconstruction. The psychoanalyst's task is far more complicated; whenever he has been able to reconstruct some part of his patient's forgotten past, he must go on to the next essential step in his work. For, as Freud (1917) put it: "The time and manner in which he conveys his constructions to the person who is being analyzed, as well as the explanations with which he accompanies them, constitute the link between the two portions of the work of analysis, betwen his own part and that of the patient."[7]

And both parts of this work are encompassed in what we call interpretations in the therapeutic procedure. Indeed, the analyst's interpretations stand in a twofold relation to the part of the patient.

6 In a personal communication, Heinz Hartmann mentioned still another difference between archeological and psychoanalytic reconstruction. The latter makes use of the known existence of maturational and developmental stages in the individual human being. Archeological research cannot avail itself of such scientifically established, regular historical processes.

7 Freud distinguished interpretation of isolated parts of a patient's material, such as a parapraxis or a dream, from the reconstruction of important events in the patient's past for which he proposed to use the term construction. Thus most of what we call genetic interpretations should, according to Freud, be called constructions or reconstructions. However, we shall not here follow this rigid distinction, but rather use the term interpretation in the customary and more comprehensive sense.

(1) The patient's material enables the analyst to make interpretations which in turn bring new material to the fore. (2) In the patient these interpretations must have their counterpart, the gradual gaining of insight, which is decisive for the outcome of the psychoanalytic work.

Until now we have examined only one aspect of our interpretative work in analysis. The analyst's concern with the counterpart of his work in the patient leads to yet another set of considerations about interpretations, which frequently is viewed in the context of the psychoanalytic technique proper. I do not intend, however, to discuss practical problems arising in connection with the technique of interpretation, but want rather to highlight some questions of a more general nature.

The question raised by Freud's statement about the time and manner in which the analyst communicates his constructions to the analysand has in part been answered in various writings on technique, particularly by Freud himself. In more recent years the development of ego psychology has permitted us to sharpen and to refine our knowledge in this area, and indeed has helped considerably to improve the efficiency of our technical skill. On the other hand, as Hartmann (1951) pointed out several years ago, actually a large body of knowledge on matters of psychoanalytic technique is being transmitted by one generation of analysts to another without having been theoretically formulated.

It happens not infrequently that in the material of the patient presented by a younger analyst, the supervisor perceives a meaning or a trend which the candidate did not suspect but can confirm from material appearing in subsequent sessions. To the beginner such an achievement seems not only amazing but sometimes a result of uncanny intuition. It cannot be denied that the work of some analysts has a quality reminding us of the work of an intuitive artist. But as a rule one can say that this apparent intuition is based on experience which has taught the older analyst to grasp slight signs presented by the patient and not yet perceived by the younger colleague. It would seem desirable for us to be able to supplement this intuitive, often preconscious grasping of clues by a more systematic study of the latter and of the implicit method which leads the analyst to draw conclusions from them.

Such a study might be considered a special branch of what Bernfeld termed our science of traces. On the one hand, this science of traces hinges on the knowledge about the existence in every person's past of processes, developments, typical conflicts, their vicissitudes, derivatives, transformations and recombinations they undergo in the course of years. It thus hinges, on the other hand, upon the acquaintance with signs that permit us to infer their existence.[8] Information concerning these processes derives from reconstructions in other analyzed cases and from direct observation. In recent years the latter source of information has greatly gained in importance for our knowledge of very early instinctual and ego development. I should like here particularly to mention the work of Anna Freud and Dorothy Burlingham, of Ernst Kris and his co-workers at Yale, of René A. Spitz, of Margaret E. Fries, and of John Bowlby.

In a recent paper, "The Recovery of Childhood Memories in Psychoanalysis," Kris (1956b) gives an account of the way a little girl, "Dorothy," observed at the nursery school of the Child Study Center in Yale, reacted in her third year to a series of events important for her life: the birth of a sibling, the death of her grandfather and of her pet dog. Kris then proceeds to engage our interest in an "experiment in thought: let us imagine," he writes, "how after twenty years the recollection of the material here reported in considerable simplification may appear in Dorothy's analysis. The network of overdeterminations seems almost infinite: the wish for a child from father, the death wish against the mother, the fear about both sexual and destructive impulses, and finally the fear of castration which . . . age adequately added and superimposed, are likely to baffle the future analyst's imagination." He adds that reconstructive work in analysis might in one sense be "a hopeless task" if its aim were to reconstruct exactly "what had happened." "But," he continues, "reconstructive work in analysis cannot aim at such a goal: its purpose is more limited and yet much vaster. The material of actual occurrences, of things as they happen, is constantly subjected to the selective scrutiny of memory under the guide of the inner constellation. What we here call selection is itself a complex process. Not only were the events loaded with meaning when they

---

8 This in turn hinges on the assumption, which may not always be justified, that all processes leave traces or that there is a regular relation between each process and the trace it leaves.

occurred; each later stage of the conflict pattern may endow part of these events or of their elaboration with added meaning. But these processes are repeated throughout many years of childhood and adolescence and finally integrated into the structure of the personality. They are molded, as it were, into patterns, and it is with these patterns rather than with the events that the analyst deals."

This greater importance, in our work, of patterns rather than of exact events is the reason why unconscious fantasies were regarded by Freud as approximate equivalents of actual traumatic events. Yet we also know since Freud that in many cases we are not or should not be satisfied with this equivalence. Not only do we feel impelled to distinguish between them in our work of reconstruction of the past, but we also have indirect reasons for assuming that unconscious fantasies and real events are not to be treated as psychological equals in their present effects. I am alluding here, for instance, to the transference reactions of patients when faced with some correctly perceived peculiarities of their analyst's behavior. In most instances, these perceptions simply trigger off some fantasies and transference reactions that can be traced back to the past, i.e., analyzed. But there are some cases where it does not seem to work that way, where the patient feels his reactions to be so well justified by the analyst's actual behavior that such reactions may become unanalyzable (Bibring-Lehner, 1936).

And yet, not until this year did we have any thorough study on the signs permitting us to distinguish, in analysis, the existence of actual traumatic events in the patient's past as opposed to unconscious fantasies. I refer here to Greenacre's (1956) important work on the subject. It was also she who drew our attention in recent years to the particular importance of actual traumatic events in the pathogenesis of severe neuroses (1952).

We must confess that notwithstanding the considerable amount of knowledge we have acquired, we are still far from possessing a satisfactory "science of traces" in Bernfeld's sense. Let me give an example from my recent experience.

A young man of twenty-six seeks help from psychoanalysis for his severe inhibition in work and social relations. He is the youngest of four children and the only one still living with his parents. From the beginning he complains about his inability to do any work, in spite of ambitious fantasies, and soon he illustrates his inhibition by stressing his inability to comply with the requirements of analysis: he can neither remember anything of his life, nor can he tell what occurs to him. After two months this difficulty becomes increasingly strong. One day, while begging me to tell him what to say, he violently and somehow provokingly rejects any help I offer and at the same time smilingly asks me to declare that I am not at all interested in his talking and would not even listen to him if he did. These latter words reminded me of the behavior of a mother driven to violent anger by the passive, stubborn refusal of a child to do what she has asked. I suggested that he must have been a bad eater as a child and must have had many fights with his mother when she tried to persuade him to eat. The patient laughingly acquiesced. And although he could remember no specific incidents, some details of more recent fights with his mother then came to the fore, where both would display an equal degree of stubborn, defiant sulkiness.

The interpretation I proposed to this patient thus seems to have been correct and to the point, and yet I would be hard put to it to explain on what grounds I made this inference. It must have been arrived at by way of many small signs which remained pre-conscious to me, until the conclusion suddenly was brought to my conscious awareness by the patient's invitation to declare that I would no longer be interested in his talking to me. What these little signs are, which in this case permitted me to draw a correct con-clusion, but which in many other instances may be entirely lost, could be the subject matter of a highly rewarding research for the systematization of our "science of traces."

In two of his recent papers Ernst Kris contributed fundamentally to the theory of psychoanalytic technique by studying the effects of interpretation on two phenomena most essential and characteristic for the psychoanalytic process: recall and insight.

In his study on the recovery of childhood memories, which I mentioned above, Kris (1956b) takes up an idea he developed before (1950), on the relationship between recollection and the recognition of what has become familiar through an interpretation or recon-struction. He adds that "the communication with the patient is never exclusively regulated by the secondary process. Our inter-pretations may stimulate linkages between various strata of the mind which reawaken the flow of primary process connections." According to Kris, the process of recollection is set in motion by interpretations not because they directly produce recall, but rather because they establish conditions under which recall becomes possible: "conditions more similar to those which existed when the recalled scenes and events occurred."

We may say that these conditions are gradually achieved through the fact that interpretation effects a regrouping of the material available to the patient. We know that with the use of classical analytic technique the dramatic reappearance of forgotten memories, so conspicuous in Freud's early experience, is quite rare. Kris, discussing this point in his paper, mentions that a recall occurring in analysis is often accompanied by the experience of *déjà raconté*. Here I should like to bring an example which illustrates another variant of recall experience during analysis.

Many years ago I analyzed a young man suffering from severe premature ejaculations which caused him no end of humiliation and anxiety. In the fourth month of his analysis he told me of an experience at the age of nine. His father had taken him along to a swimming pool where only men were admitted and where it was customary to swim in the nude. The patient recalled how, while lying in the sun, he had felt terribly humiliated when one of the grownups looked at him. He attributed his embarrassment to the fact that he had a mole on the thigh. Shortly after this session, the analysis entered a period of intense transference resistances. This culminated after several months in the patient's becoming aware not only of his competitive reactions toward the analyst, but also of his unconscious fear of retaliation, the fear that the analyst might wish to keep him impotent. A calmer period then ensued in the analysis, during which he once more recounted the incident of his embarrassment at the swimming pool. This time he told it differently: his humiliation, he recalled, had been due to the comparison between the large penis of the grownup and his own penis which appeared so small to him. When I reminded him of having related this incident to me incompletely, he responded indignantly: he had always recalled it exactly as he just told it to me, and he was absolutely certain he had never before mentioned it in the analysis.

This example permits us to draw a number of conclusions. In one respect my patient was different from those described by Kris: his recall was accompanied not by the experience of *déjà raconté*, but of its opposite, *jamais raconté*, which is not very common. But in some respects, I believe, this patient resembled Kris's patient and many others. Indeed I think that recall of previously unavailable, warded-off memories or of some details occurs regularly in our cases; but much of it occurs in such an inconspicuous way that neither the patient nor the analyst can become aware of it. My patient was right in saying that he had always known all the details of the event recalled; except, we must add, that some of them were not conscious, not available to him when he first described it. The reappearance in his awareness of these previously unavailable details could be ascribed to the preceding analysis of transference resistances. This case is but one example of the well-known fact that interpretations rarely have an immediate and direct effect upon recall. Here one must even assume that the re-emergence of memory traces was due to an interpretation which in its content had only indirectly and remotely to do with the scene involved. It was, I believe, the partial diminution of the patient's fears of competing with a man—the analyst—that permitted the re-emergence of similar reactions toward a man in the childhood scene. Indeed, it is a remarkable fact that although our interpretations deal directly and explicitly with only some of the facets and aspects of the conflict involved, they implicitly encompass and indirectly affect a much larger number of them. This is the fact to which Hartmann (1951) referred when he spoke of the "multiple appeal" of interpretations.

Complex consequences indeed may ensue when, due to analytic work, some resistance of the patient is overcome. We are not dealing with isolated defenses or resistances, but with "defensive structures" (Hoffer, 1954; Kris, 1956). I believe that this is the state of affairs to which Freud (1917) alluded in his *Introductory Lectures* where he compared the psychoanalytic technique with the then raging First World War and spoke of the important consequences of winning a battle on a piece of territory that in itself is insignificant.

In his study "On Some Vicissitudes of Insight in Psychoanalysis," Kris (1956a) describes convincingly that what he calls a "good analytic hour," in which real insight is achieved, is the result of a long drawn-out process in which "energies attached to the repressed material have been set free," and he says: "The reorganization which takes place is the essence of the analytic process with its vicissitudes and changing facets. As part of this reorganization some of the energies set free are . . . at the disposal of the ego." We will add: at the disposal of the autonomous ego functions.

We know that this result is attained by way of a complicated preparatory work, a work which comprises many steps of various kinds. Some of them have to deal with immediate tasks of facilitating the patient's communication. Others involve a forming of provisional hunches which later may be corroborated or, on the contrary, modified or even discarded when confronted with additional material. Still other steps consist in communicating to the patient some observation derived from his associations, hoping that it may group or organize the material in such a way as to elicit additional material ultimately leading us to an understanding and thus to an interpretation of the patient's behavior. For a long time usually these interpretations are only of limited scope, until a more comprehensive one becomes assured.

This grouping of the material, as we are all aware, is being achieved in a number of ways; for instance, by bringing out similarities in the patient's reactions to various important events of his life, or similarities of mechanisms in dealing with situations, with people, with impulses or with the analyst. We know the importance this type of work assumes when the analyst can point to the similarity of such behavior patterns to the patient's mode of resistance (A. Freud, 1936). Let me give an example of a less frequent, though also well-known type of preparation. The stressing of a time sequence of some reactions may bring a patient a considerable step forward in understanding his reactions. Thus to a college girl, say, who has always been preferred by her father, it may bring a sudden insight into the reasons for her wish to quit college when she is shown that the decision to abandon her studies and return home coincided with receiving a letter from the father telling her that his relation with her mother had improved.

By and large, the nature of the preparatory work we perform every day is incompletely defined and has not been described in sufficient detail. And yet it is on this gradual and painstaking work that the outcome of an analysis usually depends. It would be a worth-while task to make a careful study of this preparatory work in analysis, as a counterpart to the one on traces which I mentioned before.

As my next illustration I have chosen an example that may serve as a link between preparation and interpretation proper.

A patient of mine, a girl in her twenties who had recently become acutely distressed by her boy friend's unfaithfulness, spoke of the following matters within one session. She described at length her enjoyment at listening to Gluck's aria "I lost my Euridice," then talked about the special enjoyment she used to get in her childhood and adolescence from playing records of sad songs. She then shifted over to the painful events of her prepuberty when, after having been a tomboy among boys, one day she realized that these boys were running after a girl who was girlish and pretty, and that she herself could not run as fast as the boys; then she again related a painful incident of having been humiliated and threatened by a nurse in childhood, adding: "I feared I might lose the respect of my younger siblings." At the end of the hour I pointed to the importance of the notion of a "loss" in her associations. I thought, rightly or wrongly, that this word might help in grouping her memories and reactions. This word could form a bridge between several chains of memories and developments in her life: the enjoyment of a loss, leading toward her masochistic fantasies of prepuberty and centering around that precise childhood event in which she feared the loss of her siblings' "respect"; the loss of her illusion of masculinity as a tomboy, with feelings of inability to compete with a pretty girl, in its turn is a link to that of her boy friend who prefers another girl. May I add that my choice of this common denominator of the session was not made arbitrarily; it derived from the material of the session and, moreover, must have been prepared in me by my thorough acquaintance with the patient.

We must realize that in speaking of preparatory work a distinction cannot always be clearly drawn between preparation (Loewenstein, 1951a), confrontation (Devereux, 1951), clarification (in E. Bibring's sense, 1954) and interpretation proper, and that interpretations themselves have various structures and functions.

From experience we know that the effectiveness of interpretations as well as of the various interventions which prepare them is contingent upon certain conditions, such as dosage, hierarchy, timing, and the wording of interpretations. These are sometimes classified under the more general and less precise heading of psychoanalytic tact (Loewenstein, 1930/31, 1951a), a term which by its very vagueness, by its allusion to intuition, betrays our lack of well-established knowledge.

Since interpretation aims at helping the patient to uncover what he does not know by means of what he knows about himself, tact in interpretation often consists in choosing a wording that will permit the material to be regrouped in a significant way. Among the various ways in which the material is thus being reorganized during the analytic process, I should like to stress a particular one. Genetic interpretations essentially are reconstructions of psychological events considered to be the prototypes or the causes of later psychological manifestations whose significance or determinants are thus being explained. But genetic interpretations can also move in the opposite direction, as it were, when it is necessary to find the more recent derivatives of a known event or pattern in the past. In other words, genetic interpretations aim at the establishment of a reciprocal relationship between the present and the past. If the term reconstruction is used for the establishment of a forgotten childhood event from its more recent derivatives, one might use the term reconstruction *upward* to denote the type of interpretation we employ in reconstructing the more recent consequences of a former event (Loewenstein, 1951a). Permit me to give an example of this not infrequent type of interpretation.

A medical student had a fear of dropping to the floor when looked at by the professor in class. While relating this symptom he remembered that in his adolescence, when he was very religious and had to lift the Torah in the synagogue, he was terrified lest he might drop it on the floor. He added that he was so worried lest in the eyes of the assembled religious community the dreaded accident might represent a disgrace to his father. His next thought was that while afraid of dropping to the floor during the lecture, he was preoccupied with what his classmates might think, who knew that he was in analytic treatment. The conclusion is obvious to any analyst that the patient at this time was under the impact of an ambivalence conflict toward his analyst, resembling the one toward his father when he had feared to let the Torah drop to the floor; that he was under the influence of his fear and unconscious wish to disgrace the analyst, as in adolescence he had been afraid of his unconscious wish to disgrace the father. A more complete interpretation, in this case a reconstruction upward, would have to take into account some differences between the two situations, as for instance the change from an active dropping of a revered object, the Torah, to a passive dropping to the floor under the gaze of a teacher. Such reconstructions upward often have great importance in the analysis of transference resistances.

The interpretation in this case was based upon the use of three key ideas: dropping, being seen, and disgrace. In adolescence, the disgrace would have ensued from being seen dropping the Torah; in the analytic situation, the presence of idea of disgrace had to be inferred from the fantasy of being seen dropping to the floor by those who knew the patient to be in analysis. The use of key ideas in the wording of interpretations derives its importance from several reasons. They are ideas used by the patients themselves and thus facilitate recognition. They also are those which emerge as compromise formations into the preconscious and therefore bear traces of the interplay of forces that led to the compromise. Interpretations aim at reflecting the work not only of the id, but also of the superego and the ego. Thus, when they use key ideas in their wording they have the ability to promote that regrouping of the patient's thoughts and emotions which leads to recall and insight (Kris, 1951; Loewenstein, 1951a).

In many a case insight in the patient is made possible only if the wording of interpretations contains words corresponding to some particular derivative of his conflicts.

I remember a case of a patient whose symptoms centered around obsessional fears about the health of her grown-up son. These anxieties had started shortly after the death of her mother, approximately twelve years before the patient came for analysis. They were actually a continuation of previous, similar anxieties about her mother's health. This continuity also was attested by frequently recurring dreams in which the mother was still alive but ill, and the patient had to worry lest something happen to her mother. After some time the analytic work, which then centered around the nature of her relationship with her mother and its influence on her present obsessional fears, bogged down. The analyst's emphasis on her love or attachment or submissiveness to her mother, which were all facts, seemed no longer to help the progress of the analysis. One day I picked up a word the patient herself had used; faithfulness to her mother. This term struck her as expressing the exact nature of what had remained after a period of violent and prolonged struggles between daughter and mother. And the term faithfulness helped the patient considerably in gaining insight into her complicated, ambivalent reactions to her dead mother and into their continued impact on her obsessional preoccupation with her son's health.

But there are other cases where it takes the patient a long time to accomplish the change in the wording of a thought. One patient, for instance, who suffered from the consequences of extended phenomena of isolation of affect, always spoke of his mother as a rather harsh, unbending, and sarcastic person. Yet when first confronted in his analysis with the idea that he might have wished for his mother's love, he remained completely incredulous. Such a thought was entirely foreign to him. It took several years of analytic work and a gradual reconstruction of his childhood history until the existence of this wish became conscious to the patient. He himself remarked, correctly, that it took so much work simply to turn the knowledge he always had a few degrees to the side.

The reason for the importance of the wording in an interpretation resides in the function of speech in the analytic procedure. Speech, in the communication between patient and analyst, is the main vehicle that permits the lifting of psychological processes out of their unconscious state into the preconscious and finally into consciousness.

While interpretations decisively influence the process of analysis and while, to be effective, they have to be timed and worded in certain ways, they are continuously influenced in their turn by the psychological processes taking place in the patient. It is not, as it may seem, that the analyst knows it all in advance and but judiciously chooses the moment and the way to impart this understanding to his patient. To be sure, frequently the analyst sees or knows something long before the patient is able to remember or to grasp it. But he acquires this knowledge gradually from his patient. If the analyst's interpretations enable the patient to gain insight, the latter's communications and interpretations, in their turn, create insight in the analyst. Moreover, an interpretation is meaningless as a one-sided act and acquires its full significance only through its counterpart, the effects it produces on the patient. This subtle interaction between patient and analyst is an essential feature of the analytic process.

Actually this interaction between analyst and analysand can exist only in the type of psychological process which we call a psychoanalysis, since to acquire its full significance an interpretation must be followed by its counterpart; namely, dynamic change leading to recall and insight in the patient. But this condition need not obtain in an analytic investigation in a narrow sense; and it is certainly absent in those explanatory interpretations which I mentioned earlier, in contrasting the scientific explanation of a symptom with its concrete interpretation in the analysis of an individual.

To underscore these differences somewhat more sharply, I should like to remind you of certain forms of resistance in analysis.

Analytic interpretations have always been opposed by the patients on rational or intellectual grounds. In the last decade a particular variation on this theme has appeared with increasing frequency. The patients who present this type of resistance seem overeager to accept analytic interpretation, and they express this by jumping to conclusions couched in psychoanalytic terms. These patients will immediately translate the meaning of their dreams into such terms as, for instance, oedipus complex, homosexuality, castration, etc. The use of psychoanalytic jargon or of the cliché, as Martin Stein (1957) recently described it, is quite frequent nowadays.

I learned most about this form of resistance from a patient whom I analyzed some twenty-five years ago. This was the obsessive-compulsive patient already mentioned, who had been analyzed for many years before she was referred to me. She had entered that previous treatment as an agoraphobic and during its course had developed the symptoms of a severe obsessive-compulsive neurosis. From the start of her treatment with me she would bring daily dreams and would "associate" to them in a particular way which clearly indicated that she continued a style of analysis established by her former analyst. She did not use analytic terminology in the crude way, just described, but somehow more subtly spoke in her associations of fantasies and events that left the analyst no choice, at first sight, but to interpret them in terms of direct derivatives of typical early childhood conflicts. These were the interpretations which she would then ask me to repeat many times at the end of the hour.

I shall not go into the details which permitted me to understand the meaning of this patient's type of resistance. Suffice it to say that she used the analytic procedure and the analyst's interpretations, not as a means of understanding herself but as a magical conjuring away of her main obsession: the dread of having "touched the old woman." The repetition of the interpretations had the same meaning of a magical procedure. I mentioned before that underneath this magical function of her analysis there existed another one, that of a mocking parody of her previous treatment.

In this case, as in many another instance of the misuse of analytic concepts by the resistance, the patient's style of resistance was but a slight variation of the analyst's mode of interpreting. What strikes one in those pseudo interpretations so eagerly suggested by the patients is that they are not completely wrong; nor are they completely correct. And if one examines them as well as the somehow awkward interpretations of the analyst which may have led to this state of affairs, one is struck by the peculiar language of these statements; by a paucity in the choice of verbs, mostly limited to the verb "to be." However, and this is their most conspicuous distinction, these statements are characterized by the absence of an adverb of time; as for instance: "this is homosexuality," "this is a father figure," etc. While such statements fit very well into a scientific paper describing the general category of phenomena into which a dream might be placed, they are not adequate to describe any concrete psychological phenomenon which, in order to be placed into its genetic and dynamic context, requires qualification by a temporal adverb.

This peculiar state of affairs can be understood if one considers the function of speech in analysis.

Although nonverbal communication may flow from the patient toward his analyst and to some extent also from the analyst to the patient, the essential interchange of communication in psychoanalysis is by speech. This peculiar and protracted dialogue, which constitutes the analytic process, can also be characterized by its division of certain functions of speech between patient and analyst. I discussed these speech functions rather extensively in another paper (1956), using the classifications proposed by Karl Buehler (1934). Here I may repeat, briefly: whereas the analyst is supposed not only to limit his speech to its so-called cognitive function, but to that part of it which refers to his understanding of the patient, we expect the patient in analysis to use the expressive function of speech and that part of its cognitive function which deals with the knowledge of one's own self.

Recall and insight in the patient use a kind of thought and speech function which combine the cognitive and expressive functions in a particular way. Of patients who present intellectualization of the type mentioned before, i.e., analytic jargon, one might say that they make use of the cognitive function devoid of its expressive counterpart. Thus their verbalized thoughts concern phenomena that are not theirs personally, but are impersonal and possibly valid for a large number of individuals whose symptoms or dreams fall under the same heading of, for instance, oedipus complex, or sibling rivalry, or whatever it may be. The absence of the expressive function in the speech of these patients is the result of their resistance. The analyst's use of psychoanalytic jargon in interpretations reveals a shift of the cognitive function from the patient's individual problems to more general phenomena. As a matter of fact, while analyzing we always do, consciously or preconsciously, work with these concepts as a general framework. But when actually interpreting we retranslate them into the patient's concrete experiences.

This brings us back once more to the problem of the difference between interpretations of specific psychological phenomena in an individual case and those interpretations which present a more general, explanatory, scientific character. By using particular interpretations in the individual analysis, which enable us to uncover further data, we reach more generalized, explanatory interpretations of mental phenomena. But the obverse likewise is true and characteristic of psychoanalytic work: we use explanatory concepts in order to arrive at concrete interpretations and thus, in turn, are led to discover new data.

But should we assume that concrete interpretations in therapy do not have the character of an explanation? This assumption would certainly be wrong; some of them undoubtedly possess this quality, even though their validity is limited to a given patient. For instance, the reconstruction of a forgotten childhood event out of symptoms, dreams, etc., states that this event caused or codetermined the existence of such symptoms or dreams. A scientifically valid explanation need not make explicit the assumptions on which it is based, and the assumptions implied in such interpretations are contained in the psychoanalytic theory.

In each individual analysis there is an interplay between observation and the application of some theoretical assumption or hypothesis, without which the observational data would simply remain in a state of chaos (Hartmann, Kris, Loewenstein, 1953). And yet, every psychoanalysis can and perhaps ought to be conducted as though the theory were never completely taken for granted. This is a way to make new discoveries; it was the way Freud, in the past, discovered most of what we know now. It may also enable us in the future to effect possibly necessary realignments or modifications of our theoretical assumptions on the basis of new observations. The essence of psychoanalysis is that particular interplay between observational data, gathered from clean clinical work, and their interpretation within a scientifically valid conceptual framework—be it the one we have now or possibly a future, better one.

BIBLIOGRAPHY

Bernfeld, S. (1932), Der Begriff der "Deutung" in der Psychoanalyse. *Ztschr. f. ang. Psychol.*, XLII.

Bibring, E. (1954), Psychoanalysis and the Dynamic Psychotherapies. *J. Am. Psa. Assn.*, II.

Bibring-Lehner, G. (1936), A Contribution to the Subject of Transference Resistance. *Int. J. Psa.*, XVII.

Brenner, C. (1955), The Validation of Psychoanalytic Interpretation. Summarized in Panel report: Validation of Psychoanalytic Techniques. *J. Am. Psa. Assn.*, III.

Buehler, K. (1934), *Sprachtheorie. Die Darstellungsfunktion der Sprache.* Jena: Gustav Fischer.

Burlingham, D. T. (1935), Die Einfühlung des Kleinkindes in die Mutter. *Imago*, XXI.

Devereux, G. (1951), Some Criteria for the Timing of Confrontations and Interpretations. *Int. J. Psa.*, XXXII.

Eissler, K. R. (1953), The Effect of the Structure of the Ego on Psychoanalytic Technique. *J. Am. Psa. Assn.*, I.

Ekstein, R. (1955), Discussion remarks in Panel: Validation of Psychoanalytic Techniques. *J. Am. Psa. Assn.*, III.

Fenichel, O. (1939), Problems of Psychoanayltic Technique. *Psa. Quart.*, VIII.

Freud, A. (1936), *The Ego and the Mechanisms of Defense.* New York: International Universities Press, 1946.

Freud, S. (1900), The Interpretation of Dreams. *Standard Edition*, IV, V. London: Hogarth Press, 1953.

—— (1917), *Introductory Lectures on Psycho-Analysis.* London: Allen & Unwin, 1922.

—— (1937), Constructions in Analysis. *Collected Papers*, V. London: Hogarth Press, 1950.

Glover, E. (1955), *The Technique of Psycho-Analysis.* New York: International Universities Press.

Greenacre, P. (1952), *Trauma, Growth and Personality.* New York: W. W. Norton.

—— (1956), Re-evaluation of the Process of Working Through. *Int. J. Psa.*, XXXVII.

Hartmann, H. (1927), *Die Grundlagen der Psychoanalyse.* Leipzig: Georg Thieme.

—— (1951), Technical Implications of Ego Psychology. *Psa. Quart.*, XX.

—— & Kris, E. (1945), The Genetic Approach in Psychoanalysis. *This Annual*, I.

—— —— & Loewenstein, R. M. (1953), The Function of Theory in Psychoanalysis. In: *Drives, Affects, Behavior*, ed. R. M. Loewenstein. New York: International Universities Press.

Hoffer, W. (1954), Defensive Process and Defensive Organization: Their Place in Psycho-Analytic Technique. *Int. J. Psa.*, XXXV.

Isaacs, S. (1939), Criteria for Interpretation. *Int. J. Psa.*, XX.

Kris, E. (1950), On Preconscious Mental Processes. *Psa. Quart.*, XIX.

—— (1951), Ego Psychology and Interpretation in Psychoanalytic Therapy. *Psa. Quart.*, XX.

—— (1956a), On Some Vicissitudes of Insight in Psycho-Analysis. *Int. J. Psa.*, XXXVII.

—— (1956b), The Recovery of Childhood Memories in Psychoanalysis. *This Annual*, XI.

Loewenstein, R. M. (1930/31), Le tact dans la technique psychanalytique. *Rev. Franç. Psychanal.*, IV.

—— (1951a), The Problem of Interpretation. *Psa. Quart.*, XX.

—— (1951b), Ego Development and Psychoanalytic Technique. *Am. J. Psychiat.*, CVII.

—— (1956), Remarks on the Role of Speech in Psycho-Analytic Technique. *Int. J. Psa.*, XXXVII.

Reich, W. (1945), *Character-Analysis*. New York: Orgone Institute.

Schmidl, F. (1955), The Problem of Scientific Validation in Psycho-Analytic Interpretation. *Int. J. Psa.*, XXXVI.

Stein, M. (1957), The Cliché: A Phenomenon of Resistance. Summarized in Panel report: Clinical and Theoretical Aspects of Resistance. *J. Am. Psa. Assn.*, V.

Sterba, E. (1945), Interpretation and Education. *This Annual*, I.

Waelder, R. (1939), Kriterien der Deutung. *Int. Ztschr. f. Psa. & Imago*, XXIV.

PSYCHIC ENERGY AND MECHANISMS
OF DEFENSE

SEYMOUR L. LUSTMAN, Ph.D., M.D. (New Haven)[1]

This discussion will address itself to three problems facing psychoanalytic theory today. These are questions of quantity and source of neutralized psychic energy, and the basic mechanisms of defense. It will not be the purpose of this paper to evaluate the current controversial thinking in regard to these areas, but rather to make certain speculative postulates based on observational and experimental studies of neonates and infants. However, some of the basic assumptions upon which this communication rests should be stated at this time.

The first of these is that in psychoanalysis, the ego is defined in terms of functionally related mental processes. As Freud (1923) stated, "the ego is a cohesive organization of mental processes," a statement most readily understood in terms of a mature ego. While Freud took cognizance of inborn ego factors, it was Hartmann (1939) who developed the concept of a "conflict-free sphere of ego development" with a clearer recognition of an inborn "ego constitution." Within this sphere, Hartmann places such ego functions as "perception, intentionality, object-comprehension, thinking, language, recall phenomena, and productivity" as well as motor development. In regard to the newborn, Hartmann felt that these inborn ego apparatuses cause a state of "adaptation to exist before processes of adaptation begin to function." Contrary to lower animal forms, adaptation and survival in man does not rest in instinctual behavior but rather in the ego. Thus the ground is laid for the concept of a functioning, rudimentary ego in the neonate. This arises from the "undifferentiated phase," as proposed by Hartmann, Kris, and Loewenstein (1946), from which, to quote Rapaport's summary

[1] Yale University School of Medicine, Child Study Center.

(1951), "both ego and id differentiate in the course of maturation and development from a common matrix that already contains the inborn ego apparatuses which guarantee adaptedness and adaptation."

In an earlier paper (1956) I have presented evidence from the three-day-old neonate of the existence of a rudimentary ego which functions demonstrably in perception. Inherent autonomic endowment was presented as one of the inborn precursors of ego, which in the neonate demonstrates remarkable discriminatory power both in terms of inter- and intraindividual differences. This is felt to support the concepts of an undifferentiated phase of ego-id development, with already functioning inborn ego apparatuses, which operate in a conflict-free sphere. Implications were drawn relating to subsequent autonomous and conflict-involved ego development. The presence of this rudimentary ego in the neonate is one of the basic hypotheses upon which this discussion rests.

The next fundamental concept of import to us is the fact that the ego, mature or primitive, must have available to it energy in order to function. The question of source of this energy, already raised by Hartmann, Jacobson, and Kris, will be discussed in detail below.

The next basic assumption is that the mechanisms of defense, described in current ego psychology as ego functions, must use psychic energy for their operation.

To summarize my basic hypotheses: from at least the age of three days, we already have a primitive or rudimentary ego, functioning in a perceptually discriminating fashion, which is dependent upon such inborn apparatuses as inherent autonomic endowment. The very fact that this ego is functioning, although in a primitive fashion, implies that these apparatuses already have available to them psychic energy. The assumption is made as stated by Hartmann (1955), "that all ego functions are fed by desexualized or sublimated energy (by neutralized energy)," a proposition advanced by Freud (1926), but amplified now so as to define neutralization as the desinstinctualization of both aggression and libido (Hartmann, 1955), and to the "probability that there exists a continuum of gradations of energy, from the fully instinctual to the fully neutralized mode" (Hartmann, 1950; Kris, 1950; Rapaport, 1950a). The source of this neutral psychic energy must be questioned; namely, is it instinctual or noninstinctual? Moreover, it is hypothesized that *if* this energy is derived from instinctual sources, its character in the neonate will be more closely related to its source drive (aggressive or libidinal) than is the complex fused neutralized energy seen functioning in the mature ego.

We will now concern ourselves briefly with the pleasure-unpleasure continuum, since it will enter into the later discussion of the questions here raised. In terms of the newborn, existing observational and experimental data make it justifiable to consider active nursing as close to the extreme of pleasure. Classically, the pleasure-unpleasure continuum was originally related to the discharge or accumulation of psychic energy bearing a direct relationship to tension. However, in exploring Freud's suggestion of the import of rhythm and timing to this problem, Jacobson (1953) has advanced the concept of relating the perception of feeling not to tension or discharge per se, but rather to "the flux of mobile psychic energy released, the changes in the level of tension—or in the amount of excitation respectively . . ." Thus, while satiation may remain the basic model for the extreme of pleasure, the change from restless, hungry infant to active nursing will come close to this.

The other end of the continuum presents a more difficult problem. Logically, deprivation of sucking-feeding should fit here. However, this presents such insurmountable problems of intensity or degree of deprivation, and of experimental license, that instead we will limit this paper to the consideration of extreme pain of clinical colic as our other end of the spectrum.

We may now turn to our data on the newborn and the infant. While much of the material has been presented elsewhere in relation to psychosomatic disease (1953, 1955, 1956), it will be included in our considerations. For our present purposes, I would like to review briefly a study of hearing in the neonate with emphasis on its pertinence to nursing.

Richmond, Grossman, and Lustman (1953) made 292 observations on forty-six infants, of which thirty-nine were full-term infants ranging from half hour to eight days in age. Seven were premature infants ranging in age from one day to fifteen days. Each infant was classified into the following testing conditions: (1) light sleep, (2) deep sleep, (3) awake, (4) active nursing; in addition (5), there was a poststimulation group comprising those infants from the other groups who did not respond to their first auditory testing stimulation under the first four conditions listed. Each infant was stimulated an average of three times by striking a bell held 33 cm. from its head while it was observed by two observers for reaction to sound. Palpebral or startle reflex or both were taken as evidence of hearing. For the details of the study, the reader so interested is referred to the original paper. For our purposes only the pertinent results will be presented.

All forty-six infants in this series gave evidence of hearing in the form of a positive palpebral or startle response or both. Thus all of the infants were able to perceive sound; however, with dramatic differences related to the conditions under which the testing was done. Active nursing proved to be the poorest condition under which to test for hearing. Only 17 per cent of the resulting reactions to sound were positive in this condition. This is in contrast to 91 per cent positive responses during light sleep. It is interesting to note that the only circumstance in which no startle responses were elicited was during active nursing. Yet, under other circumstances, all responded to sound and the majority manifested a startle response. Thus, while nursing, many infants, although not deaf, are unaware of, or unable to respond to, sound stimulation.

Apart from our experimental findings there is other evidence which has bearing on the effect of active nursing on ego function. Wolowik (1927) demonstrated that three times as much electrical stimulation was required to make the nursing two-month-old infant cry as was required under other conditions. Jensen (1932) and others have shown that general activity and sucking bear an inverse relationship. It might be noted in passing that sucking is not purely a reflex action, but that discriminatory perception of some sort is involved, as suggested by the observations that salt solutions and critical temperature of milk cause the response to deteriorate or cease.

On the other end of the continuum, few experimental data are available for speculation in spite of the amount of work done with painful stimuli. It would seem, however, that the infant with severe pain of colic comes pretty close to the extreme of unpleasure. It has been my experience that the introduction of the most pleasurable stimulus, the nipple, at moments of great pain goes unnoticed by the infant. Indeed, any combination of comforting, pleasurable stimuli may go unnoticed, and frequently the infant will scream until the intervention of physical exhaustion. Thus, at moments of great unpleasure, the infant is as unaware of the nipple as is the nursing infant of sound or electrical stimulation. Yet, under other, more neutral conditions in the pleasure-unpleasure spectrum, the same infants will obviously perceive such stimulation.

The speculative conclusions which I will draw from such data are based on the acceptance of the basic psychoanalytic hypotheses outlined above. In the neonates and infants described, we can think of the awareness of auditory, tactile, electrical stimulation, as manifested by various responses, as evidence of the functions of a primitive or rudimentary ego. As previously brought out, this falls within the "conflict-free" sphere of perception. In addition, the fact that this primitive, but unquestionably present perception occurs, means that energy is available to this ego to operate these functions through inborn ego apparatuses. When one considers that the newborn has as yet no voluntary or conscious control over the manifestations of its awareness (i.e., reflex-like reactions of startle response, palpebral response, autonomic response, etc.) to stimulation, the presence, diminution, and absence of such reactions in the same infant under different circumstances take on great significance.

We have, then, infants and neonates who, although they manifest a differentiated response to auditory, tactile, and electrical stimulation (as evidence of ego function), do not manifest this perceptual discrimination under conditions at the extremes of the pleasure-unpleasure continuum. This leads us to our first conclusion. That is, the newborn is at these moments unaware of, or unresponsive to, such stimuli because at that particular moment there is insufficient energy available to the ego to enable it to operate its apparatuses of external perception. The details of this will be discussed presently.

This in turn leads us to our second conclusion, which is that *at any given moment,* regardless of its distribution, the total quantity of mobile psychic energy available to the ego is fixed. This latter conclusion is frequently implied by Freud. There is, furthermore, the implication that the ultimate amount of energy is fixed, an implication inherent in the concept that as the ego is strengthened by neutralization of instinctual energy, the strength of the instinctual drives is reduced. It would thus appear that in some ways the energy system postulated by Freud was related to thermodynamic energy concepts. This implication of fixed quantity is perhaps most definitively stated by Ives Hendrick (1944) who asserts that the kinetic implication of psychic energy "closely parallels the conception of thermodynamics in that it hypothecates a constant and indestructible energy." In terms of ego function, the concept of fixed amounts of highly mobile neutral energy has long existed as an extremely valuable clinical tool, since it permits one to understand, by virtue of shifting cathexes, fluctuation in ego richness and impoverishment as manifested in therapeutic work.

In this regard, however, one must remain aware of the current concern with the nature of biological systems, more specifically with the question of "open" versus "closed" systems. While many have stated that man as a biological system is an "open system," the applicability of such concepts as entropy, open system, negative entropy, communication theory, to mental processes is not yet at hand. Rapaport (1950a, 1951b) has clearly indicated the complexity of the problem in reviewing the increasing concern of physicists with biology. He has emphasized that biological events are unlike physical events in that they are "timebound and historical, and therefore cannot be treated with the usual methods of physics."

Thus, in speaking of fixed or limited amounts of psychic energy, I refer to a given moment of time, and not a thermodynamic principle. Such limitations will be most apparent in the neonate who has not the sources and apparatuses for neutralization and mobilization of psychic energy that are available to the adult. But even in the adult, psychic energy is not inexhaustible, and even though the quantity may vary from moment to moment, *at a given moment* the quantity available is fixed or limited.

Thus, in trying to understand the fluctuation in the responsiveness of the infants cited, it is my supposition that at moments of extreme pleasure or unpleasure, all or relatively all of the available psychic energy is mobilized and invested in those ego apparatuses particularly involved. Since the supply of energy is fixed, other ego functions cease or are dramatically curtailed because of the then insufficient energy to permit their function. In the examples above, it is apparent that the ego functions dealing with external excitation suffer at the hand of those ego functions dealing with stimulation from within the individual. Actually, these statements are in accord with Freud's (1920) discussion of the vulnerability of the cortex to stimulation from within and without, in which he assumed the position that protection was effective *only* to excitation from without, a view modified by Anna Freud (1936). However, Freud (1920) continues: "Toward the inside there can be no such shields; the excitations in the deeper layers extend into the system directly and in undiminished amount, in so far as certain of their characteristics give rise to feeling in the pleasure-unpleasure series. The excitations coming from within are, however, in their intensity and in other, qualitative respects—in their amplitude, perhaps—more commensurate with the system's method of working than the stimuli which stream in from the external world. This state of things produces two definite results. *First, the feelings of pleasure and unpleasure (which are an index to what is happening in the interior of the apparatus) predominate over all external stimuli*" (my italics). Freud then proceeds to relate this to the mechanism of projection whereby the externalization permits more effective shielding.

I will now amplify my hypotheses as follows: perception of excitation coming from within is an ego function and one that will predominate or take precedence over external perception. Therefore, when excitation from within reaches great magnitude, as it does at the extremes of the pleasure-unpleasure series, the ego will invest all of its mobile energy, in a preferential manner, to the perception of, and attempts to cope with this excitation—leaving the ego apparatuses which deal with external perception without energy and thereby rendering them completely or relatively nonfunctioning. A suggestion of this is in Freud's statement (1916): "With our scanty knowledge of the metapsychological conditions of mental processes, we may perhaps see in this fact a hint that complete absence of cathexes in a system renders it less susceptible to stimulation."

I will now turn to the application of these admittedly conjectural conclusions to the problems of mechanisms of defense. Again, we start with the basic assumption that the mechanisms of defense are ego functions and as such partake in the fixed amount of energy available for their operations. As indicated above, Freud felt that the organism could defend itself, and the importance he placed on such defense is clearly apparent in the following statement (1920): "Protection against stimuli is an almost more important function for the living organism than the reception of stimuli . . . The protective shield is supplied with its own store of energy and must above all endeavor to preserve the special modes of transformation of energy operating in it against the effects threatened by the enormous energies at work in the external world."

With reference to the newborn, Anna Freud (1936) states, "The infantile ego experiences the onslaught of instinctual and external stimuli at the same time: if it wishes to preserve its existence, it must defend itself on both sides simultaneously." At the same time, she emphasizes the fact that little is known of the basic mechanism of defense, or perhaps of the precursors of defense. Some hints of this come from Freud (1926) in his statement: "It may well be that before its sharp cleavage into an ego and an id, and before the formation of a super-ego, the mental apparatus makes use of *different methods of defense* from those which it employs after it has attained those levels of integration" (my italics).

I would like now to speculate that the experiments described above, and the conclusions drawn from them, have within them the first, basic, inborn defense mechanism of the ego. This defense is the very fact that the amount of energy available to ego function is mobile, and that at any given moment the amount is fixed. What I propose is that these two factors operate in what I call the *defense of imperceptivity*. In terms of a system composed of connected inter-related ego apparatuses, all dependent upon the same source of mobile but limited quantities of energy, the channeling of all of this energy into one or several of the apparatuses will automatically shut off the remainder for lack of energy to operate. So the newborn is rendered impercipient by the inability of those apparatuses concerned with external perception to function, because all of the psychic energy is invested in other apparatuses concerned with internal perception and control. This may be thought of as an inborn regulator or control which not only permits of more efficient usage of small amounts of energy, but also defends against overloading.

Overloading is here thought of in the same sense as indicated by Freud (1920), as quoted above with reference to the danger of the "enormous energies at work in the external world." In addition, during moments of crises, pleasurable or unpleasurable, overloading takes on increased significance.

Fenichel (1945) suggests a similar defense with a different mode of operation, which comes into being after the "differentiation of systems of perception and systems of memory, and the origin of a more differentiated consciousness. After the completion of this differentiation, the organism is in a position to protect itself against too much influx of stimuli by shutting off the function of perception. The newly formed ego can again sink back into the id."

It is conceivable that this mechanism of imperceptivity continues to function in greater or lesser degree throughout life. In this regard, I would like to direct attention to the infant suffering with "anaclitic depression." It is appropriate to quote directly from the classic description of Spitz and Wolf (1946):

> In the second half of the first year, a few of these infants developed a weepy behavior that was in marked contrast to their previously happy and outgoing behavior. After a time this weepiness gave way to withdrawal. The children in question would lie in their cots with averted faces, refusing to take part in the life of their surroundings. When we approached them we were ignored. Some of these children would watch us with a searching expression. If we were insistent enough, weeping would ensue and, in some cases screaming. . . . This behavior syndrome lasted three months. Then the weepiness subsided, *and stronger provocation became necessary to provoke it. A sort of frozen rigidity of expression appeared instead. These children would lie or sit with wide-open expressionless eyes, frozen immobile face, and a faraway expression as if in a daze, apparently not perceiving what went on in their environment.* This behavior was in some cases accompanied by autoerotic activities in the oral, anal, and genital zones. Contact with children who arrived in this stage became *increasingly difficult and finally impossible.* At best, screaming was elicited [my italics].

Spitz and Wolf state that this syndrome appears "only in children who were deprived of their love objects for an appreciable period of time during their first year of life"—a period characterized by an

immature almost nascent ego.[2] I feel that here might be the classic
example of the infant, who in the early period of the illness is
attempting desperately to cope with the mounting unpleasure from
within. As his immature mechanisms of defense prove inadequate
to militate against the increasing magnitude of unpleasurable excitation from within—more and more of his limited amount of psychic
energy is invested in the struggle until by virtue of near total investment, he is rendered impercipient and, as described above, does not
perceive the environment. In addition, we can here see not only the
apparatuses for perception involved, but even the apparatuses for
expression, thinking, language, and motor activity.

Since the mature or adult ego has available greater amounts of
psychic energy and many more effective and efficiently operating
mechanisms of defense, it is logical that the defense measure I
propose could be demonstrated only in those emergency or crisis
situations which are capable of arousing such overwhelming feelings
of pleasure or unpleasure. One must caution against too literal application of this measure to the adult ego because of its tremendous
complexity of fused libidinal and aggressive energies, and the complexity of pleasure-unpleasure feelings. However, in terms of overloading, it may be operative in the greater comfort of the patient
with migraine who is placed in a quiet, darkened room; or the oft-
quoted obliviousness to external stimulation during intercourse.
As a measure of defense it might make more comprehensible neuro-
genic shock following emotional catastrophe, or the soldier's un-
awareness of severe physical injury to himself sustained during the
heat of battle. To a lesser degree, its function might make more
comprehensible the plight of the music lover, who is so enraptured
by the internal pleasurable excitations brought to him through his
auditory sensibilities and his varied internal reactions to it that he
becomes imperceptive to the hardness of his bench, or the fact that
his leg has "fallen asleep." It might be conceivable that this is the
mechanism which accounts for the compensatory increase in sensitivity by one sensory modality following the loss of another, as has
been reported in blindness.

This defense of imperceptivity must be sharply distinguished

2 Coleman and Provence (1957) have reported that such deprivation may occur in
infants living in families as a result of insufficient stimulation from the mother.

from other mechanisms of defense, especially denial (in its original sense of denying entry of external stimulation of a *painful* sort), on the basis that all other defense mechanisms require energy for their operation, whereas the defense of imperceptivity consists in the unavailability of psychic energy. In addition, it functions without regard to the pleasure or unpleasure of the stimuli excluded.

It seems to me that the above conclusions and considerations have some limited applicability for instinct theory. Let me say at the outset that these data have no applicability to a discussion of the existence of the controversial death·instinct. The implications of which I speak have only to do with the behavior in the newborn period and its relation to Freud's statement (1922), "Both classes of instincts, Eros as well as the death instinct, would in this view, *have been in operation and working against each other from the first origin of life*" (my italics).

The major theoretical problem has to do with the source of this energy and the process by which it is made available to the ego. Freud, Hartmann, Kris, and Rapaport all indicate the acceptance of a concept, according to which the neutralization of instinctual drive energy into psychic energy is a continuous process. Rapaport (1956) describes the mechanism of this operation as follows: "Hartmann indicates that the paradigm of neutralization is the process described by Freud (1923); the identifications built up as structures in the ego in the wake of object loss—on the pattern of the object— are invested with id energy, which thus comes to be at the disposal of the ego. Hartmann (1950, 1954) implies that all sublimations and desexualizations may follow this pattern, and extends this to the neutralization of aggressive energies also." Even if one assumes that neutralization starts very early (Hartmann, 1955), it is extremely unlikely that such a mechanism can be functioning in the three-day-old neonate. That instinctual drive might not be the only source of neutralized energy is clearly stated by Hartmann (1955), in his discussion of sublimation:

> Here I want to add a few words to what was also hinted at before: the possibility that there exist other, noninstinctual sources of neutralized energy. Most of the energy active in the psychic apparatus originates, according to Freud, in the drives. But a later hypothesis of his which may be relevant for this ques-

tion assumes that there exists a hereditary core not only of instinctual, but also of ego functions. This idea I have developed, as to some of its implications, in my work on the primary autonomy of the ego (1939, 1950, 1952), which prepares the ground for the possibility just presented: namely that part of the mental energy—how much or how little we can hardly estimate— is not primarily drive energy but belongs from the very first to the ego, or to the inborn precursors of what will later be specific ego functions, and maybe also to those apparatuses that come gradually under the influence of the ego and in turn influence its development.

The relationship of this to original energy sources has been the concern of both Jacobson (1954) and Kris (1955, 1956). With reference to the possibility of noninstinctual origin, Kris (1955) states: "When Freud hinted at the existence of such energy sources, it seemed difficult to find a place for them in psychoanalytic thinking. Now this assumption seems to have become eminently useful. *The energy might be thought to stem from the apparatus of the ego,* and we might add that, by its quantitative variations, it may influence the investment of the ego with neutralized energy" (my italics).

To return to the neonate, it is unlikely that the above-described mechanisms of neutralization, rooted as they are in identifications, are operative in this period. If such were the case, it is likely that the kind of psychic energy would show more clearly its similarity to its instinctual source. Our observations do not support any clear-cut statement of the presence of both drives at birth, or of their being the source of the initially present psychic energy. Yet, psychic energy is present and partakes in the *primary autonomy* of the ego. There would appear to be two possible sources for the neutralized energy. First one could postulate an inborn supply of undifferentiated psychic energy, very small in quantity, as part of the inborn ego apparatuses. Second, and I consider this most likely, one can postulate an undifferentiated phase of instinctual development corresponding to the undifferentiated phase of ego-id development. Since ego and id are as yet undifferentiated, the rudimentary ego will also have access to this source of undifferentiated energy which appears to be primitively neutralized. As suggested by Hartmann (1955), this might be called "primary ego energy." Kris (1956), in his concern about developmental sequence and especially negativism, has also come to consider the possibility of an undifferentiated phase in instinctual development. Jacobson (1954) postulates this in her statement, "Consequently, we might wonder whether the observable facts could not be explained more easily by the assumption that, at the very beginning of life, the psychic energy is still in an undifferentiated state and develops into two kinds of drives with different qualities only under the influence of external stimulations with the opening up and increasing maturation of pathways for outside discharge." She further feels that this is confirmed by the indistinctiveness of aggressive and libidinal qualities in the instinctual manifestations of infancy and early childhood.

CONCLUSIONS

1. Our observations of the functioning of the neonate suggest the presence of a functioning rudimentary ego, whose ego function of primitive but differentiated perception is dependent upon already existing psychic energy.

2. This energy is highly mobile, and at any given moment is fixed in quantity.

3. The highly mobile nature of this energy permits its *total* investment if necessary. Such total investment is most likely to occur in processes operating at either end of the pleasure-unpleasure continuum.

4. The necessity to attend to and attempt to cope with excitation from within will take precedence over excitation from without.

5. The total investment of energy in processes from within will make it impossible for those ego functions dealing with excitation from without to function because of a lack of energy.

6. It is postulated that this lack of available energy forms an inborn primary defense mechanism which is called the *defense of imperceptivity*. Although most blatant in the neonate, it is felt that this defense operates to a lesser or greater degree throughout life, and that it will be most discernible in crises or catastrophic experiences. This can be defined as follows: when the level of excitation from within (and without) reaches such magnitude as to overwhelm the ego, the tendency is to direct all available psychic energy preferentially to those ego apparatuses which deal with internal

excitation; thereby the ego apparatuses which deal with external excitation will be automatically depleted or "closed" because of a lack of energy, rendering the organism totally or relatively impercipient to external excitation. It is further postulated that other ego functions, such as language, thought, motor activity, etc., may be so involved by more extensive chronic depletion. With chronicity during developmentally crucial periods, severe ego restriction such as "environmental retardation" may result.

7. It is felt that the psychic energy of the neonate does not function in a manner to suggest derivation from libidinal and aggressive drives. It is further unlikely that mechanisms of neutralization are available to the rudimentary ego. It is rather assumed that this supports Hartmann's suggestion that there might be other sources of neutral psychic energy. It is postulated that there is an undifferentiated stage of instinct development that is functional, and exists as a functional matrix corresponding to the undifferentiated phase of ego-id development. This energy appears to be primitively neutral, and since ego and id are not as yet differentiated completely, the ego will have access to this energy to operate its primitive functions.

BIBLIOGRAPHY

Coleman, R. W. & Provence, S. (1957), Environmental Retardation (Hospitalism) in Infants Living in Families. *Pediatrics,* XIX.

Fenichel, O. (1945), *The Psychoanalytic Theory of Neurosis.* New York: Norton.

Freud, A. (1936), *The Ego and the Mechanisms of Defense.* New York: International Universities Press, 1946.

Freud, S. (1916), Metapsychological Supplement to the Theory of Dreams. *Collected Papers,* IV. London: Hogarth Press, 1948.

—— (1920), *Beyond the Pleasure Principle.* London: Hogarth Press, 1922.

—— (1922), The Libido Theory. *Collected Papers,* V. London: Hogarth Press, 1948.

—— (1923), *The Ego and the Id.* London: Hogarth Press, 1948.

—— (1926), *The Problem of Anxiety.* New York: Norton, 1936.

Hartmann, H. (1939), Ich-Psychologie und Anpassungsproblem. *Int. Ztschr. Psa. & Imago,* XXIV. Translated in part in: *Organization and Pathology of Thought,* ed. D. Rapaport. New York: Columbia University Press, 1951.

—— (1950a), Psychoanalysis and Developmental Psychology. *This Annual,* V.

—— (1950b), Comments on the Psychoanalytic Theory of the Ego. *This Annual,* V.

—— (1955), Notes on the Theory of Sublimation. *This Annual,* IX.

—— & Kris, E. (1945), The Genetic Approach in Psychoanalysis. *This Annual,* I.

—— —— & Loewenstein, R. M. (1946), Comments on the Formation of Psychic Structure. *This Annual,* II.

Hendrick, I. (1944), *Facts and Theories of Psychoanalysis.* New York: Knopf, 1944.

Jacobson, E. (1953), The Affects and Their Pleasure-Unpleasure Qualities, in Relation to the Psychic Discharge Processes. In: *Drives, Affects, Behavior,* ed. R. M. Loewenstein. New York: International Universities Press.

—— (1954), The Self and the Object World. *This Annual,* IX.
Jensen, K. (1932), Differential Reaction to Taste and Temperature Stimuli in Newborn Infants. *Genet. Psychol. Mon.,* 12.
Kris, E. (1955), Neutralization and Sublimation. *This Annual,* X.
—— (1956), Personal communication.
Lustman, S. (1956), Rudiments of the Ego. *This Annual,* XI.
Rapaport, D. (1950a), Review: Cybernetics of Control and Communication in the Animal and the Machine. *Psa. Quart.* XIX.
—— (1950b), On the Psychoanalytic Theory of Thinking. *Int. J. Psa.,* XXX.
—— (1951a), The Autonomy of the Ego. In: *Psychoanalytic Psychiatry and Psychology,* ed. R. P. Knight & C. R. Friedman. New York: International Universities Press, 1954.
—— (1951b), The Conceptual Model of Psychoanalysis. In: *Psychoanalytic Psychiatry and Psychology,* ed. R. P. Knight & C. R. Friedman. New York: International Universities Press, 1954.
—— (1956), Present-Day Ego Psychology. Unpublished Manuscript.
Richmond, J. B. & Lustman, S. (1955), Autonomic Function in the Neonate: Implications for Psychosomatic Theory. *Psychosom. Med.,* XVII.
—— & Grossman, H., Lustman, S. (1953), A Hearing Test for Newborn Infants. *Pediatrics,* XI.
Spitz, R. A. & Wolf, K. (1946), Anaclitic Depression. *This Annual,* II.
Wolowik, A. B. (1927), Über die gegenseitige Wirkung der Schmerz- und Nahrungsreflexe bei Kindern. *Jb. Kinderheilk.,* CXV.

ASPECTS OF EARLY DEVELOPMENT

ANXIETY RELATED TO THE "DISCOVERY" OF THE PENIS

An Observation

GABRIEL CASUSO, M.D., D.Psych. (London)

With an Introduction by
ANNA FREUD, LL.D. (London)

Introduction

Analysts who have followed the publications in our psychoanalytic journals from their beginnings may remember a column in the original German issue which was reserved for observations made on children. The communications selected for it were written by parents or teachers who had undergone analysis themselves and, thereby, had their eyes opened for signs of happenings in the child's mind which escaped the notice of unanalyzed observers. Sayings, and forms of behavior were recorded which showed the child under the impact of his sexual strivings. These descriptions ceased to be published later on when the existence of infantile sexuality had been established beyond doubt, and no further evidence from direct observation seemed necessary to validate the analytic findings in this particular respect.

After reading Dr. Casuso's description of certain events in the life of his infant son, which follows here, readers may feel that the publication of communications of this kind should be begun again in our days and that the observing and recording activity of analytic parents might help toward filling an important gap in our analytic knowledge. Although in recent years the interest of many analysts and child analysts has concentrated on the first year of the child's life, there is much uncertainty still concerning the ways and means which should be employed to unearth suitable material. Reconstruction from the analyses of later stages of development has provided us with all we know about the libidinal phases, the oedipus and the castration complex; but reconstruction becomes less certain, and less fruitful, where the preverbal period is concerned. Even though analysts may expect the complications of the early mother relationship to be repeated in the transference, they will be less confident concerning the reappearance of past happenings where, for example, the intricacies of building up the body ego are in question.

Direct observation of developmental steps may, therefore, prove invaluable and indispensable. But to take cognizance of an infant's changing mood swings, of his fleeting moments of anxiety or pleasure, interest, or need for comfort, is no easy matter. It is done best on the basis of the type of twenty-four-hour contact which is denied to the objective, academic, scientific observer. Motherless children who are cared for by objective strangers labor, as we know, under disadvantages which confuse the issues. This points to the parents as the only people who are sufficiently in contact with the infant and knowledgeable about him to observe minutely. The recording of their observations will be all the more valuable, the more their attention is alerted and any inevitable subjectivity corrected by their analytic experience.

Dr. Casuso's short paper may convince readers that the latter can be done.

Anxiety Related to the "Discovery" of the Penis

This communication deals with a series of observations made by my wife, who first noticed the "discovery," and by myself, on our son G., who at the time was a little over ten months old. The reports cover roughly the seven or eight weeks between that time and his first birthday. The first report was written for a consultation with Miss Anna Freud, and the next two at her suggestion that we follow it up to record the length of the initial fear, its development and its aftereffects, if any.

First Report

About five days ago G. discovered his penis. At the time he was sitting on the bed, dressed in just a vest, playing with a toothbrush.

Accidentally he looked down, the toothbrush fell from his hand and very gingerly he touched his penis with one finger; he was simply "frozen" with intensity. Very carefully he pulled it a little, then gave a small frightened sigh, turned around, crawled toward his mother as fast as possible, pulled himself up, crying pitiously and pushed his face against her. She comforted him and then examined his penis, thinking that maybe it was hurting; but everything looked alright, and his nails were cut short so he could not have hurt himself that way. The first thing he did when he had his clean nappie [diaper] on was to look down, and he seemed relieved to see nothing but white plastic.

The next day the same thing happened, and the next. This time the mother picked him up, touched his penis and told him that it was also part of him, just like his hands, his feet and his nose, touching everything when she named it. Naturally he did not understand what she was saying, but he was very interested in what she did; and this time he did not look down when he had his clean nappie on and played cheerfully with a toy.

For two days nothing happened, he was too busy with rattles and toys to be thinking of the "strange" thing he had discovered, but then it attracted his attention again. He was still a bit frightened and still crawled quickly toward his mother, but his reaction was not nearly as violent as before. Again the mother pointed things out to him and very soon he began making happy noises and grabbed a toy.

About a week before the "discovery" he stood unaided for the first time.

Second Report (a fortnight later)

Since the first report was written G. has lost the fear of his penis. For a few days he had little interest in the "new thing," but gradually the interest returned, this time without fear or tenseness.

His mother made a point of being near him when he was playing with it, in case he would feel like running to her again but did not pick him up as he did not seem to need comforting. The interest increased and some days ago he started to look for his penis as soon as his leggings were removed; he looked down and tried to feel it through his plastic pants and nappie. Immediately after those obstacles were out of the way, he became absorbed in the contemplation of and playing about with his penis. Yesterday, when this was once more in full swing, he suddenly looked up at his mother, smiling broadly.

Today he had another "fantastic" experience: while he was sitting on a towel after his bath, as usually gently pushing and pulling his penis, he urinated. It trickled over his foot and he was terribly interested, watching keenly how the stream appeared and then formed a puddle on the towel. One drop remained hanging from his penis; after a moment's hesitation, he touched it with a stiff forefinger and was obviously somewhat baffled that it fell and disappeared in the puddle. He then poked his finger in the wet spot on the towel, giving happy little grunts.

Throughout the period covered by these two reports his handling of his penis has not produced any erections; nevertheless it appears to be pleasurable. On the other hand erections have occurred occasionally for some time when his mother cleans him.

Third Report (a month after the second report)

Yesterday G. was one year old.

The fear of his penis has not returned, the interest in it has not lessened, if anything it has increased. Not that he plays with it more often than before, but when he plays with it now he really concentrates on it and any interference by his mother is met with black looks and makes him thoroughly angry. It happens that he starts playing with it when he lies on his back while he is being cleaned and powdered and then he pushes his mother's hand away impatiently. He is usually allowed to go on until he stops by himself.

There have been a few weeks that washing made him absolutely shriek with laughter, he simply doubled up with mirth and pressed his legs together so that his mother could not go on. This, however, has stopped as suddenly as it began.

During the period covered by this report, erections while being handled by his mother have been more frequent, accompanied by a sort of faraway look on his face, the whole experience obviously being very enjoyable to him. No erection has occurred when he plays with his penis.

I think I should add that G. has very much a "one-track mind."

Interference when he is playing with his toys also makes him angry. And when, for instance, he is grabbing something he had better not play with and one tries to divert his attention by giving him something else, he may give the new object a fleeting glance, but he will go back immediately to the old one.

A few days before his birthday he took a couple of steps all by himself and today he "walked" from one end of the playpen to the other.

Appendix

At the time this communication is written G. is sixteen months old. The fear related to his penis has not recurred, nor has fear appeared in relation to any other part of his body, although fascination reappeared in connection with knees, his own and other people's. Also he shows interest in his toes.

About a month after the third report was written erections began to appear when he was playing with his penis. By now he shows only occasional interest in it.

Walking has now really become a source of great pleasure.

I think it is relevant to mention that a fear of the big bathtub in the bathroom preceded by about four weeks and overlapped the onset of the fear described in this communication. It was dealt with by bathing him in a small tub in the kitchen.

I should like to add that since G. was born and after the first twelve days in hospital, his mother always changed, bathed and handled him, with some assistance on my part during the first three months. At around the age of four months the standard type of nappies were substituted by the throw-away type, covered with plastic pants.

Tentative Explanation

Loewenstein (1950) describes a somewhat similar observation by a patient of his on her baby, although in the case of G. the anxiety was far more apparent. Perhaps the explanation for this difference could be sought along the lines of the timing (which is probably variable in each individual) of the discovery of the penis in relation to the discovery of other parts of the body, which leads to the infant's formation of his concept of body image. In other words, my idea is that for him, at that time, through his discovery of body boundaries by sight and hand, the penis was not only alien but also particularly disturbing in its strong sensations because of its erotic sensitivity; hence the child's relief of finding the plastic pants back on again. It could also be a difference in the ways the two babies dealt with anxiety. Loewenstein contends that this anxiety, this uncertainty whether or not the penis is part of the body, sets the model for what at a later stage of development and under different circumstances is felt as castration anxiety.

On writing this communication I am fully aware that there are many things which I have not tried to explain, such as the connection between the fear of the bath tub and that of the penis, or what effect his observing himself urinating had on his assimiliation of the "discovery," etc. But I feel that in this communication the emphasis should remain on the observation itself.

BIBLIOGRAPHY

Loewenstein, R. M. (1950), Conflict and Autonomous Ego Development During the Phallic Phase. *This Annual*, V.

THE USE OF PREDICTION IN A
LONGITUDINAL STUDY

MARIANNE KRIS, M.D. (New York)[1]

Given some information about a young expectant mother and her infant's behavior during the first months of its life, one feels tempted to predict the future development of this mother-infant relationship. For instance, Mrs. A. was happy during her pregnancy and eagerly anticipated the arrival of her first baby. Billy was born after a labor which Mrs. A. experienced as being much less painful than she had expected. From the very beginning she handled the baby competently, seemed particularly responsive to clues from him, and had great success in satisfying him. When Billy was three weeks of age the pediatrician noted that Mrs. A.'s way of comforting him seemed to be "all he needed and no more."

During the first nine to ten months Mrs. A. was described by everyone who saw her as a particularly warm and skillful mother, and the impression of unity and understanding between her and Billy was repeatedly commented upon. She seemed to set her limits in a way that aroused a minimum of protest from the baby. She anticipated no difficulty and seemed to feel perfectly sure that everything would go well between them, and so did everyone who observed them together. The prediction was made that Billy would fare well in his further development, especially since he showed surprising adaptability and smoothness in many of his physiological and maturational patterns.

As a newborn he was described as mature and moderately active. He expressed his wishes so clearly that they could easily be understood. He developed well, slept soundly and ate vigorously, and could

[1] From the Child Study Center, Yale University School of Medicine. The research project has been supported by a grant from the Commonwealth Fund.

Presented at the special meeting celebrating the 35th Anniversary of the Youth Guidance Center, Worcester, Mass., on September 19, 1957.

usually be persuaded to "take one more bite for mommy" if she wished it. He was responsive to every adult, but most of all to his mother. He smiled readily, babbled freely and gave an impression of great amiability.

Those first nine to ten months, then, presented such an untroubled, conflict-free, mutually satisfying and stimulating mother-child relationship that the period of "crisis" which arose during the tenth month came as a surprise. At that time Mrs. A. scolded Billy sharply, looked harassed and tired, and said about Billy, "I really work up a sweat trying to figure out what he wants now." She reported that Billy was now so active that he grabbed the spoon when she fed him, and always seemed to want to be down on the floor, out of his crib or chair. She spoke of him as though his activities were primarily aimed at provoking her. At that point Billy would permit no one except his mother to feed him his meals, which both pleased and irritated her.

Shortly thereafter she began to express dissatisfaction with other circumstances in her life situation, which previously had not disturbed her. She complained particularly about living with her in-laws and Billy's interest in his grandmother. Her problems with Billy continued. She became increasingly displeased about the fact that Billy could no longer be persuaded to comply with her wishes, and summarized her difficulties by saying: "I can't figure him out any more." Under the pressure of her dissatisfaction Mrs. A. returned to work and left the care of Billy to her sister.

The preceding case is from an article written by Coleman, Kris and Provence (1953), using the observations of the longitudinal study in child development initiated at. the Yale Child Study Center in 1949 by Ernst Kris and Milton Senn. One of its aims has been to develop methods of evaluating what might be referred to as "varieties of health" rather than to focus on pathology. Our data have come from various contacts with the children and their families over a six- to seven-year period. During their first pregnancy, most mothers were given psychological tests, and all were regularly interviewed by the social workers who continued the contact with the family mostly in home visits. The pediatrician saw both mother and child at well-baby clinics, administered infant developmental tests at regular intervals, and also visited the home when the children were sick. The well-baby clinics were observed by all members of the staff. The analysts began to have direct contact with the children when they entered nursery school at the age of a little over two years. I myself joined the staff only at that time. When the children were about three, individual explorative play contacts with the analysts were initiated, and some of the children were taken into psychoanalytic treatment. No attempt will be made here to describe the study, its methodology or its procedures in any comprehensive fashion. We will focus primarily on a single aspect; namely, the use of prediction as a research device. Ernst Kris wrote about this as follows:

> One way in which we have viewed our data is in terms of their use for prediction. We not only try generally to anticipate "what will happen next" but we try to focus on specific problems: what kind of predictions are being suggested by any given material; at what point are these predictions expanded; when do new areas of prediction suggest themselves; when are general predictions replaced by more specific ones; what predictions could have been made in the past had we properly evaluated clues. What can be predicted at any given time, that is, the *range* of predictable events is to us more significant than the correctness or incorrectness of any specific prediction. . . .
>
> Past predictions become part of the material for retrospective evaluation. In rediscussing a case we turn to the past material in search of clues which would have suggested a different or more specific prediction. Thus prediction and retrospective evaluation interact.[2]

It is evident that all clinicians employ prediction implicitly or explicitly in their work with patients. It is inherent in diagnosis and prognosis and employed so routinely that it is taken for granted. This is, of course, equally true for the analyst who, in making an interpretation, has a prediction in mind, though it may be more often preconscious than conscious. Perhaps the major difference between the use of prediction in such a study as ours and in individual practice lies in our effort to systematize the procedure: to re-examine

2 Quotes are excerpts from papers by Ernst Kris (1957) and Coleman, Kris, Provence (1953), but have been rearranged somewhat.

The method described above was devised independently by Ernst Kris before he was familiar with Benjamin's (1950) views. Benjamin's views coincide with his in many respects, except that Benjamin's are aimed more at validating psychoanalytic theory, whereas the Yale study uses prediction as a tool for refining propositions and for developing new hypotheses.

the correctness of the predictions in terms of the relevance of data
and assumptions on which they are based.

The bulk of predictions was made during the first two years of
the children's life; it seems the infant's early stage of development—
the lack of differentiation—invites prediction. Later on, partly also
for practical reasons, fewer predictions were made.

Actually the first attempts at forecasting the future were made
already during the period of the mother's pregnancy. On the basis
of data gained in interviews with the mother and from a Rorschach
test the staff tried to evaluate the mother's personality, and to predict
its influence on the infant. For example, in one of our families, Mrs.
C. and Margaret, we inferred that Mrs. C.'s own reaction formations
toward dirt and messiness would result in attempts at *early* toilet
training, and in her adopting an overstrict attitude, which would
produce similar tendencies in the child. What we later observed,
during the third year of the child's life, was that the child could not
bear to see the tiniest spot of dirt on her dress or tolerate the slightest
bit of paint on her hands without immediately wanting to have the
dirt washed away. In playing house with other children she became
quite upset and bossy when things were not put exactly where "they
belonged." At that time, however, the mother had not yet made any
real attempts at toilet training. In the beginning of the fourth year
the mother's inconsistent attempts at bowel training were resisted by
the child. The mother continued the diapering with such an expression of distaste on her face that the little girl once said, "Please don't
make a face, mommy." The child looked troubled, but went on
soiling. Training was achieved very quickly a few months after
Margaret's fourth birthday when at last the mother was helped by
her therapist, also a member of our team, to make a determined
effort in this direction.

In examining the assumptions on which this prediction was based,
I should like to point to some factors which might be of general
applicability. We observed the rigidity of the mother's character in
her traits of overcleanliness and orderliness, which are, as we know,
associated with anal conflicts. Then we assumed that in handling the
child's bowel functions, she would show the same or even greater
overstrictness, in view of the fact that the direct contact with the
child's anal activity might aggravate her own anal desires and there-

fore intensify her habitual defenses. This assumption was incorrect. The mother's concern with dirt persisted unchanged, and indeed the child developed the same traits quite early—long before toilet training was attempted.[3] But the conflict inherent in toilet training—and this conflict is a ubiquitous one—did not lead, as was assumed, to an intensification of this mother's defensive processes, but rather to a breakthrough or indulgence of her original impulses, in that they were given free reign in the child. One wonders whether similar circumstances may not be involved in the frequently encountered inconsistencies in toilet training. It seems that the direct contact with the anal activity of the child—the seduction thus coming from the child—stimulates the mother's own old conflicts and induces her at times to relinquish her role as mother. Temporarily she can thus gratify her old pleasure in uncontrolled soiling through identification with the child.

This example illustrates something we have repeatedly encountered: we have often been able to outline correctly a broad area of difficulty but incorrectly predicted the specific details of maternal behavior.

The predictions in this case were made on the basis of what Mrs. C. told us—that is, what she consciously knew—at a time when the staff had had only few contacts with her. Yet it was probably not a matter of paucity of information alone, but also one of its quality, that prevented us from making the more specific prediction. Our data were not derived from an analytic contact; the repressed and unconscious material which would have been helpful was not available to us. Yet even if we had had more information about her conscious attitudes and had been familiar with her unconscious fantasies, I am not sure that we could really have "hit the mark." Though we often speak of the influence of the mother's unconscious tendencies upon the child, we know very little in which areas and in what form these influences will manifest themselves in the child. Thus we can only ask a question: if we knew more of the unconscious material, would we then predict more accurately the influence of the conscious and

---

[3] In 1950, Hartmann suggested, mainly on theoretical grounds, that "reaction formations, like orderliness or cleanliness, . . . which we are accustomed to find correlated with the anal phase, may appear before problems of anality have come to dominate the child's life." The case of Margaret (as well as those of other children in our study) furnishes evidence for the correctness of his suggestion.

of the unconscious attitudes of the mother upon the immediate behavior of the child and upon the formation of his character? Perhaps
such studies as those of Burlingham et al. (1955) on the concomitant
analyses of mother and child might furnish some answer to this
question.

There are several more reasons for the fact that some of our
predictions were wrong or only partially correct. One of them is that
in making our predictions we did not properly evaluate and utilize
all the information we had at a given time.

Let us return to our first case, Mrs. A. and Billy. Could we have
known that the mother who related so perfectly to the helpless infant
would become so exasperated by his first attempt at independence?

Unfortunately we were not sufficiently impressed by our own
description of her as "uninterviewable," and indeed she was one of
the few who was not given a Rorschach test. She was one of the least
communicative mothers in the study. We know from our clinical experience that abundance or paucity of information at any given time
are as significant as the content of the communication. We missed
this clue to a disturbance in her personality, and therefore we failed
to make the relevant predictions. Had we been able to understand
her conflicts better—particularly what significance a baby, especially
a boy, had for her—we might possibly have been able to predict and
prevent by active assistance the crisis that ensued.

Another reason why our predictions were bound to be inaccurate
at that time is the following: we were predicting mother-child rela-
lationships with no knowledge of the reality of the child himself.
The importance of the child's equipment in influencing the relationship and sometimes in changing parental attitudes was fully appreciated by us only when we were faced with it. In our second case
Margaret's individuality as it influenced the mother-child interaction
was of interest from the beginning. She was a well-formed, vigorous
7-lb. baby, born after a prolonged and exhausting labor. However,
at the age of 12 hours there were symptoms which were of concern
to the pediatrician: "She had a high-pitched cry of poor quality,
reacted minimally to stimulation, had poor sucking and rooting
responses and some degree of stupor. Over the next three days these
subsided so that she seemed again active and normal and by age 6
days was described as an attractive, well-formed, active baby who was

hypertonic, startled easily and was sensitive to external stimuli. She cried loudly for feedings and was difficult to comfort."[4] It was felt at the time that because of her physiological make-up she would be a difficult baby, and it seemed unfortunate that this infant, whose needs seemed to overwhelm her, was to be cared for by such an anxious mother.

The prediction of difficulty was eminently correct. Mrs. C. described the first three months as the worst months of her life, a period during which she lost all confidence in herself, was incapable of making decisions, and was repeatedly confused by suggestions from neighbors and relatives. The baby grew and developed fairly well, but she was physiologically somewhat unstable and hard to satisfy, and there was no doubt that these characteristics exaggerated her mother's problems in caring for her.

The hypersensitivity of this infant led some members of the staff during the first year to suggest the possibility that Margaret would later develop along psychotic lines, as described by Bergman and Escalona (1949) in regard to infants with unusual sensitivities. There was disagreement on this point from the pediatrician, who felt that such an outlook was not justified, but the reasons for the more optimistic prediction could not be formulated clearly. The alternate idea was that some minimal central nervous system damage had resulted in exaggerated responses to stimuli without other developmental or neurological signs.

I can well understand the prediction of psychosis. Even when I first saw Margaret at the age of two years and four months, I was struck by her complete immobility of posture and rigidity of facial expression. She was standing quite close to her mother, staring at the sandbox in the courtyard of the nursery school. I could not make out whether her stare indicated a desire for a toy, a desire she did not dare to express; or whether she was terror-stricken at the sight of a stranger or frightened by the idea that her mother might move an inch away. I tried to hand her a spoon to play with the sand, but at my mere approaching gesture she recoiled. Knowing her early history and about the indirect way in which her mother had handled her, I placed the spoon within her reach on the sandbox. She remained

4 This description has been taken from the article previously referred to, by Coleman, Kris, Provence (1953, pp. 37, 38).

apparently immobile and unresponsive for a considerable time until
at last, with some additional help from her mother, she gingerly
picked up the spoon. This first encounter with Margaret made me
too wonder whether she was a psychotic child. Afterwards we understood that her behavior was partly a reaction to her mother's rejection
who just at that time was frequently absent from the home and often
shipped Margaret out of the house.

Margaret's further development proved the early prediction of
psychotic involvement to be erroneous. Retrospective evaluation of
the same data toward the end of the first year led to the realization
that an important clue had been overlooked in the original prediction—namely that the infant had revealed a capacity to organize and
integrate stimuli and to gain from them developmentally, in spite
of her extreme sensitivity. The correct recognition of this, as a
strength or asset in the early months, would have enabled us to make
a more accurate prediction. In contrast to the clues to pathology
which we overlooked in the case of Mrs. A. and Billy, where I said
that we should have been able to predict her reactions, I do not believe that we could have known the significance of such early signs
of ego assets in Margaret's case. It was only in the course of this study
that we began to recognize the importance of such clues and to
appreciate their predictive value.

Retrospective evaluation, however, does not always so readily
provide answers to the questions raised. When the staff discussed the
possibility of a future psychotic development in Margaret, it also
noted that the infant easily found her thumb and sucked it. The suggestion was made that thumb sucking in an infant might possibly be
of predictive significance in the differential diagnosis of normal or
neurotic versus autistic development, based upon the idea that the
shift of cathexis from the breast or nipple to the thumb may represent the nucleus of the capacity to establish object relations.[5]
Margaret's subsequent development has supported this suggestion,
but in order to prove a definite connection many more cases would
have to be studied.[6]

[5] This formulation can, of course, not be reversed: the mere absence of thumb
sucking does not imply autistic development.

[6] In a personal communication, Dr. Mahler told me that in her observation autistic
children generally do not suck their thumbs, whereas in symbiotic infants she has
observed thumb sucking.

Another event in the first year of Margaret's life will serve to illustrate an additional point in regard to the difficulties of prediction: not only the equipment but also the growth and maturation of the child can bring about modification in maternal attitudes.[7] Mrs. C. feared during the first five months that Margaret would be a mentally retarded child in spite of the fact that her physical growth and her performance on the infant tests had been excellent from the first month. Moreover, Margaret had become infinitely less irritable and demanding. At five months, two things happened which brought about a change in the mother's attitude: the baby became more active motorwise, and also developed a distinct apprehensiveness about strangers and a preference for her mother. This seemed to banish the fear that the child was damaged or defective and gave the mother the reassurance she had been unable to accept from the pediatrician. The child's turning toward her also proved to her that she was not a "defective mother." During the following months her pleasure in the child increased and she now was able to assume responsibility for making many everyday decisions which came up in regard to Margaret's care. We had not foreseen the positive effect that the baby's maturation would have on the mother's attitude and had made no such prediction.

In this instance, the reassessment of data permitted us to see some details of the vicissitudes of the mother-infant relationship, and to suggest the child's maturation as one of its determining factors. In Margaret's case, we said that it gave a positive turn to what we would characterize, on the whole, as a very precarious and poor relationship. Now, a few years later, we would once more qualify our statement and say that *certain* maturational factors in the child *temporarily* exerted a positive influence upon the mother's attitude. They were not sufficiently strong, though, to withstand the impact of the mother's ambivalence, covertly and overtly expressed in so many areas. In other words, the first impression proved in the long run to be correct. But in the process of predicting and re-evaluating we have learned why our first impression was right in a much more specific way.

First impressions are sometimes not taken seriously enough. During the pregnancy, Mrs. C.'s repeatedly expressed concern for the

[7] See Coleman, Kris, Provence (1953).

welfare of the infant, and her doubts about her ability to care for an infant suggested to us that her ambivalence would negatively affect the handling of her child. This impression was forgotten when the mother seemed to have found a way of comforting this baby who showed hypersensitivity to almost all stimuli and was indeed difficult to care for. Mrs. C. avoided touching and handling her, and instead talked to her quietly and softly at a distance, thus exposing the child to few stimuli of low intensity. The staff interpreted this as a sign of the mother's perception of the child's needs. But when a second child with very different equipment and very different needs was born, the mother behaved in exactly the same way. We then realized that her behavior was dictated by her own unresolved conflicts. It was her own need to avoid close physical contact with the children which made her incapable of stimulating them appropriately.

As we gained more information about mother and child, our predictions became more specific. For instance, Margaret's particular competence in the area related to intellectual functioning, as shown by the infant tests, became increasingly apparent during the latter half of the first year of life. The first prediction followed the recognition that she was interested not only in the test materials as such but in what could be done with them. Her curiosity and imaginativeness led Ernst Kris to hypothesize that this behavior demonstrated a shift of cathexis from the object to the process, reflecting the first steps of intellectual activity in the conflict-free sphere of the ego. That is, the need to *possess* the object was superseded by the desire to make it *function* in some way. He predicted that she would be "a passionate intellectual." Further observation led him five months later to modify this prediction. While Margaret continued to demonstrate high intellectual performance, it became apparent that much of her shift away from the object to the process was stimulated by anxiety. The use of intellectual activity as a defense against danger was then clearly visible. At that point he predicted that this would continue to be a characteristic part of her functioning.

This latter prediction, first made when the child was less than a year and a half old, has proved to be correct in so far as it implied a heightened power of observation and a narrowing of genuine intellectual capacities. At present Margaret who is now six years old appears to be an intelligent but not very imaginative child, always on the alert for danger, and keenly observant in very circumscribed areas. In evaluating this long-term prediction, however, a new factor must be taken into consideration. She has been in analytic therapy since the age of three and a half. This, we think, has greatly modified her enormous fear of new situations and with it the need to use her intellectual endowment to minimize danger. Nevertheless, the main goal of therapy still is to free her of her intellectual inhibitions. The analyst in this case must deal not only with the internalized conflict in this child but also with the persistent inhibiting influence of the mother who in many subtle, devious, and confusing ways forcefully stifles the unfolding of the child's normal curiosity and intellectual development.

I have just mentioned the fact that in re-examining our predictions, we must now take into account the effect which we ourselves had on the development of these children. That we influenced their development is of course quite obvious in those children who are in analytic treatment. Yet we have influenced their development, and thus our predictions, from the very beginning. The pediatrician gave active advice in child care; the social worker, and in the case of Mrs. C., her therapist, attempted to modify her attitudes. The nursery school teacher educated not only the child but also the parents. All our predictions, therefore, had to be based not only on our knowledge of the families but also on an assessment of our own influence on them.

Our services to the families were not merely a factor to be considered in making and re-evaluating predictions. In some cases, an active intervention which, as already stated, is always based on a prediction, may possibly have been the factor that prevented the development of pathology and in this way furnished us with an opportunity to view our data in a different way.

Re-reading the records of Margaret's early feeding history, I began to wonder why the child did not develop an eating disturbance. I would be inclined to venture such a prediction if I hear that a mother gives an infant one ounce of milk, then removes the bottle from the vigorously sucking baby and waits until the baby has burped three times, even if it takes several minutes, before she continues the feeding, only to repeat precisely the same sequence after the infant has sucked another ounce. Margaret very soon began to spit up her food, to which the mother reacted with extreme disgust. Mrs. C. herself, we learned later, had had an eating disturbance as a child until she was about twelve years old. She once compared herself with Margaret in this respect, telling me, "She is just like me . . .?" Even now Mrs. C. who tends to be obese has great difficulties with her diet.

In attempting to answer the question why Margaret did not develop an eating disturbance, many factors must be considered. But one of them, I trust, was the influence exerted by the staff. The pediatrician attempted to change the obsessive feeding pattern, and gave detailed advice about the baby's diet, which somewhat reassured Mrs. C. In addition, the special attention given to Mrs. C. in those early days must have been very meaningful to her. We now know that she relates to her daughter as though she were competing with a sibling, jealously watching that the child is not given more than she. The fact that during the child's first year of life all the help was given to the mother may have enabled her to accept the pediatrician's advice and change her behavior in the feeding situation.

Perhaps these illustrations indicate something of the process of predicting. As time and experience have accumulated it has become apparent to us that in general we have been more accurate in predicting areas of conflict, difficulty and pathology that we have been in predicting conflict-free functioning and the use of normal defenses. This may be due to a general tendency in many of us to look for the "defect." But then also, most members of our team come from clinical fields, and are, by training and motivation, oriented to pathology and to the diagnosis and treatment of disease. Therefore we readily recognize the familiar signs and configurations of pathological phenomena. Knowing that neurotic behavior is repetitive and relatively immune to outside events, we tend to select as having predictive value those characteristics of the mother's personality which reflect the greatest inflexibility. We assume that her behavior with the child is then dominated by her own inner conflicts which make her less aware of the child's needs and therefore less responsive to clues from the child—in other words, that she will, with her pathology, disturb the natural rhythm of the child's evolving endowment and narrow its potentialities. In describing and looking at our children and their parents, it has been easiest for us to start with this

frame of reference. In the positive sense, we have tried to train ourselves to focus equally on those areas in which the mother is least
rigid, and where she is most likely to respond to the child's needs
and to foster the development of his own innate capacities. In this
case, therefore, the specific individuality of the child is relatively
more relevant for our predictions.

On the whole we have had to work hard at recognizing nonpathological aspects of behavior and finding tools for studying them.
In the search for additional methods we have found infant tests very
helpful, particularly in the way in which Drs. Coleman and Provence
have utilized these tests to assess ego functions and modes of adaptation. In addition, this project has sharpened our awareness of and
alertness to what constitutes a clue to ego capacities and healthy
assets. All staff members in all of the observational situations have
learned increasingly to include these important aspects in their descriptions. This has perhaps come more naturally to the nursery
school teacher who is accustomed by training to be aware of the areas
of mastery and of skill. Though much remains to be learned, in this
respect, we may say that in principle health is as predictable as
pathology.

We should also mention that the predictions made have been of
various kinds: short-term, long-term, simple and complicated. A
short-term prediction of a simple nature would be one in which current observations of the child's behavior resulted in the expectation
that in a parallel situation the child would react in a similar way;
e.g., that a child in whom anxiety about strangers persisted through
the second year would show separation anxiety on entering nursery
school. These predictions certainly have practical value, but we are
not likely to learn much from them unless they prove to be incorrect.
Actually, many such simple short-term predictions are merely a
common-sense application of what we already know.

The more complex and long-term predictions result from our
evaluation of the mutual interaction of the child's equipment with
his environment, as we have tried to illustrate in this paper. They
were based on (1) what we knew about the mother's conscious attitudes and what we inferred about her unconscious tendencies, and
(2) on what we knew about the child's innate capacities.

There are some factors, however, which we cannot foresee. We know very little about the nature and intensity of a particular child's drives.[8] In addition, we do not know what new facets of the equipment the maturational impact will bring to the fore.[9]

Another factor which we cannot foresee are the real incidents that life brings along: for instance, the birth of siblings; a friendly or unfriendly teacher when entering school; the role of classmates; grandparents moving in or out of the house; the prolonged absence, or death of a parent. Though we cannot predict the occurrence of such reality events, we nevertheless could make a systematic attempt at prediction, as if we knew the future, by assuming such typical and accidental situations and picturing how the child would react to them at different stages of development. When such incidents then actually occur, we would be able to learn from these "as if" predictions. Unfortunately we did not use this type of systematic prediction ourselves, but only realized its possibility in the course of the study.

At this time we cannot go further than this fragmentary presentation. The definite evaluation of our methodology—the use of prediction and of the other procedures as well as the findings of our research study—can be made only after we have worked through all of our material.

In conclusion I would say that the use of prediction seems to us an important and useful tool also for this kind of research. It delineates the areas in which we are on firm ground and helps to expose the areas in which our knowledge is scanty. It sharpens our capacity for observation as it constantly forces us to evaluate and re-evaluate our data and our assumptions of what is relevant. We feel that this procedure is one of the safeguards against the attempt to resort to oversimplified theories of personality development.

BIBLIOGRAPHY

Benjamin, J. (1950), Methodological Considerations in the Validation and Elaboration of Psychoanalytical Personality Theory. *Am. J. Orthopsychiat.*, XX.

Bergman, J. & Escalona, S. K. (1949), Unusual Sensitivities in Very Young Children. *This Annual*, III/IV.

[8] A recent attempt to learn more about drive endowment has been made by Alpert, Neubauer, Weil (1956).

[9] Ernst Kris frequently reminded the group that equipment is not a static but a dynamic force.

Burlingham, D., Goldberger, A., & Lussier, A. (1955), Simultaneous Analysis of Mother and Child. *This Annual*, X.

Coleman, R. W., Kris, E., & Provence, S. (1953), The Study of Variations of Early Parental Attitudes. *This Annual*, VIII.

Hartmann, H. (1950), Psychoanalysis and Developmental Psychology. *This Annual*, V.

Kris, E. (1957), A Longitudinal Study in Child Development: Notes on Purpose, Methodology, and Relevance of Data. Paper read at the International Psychoanalytical Congress, Paris.

THE EARLIEST DREAMS OF A YOUNG CHILD

WILLIAM G. NIEDERLAND, M.D. (New York)

A former patient, mother of three children, provided me with a record of the dreams of her eldest son, Johnny, between the ages of seventeen and forty-seven months. The child, now four years of age, has two younger siblings, two-year-old Charlie and ten-months-old Sandy. The mother, a very intelligent and reliable observer, recorded the child's dreams verbatim each time they were communicated to her or to her husband (or both) by the young dreamer, usually after the latter's awakening in the morning. The dreams, as reported by Johnny, were brought to my attention the same day; their content and wording (if any), mode of appearance, the ascertainable circumstances under which they occurred, accompanying experiences, etc., are presented in the account that follows. Because of their small number—eleven dreams altogether—no attempt will be made to classify them or to use them as the basis for specific formulations on the nature, function, and significance of childhood dreams. A short discussion, in the second part of this paper, is limited to some observations on the child's experiences as well as their relation to the relatively few comparable data in the analytic literature.[1]

THE DREAMS AND THEIR CIRCUMSTANCES

Dream I. The first experience reported as a dream was a nightmare and nonverbal. It occurred when Johnny was seventeen months old. The child, usually a sound sleeper, woke up screaming during the night. It took some time, perhaps an hour or so, until the parents were able to calm the crying and obviously frightened child. During the day preceding this nocturnal experience Johnny had been taken

---

[1] I am indebted to Mrs. Berta Bornstein for her helpful suggestions in the preparation of this paper.

by his grandmother to the Museum of Natural History. In great excitement and with shouts of apparent joy he had been running, for about twenty minutes, from exhibit to exhibit, looking at the bears, buffalos, and other large animals which he saw in the museum hall. He did not want to leave the museum and was finally led out by the accompanying adult.

Dream II. Johnny experienced the next dream when he was twenty months old. It also was a nightmare and nonverbal. At that time his mother was in the seventh month of pregnancy with the second child. Johnny awoke during the night screaming wildly. When his mother entered his bedroom (where he slept alone), she found him standing in his crib, pressing his right fist tightly against his teeth. After being held for a little while in his mother's arms, he calmed down and fell asleep again. During the preceding day, according to the mother's account, about seven or eight hours before what may be presumed to have been a nightmare, his mother had been playing with him, whirling him about in her arms and holding him against her body. The mother considered it likely that he might have felt fetal movements in her abdomen. While the correctness of this idea cannot be ascertained, it was quite apparent that the child thoroughly enjoyed this game with his mother, when suddenly and vigorously he bit her nipple through the clothing. He had never done this before. The mother's pain was so intense that she slapped him and instantly put him down. She, too, had never done this before. Johnny cried, and may have become aware of the acute pain (or, at least, abrupt change in the mother's behavior) produced by his biting. That night he awoke screaming and holding his fist in his mouth, pressing it against his teeth—something not observed in him before. As indicated above, Johnny had always been a sound sleeper and very rarely awakened during the night.

Dream III. This dream had a verbal content. It occurred when Johnny was two and a half years of age. His first words, on awakening one morning, were: *"Jimmy was at the waterspray, Jimmy was at the waterstream. Estelle was there too."* He repeated these words several times loudly and cheerfully. Jimmy was the dreamer's older playmate with whom he had happily played near a fountain on several recent visits to a playground in the park. This fountain had been called by him "waterspray" or "waterstream," and he had been drinking from it, holding his hands in it, splashing the water, sprinkling it over the ground, with great gusto. During the three days preceding the dream Johnny had had to be kept at home because of an acute tonsillitis. On the day of the dream he had repeatedly asked to be taken to the playground, but had been kept at home because his temperature was still above normal. As in Freud's (1900) examples of children's dreams, Johnny's dream directly represented the fulfillment of his wish which had been frustrated in reality. But there was more to it, as evidenced by the names included in the dream. Jimmy was not only the name of the dreamer's older playmate, but also of Johnny's own father (Jim). Estelle was the name of the baby nurse who had taken care of Johnny's brother Charlie through the first six weeks of Charlie's life. Charlie had been born eight months ago. Johnny had seen and recognized Estelle, Charlie's former nurse, in the playground where he had been playing with his friend Jimmy near the fountain. Johnny had been surprised to see that Estelle was now wheeling around another baby in a carriage, occasionally taking it out of the carriage, holding it in her arms, and feeding it. The dream, then, appeared to contain references related to birth, nursing, and the sibling situation. In addition to these elements, it is probable that the dream also refers to a traumatic episode which Johnny had experienced two months before the actual dream. The essential element of this experience—water—appears in this dream as well as in several subsequent ones.

During a brief stay in the country, Johnny had been playing in a pool which was divided into two areas, a wading pool for small children of his age and a deeper pool for older children. At a moment when he was not being watched, he ran from the shallow pool where the water had hardly reached his ankles to the deeper pool, dashed into it, and disappeared beneath the surface. He was almost immediately pulled out of the water. The child was fully conscious and cried. He showed no signs of shock and no medical treatment was necessary. A few days later, however, he developed an acute tonsillitis with fever, pain, and general malaise. It was the child's first tonsillitis and it was of brief duration. Whether this illness was *causally* connected with the fall into the pool cannot be known, of course; *chronologi-*

cally it undoubtedly was and presumably remained so in the child's mind. It is worth noting that the above dream occurred during the second tonsillitis the child experienced.

The reaction to the pool episode was expressed in a series of later water dreams and, by play and action, in two more ways. During the following fall and winter Johnny was repeatedly taken to the local zoo where he soon developed a keen interest in the sea lions. On entering the zoo he would immediately go to the pool where the sea lions were kept, would attentively watch them swimming, diving into and emerging from the water. He would often express wonderment about the sea lions, especially their swimming capacity, and would ask how sea lions could hold their heads under water so easily and for long periods of time. At home Johnny would attempt to swim in the bath tub, imitating a sea lion, trying to growl and gurgle like one, and exclaiming many times, "I am a sea lion." Through his observation of the sea lions' behavior and his repetitive active play of being such an animal himself, Johnny obviously was striving to attain mastery over the traumatic experience in the pool. His former fondness for water remained unchanged. In fact, he developed an extraordinary and active interest in fishing, boating, and other aspects of water life. The following summer at the beach he nevertheless showed a marked fear of entering water more than ankle deep. Whereas formerly he had been almost delirious in his play with waves and had to be restrained from dashing into deeper water, he now fled from bigger waves. He also spoke repeatedly of his experience during the previous summer when his "head went under the water" and he often said that it was "bad water" where that had happened.

Dream IV. Johnny reported the next dream when he was two years and ten months old. At that time he had become aware that his mother's belly was getting bigger again and had been told that a new baby would come into the house. The day before the dream he had spoken a great deal about the anticipated "new baby." During the night he was restless, woke up repeatedly, and in the morning told his parents: *"I saw a child in a tunnel; the child fell into the water."* In contrast to his usual way of speaking clearly and distinctly, and in contrast also to the open and cheerful manner in which he had reported the preceding dream, this was told in a low, indistinct, almost mumbling voice. On being questioned about the child in the dream, he first replied that he did not know, then that it was his brother Charlie, and finally said that the child was himself, Johnny. After a pause he added, apparently referring to the incident described above: "I fell into the water; Daddy took me out." It had actually been his father who pulled Johnny out of the pool. The unmistakable reproach addressed to the mother seems here expressed in an almost Janus-like fashion by the child: one part of the reproach reaches back into the past and the traumatic episode referred to; the other part points into the future, apparently expressing the child's resentment over the mother's pregnancy and the expected arrival of a new child.

Dreams V, VI, VII. These dreams occurred during the last fortnight of his mother's third pregnancy. They were all water dreams. Johnny, now three years and two months old, woke up in the morning at his usual time and reported excitedly: *"I had a special kind of sleep.[2] It was raining and there was water jumping up and down, up and down. There were cars coming in the street, many cars."* A little later, he repeated this in the same words, adding: "The special kind of sleep was fine. I liked it very much." One week later, shortly after awakening in the morning, Johnny said that he had had *"another special kind of sleep, water was jumping up and down the street, jumping up and down."* While relating this with great excitement, he started jumping up and down on the floor himself in an effort to explain how the water had been moving and jumping in his dream, and then added that it had been raining hard. (No rain had fallen during all these days and nights.) Two days later, shortly after midnight, Johnny awoke suddenly, left his bed, and wanted to go to the window to see the rain outside. Asked why he wanted to do that, he replied: *"I again had a special kind of sleep. It was raining hard and I want to see the rain. The water was jumping up and down in the street where the cars go."* He insisted on going to the window of his bedroom and looking out of it. (No rain was falling.)

The notable aspects of this series of dreams which, in effect,

2 Johnny had recently heard and used the expression "a special kind of . . ." in various connections, e.g., "a special kind of bread," "a special kind of book," and the like.

appear to be a reduplication of the same dream over a period of almost two weeks, can be summarized as follows:

1. They were water dreams.

2. No bed wetting took place at any time before, during, or after these experiences.

3. The dreams occurred during the last fortnight of the mother's pregnancy.

4. In preparation of the mother's forthcoming hospitalization Johnny had been told by his mother on several occasions that she would soon go to the hospital and bring back a new baby.

5. About the same time Johnny had noticed that a bathinette had been placed into the same room in which his brother Charlie had slept during the first year.

6. Prior to this dream series Johnny had begun to visit this room several times a day, apparently in order to check whether the new baby had not secretly arrived in the meantime. He continued to inspect this room frequently through the period of the three dreams.

7. A few days preceding the fifth dream Johnny, now under the full impact of the baby's imminent arrival, had begun to act like a baby himself, stating again and again: "I am a little baby, I am Charlie," imitating the behavior and noises of an infant, using baby talk, and crawling on the floor.

8. The day preceding the sixth dream he had sat on his mother's lap for a while. She is convinced that he perceived fetal movements in her abdomen on this occasion. He then said to her: "The baby is inside you, around you, all around." He repeated this emphatically and, while saying so, he pointed to his mother's arms, chest, legs, hips, shoulder, and only much later to her abdomen.

Dream VIII. A day or so after the seventh dream the mother entered the hospital from which she returned within a week with the new brother Sandy. Two weeks after the baby's arrival Johnny reported his next dream, which he had had while sleeping at his grandmother's house, where he slept in the latter's bedroom. During the night he suddenly awoke and shouted: *"A parakeet bit me in my hand."* He pointed to the back of his right hand between the thumb and index finger and urgently demanded to be allowed to sleep "with grandma in her bed." This was granted and the child soon fell asleep again. The dream was so vivid that on his awakening in the morning when he saw his grandmother in the other bed (where he had originally slept), Johnny exclaimed: *"Get out of the bed, grandma! There is a parakeet in the bed. He will bite you!"* He then explained in vivid detail that *"the paraket flew out of the tunnel zoo from the cage where the sea lions are. The parakeet flew first to my house. He did not find me in my house, because I slept in grandma's house. The parakeet then flew all the way to grandma's house into my bed and bit me in my hand. He came in through the window."*

Johnny's absorbing interest in the sea lions at the zoo was mentioned above. There was, in fact, a bird cage with parrots a short distance from the pool where Johnny had often watched the sea lions. With his attention focused on the pool and the sea lions, he had hardly ever taken notice of the bird cage nearby or of its winged inhabitants—except on one occasion, when the birds in the cage had been screeching rather loudly and flapping their wings violently. Johnny, standing close to the pool and listening to the noise made by the birds, had then looked attentively in the direction of the cage without saying anything. Moreover, when Charlie had been born and for a number of months thereafter, Johnny had shown keen interest in a parakeet whom he had seen in its cage in the window of a neighboring house. When his mother took Johnny and Charlie (the latter in the baby carriage) outdoors for a stroll, Johnny had often insisted that they first go to see the parakeet in the window down the street. Sometimes there were two or three parakeets in the cage. This fact greatly excited Johnny. Where did the other parakeets come from? Were they new parakeets? Johnny asked many questions. On the day preceding the parakeet dream Johnny had taken physical possession of Charlie's stroller, sat himself in it, and refused to leave it, saying again and again: "I am a little baby, I am Charlie, I am Charlie. . . ." He had only relinquished the stroller when his grandmother to whom he was very much attached (and had become more so lately) had promised to take him to her house by subway— a mode of transportation he loved—and let him stay with her overnight.

Dream IX. At the age of three years and eleven months Johnny reported the following dream to his parents: *"Rose had a new puppy.*

The puppy was white. It was talking and jumping up and down on the bed. Then the puppy was running and broke a leg." A little later he changed this version somewhat and said: *"The puppy broke its leg off. It was dead and could not walk and could not talk."* To understand this more complex dream, a detailed account of the accompanying circumstances is necessary. During the night of the dream, about midnight and almost certainly before the dream, Johnny had been awakened by the crying of his brother Charlie (who now slept with him in the same room). When the parents entered the childrens' room, Johnny had pointed angrily at his brother Charlie and had complained: "He disturbs me. He cries, and I cannot sleep." Thereupon Charlie was taken to another bedroom and Johnny, now alone in his room, was soon asleep again in his bed. At five A.M. he came running into the parents' bedroom and related the above dream. Thus it may be legitimately assumed that the manifest dream occurred between midnight and five A.M. It also seems permissible to think of the dream, at least in its immediate setting, as having been stimulated by the disturbance caused by his brother Charlie.

A number of other factors, based on a thorough evaluation of the ascertainable circumstances, could be identified as components of the dream's manifest content. Two days prior to the dream Johnny, while walking with his mother in the street, had seen two little dogs, one of which, a white one, was limping. This caught the child's attention and he questioned his mother about it. She explained that the dog's leg must have been injured by something and that it was such an injury which caused the dog to limp. That day was Washington's birthday. When Johnny heard the adults mentioning this fact, he wanted to know all about it, what it means, and who Washington was. He was briefly told about it and, in passing, it was also mentioned that Washington was long dead. This produced considerably anxiety in the child. Many times that day he questioned his parents, grandmother, and other adults about Washington being dead and how it had come about. (One of the disturbing factors seems to have been the close and, to the child, incomprehensible connection between birthday and being dead at the same time.) During recent visits to the Museum of Natural History he had found out that the animals there were dead, that they could not walk or talk, and he had spoken about this frequently. Noticeably concerned about death, he had repeatedly said: "When I die, I don't want to be dead." His concern was further related to his forthcoming (fourth) birthday for which some arrangements for a party were being made just then.

Furthermore, about a week before the dream Johnny had told his mother that he very much wanted a new baby. His mother felt that this was an attempt on his part to test her. Therefore she had told him that he might perhaps want to have a new baby, but that she certainly did not want one herself, because it would mean spending too much time on a new baby, time and love and care which she wanted to spend on him and his brothers. At this, the mother reported, his face brightened and, visibly relieved, he repeated: "If a new baby came, mummy would not have enough time for me and my brothers. Mummy will not have a new baby." For several days he repeated this statement in various versions, always with glee and always seeking his mother's further reassurance that she would not have a new baby. His concern about childbirth manifested itself also in such frequent questions as "Where did Sandy come from?" or "Where do bunnies come from?"

Other source material used by the dream work was apparently derived from the fact that, some weeks preceding the dream, Johnny's uncle had broken his leg during a ski accident. The child had repeatedly visited the bed-ridden uncle in his home, had seen and touched the plaster cast, and spoken about the uncle's broken leg.

Rose is the girl friend of Johnny's mother, and Rose's son Erwin, who is about the same age as Johnny, is his favorite playmate to whom he has become greatly attached in recent months. There are no other children in Rose's family. Rose and Erwin have a little dog, however, a black poodle. The dog follows Erwin around in about the same manner Charlie follows Johnny from room to room, from toy to toy. Though the "new puppy" in the dream was white (like the limping dog seen in the street), it was "jumping up and down on the bed." It also was talking. These qualities identify the dog in the dream as Johnny's brother Charlie whose most recent and most active play has been to do precisely what the dream ascribes to the dog, that is, talking and jumping up and down on the bed. According to the mother's detailed description of the situation between the brothers, Johnny has lately also taken to jumping up and down on the bed just as Charlie does. Often the children play this game on the same bed side by side, as if they were "in unison," the mother says, and she has occasionally told them to be careful "because the bed may crack and they may get hurt." The hostile wish expressed in the dream (that Charlie should break his leg and die) thus relates to the dreamer, too, who fears via *lex talionis* the same fate for himself, a fate modeled on his bed-jumping and getting hurt, the uncle's ski-jumping and his getting hurt, the observation of the limping dog in the street, and ultimately to the question of birth and death, as evidenced by Johnny's worried ruminations about Washington's birthday, the dead animals at the museum, and his statement: "If I die, I don't want to be dead." It is possible that the death wish also extends to the younger sibling Sandy about whose soft and delicate appearance Johnny has heard many comments, and perhaps also to an anticipated new baby ("a new puppy" in the dream) the fear of which may not have been fully dispelled by the mother's reassurances Johnny has so eagerly elicited from her during the days preceding the dream. This fear, of course, may already represent Johnny's beginning oedipal attachment to his mother and contain the wish to have a baby with her. The next dream seems to throw further light on this situation.

Dream X. About a week later Johnny told his father in the morning that he had had another dream, but immediately added: "I don't want to tell you." He appeared to be considerably embarrassed, talked very little for a while, kept away from his father, but finally volunteered: "I'll tell you later when Grandma gets up." This seemed to be an important point as far as Johnny and his dream were concerned. In fact, his grandmother had spent the night in Johnny's house and he had been allowed to sleep in the same bed with her. In striking contrast to his usual spontaneity in communicating a dream (or other experiences), this time it took him an hour or more to get around to telling it. With a sort of embarrassed smile and in a lowered voice he finally reported: *"Tonight I was a pigeon and*

I was flying." He then added, still smiling in an embarrassed and subdued fashion: *"I was not really a pigeon. It was just a dream."* This frankly oedipal dream was supplemented by some comments from the later awakening grandmother who volunteered the information that "Johnny was restless all night long; he was moving and tossing about in bed most of the time." Unfortunately, on the dreamer's part no further data were forthcoming regarding this dream, nor were any other clues reported by my former patient.

This dream, then, and its oedipal meaning further clarify the mutilation and death aspects of the preceding one. Besides sibling rivalry, hostility feelings related to it, and concern with birth, they express the essential characteristics of the oedipal situation in the typically symbolized manner of this constellation: the wish to be a bird and to fly[3] as direct manifestations of the oedipal strivings, and the castration anxiety connected with it appearing in such well-known dream symbols as limping, breaking a leg, losing the capacity to talk, walk, etc.

Dream XI. As if to corroborate this view, two days later Johnny reported the following dream to his father, again rather reluctantly and with repeated protestations, "I don't want to tell you." The dream was terse and unmistakable: *"I had another daddy."* As an afterthought the dreamer then said, again turning to his father: *"The daddy was taller than you."* During recent weeks and months Johnny had in many ways voiced his wish to be taller and stronger than his father. Here, then, it becomes apparent that part of the oedipal strivings have run their full course: the father is eliminated and is superseded by "another daddy" who is taller than the father, that is, by the dreamer himself who now sets out to take the former's place with mother.

DISCUSSION

The dreams reported here cover a period of thirty months in the child's life. For reasons of clarity, they are summarized in the following table according to age and manifest content:

[3] The phallic meaning of the pigeon symbol is well known. It has been discussed by Jones (1914). In Italian slang *uccello* means penis. In Bocaccio's *Decamerone* the verb *uccellare* is used throughout as synonymous with cohabit.

DREAM	AGE			BRIEF CONTENT	MANIFEST ACTIVITY	DREAM POPULATION
I	1 yr.	5	mths.	nonverbal	nightmare	
II	1 "	8	"	nonverbal	nightmare	
III	2 yrs.	6	mths.	water		Jimmy, Estelle
IV	2 "	10	"	water, tunnel	falling into water	child
V	3 "	2	"	water, cars	raining, water jumping, cars coming	
VI	3 "	2	"	water	water jumping, raining	
VII	3 "	2	"	water, window	water jumping, raining hard	
VIII	3 "	3	"	parakeet dream	flying, biting	parakeet
IX	3 "	11	"	puppy dream	jumping, breaking a leg	Rose, puppy
X	3 "	11	"	oedipal dream	flying	pigeon
XI	3 "	11	"	oedipal dream	increased body size	"another daddy"

A further discussion of these dreams may be facilitated by a few clarifying remarks:

1. The full biographical background of the dreamer and his immediate environment is known to this author through the analysis of his mother.

2. The dreams were experienced in a nontherapeutic situation and were communicated by the child spontaneously and verbally, except in those instances especially noted in this report. At no time were interpretations given to the child, directly or indirectly.

3. The eleven dreams here reported are all the dreams communicated by the child during this period. In a sense they represent a sort of *recorded longitudinal dream history* during the first years of life.

With these premises in mind, it appears legitimate to assume that this series of eleven dreams is neither complete nor fully representative of the child's entire dream life. It is, in fact, quite possible that the child had more dreams than those actually related by him. It also should be mentioned that Johnny's parents observed certain phenomena such as giggling, laughing, facial and other muscular movements during sleep, especially during the nonverbal period of Johnny's life, phenomena which frequently lend themselves to be regarded as dreams or dreamlike experiences, but which are omitted in this study because of their nonverifiable nature.

The chronologically earliest dreams described in the analytic literature concerned children less than one year of age (Hug-Hellmuth, 1919; Milton Erickson, 1941) where such observations of facial and other muscular movements were made and interpreted as possible dreams by the observers. In Hug-Hellmuth's case, an infant less than one year of age had 'spent most of the preceding day play-ing and splashing in water. During the night the child was seen making splashing movements with its hands in its sleep. Although similar observations were made during Johnny's first year of life, they were not included here, since it could not be ascertained that such movements were derived from or related to an actual dream. In view of these reservations, there is some question whether the first two experiences which were described as nonverbal and night-mares, can be legitimately regarded as dreams. Indeed, at the present state of our knowledge, this question must remain unanswered. In including these nocturnal experiences as Dreams I and II in the above list, I was guided mainly by the ascertainable circumstances to which they could be related, and in part also by the dramatic quality of the experiences themselves.

The first verbalized dream (Dream III) as well as the rest of the series corroborate Freud's principal statements about dreams of young children: "The dreams of little children," Freud (1900) ob-serves, "are often simple fulfillments of wishes . . ." In a detailed footnote he further explains that "young children often have more complex and obscure dreams" and also indicates "how rich in un-suspected content the dreams of children" sometimes are. I believe that this unexpected wealth of manifest and latent dream material, of symbolism, of immediate and remote sources used by the dream work can be found in some of Johnny's dream experiences. More-over, it seems to me that the obscurities in a young child's mental productions can be largely clarified by a full knowledge of the various circumstances, family setting, external and internal influences oper-ative in the child's life, and their proper evaluation, as clearly shown by Brenner (1951) in a case of childhood hallucinosis in a three-and-a-half-year-old girl. Though all of Johnny's verbalized dreams con-tained the element of wish fulfillment, it was not the only one at work, a fact to which Grotjahn (1938) had drawn attention in his dream observation of a two-year-four-months-old girl.

Of particular interest is the frequency of water dreams in Johnny's dream history. Despert's (1949) notion that water dreams are especially important in bed wetters, could not be borne out in this admittedly very small series which, however, has a high percentage of such dreams (almost 50 per cent). It is my impression that the water dreams here reported (Dreams III to VII) refer, in addition to the traumatic episode at the pool, to the birth of a sibling. According to Freud, water dreams are parturition dreams. Freud (1916/17) states: "Birth is almost invariably represented in dreams by some reference to water: either we are falling into water or clambering out of it . . ." Dream IV was such a dream; it dealt with a child falling into water and occurred after Johnny had become aware of his mother's pregnancy. Dreams V to VII, representing a dream sequence characterized by the frequency of the water symbol, occurred during the last fortnight of this pregnancy. Here an interesting question poses itself. Is the use of the water symbol by the dream work, and the outspoken activity element connected with it (water jumping up and down, raining, raining hard), in any way related to the child's perception of fetal movements in the mother's abdomen? Certain aspects of water symbolism, which have been discussed by me elsewhere (1956, 1957), seem to point to the importance of what I have described as the "water in motion" factor during the birth process.

In two of Johnny's dreams another symbol appears—besides water—namely: cars. Dream V has ". . . cars coming in the street, many cars," and in Dream VII the water is "jumping up and down in the street where the cars go." Though I had been assured by Johnny's parents that he slept in a room distant from theirs and had never seen or heard primal events, I took this dream detail for a long time as proof of primal scene content, until Johnny himself gave it a different or, at least, additional interpretation. Telling his father one day about a horde of children invading the playground where he and his friend Erwin had played, he suddenly became greatly excited, ran to the window from where the street could be seen, and exclaimed: "Cars, cars, cars, coming in the street, many cars!" His excitement and usage of the same wording, months later, as in Dream V struck me when it was reported to me. In the present setting cars undoubtedly referred to the sudden, rude and, as far as Johnny was concerned, irresistible invasion of his playground by a horde of unwanted children. Should the same meaning, i.e., cars =

children, also apply to the arrival of unwelcome and intruding siblings in his own home, who take over mother, food, toys, playground, and all? Johnny's behavior is here reminiscent of "Little Hans" and the latter's reaction to heavily loaded carts, furniture vans, and buses —interpreted by Freud (1909) as "symbolic representations of pregnancy."

There still is another detail to consider which belongs to the events preceding Dream VII. During the day prior to that dream the mother recorded that Johnny in all probability perceived fetal movements in her abdomen and that, thereupon, he pointed at many parts of her body and said emphatically to her: "The baby is inside you, around you, all around." This remark seems to indicate the possibility that the pregnant mother is perceived by Johnny not only as the carrier of the dreaded rival, but as actually equated with the baby herself. In this way the mother, besides being the baby's container, may be viewed by the child as the rival and therefore the "bad mother." Such an impression may then well become concretized by the perception of bodily changes in the maternal physique, of fetal movements in her abdomen, even by her talking about her pregnancy and the new baby within her.

Of interest is further Dream VIII, the parakeet dream. It occurs less than a fortnight after the mother's return from the hospital with the new baby, Sandy. It seems permissible to explicate from this dream what appears to be the infantile, condensed, symbolized, but basically correct version of the process of childbirth as reflected in the little boy's mind. The *parakeet,* that is, the baby, flew out of the *tunnel zoo* (the female genitals) from the *cage* (the maternal abdomen) near the pool where the sea lions are (*water*). If we try to understand this particular sequence, it is well to remember two significant experiences in the dreamer's life which appear to have undergone a typical fusion through the dream work. The child's perception of fetal movements in the mother's body seems to be fused with his experience in the zoo where he saw and heard the birds beating their wings against the cage. What he had felt in mother's abdomen thus became amalgamated with what he had seen and heard near the cage at the zoo. The parakeet is relentless. His arrival cannot be undone. He first flies to Johnny's place. When Johnny, self-exiled to his grandmother's house, sleeps away from his own home in an

attempt to find some safe haven elsewhere, the parakeet follows him
even there. Moreover, the parakeet does to Johnny what Johnny did
to his mother when he was a little baby (Dream II).

It is further worth noting that the parakeet dream has one element in common with the preceding Dream VII—the window. In
the former the parakeet enters through the window to attack Johnny;
following the latter Johnny insists on going to the window to see the
rain and the cars in the street. Perhaps this looking out of the window at night can be understood in the same way as his looking into
the room with the bathinette during the day, both in response to
the same disturbing question: Has the new baby arrived already, or
has it not? Dream VII causes Johnny to look out of the window into
the street where it is raining hard and the cars are going; but the
mother is still pregnant and the baby has not yet arrived. In Dream
VIII, after the sibling's birth, the parakeet makes its appearance,
enters through the window, arrives in Johnny's room and bed. The
parakeet dream has a common element also with Dream IV, though
in a different setting. In Dream IV Johnny sees a child in a tunnel,
and he relates this dream in a hazy, indistinct, almost faraway manner, as if to indicate that he dimly perceives the relationship between
female genital (tunnel), pregnancy, and childbirth. In Dream VIII,
which has the vividness of an actual experience, the mystery is all but
solved; the parakeet flew "out of the tunnel" and is here to stay.

Not so long ago I analyzed the dream of an adult patient which
in some way was comparable to the parakeet dream. The patient,
son of a musician, dreamed about an opera by the Venetian composer Wolf-Ferrari. He could not recall the opera in the dream,
which appeared to him like "an empty gap" and this gap was filled,
as it were, by another opera of the same composer named *I quattro
Rusteghi*. He then found himself on an island and suddenly saw
three or four small birds approaching the island from far out at
sea. He tried to prevent the birds from reaching the island and to
chase them away. But the birds kept coming—"irresistibly," he said
—and took the island over. In his associations the patient spoke of
Venice, which he called "the sea-born city," of the three siblings he
had, and that there had been four children in the family, including
him—*I quattro Rusteghi*. He wanted to get rid of the siblings, but
they kept coming and coming to the island, the mother. They kept
coming from the sea like the birds in the dream and took mother
over. During that analytic hour the name of the original opera in

the dream remained unknown. The patient felt extremely disturbed about this gap in his knowledge, spoke of "vagueness" and "dim feelings" in his eyes and forehead, and when he came to his next session, he reported that he had had the irresistible need to look up the biography of the composer Wolf-Ferrari. There he found the name of the opera he had dreamed about: *Il Segreto di Susannah*. Further analysis revealed that the "secret" was the pregnant mother's naked body.

To return to the significance of the window in Dreams VII and VIII, Freud, in his paper on Goethe's earliest childhood recollections from *Dichtung und Wahrheit* (1917), mentions, in a footnote, the "pregnancy symbolism" of the window. He adduces the example of a middle-aged woman who "as a little child, when she could hardly talk, *used to drag her father to the window in great agitation whenever a heavy lorry was passing along the street* . . . At about that time the brother next to her was born . . ." (italics added). In the same paper Freud (1917) explains Goethe's recollection about hurling crockery out of the window in these words: "At the time of the birth of the first little brother . . . Johann Wolfgang was three and a quarter years old . . . The new baby must be thrown out, *through the window, perhaps he came in through the window*. The whole action would thus be equivalent to the familiar things said by children who are told that the stork has brought a little brother or sister" (italics added).

To be sure, Johnny as a child of the twentieth century was not told any stork fable. When he asked "where the new baby comes from," he was told by his mother that the baby comes out of a special opening in her body. The opening, thus, in the dreams becomes the window, the latter also representing Johnny's wish to see this very opening (window = *Windauge),* a wish repeatedly verbalized by Johnny and addressed by him to his mother who, however, did not gratify this wish. A window, of course, is not merely an opening to be inspected, but also a medium through which other objects, especially new and moving objects, can be seen and beheld. Freud's middle-aged woman dragged her father to the window in great agitation whenever a heavy lorry was passing outside; Johnny saw cars passing in the street and became excited. The reaction of "Little Hans" to heavily loaded carts was mentioned above. In all these cases the window played a role and the mani-

festations occurred about the time siblings arrived. The window
in the Wolf Man's dream also belongs here, as mentioned by
Bertram D. Lewin in a personal communication. If we remember
Freud's analysis of this dream (perception of parental coitus *more
ferarum*) and the prominent part of the female buttocks under such
circumstances, the symbolic significance of the window as representing part of the mother's body becomes clear. Elsewhere (1956) I
discussed the relation of breast, buttocks, birth, and water in some
detail.

The prevalently oedipal strivings characterizing Dreams IX to
XI and the castration anxieties connected with them were already
discussed in the first part of this paper. Condensed into the relatively short span of thirty months, this longitudinal history of early
childhood dreams—as fragmentary as it is—brings into sharper
focus some of the landmarks in the child's development: from the
early nonverbal productions of the psyche, as yet poorly understood,
through the vicissitudes of trauma, mastery of traumatic events,
impact of pregnancy and birth, crises of physical illness and sibling
rivalry, to the threshold of genitality and the sexual conflicts of the
oedipal period.

Postscript: As I corrected the proofs of this paper, the latest of
Johnny's dreams was reported to me. The dream is, in the words of
the dreamer, about *"one man who is made dead by another man. A
little man made the bigger man dead by hitting him with a big
stone over his head."* The oedipal meaning, in direct continuation
of Dreams IX through XI, is unmistakable. It was confirmed by the
dreamer himself who spoke of the David-Goliath story and quoted
some lines from *Porgy and Bess*, which he had just learned to sing:
"Little David was small but oh my, he slew big Goliath who lay
down and dieth . . ."

BIBLIOGRAPHY

Brenner, C. (1951), A Case of Childhood Hallucinosis. *This Annual*, V.
Despert, J. L. (1949), Dreams in Children of Preschool Age. *This Annual*, III/IV.
Erickson, M. (1941), On the Possible Occurrence of a Dream in an Eight-Months-Old
    Infant. *Psa. Quart.*, X.
Freud, S. (1900), The Interpretation of Dreams. *Standard Edition*, III, IV. London:
    Hogarth Press, 1953.
—— (1909), Analysis of a Phobia of a Five-Year-Old Boy. *Collected Papers*, III. London:
    Hogarth Press, 1925.

—— (1916/17), *A General Introduction to Psychoanalysis.* New York: Liveright, 1935.
—— (1917), A Childhood Recollection from *Dichtung und Wahrheit. Collected Papers,* IV. London: Hogarth Press, 1925.
Grotjahn, M. (1938), Dream Observation in a Two-Year-Four-Months-Old Baby. *Psa. Quart.,* VII.
Hug-Hellmuth, H. (1919), *A Study of the Mental Life of the Child.* New York: Nervous and Mental Disease Publ. Co.
Jones, E. (1914), The Madonna's Conception through the Ear. *Essays in Applied Psycho-Analysis,* II. London: Hogarth Press, 1951.
Niederland, W. G. (1956), River Symbolism. Part I. *Psa. Quart.,* XXV.
—— (1957), River Symbolism. Part II. *Psa. Quart.,* XXVI.

INCONSISTENCY IN THE MOTHER AS A FACTOR IN CHARACTER DEVELOPMENT: A COMPARATIVE STUDY OF THREE CASES[1]

ANNE-MARIE SANDLER, ELIZABETH DAUNTON, and ANNELIESE SCHNURMANN (London)

With an Introduction by
ANNA FREUD, LL.D. (London)

Introduction

There is a variety of ways in which a mother's neurosis or personality disturbance can act unfavorably on a child's development; and there is a variety of ways in which the interaction of the partners in the preoedipal mother relationship can be explored. In our Hampstead Child-Therapy Clinic the method of choice is the procedure outlined by Dorothy Burlingham in her paper "Simultaneous Analysis of Mother and Child."[2] This implies that mother and child are analyzed independently of each other, by two different workers; that the analysts do not communicate with each other so as not to exert any influence on the treatment of the other partner; and that they report to a third analyst who coordinates the material and scrutinizes it for whatever types of interaction may emerge.

The following "Comparative Study of Three Cases" of the Hampstead Child-Therapy Clinic, on the other hand, has not been carried out on the basis of this exacting method, nor is it equally ambitious in its aims. It represents the independent effort of three analytic

[1] This investigation has been carried out in the Hampstead Child-Therapy Clinic, London, which is maintained by the Field Foundation, Inc., New York. It has been aided by a grant from the Foundations' Fund for Research in Psychiatry, New Haven, Conn.

[2] Published in Vol. X of *This Annual*, in cooperation with Alice Goldberger and André Lussier, Ph.D.

child therapists who were struck by marked similarities in the manifest behavior and symptomatology of their patients and entered into discussion with each other, wondering whether similar environmental factors in the children's background might be held responsible for the result. Their exploration convinced them that the harmful factor at work in all three cases was to be found neither in a similarity of the mothers' personalities (of whom one only was in analysis), nor in the family circumstances or historical events which differed with each child. The point of identity lay in a particular type of fear of the mother which was present in all three children and reinforced in them the same archaic and fantastic anxieties. The similarity between the mothers, summed up by the authors under the term of "inconsistency," went no further than the fact that they aroused this fear.

The three authors of this paper are aware of the limitations of a comparative study of this nature; it cannot elicit all the details of interchange between the id content of two personalities by way of following the processes of identification, internalization, or positive and negative response to subtle provocation. On the other hand, they are confident that their paper may be useful in trying to trace the ways in which external, environmental influences are translated into internal pathogenic agents. In their cases the path led from the threatening quality of the first love object to an increase of id anxieties. This, in its turn, produced an overstressing of defenses, alternating with complete breakdowns in defense activity; and further the inhibitions, the lack of control, and with them the inconsistencies of personality development by which the three children are characterized.

Inconsistency in the Mother as a Factor in Character Development

In this paper we will attempt to show how the extent and nature of maternal disturbance can affect the development of the child's character. The clinical material upon which this study is based was derived from the analyses of three children who showed certain marked similarities in both their behavior and personal appearance. In joint discussions of the therapists, the attempt to understand the underlying reasons for the similarity in the children has led to certain ideas about the role of inconsistency and unpredictability of maternal behavior, and the influence of the child's own anxiety on his character development. It is not enough, we feel, to accept at face value the proposition that a disturbed mother will create a disturbed child. We ought to know how the disturbance in the mother modifies the child's character development, and at the same time we should not underestimate the importance of endopsychic factors in this process.

THE COMMON CHARACTERISTICS OF THE THREE CASES

The three children—Roberta (aged six), Elizabeth (aged seven), and Mary (aged eight)—were in individual treatment, five days a week, at the Clinic. They were each neat and tidy, were light and deft in their movements, and all showed great pleasure and skill in bodily activity. They often gave the appearance of being highly excited, and were controlling and domineering in their relations with others. In addition, they shared certain social difficulties—they could not make friends, nor could they adapt adequately to school. Each child also had learning difficulties. When meeting, they were clearly attracted by one another and preferred to play together rather than with other children.

Each child had a mother who was highly disturbed but who was at the same time a "good mother," much concerned about the care of her child. Each made her daughter's clothes and wanted her to look nice, and each was concerned about her child's difficulties and blamed herself for contributing to them. All the mothers frequently reproached themselves, for example, for the separations they had had from the children.

When we came to compare the children, with these quite strikingly similar external impressions as our starting point, we noticed certain inner similarities. These were children with strong instinctual impulses, particularly on the oral and anal-sadistic level of development, which the ego, in spite of an attempt to build up strong defenses, was not powerful enough to control, with the result that the children were acutely anxious. Anxiety was easily aroused either by fantasy or by new external situations. Typically, these children attempted to deal with their anxiety by the mechanisms of identification with the aggressor, of projection, and of counterphobic behavior. It was noticed that anxiety was also highly sexualized and that this contributed to the excited behavior mentioned above. Object relationships were highly ambivalent, and the ego was restricted because of poor neutralization and inadequate fusion of instinct. Of their ego functions, the least restricted was motility (their pleasure in movement has been mentioned previously). We also noticed the fierce but inadequate superego of each of the children and the erotization of guilt, as shown in their sadomasochistic behavior.

While certain aspects of the children's personalities seem similar to us, we do not wish to understress the individual differences in their development, nor the fact that each of these children found a different solution for her conflict in a different symptom; e.g., Roberta developed a sleeping disturbance, Mary a nervous cough, and Elizabeth general backwardness. In the same way, while we can relate some aspects of the children's personalities to the mothers' disturbances, it is necessary to emphasize the fact that each of the children had her own individual internalized conflicts, which must be understood as such, and not by an attempt to relate all their problems to the mother. We should like, however, to highlight those common trends in the children's personalities, which we think were closely related to the mothers' disturbances.

THE CHILDREN AND THEIR PARENTS

A short description of each child and her mother follows. These descriptions portray the child at the time of referral and do not take into account changes which occurred in the children during their treatment; nor do they take into account those changes in the mothers which occurred as a result of their talks with the therapist and the psychiatric social worker.

Mary and her Mother

Mary was five when she began treatment, having been referred for a nervous cough and for generally difficult and aggressive behavior. This had become more pronounced following a tonsillectomy when she was nearly five, and her mother's hospitalization a few months later. In the first months of treatment Mary behaved in a very excited manner, which was really an expression of her extreme anxiety. She had to rush from the room or occupy herself with routine tasks whenever she felt afraid of her aggressive thoughts. She showed great fear of her mother, yet was very provocative and demanding with her. She was also quarrelsome with her sister, and her relationships generally were very ambivalent. However, she got on well with her father, who was both more positive and more consistent than the mother. At school she could not settle down but constantly needed to claim the teacher's attention. She was frequently left by teachers and children to herself at playtime.

Mary's mother, who already had one daughter aged twelve, had been extremely upset when she became pregnant with Mary at the age of thirty-nine. This pregnancy made her feel self-conscious and ashamed. She told of her extreme feeling of hostility toward the baby after its birth, and in the interviews she always reproached herself for her adverse treatment of Mary. She was particularly guilty about her compulsive thoughts of injuring the child; for example, she pictured Mary falling under a bus or onto the railway lines. She partly dealt with her anxiety by being overprotective. She was ashamed of her periodic violent outbursts toward the child, although it was apparent that she also derived satisfaction from this sado-masochistic relationship. She had many cleanliness rituals connected with the preparation of food and was compulsive about time. In addition she had suffered from arthritis of the hands for some years and had many hypochondriacal anxieties.

Roberta and her Mother

Roberta was referred, just after her third birthday, for marked sleeplessness. She had found it difficult to fall asleep and would wake many times during the night wanting the pot or a drink. She was very restless and talked in her sleep, but did not have night terrors or nightmares. Other symptoms were: daytime wetting, nail biting and nose picking; marked fears and anxieties about the dark, about boys, trains, post-boxes, tunnels, etc. Roberta appeared to be a lively, rather uninhibited and restless child, who had a very anxious look and thus seemed to confirm her mother's statement that she was a worried child. She was obviously overactive and excitable. Roberta was a good eater, but very thin and light for her age. She was very greedy and forever demanding sweets.

Roberta was an only child, born after seventeen years of marriage. When she was nine months old, the mother decided to go out to work to supplement the irregular earnings of her husband who played in a band, and she fostered Roberta out. Between the age of nine months and two years nine months, the mother placed the child in three different foster homes; then she took her home for good. The mother reported that at this age Roberta was "spoiled and filthy" and undertook to train her.

Roberta's mother was comparatively old when Roberta was born. She had not wanted a child; but if she was to have one, she would have preferred a boy, whom she meant to call "Robert." The mother seemed to have enjoyed Roberta when she was a small baby whom she could control fully, but apparently she felt unable to cope with the more specific demands of a growing baby and toddler. After boarding Roberta out, she felt very guilty, and had to "rescue" her after a few months from each of the three different foster homes, realizing that they were unsatisfactory.

The mother had only been seen on a few occasions by the therapist and later also by the social worker. It soon became apparent that this mother was fighting, through overactivity, against her inner awareness of a potential breakdown. She also complained about her very unsatisfactory marital relationship, her wish to weep all the time and her worry that she herself might die. It was clear that Roberta was often used as a pretext for quarrels between the parents. The mother seemed to have had a very unhappy childhood, and to be compelled to repeat on Roberta what she herself had experienced. For example, she said that the child would one day see that her father was "no good," just as she had realized it with her own father, and that her own mother was everything to her. Moreover, the mother wanted to send Roberta to a convent boarding school, where she herself had been sent, and where she had been very unhappy. This was also in keeping with her social ambitions ("It will make a lady out of her"). The mother had felt very guilty about not giving Roberta enough affection and tried to make up for it by material things, and by working to earn the fees for a private boarding school.

Roberta's mother was the daughter of a publican and inclined to immoderate drinking. On several occasions she came to the Clinic in a drunken state. In the Clinic she often behaved like a naughty rebellious child, as if to inform us what a horrible mother she really was and to provoke a telling off. She also appeared to be very fond of her child and was proud of Roberta's intelligence and good appearance.

The mother had been complaining of pains in the chest for years, but the doctors did not seem able to diagnose any known disease and told her that the pains were due to "worry."

Elizabeth and her Mother

Elizabeth was an attractive, graceful little girl with fair hair and blue eyes. She was referred at the age of five years for backwardness and for aggressive and destructive behavior at home which contrasted strangely with her overwhelming shyness in the presence of strangers. Elizabeth seemed to have had a satisfactory period of life up to the age of one year, when her mother was suddenly called away to her own mother who was seriously ill. After the grandmother's death, Elizabeth's mother, who before had inclined to depressive moods, developed a state of great emotional upset which prevented her return home for several months. In the hope that a change of surroundings might improve matters, the father then accepted a job in London and moved there with his family from the north of England.

The mother's depression eventually decreased, but she became very quarrelsome and at times was quite unable to control her aggression; small provocations gave rise to violent outbursts of rage. Her hostility was directed mainly toward various female members of her own and her husband's family. But also the relations between Elizabeth's mother and her husband became very strained, and the child herself could not quite escape the mother's outbursts. A slipped disc, which caused the mother constant pain and impeded her movements for many months, added to the difficulties.

Elizabeth's mother was always very neat and carefully dressed. She was an efficient housewife and tended to wear herself out in household tasks. Her behavior toward people in the Clinic was either one of withdrawal or else of overexcitement. In her relation to the therapist she showed an excited type of behavior. She was jealous of the therapist who, she felt, was destroying her own educational efforts by "contrary" permissiveness. But she confessed with obvious guilt feelings to certain of her actions toward Elizabeth (e.g., hitting her, forcing her to eat, keeping her waiting in school, etc.), of which she thought the therapist would disapprove. In this way she seemed to be saying: "Look what a bad mother I am." She also showed that she felt guilty about her uncontrolled outbursts of rage, which were in the main directed against her husband and his sister. The mother was, however, fundamentally very fond of Elizabeth.

The Fathers

We should like to add a word about the children's fathers. In Mary's case the father was a stable person who took a great deal of responsibility in the family. He managed to maintain a good relation with his wife as well as with his child and was the head of the household. The other two fathers, less stable personalities, were more or less dominated by their wives. In these two households there were constant quarrels between husband and wife.

SIMILARITIES AND DIFFERENCES

We think that, while even a casual observer would have noticed the resemblance between the children, the mothers did not give the same impression of similarity. As far as overt behavior was concerned, they had few features in common, the most outstanding being their domineering attitude and their uncontrolled outbursts of aggression. As has been shown, there were also other traits shared by these three mothers, which would not be obvious to the outside observer, e.g., their conviction that they were unsatisfactory mothers, as well as their guilt feelings about this. Although their problems and conflicts were different, these resulted in a number of similar attitudes toward their children.

It seemed to us that there were three aspects of the mothers' disturbances which particularly affected the personality and development of their children. The first aspect was the mothers' problem in dealing with aggression; the second was their marked inconsistency of handling; lastly the mothers had certain mental and physical disabilities to which their children reacted.

Aggression in the Mothers

When the problem of aggression was considered, it was found that all the mothers had rather frequent sadistic outbursts during which the children were smacked or beaten; these attacks on the children clearly aroused anxiety in the mothers and led to self-reproaches, but were at the same time gratifying because of the close physical contact with the child.

The effect on the children could in each case be studied in the transference. All three children tried to introduce highly exciting games in which they would be chased or beaten by the therapist. We could see that the attacks had both a frightening and a seductive effect on the children, making anxiety and pain pleasurable, and pleasure frightening.

Apart from their aggressive outbursts, these mothers maintained a fighting relationship with the children; in each case there were demands and regulations about eating and cleanliness, to which the children responded with defiance, sensing the provocation in the mother. It was apparent that in this way the children's fixation to the oral and anal levels and the preoedipal attachment to the mother were strengthened.

Two of the children, Mary and Roberta, showed strong counterphobic defenses, while Elizabeth did not show them to any marked degree. It was clear that these two children were in fact counterphobic toward their mothers; they were compelled to test out the reactions in the mothers which most frightened them. For example, Roberta looked frightened in the session as she told of a witch who was very cross with children who got dirty. Before going to the waiting room, she deliberately wet her dress, inquiring from the therapist whether her mother would hit her. Downstairs, she rushed straight to her mother to show her wet dress, looking most relieved when the scolding was over. This mother often remarked to the therapist that she would "murder the child" if she continued to provoke her, and Roberta's behavior was understood as a testing of the mother's reactions, to reassure herself that she would not in fact be harmed. A comparable example for Mary would be her compulsive climbing onto bannisters and window ledges although she was afraid of falling, knowing well that her mother would be provoked to a frenzy. As mentioned previously, Mary's mother had fantasies of the child being killed by falling, particularly onto the railway lines. By her climbing, this child also seemed to be testing out her mother's fantasy. It was thought that perhaps Elizabeth did not show these counterphobic mechanisms to the same degree because of an important difference in her relationship with her mother. She was not the main focus of the mother's hostility, which was directed more toward her aunt; whereas Mary and Roberta were the objects of the mother's hostile fantasies and behavior.

We have noticed that fear of their mothers influenced the ego development of these children in two outstanding ways. To consider their defense mechanisms first: all the children identified with their frightening mothers, adopting the same angry manner of speech, were often violent as well as bossy and controlling. In each case the therapist could tell at once from the behavior of the child in the sessions when the mother was particularly angry or upset. Elizabeth, for example, was more aggressive to the therapist whenever her mother was aggressive to the aunt.

Each child clearly expressed the fear in the treatment that the therapist would kill her or swallow her up. This fear of their mothers influenced the egos of these children in the following way: they were like much younger children in their inability to distinguish fantasy from reality, and consequently there was considerable ego restriction. For example, Roberta asked for repeated reassurance from the therapist that witches did not really exist and that the therapist was not a giant. Elizabeth inquired seriously whether her mother and aunt meant to kill each other. Mary could not listen to a story to be remembered in an intelligence test because, when she heard that a pony was frightened and ran away, she had to stop and ask what had frightened the pony. When she was taken to the theater, Mary was genuinely frightened by the bad characters in the play, as though they were real.

The Inconsistency of the Mothers

All these mothers had frequent and intense changes of mood; particularly in the case of Mary's and Roberta's mothers, where out-

bursts with the children were followed by reconciliations and undoing, in which the giving of sweets played a large part. In this
respect, too, the children identified with their mothers. Thus Mary,
for example, after angrily throwing bits of paper on the floor,
offered to sweep them up, saying, "I will help you now, because I
hindered you." Roberta, having shouted at the therapist for being
silly and slow, rushed to her to kiss her and gave her a sweet.

All these children were not only anxious about their mothers'
unpredictable attitudes (e.g., Roberta often asked her therapist:
"Will Mummy be cross today?"), but they did not know how to
predict other people's reactions. This made them quite apprehensive
in meeting new situations, increased their separation anxiety, and
consequently led to a retardation of ego development. All three children were more than usually upset by a change of class and teacher.

The mothers seemed to show many inconsistencies in their educational attitudes toward their children. They were both restrictive
and seductive in the ways in which they reacted to the children's
search for direct instinctual gratification. On the oral level, for
example, both Elizabeth's and Mary's mothers tried to force the
children to take food which was distasteful to them, but all used
food as a token of love and reconciliation. Thus the mothers' inconsistent attitude toward the children's oral demands paved the way to
oral fixations and regressions, to oral disturbances of various kinds,
as well as to frequent battles between them and the children about
eating.

On the anal level, all the mothers demanded a high standard of
cleanliness from the children, but the fight to maintain this was continually gratifying to both mother and child. In addition, each
mother accepted the child's demands for anal gratification in one
form or another; for instance, by regularly accompanying the children to the lavatory and wiping them. Anal erotism was also increased by the mothers' concern about constipation and the giving
of aperients.

Two of the mothers, Roberta's and Mary's, were also markedly
inconsistent in their treatment of curiosity. Roberta's mother could
not bear the child to express any interest in the mother's body.
Sometimes she sent the child out of the room when she changed her
dress, while at other times she bathed with her. She was angry when

Roberta asked questions about her activities, but at times discussed with her her most intimate worries, for example, her quarrels with her husband or her money problems. Mary's mother displayed herself in front of the child in the bathroom, but regarded her wish to see her father in the nude as "rude." Elizabeth's mother had a more consistent and rather less seductive attitude to the child's curiosity.

Coming now to the children's general reactions to the mothers' inconsistent behavior, it was characteristic of these children that they sought direct instinctual gratification in particular from their mothers. This was one of the reasons why these children found it almost impossible to detach themselves from their mothers. This need for direct gratification also impeded the desexualization of ego activities. For instance, Mary had difficulties in learning to read, because looking was in itself so highly sexualized. Roberta found painting very difficult because of her strong urge to mess, while Elizabeth was unable to play lest she become dirty and destructive.

On the other hand, the mothers' more restrictive attitudes were also internalized, leading to conflicts between id and superego. The children blamed themselves for messiness and were intolerant of their own and other people's mistakes. Mary was ashamed of her scoptophilic impulses, and Elizabeth could not bear her dirtiness.

Another aspect of the mothers' inconsistencies was seen in their attempts to impose standards of behavior on the children which they could not themselves maintain. This was shown particularly in attitudes toward verbal aggression and swearing. For instance Roberta's mother scolded her severely for complaining about a school friend, but immediately began to tell the therapist how disagreeable this girl and her mother were. The mother would use bad language in her quarrels with the husband and neighbors, but became disproportionately upset when Roberta used the same words. The other two mothers also had angry outbursts of swearing while expecting their daughters to speak in a proper and controlled manner. In fact, these children identified with their mothers in quarreling, and in the use of swear words, although not without guilt feelings. It was apparent that the mothers' dual standards confused the children and affected their superego formation. Roberta seemed to show this problem clearly in relation to swearing. Once on her way up to the treatment room she heard a child using bad language. She looked at her therapist very reproachfully and said: "It is very rude to talk like that. My mummy says so. She doesn't let me say those words." Later in the session, however, Roberta suddenly asked the therapist: "Why does mummy use dirty words when she quarrels?"

The mothers were also inconsistent in the roles they wanted their children to play, and found it hard to adapt their treatment of the children to the appropriate age and stage of development. It seemed that their own fantasies and narcissistic cathexis of the children interfered with their ability to support the girls in their progress from one stage of development to another. All the mothers treated the children in some respects as babies. Elizabeth's mother engaged in the physical care and close bodily contact that were appropriate to a much younger child, thus prolonging the girl's dependence on her. The attitude of Roberta's mother was rather similar, and Roberta told the therapist, "My mother likes babies and boys best, but not girls." For Mary, being the mother's baby mainly meant restrictions; having to eat baby food, and being sent to bed early.

These children reacted to being treated as babies by the mother, either by trying in a rather anxious way to prove that they were big, or by giving in to their own oral passive wishes. Roberta often said to the therapist that she was big, and not a baby, and showed how she could pour tea or skip. At those times she always insisted that what she did was up to adult standards, thus denying her fear and wish that she might still be a baby. In the transference all three girls showed their liking for oral passive gratification; they all spent part of their sessions lying down and asking to be fed.

On the other hand the mothers sometimes treated the children as adults; Roberta's mother treated her as her confidante and took her to grownup parties, while Mary was often required to behave in a controlled way as though she were an adult member of the family.

Roberta's and Elizabeth's mothers also felt that their children belonged to them and not to their husbands whom they regarded as adversaries. Roberta's mother expressed this openly, showing the child that if she were the father's friend, she could not be hers. Elizabeth's mother, although not opposing any friendly advances by Elizabeth toward her father, still conveyed her feelings about it to Elizabeth who was convinced that loving the father meant losing the mother. In this way the mothers supported their daughters' wish to take the place of the father. For neither of the two children has it so far been possible to take the step toward a passive oedipal attachment to the father. While this aspect seems very important in the case of Roberta and Elizabeth, Mary's mother, who felt that everyone else was more competent to deal with her daughter than she herself, in many ways encouraged Mary's attachment to the father.

There were also some indications that the body-phallus equation in these children was heightened by the mothers' attitudes, particularly by the close physical contact. When skipping, Roberta remarked to the therapist: "Mummy likes me like that, it makes her feel good." On the other hand, Mary's mother explained to the therapist that she was terribly upset when any of her own possessions were damaged, and worried in the same way about any injuries to the child. She thought this was because she herself had acquired some scars in childhood "which I will carry to the grave."

The Mental and Physical Peculiarities of the Mothers

Under the heading of mental peculiarities we include certain fears and irrational beliefs of the mothers relating to eating, elimination, and to illness. Mary's mother would observe the most strictly hygienic precautions about food, washing all utensils before use. Mary repeatedly voiced the fear that she would be poisoned by dirty water or food and sometimes used counterphobic methods to deal with her anxiety. Elizabeth's mother expressed the concern that her child would grow weak and ill if she did not eat enough. Elizabeth in turn was afraid that these things could happen to her. The mother's strong convictions again made it more difficult for the children to distinguish fantasy from reality.

These mothers either had real reasons to be worried about their health, or had hypochondriacal fears, or both. Mary's mother had arthritis of the hands and was frightened of becoming blind and insane. Roberta's mother was constantly seeking medical care for chest trouble. Elizabeth's mother was for a considerable time handicapped by a slipped disc which worried her extremely.

It is interesting to see the children's similar reactions to their mothers' disabilities. Each saw her mother as castrated, held herself responsible for this condition, and feared retaliation. When she spoke of her mother's arthritis, Mary said she had made it worse by her naughty behavior and that when she grew older she would have arthritis and "give it to her children." When her mother had a chest ailment, Roberta played in her session that a horrid little girl was sent to hospital with a chest ailment. When Elizabeth's resentment of her mother's restricted motility caused by the slipped disc was discussed in treatment, she burst out: "How did she make her back bad? I made it bad. I broke my mummy." Later on she brought the fantasy that she was mad and could not learn, as a punishment for having made her mother ill.

The mothers' illnesses also heightened the children's sadistic fantasies of intercourse. When Roberta played doctor and patient with the therapist, she had either to be the doctor or, as a patient, to control the doctor's every move. Mary was afraid to grow up to be a lady and inquired whether it hurt to have ears pierced for earrings. Elizabeth initiated many fantasy games and later verbalized theories in which she showed that she understood the parents' sexual activities as a mutual poisoning, castrating, and infection with germs. It also became clear that like the other two girls, Elizabeth thought the mother was getting the worst of it. We realize that all children have some sadistic fantasies of intercourse, but the intensity of the anxiety which accompanied these fantasies in our three children was striking.

The children's fears and fantasies about their mothers' illnesses had certain very marked effects on their ego functioning and object relationships. Their frightening intercourse fantasies made them retreat from the passive attachment to the father and strengthened the homosexual attachment to the mother. In the same way the masculine identification with the father was strengthened. In the sphere of the superego, the feeling of being responsible for the mother's illness as well as the sadistic intercourse fantasies greatly increased the children's feeling of guilt. They repeatedly expressed the belief that they were horrible, naughty, or no good, and could not believe that they could attain pleasure in adult life.

CONCLUSIONS

In conclusion we should like to advance the hypothesis that the similarities we have noticed in these children are due mainly to the similar ways in which they have dealt with their anxiety. We have tried to show how each child's anxiety, whether aroused by the instinctual impulses of the id or by the demands of the superego, had been pathologically reinforced by the very real fear of the mother, who combined in her behavior to the child both seductive and aggressive attitudes. Thus the anxiety felt by the child's ego was a combination of neurotic anxiety and a real fear based upon the mother's unpredictability. The child's anxiety was continually aroused not only by the demands of id and superego, but by the external world as well. These three sources of anxiety constantly interacted, for the inconsistencies and seductions of the mother in turn reinforced the instinctual wishes of the id, leading to increased anxiety. The mother's aggressive behavior similarly reinforced the prohibitions of the superego, which was in any case faulty in its structure because of the mother's inconsistencies.

The situation was further complicated by the projection outward of the internalized picture of the mother, which carried with it the full weight of the child's own libido and aggression. All this conflict, we feel, arose from the instability of the real mother, who because of her very unpredictability did not provide that solid basis in reality upon which a stable ego structure could be built. We might venture to say that if these mothers had been consistently aggressive or seductive, these children would have been less liable to anxiety; partly because the internalized mother figure would be either consistently prohibitive or permissive, and partly because the child would be able to predict with fair accuracy the real reaction of the mother. This perhaps explains why some children who have grossly disturbed parents manage to develop stable character structures: so long as the parents are at least consistent in their behavior and attitudes toward the child, he can base the development of his character structure, even though one-sided or distorted, upon the very consistency and predictability of the parents' attitudes.

We feel that our three children have tried to build up stable defenses, but their efforts were constantly undermined, for the reasons given. Because of their instability, the smallest provocation could lead to acute anxiety, which the children attempted to deal with primarily by identification with the aggressor. Their defenses were insufficient, and when the stress became too great, these children tended to regress. The ease of regression which we have noticed would appear to be due both to the magnitude of the threat from id, superego, and reality, and to the strong fixation at the anal-sadistic and oral levels of development. Not only had there been fixation at these stages in the past, but the alternating gratifications and prohibitions of oral and anal-sadistic wishes had continued beyond the age when such attentions by the mother normally cease to play an important part. We have noticed that in all three of our cases the closest relationship between mother and child seemed to take place on the anal or oral level.

The sadomasochistic relation obtaining between each mother and her daughter led further to an erotization of anxiety, and this in turn increased the degree of anal-sadistic fixation. The lack of external support contributed to the difficulty these children had in passing to a further stage of ego and libidinal development. They tended to cling to what they had achieved, to what they knew, and to the sources of direct instinctual gratification. The inadequacy of the superego, based as it was upon the inadequate support of the mother, facilitated this tendency to regressive behavior.

Finally, we feel that the heightened anxiety of these children found discharge, in the main, through bodily excitement. We wonder whether the bodily skill which was apparent in these three children could be related to this need for discharge or how far it is a characteristic feature of children of this type. It is interesting, though, that these children have achieved such excellent control over their body in contrast to the fidgety behavior one might have expected. It may be that the development of bodily skills was the result of a defensive turning to the only form of instinctual gratification which was relatively free of conflicts for these children; that is, the gratification in bodily movement, which did not evoke unpredictable responses of approval and disapproval on the part of the mother. On the contrary, this seemed to be the only form of pleasure which was consistently permitted and had, therefore, tended to become conflict-free. Perhaps the most important factor was, however, that in skillful bodily activity, the child, through the body-phallus equation, satisfied both her own and her mother's desire for a penis.

CLINICAL CONTRIBUTIONS

PREOEDIPAL FACTORS IN THE ETIOLOGY OF FEMALE DELINQUENCY[1]

PETER BLOS, Ph.D. (New York)[2]

In the study of delinquency we can distinguish two fronts of inquiry. I refer to the sociological determinants on the one hand, and to the individual psychological processes on the other. These two fronts of inquiry are essentially different; yet by the very fact that they study the same phenomena, they become readily confused with each other to the detriment of clarity and research. Both aspects are intrinsically and essentially interwoven in each case. However, our understanding of a case would be incomplete as long as we fail to distinguish between the "early unconscious predisposing factors (so-called endopsychic factors)" and the "constitutional and precipitating factors" (Glover, 1956); due to this differentiation it has become customary to speak of latent and manifest delinquency. In this communication I shall restrict myself to a discussion of some predisposing psychodynamic factors as they can be reconstructed from the overt delinquent behavior and supported by the historical data in the case.

Delinquency, by definition of the term, refers to a personality disturbance which manifests itself in open conflict with society. This fact alone has pushed the social aspect of the problem into the forefront, has stimulated sociological research which in turn has thrown light on those environmental conditions which are significantly related to delinquent behavior. My concentration in this paper on the individual process shall not, I hope, be construed as an expression of my disregard for the contribution which sociological

1 Some material on which this paper is based has been presented at the Annual Meeting of the American Orthopsychiatric Association, Chicago, March, 1957; and the American Psychoanalytic Association, Chicago, May, 1957.

2 Madeleine Borg Child Guidance Institute, Jewish Board of Guardians, New York, N. Y.

research has made. The study of delinquency has by necessity always been multidisciplinary and it should not be claimed by any one discipline as its exclusive domain of inquiry.

Delinquency statistics tell us that antisocial behavior has been on the rise for some time; this goes hand in hand with a general rise in adaptive breakdowns in the population as a whole. This rise in delinquency can not be considered as an isolated phenomenon but must be seen as part of a general trend. This view becomes even more convincing if we accept the opinion supported by Healy, Aichhorn, Alexander, Friedlander and others, namely "that the differences in the psychological make-up of the delinquent and the non-delinquent are of a quantitative rather than of a qualitative kind" (Friedlander, 1947). We have also become familiar with a change of symptom picture in the field of the neuroses; the classical conversion hysteria is less prevalent nowadays and has given way to other forms of personality disturbances, best summarized as pathology of the ego. Anxious parental gratification readiness and even gratification anticipation of children's instinctual needs seem to account for many cases of low frustration tolerance and dependency which we observe in children's clinics; contributing to this confusion is the parents' surrender of their own intuitive know-how to advertisement and extraneous controls. Under such conditions the child's ego is exposed to insufficient and inconsistent stimulation with the result that more or less permanent ego defects ensue; they become apparent in the malformation of delaying and inhibiting functions. The powerful drive toward immediate discharge of tension is typical of the delinquent, and the age of instinctual tension-rise is puberty. At this time the individual normally re-enacts his personal drama on the wider stage of society, and it is of course at this juncture of maturational stress that the inadequacy of the ego becomes apparent.

If I compare the cases of delinquency which come to our clinics today with those cases I remember from my work with Aichhorn in Vienna in the twenties, I am struck by the difference, namely the predominance of poor ego integration and impulse disorders which we see today. Aichhorn's classical saying (1935), namely that the delinquent has to be turned into a neurotic in order to make him accessible to treatment, seems applicable today only to a small portion of the delinquent population.

The study of the psychodynamics of delinquency has always been prone to fall prey to general and over-all formulations. Prevalent ideas in the field of human behavior and its motivation have a tendency to provide the master plan for its solution. In fact, etiological determinants change with prevalent psychoanalytic research; the instinct-gratification theory as well as the theory of the missing superego have been left way behind; considerations of ego pathology have moved into the foreground. I do not question Kaufman's and Makkay's opinion (1956) when they say that an "infantile type of depression" due to "actual or emotional desertion" is found to be a "predisposing and necessary element in delinquency"; but it is equally correct to say that depressive elements are to be found in all types of emotional disturbances of children. What puzzles us most in the delinquent is his incapacity of internalization of conflict, or rather the ingenious circumvention of symptom formation by experiencing an endopsychic tension as a conflict with the outside world. The exclusive use of alloplastic, antisocial solutions is a feature of delinquency which sets it apart from other forms of adaptive failures. It stands in clear contrast to the psychoneurotic or to the psychotic solution, the former representing an autoplastic and the latter an autistic adaptation.

Up to a certain point all cases of delinquency have psychodynamic similarities, but it seems to me more profitable to study their differences. Only by this method shall we penetrate into the more obscure aspects of the problem. In expressing a warning of this kind, Glover (1956) speaks of "etiological clichés" such as the "broken home" or "separation anxiety." He continues: "It requires no great mental effort to assume that traumatic separation in early infantile years must have a traumatic effect; but to convert this into a *direct* determining environmental factor in delinquency is to neglect the central proposition of psycho-analysis that these predisposing elements acquire their pathological force and form in accordance with the effect of their passage through the varying phases of the unconscious Oedipus situation." My clinical and theoretical remarks proceed from this point, especially as far as preoedipal fixations preclude the oedipal stage from consolidating and thereby prevent emotional maturation.

It has always been my opinion that male and female delinquency

follows separate paths, indeed are essentially different. We are
familiar with the different manifestations of both, but we would
like to be better informed about the origin of the divergencies. Our
thoughts immediately turn to the divergent psychosexual development of the boy and girl during early childhood. And, furthermore,
it seems relevant to recall in this connection that the structure of
the ego depends to a significant extent on the existing drive organization which is subject to different vicissitudes in the male and
female. The study of identifications and of the self-representation to
which they lead in boy and girl explain the dissimilarities in ego
development in the two sexes.

If we review the cases of male and female delinquency of which
we have intimate knowledge, we gain the impression that female
delinquency stands in close proximity to the perversions; the same
cannot be said with regard to the boy. The girl's delinquency
repertoire is far more limited in scope and variety than the boy's;
it furthermore lacks significantly in destructive aggressive acts against
persons and property, and also concedes to the boy the rich field of
imposter-like adventuring. The girl's wayward behavior is restricted
to stealing of the kleptomanic type; to vagrancy; to provocative,
impudent behavior in public; and to frank sexual waywardness. Of
course, these offenses are shared by the boy offender; they constitute,
however, only a fraction of his transgressions. In the girl, it seems,
delinquency is an overt sexual act or, to be more correct, a sexual
acting out.

Let us look at the way this disparity comes about. In female
delinquency the infantile instinctual organization which has never
been abandoned breaks through with the onset of puberty and finds
a bodily outlet in genital activity. The pregenital instinctual aims,
which dominate the delinquent behavior of the girl, relate her
delinquency to the perversion. An adolescent boy who, let us say,
is caught in an ambivalence conflict with his father might defend
himself against both castration fear and castration wish by getting
drunk, by destroying property, or by stealing a car and wrecking
it; his actions often are, even if abortive, nevertheless an attempt
at a progressive development (Neauks and Winokur, 1957). The
boy's typical delinquent activities contain elements of a keen interest in reality; we furthermore recognize his fascination with the

struggle waged between himself and people, social institutions and the world of nature. In contrast to this, an adolescent girl who possesses an equal propensity to acting out will, let us say, take revenge on her mother by whom she feels rejected by seeking sexual relations. Girls of this type have told me of persistent fantasies during sex play or coitus, such as: "if mother knew, it would kill her" or "you see (mother), I have somebody too." Aichhorn, in a paper on sex delinquent girls (1949), considers the predisposing condition to outweigh any environmental factor. With reference to the rampant juvenile prostitution in Vienna after World War II he states that his observations led him to "believe that one of the causes of their [young prostitutes'] behavior was a certain emotional constellation. Milieu and deprivation were only secondary factors." Perhaps cases of delinquent girls which have been classified as psychopaths might be viewed as cases of perversion. Schmideberg (1956), in a recent paper, pursues similar trends of thought. She contrasts the neurotic and the perverse reaction or symptom, emphasizing the fact that the former represents an autoplastic and the latter an alloplastic adaptation. She continues: "In a certain sense the neurotic symptom is of a more social kind, while the perverse is more anti-social. Thus there is a rather close connection between the sexual perversions and delinquent behaviour, which is by definition anti-social." The impulsivity which is equally strong in acting-out behavior and in the perversions is well known. I hesitate to generalize as Schmideberg does, but would stress the point that the identity of delinquency and perversion outstandingly corresponds with the clinical picture of female delinquency, while it constitutes only one special variant in the diverse and far more heterogeneous etiology of male delinquency.

It is a justified request at this point to ask for those reasons which permit the view that male and female delinquency are differently structured. For this purpose it is necessary to turn our attention to those differences which distinguish the psychosexual development of the male and female child. I do not intend to retell a well-known set of facts, but instead I shall highlight some relevant points of difference between the sexes by focusing on selective stations in the developmental schedule of early childhood. The developmental foci which will stand out in what follows represent also potential points of fixation which shall lead the adolescent boy or girl into totally different crisis situations.

1. All infants perceive the mother in early life as the "active mother." The characteristic antithesis at this period of life is "active" and "passive" (Ruth Mack Brunswick, 1940). The archaic mother is always active, the child is passive and receptive in relation to her. Normally an identification with the active mother brings the early phase of primal passivity to an end. It should be noted here that a bifurcation in the psychosexual development of boy and girl is already foreshadowed at this juncture. The girl turns gradually toward passivity, while the boy's first turn toward activity becomes absorbed later in the identification which the boy normally forms with his father.

The early identification with the active mother leads the girl via the phallic phase into an initial active (negative) oedipal position as a typical step in her development. When the girl turns her love needs to the father, there always exists the danger that her passive strivings toward him will reawaken early oral dependency; a return to this primal passivity will preclude the successful advancement to femininity. Whenever an unduly strong father attachment marks the girl's oedipal situation, we can always suspect behind it the precursor of an unduly deep and lasting attachment to the preoedipal mother. Only when it is possible for the girl to abandon her passive tie to the mother and to advance to a passive (positive) oedipal position can she be spared the fatal regression to the preoedipal mother.

2. The first love object of every child is the mother. The girl abandons at one point this first love object, and has to seek her sense of completeness as well as of fulfillment in her femininity by turning toward the father; this turn always follows a disappointment in the mother. Due to the fact that for the boy the sex of his love object never changes, his development is more direct and less complicated than that of the girl.

In contradistinction to the boy, the girl's oedipal situation is never brought to an abrupt decline. The following words by Freud (1933) are relevant: "The girl remains in the Oedipal situation for an indefinite period, she only abandons it late in life, and then incompletely." Due to this fact the superego in the female is not as rigidly and harshly erected as it is in the male, it consolidates only gradually and remains less tyrannical and less absolute. In the girl the oedipal situation continues to be part of her emotional life throughout the latency period. Is perhaps this fact responsible for her ready turn to heterosexuality early in puberty? At any rate, we observe in female adolescence a regressive pull which exerts its influence in the direction of a return to the preoedipal mother. This regressive pull, determined in its strength by the existent fixation, is reacted against by the exercise of excessive independence, hyperactivity, and a forceful turn toward the other sex. This impasse is dramatically displayed at adolescence in the girl's frantic attachment to boys in the attempt to resist regression. A regression will result for boy and girl alike in a passive dependency with an irrational overevaluation of the mother or mother representative.

3. The question has often been asked why preadolescence in boy and in girl is so markedly different; why the boy approaches his heterosexuality which is ushered in by puberty via a prolonged perseverance in preadolescence with a lengthy and often elaborate recapitulation of pregenital impulses; nothing of comparable scope can be observed in the preadolescent girl. There is no doubt that social milieu has an accelerating or retarding influence on adolescent development, and consequently a meaningful comparison of developmental patterns can only be made between boys and girls from a similar milieu.

Preadolescence as a phase marked by heterogeneous libidinal aims in boy and girl gives cause to severe tensions in children of this age. The girl approaches heterosexuality more directly and speedily than the boy. The relative value of masturbation as a bodily outlet of sexual tension for boy and girl may play a role in the girl's ready turn toward heterosexuality. However, I think that earlier events in the girl's life by far outweigh any such consideration. The observable difference in preadolescent behavior is foreshadowed by the massive repression of pregenitality which the girl has to establish before she can move into the oedipal phase; in fact, this repression is a prerequisite for the normal development of femininity. The girl turns away from the mother, or to be more precise, withdraws from her the narcissistic libido which was the basis for the comforting overevaluation of her and transfers this

overevaluation to the father. All this is well known. I therefore
hasten to make the point that the girl, in turning away from the
mother, represses those instinctual drives which were intimately
related to her care and bodily ministrations, namely the total scope
of pregenitality. The return to these modes of gratification at
puberty constitutes the basis for correlating female delinquency and
perversion; regression and fixation appear as always necessary and
complementary conditions.

It seems then that the girl who in her adolescence cannot maintain the repression of her pregenitality will encounter difficulties
in her progressive development. A fixation on the preoedipal mother
and a return to the gratifications of this period often result in
acting-out behavior which has as the central theme "baby and
mother" and the re-creation of a union in which mother and child
are confused. Adolescent unmarried mothers and their attitudes
toward their babies offer ample opportunity to study this problem.

In contrast to the condition which prevails in the girl I want
to point briefly to the totally different situation of the boy. Since
he preserves the same love object throughout his childhood, he is
not confronted with the necessity to repress pregenitality equal in
summary sweep to the girl. Ruth Mack Brunswick (1940), in her
classical paper on the "Preoedipal Phase of Libido Development,"
states: "One of the greatest differences between the sexes is the
enormous extent to which infantile sexuality is repressed in the girl.
Except in profound neurotic states no man resorts to any similar
repression of his infantile sexuality."

The adolescent boy who returns to pregenital drive satisfactions
during transient regressive episodes finds himself still in relative
consonance with his progressive sex-appropriate development or certainly not in any fatal opposition to it. Behavior disturbances due to
these regressive movements are not necessarily as damaging to his
emotional development as I consider this to be the case in the girl.
"Paradoxically, the girl's mother relation is more persistent, and
often more intense and dangerous, than the boy's. The inhibition
she encounters when she turns toward reality brings her back to her
mother for a period marked by heightened and more infantile love
demands" (Helene Deutsch, 1944).

4. It follows that there are basically two types of female de-

linquents: one has regressed to the preoedipal mother, and the other clings desperately to a foothold on the oedipal stage. The central relationship problem of both is the mother. These two types of adolescent delinquents will commit offenses which look alike and are equal before the law but are essentially different as to dynamics and structure. In one case we have a regressive solution, while in the other there prevails an oedipal struggle which, it is true, has never reached any degree of internalization nor settlement.

Theoretical considerations tend to support the thesis that female delinquency is often precipitated by the strong regressive pull to the preoedipal mother and the panic which the surrender implies. As we can readily see there are two solutions available to the girl who is faced with an oedipal failure or disappointment which she is unable to surmount. She either regresses in her object relationship to the mother or she maintains an illusory oedipal situation with the sole aim to resist regression. This defensive struggle is manifested in the compulsive need to create in reality a relationship in which she is needed and wanted by a sexual partner. These constellations represent the paradigmatic precondition for female delinquency.

5. A few words about the latter type first. It is my impression that this type of delinquent girl did not only experience an oedipal defeat at the hands of a—literally or figuratively—distant, cruel or absent father, but, in addition, she also has witnessed her mother's dissatisfaction with her husband; both mother and daughter share their disappointment. A strong and highly ambivalent bond continues to exist between them. Under these circumstances no satisfactory identification with the mother can be achieved; instead a hostile or negative identification forges a destructive and indestructible relationship between mother and daughter. Young adolescent girls of this type quite consciously fantasy that if only they could be in their mother's place the father would show his true self, namely, be transfigured by their love into the man of their oedipal wishes. In real life such delinquent girls promiscuously choose sexual partners who possess glaring personality defects which are denied or tolerated with masochistic submissiveness.

In more general terms we might say that the delinquent behavior is motivated by the girl's need for the constant possession of a partner who serves her to surmount in fantasy an oedipal impasse—but more important than this, to take revenge on the mother who had hated, rejected or ridiculed the father. Furthermore, we observe the delinquent girl's desire to be sexually needed, wanted and used. Spiteful and revengeful fantasies with reference to the mother abound; in fact, the sex act itself is dominated by such fantasies with the result that no sexual pleasure is ever obtained. In these girls we look in vain for a wish for a baby; if pregnancy occurs, it is an act of revenge or competition which is reflected in the attitude to the infant: "It might just as well be given away."

6. In the case of female delinquency on the basis of regression to the preoedipal mother we witness an entirely different dynamic picture. Helene Deutsch (1944) has called our attention to the girl's dissolution of passive dependency on the mother as a precondition for the normal development of femininity; these "severance actions" are typical for early adolescence. Deutsch continues: "A prepuberal attempt at liberation from the mother that has failed or was too weak can inhibit future psychologic growth and leave a definitely infantile imprint on the woman's entire personality."

The delinquent girl who has failed in her liberation from the mother protects herself against regression by a wild display of pseudo-heterosexuality. She has no relationship to nor interest in her sexual partner, in fact her hostility to the male is severe. This is well illustrated by a dream of a thirteen-year-old girl who accused her mother of not loving her and spitefully engaged in sexual relations with teen-age boys; in the dream, she relates, she had 365 babies, one a day for a year from one boy whom she shot after this was accomplished. The male only serves her to gratify her insatiable oral needs. Consciously she is almost obsessed by the wish for a baby which, in its make-believe childishness, is so reminiscent of a little girl's wish for a doll.

Behavior then which at first sight seems to represent the recrudescence of oedipal wishes proves on careful scrutiny to be related to earlier fixation points lying in the pregenital phases of libidinal development; here severe deprivation or overstimulation or both had been experienced.

The pseudoheterosexuality of these girls serves as a defense against the regressive pull to the preoedipal mother and therefore homosexuality. A fourteen-year-old girl, when asked why she needed ten boy friends at once, answered with righteous indignation: "I have to do this; if I wouldn't have so many boy friends they would say I am a lesbian." This same girl was preoccupied with the idea of getting married. She related these fantasies to the social worker in order to elicit her protective interference. When the worker showed indifference to her marriage plans, she burst into tears, accusing the worker with these words: "You push me! I don't want to get married!" Here we can see clearly how the heterosexual acting out receives its urgency or its decisive "push" from the frustrated need to be loved by the mother. This girl's preoccupation with marriage masked her longing for the preoedipal mother and found a substitute gratification in the guise of heterosexual pseudo love.

It is a well-known fact that an acute disappointment in the mother is frequently the decisive precipitating factor in illegitimacy. By proxy the mother-child unit becomes re-established, but under the most foreboding circumstances for the child. Such mothers can find satisfaction in motherhood only as long as the infant is dependent on them but turn against the child as soon as independent strivings assert themselves; infantilization of the child is the well-known result.

7. One more possibility is open to the girl who is fixated on her mother and that is the identification with the father. This resolution of the oedipal conflict is often due to a painful rejection by the father. The girl who thus assumes the masculine role watches jealously over her mother and defies any man who aims at possessing her. We usually refer to this constellation as penis envy; in the etiology of female delinquency this factor does not deserve the overwhelming importance which was once awarded to it; of course its role in kleptomania cannot be denied and the preponderance of this symptom in women testifies to its etiological significance; however, the dynamic factor of penis envy cannot be separated from the underlying accusation of the mother that her seemingly willful withholding of expected gratification has prevented the child from overcoming his oral greed. ". . . in accord with the oral origin of the regulation of self-regard by external supplies, the penis or fecal symbol that was obtained by robbing, stealing, or trickery . . . is in the final analysis always thought of in all these forms as having been acquired orally by swallowing" (Fenichel, 1939).

The theoretical considerations which have occupied our attention up to this point need now to be brought back to the individual case where they were studied originally. The case abstract which follows concerns Nancy, a young adolescent girl. The treatment aspect of the case is not made part of the record here; it is the language of behavior to which we shall lend our ear in order to discern a verification of those ideas which had been voiced above.

When Nancy was thirteen years old she presented the family, the school authorities and the court with a problem of sexual delinquency; her stealing was only known to her mother. At home Nancy was uncontrollable and loud-mouthed; she used obscene language, cursed her parents, and had her own way disregarding any adult interference. "The names Nancy calls me are so sexy," were the mother's repeated complaints. Despite this seeming independence Nancy never failed to report her sexual exploits to her mother, or at least hinted at them sufficiently so they would rouse her mother's curiosity, anger, guilt and solicitude. With glee she showed her mother stories she had written consisting mostly of obscene language. Nancy was an avid reader of "dirty sex books"; she stole money from her mother for their purchase. Nancy's mother was willing to give her the money, but Nancy explained to the social worker that this was not what she wanted; she explained: "I wanted to *take* the money and not have it *given* to me."

Nancy blamed her mother angrily for not having been firm with her when she was a little girl: "Mother should have known that I acted up in order to get her attention and to have adults fuss over me." She, Nancy, will never marry a husband who says only "dearie, dearie," but a man who slaps you when you are wrong. The criticism implied in this remark was obviously directed against her weak father. She did not blame him for being a man of no education, who earned a modest income as a butcher, but for his indifference and his ineffectual role in the family. Nancy grew up in a small apartment located in a crowded city neighborhood. Nancy's family wanted for her the "finer things in life" and found ways and means to pay for them; thus Nancy had received lessons in dancing, acrobatics and elocution; with puberty came the end of all these activities.

Nancy was preoccupied with sex to the exclusion of almost everything else. This interest reached abnormal proportions soon after menarche at age eleven. She boasted of her many boy friends, of having sexual relations and asking her peers at school to join her "sex club." Nancy only liked "bad boys" who stole, lied and had a criminal record, boys who "know how to get around a girl." She herself wanted to steal and smoke, but she did not accompany the

boys on their delinquent excursions because she "might get caught."
Nancy has been puzzled why she can always get a fellow if another
girl is after him but not otherwise. She had established a position of
respect among the girls because she would challenge them quickly
to a fist fight; "I have to show them that I am not afraid of them."

Nancy admitted to the social worker that she desired sexual relations but denied having ever given in to her desire; she said that she
used her body only to attract boys and get their attention. She was,
however, observed being intimate with several boys on a roof top and
was found there dazed, disheveled and wet. It was at this time that
the case was taken to court; Nancy was put on probation under the
condition that she receive treatment. In the light of the evidence
Nancy did not deny any longer to the social worker that she had
sexual relations, but she now expressed her hope to have a baby. She
explained that she engaged in sexual relations to take revenge on her
mother. She, Nancy, would keep the baby and marry the boy. Her
mother, she was convinced, does not want her and, in fact, has never
wanted her. At this time Nancy had a dream in which she had sexual
relations with teen-age boys; in the dream, she relates, she had 365
babies, one a day for a year from one boy whom she shot after this
was accomplished.

Nancy daydreamed a great deal; her fantasies concerned marriage
and she was consumed by the wish for a baby. She was afraid of not
being attractive to boys and never getting married. Physically, Nancy
was well developed for her age, but she was dissatisfied with her own
body, especially her skin, hair, height, eyes (glasses), and ears (the
lobes were attached to the sides of her face). At home she was extremely modest and never allowed her mother to see her in the nude.
Nancy could think of only one reason for all her troubles, disap-
pointments and anxieties, namely her mother; she was to be
"blamed." She accused the mother of taking her friends—boys and
girls—away from her, of begrudging her the happiness she finds in
having friends, of putting a lock on the phone to cut her off from the
world. Nancy said she needs girl friends, close friends, who will become her blood sisters; she and Sally scratched their initials into each
other's arms with a razor blade as proof of their eternal friendship.
The mother scolded Nancy when she showed her the scars; this to
the daughter was another demonstration of her mother's not wanting
her to have any close girl friends. In disappointment she had tried to
run away from home, but the tie to her mother proved always to be
too strong; before long she returned.

Despite the vehement rejection of her mother Nancy nevertheless
needed her presence at every turn. She would, for instance, insist
that her mother accompany her on her visits to the social worker.
Being at a loss about a summer job, Nancy thought that her mother

should take a job as a camp counselor and she would assist her as
junior counselor. Nancy was totally unaware of her mother's unfit-
ness for such a job, nor was she able to assess reasonably her own
abilities.

If mother, Nancy continued her accusations, would only have
had more babies, not just one child and a girl at that, Nancy was
sure that her life would have taken a different turn. During the first
interview with the social worker who inquired sympathetically in
Nancy's purpose for seeing her, she preserved a long sullen silence
and suddenly began to cry. In her first words she expressed her overwhelming need to be loved; she said: "As an only child I have always
been so lonesome." She always wanted a baby brother or sister and
begged her mother to get one. She had a dream in which she was
taking care of babies; they were really her girl friend's babies (see
below) and Nancy's mother remarked in the dream: "It is a shame
that such cute children have no proper mother to take care of them;
let's adopt them." In the dream Nancy was overjoyed and ran to her
social worker to tell her that they were adopting babies. The worker
replied that it would cost a lot of money and Nancy answered: "But
don't you know we are loaded?" Waking up from the dream Nancy
asked her mother to take in a foster child. "The child," Nancy said,
"will have to be a boy as I only know how to diaper boys." She
fancied herself having a summer job taking care of children, in a
family, way out in the country. When she was a little older, age fourteen, she actually took a summer job with children as a helper in the
nursery school of a community center. There she was a child among
children, an older sister who helped the little ones with their play.
Nancy always liked to baby sit; she loved to hold a baby in her arms,
especially if it was very young. When her cousin became pregnant
Nancy looked forward to taking care of the baby but added: "I will
baby sit free for three months, that's fun, but later I shall get paid."

Nancy attached herself during these years of sexual preoccupation
to a young pregnant woman of twenty who had married at the age
of sixteen, had three children, and lived an erratic and promiscuous
life. Nancy vicariously shared this woman's sex life and motherhood;
she took care of the children during their mother's absence from her
home. This necessitated staying overnight when this young woman
did not return for a day or two; consequently, Nancy became a
truant. Once she brought the three children to her own home to take
care of them while her woman friend was engaged in her sexual
escapades and not heard from for three days. Nancy emphatically
sided with her girl friend against the husband with whom, Nancy
said, she was once in love. She also protested violently her mother's
accusations against her friend, commenting to the social worker:
"My mother has a mind like a sewer." Nancy knew that she under-

stood her girl friend; she knew that she was unhappy because her father had died early in her life and she never loved her mother. "It's no use," Nancy said, "arguing with Mother," and summed it up by saying: "My mother and I just don't understand each other." After such fights Nancy suddenly became afraid that the aggravation she had caused might kill her mother who suffered from high blood pressure.

Nancy had found a temporary haven, indeed a dangerous one, in the home of her married girl friend. She felt safe in the close friendship with this pregnant mother who knew how to attract men and get many babies. Nancy also relished the jealous anger of her own mother who disapproved of this friendship. Now, Nancy felt, she possessed a girl-friend mother with whom she could share everything. During this time Nancy withdrew from the girls of her own age, feeling that they had nothing in common any longer. An embarrassing testimony of the fact that she had outgrown her peers was her response to a group of girls discussing clothes; to the question, "What kind of clothes do you like best?" Nancy blurted out: "Maternity clothes." Such incidents drew Nancy more deeply into the make-believe family life with her girl friend. Nancy loved this woman and, as she said to the worker: "I can't get her out of my mind."

In her relationship to the social worker Nancy fluctuated between closeness and distance; this instability is well expressed by her own words: "When I think of coming to the office, I don't want to come; but when I am here, I am glad, and I feel like talking." She finally admitted that she would like to be confidential with the social worker but gave her a warning by confessing that she really was a "compulsive liar." She made the suggestion to the worker that they both should reveal to each other the secrets of their lives; then they could learn from each other. The need for intimacy which exerted its emotional pull toward the social worker was conversely responsible for her repeated running away from her.

Nancy finally came to repudiate the "crude, rough stuff of the teen-agers" and her fancy moved into the direction of acting. Here she drew on interests and playful activities which belonged to her latency years. Wild and childish daydreams of meeting movie actors, fainting in front of them and being discovered as the new star, gave eventually way to a more sober approach to the study of acting. From acting Nancy expected to "become a lady"; by this she meant: to be gentle, to speak gentle, to act gentle; then, she was sure, people will like her. It should be recalled here that Nancy was given the following explanation by her mother when she started to menstruate: "Now you are a lady."

Nancy clung to her acting all through her adolescence; in fact, she achieved at the age of sixteen a modest degree of recognition in

summer stock productions. The stage had become the legitimate
territory where her impulsivity was allowed expression in many
directions and where her exhibitionistic needs became slowly tamed
by the aesthetic code of acting itself. By this time Nancy had become
somewhat of a prude; she was a good mixer with her peers but only
to promote her self-interest in dramatic productions. As good a
manipulator as her mother always had been, Nancy now became
narcissistically related to her environment and learned how to ex-
ploit others. The interest in acting had become Nancy's identity
around which her personality integration took shape. The core of
this identity hails back to the "finer things in life" which Nancy's
mother had always wanted for her daughter. In adolescence Nancy
reverted to these imposed aspirations which were instilled in the
child by lessons in the performing arts during the latency years. It
was precisely this artistic endeavor which served in adolescence as
an avenue for sublimation of the unresolved fixation to the mother.
The vocational identity rescued Nancy from regression and delinquency, but it also prevented a progression to mature object finding;
it was, after all, still the mother whose desire she continued to gratify
by her artistic activity. When reminded once at the age of sixteen
of her wish for babies, she snapped back with disgust: "Babies is kid
stuff."

It seems hardly necessary to point out those aspects of the case
which were to illustrate the etiological importance of the preoedipal
mother fixation in Nancy's delinquent behavior. Her pseudo heterosexuality appears clearly as a defense against the return to the preoedipal mother and against homosexuality. The only safe relationship which Nancy found was a *folie à deux* with a pregnant mother-
girl friend; this attachment and transient identification rendered the
sexual acting out temporarily expendable. However, an advance in
her emotional development was precluded until a turn to a sublimated endeavor, namely becoming an actress, had firmly taken
possession of the girl. This ego ideal—adolescent and probably
transient—resulted in a relatively more stable self-representation,
and opened the way to adolescent experimentation and to ego-
integrative processes.

The delinquent behavior of Nancy can only be understood in
conjunction with the personality disturbance of her mother. Upon
closer inspection of the family pathology we recognize—quoting
Johnson and Szurek (1952)—"the unwitting employment of the child
to act out for the parent his own poorly integrated and forbidden im-

pulses." The diagnosis and treatment of this type of antisocial acting out has become a familiar one for those clinicians whose wits have been sharpened by the research which Johnson and Szurek have conducted over the last fifteen years. The "collaborative treatment" in Nancy's case followed the lines which were outlined by them.

My curiosity is aroused by another set of facts. From the analysis of adults who also happen to be parents we know of their delinquent, perverse and deviant unconscious fantasies, and we also know how often the parent is identified with his child and the instinctual life of his respective age. However, many children of such parents show no tendency toward acting out the delinquent, perverse and deviant unconscious strivings of their parents; in fact, many demonstrate in this respect a resistivity which in the case of Nancy is totally lacking. Children normally seek in their environment compensatory experiences which will to some degree make up for the deficiencies which exist in the emotional diet of the family. This is especially true for children of the latency period, but also of younger children who establish meaningful relationships with older siblings, neighbors, relatives, family friends, teachers and others. In contrast, children like Nancy are totally unable to supplement their emotional experiences in their broader environment, but continue to live their impoverished social life in the narrow confines of their family.

It seems, then, that a special kind of interaction between parent and child must be at work in order to prevent the child from establishing progressively his more or less independent life. This special quality of the parent-child relationship lies in a sadomasochistic pattern which has permeated not only the instinctual life of the child but has affected adversely his ego development as well. Primal ambivalence rooted in the biting stage of oral organization constitutes a nucleus from which a lasting pattern of interaction between mother and child emerges; this is carried like a *Leitmotif* through all the stages of psychosexual development. The polarities of love-hate, giving-taking, submission-domination continue to exist in an ambivalent reciprocal dependency of mother and child. The sadomasochistic modality gradually inundates all interaction between child and environment; it eventually influences ego development via the introjection of an ambivalent object. As a consequence inhibitory functions are poorly developed and tension tolerance is low. The stimulus hunger of these children represents the lasting expression of their oral greed. Does perhaps the impulsivity which we observe in the acting-out behavior of Nancy constitute an essential quality of an all-pervasive sadomasochistic drive organization? We should remember here, as Szurek (1954) has pointed out, that the "two factors, the libidinous fixations and the internalization of the parents' attitudes, determine which impulses of the child became ego-syntonic and which are repressed. To the extent that these factors interfere with the child's satisfactory experience in any developmental phase, the internalized attitudes are revengefully (i.e., sadistically) carica- tured and the libidinous impulses are masochistically distorted, i.e., the libidinous energy of both the id and the superego is fused with the rage and anxiety consequent to the repeated thwarting."

The case of Nancy is of interest in the light of these considera- tions. Therefore, we shall now turn to her early life in search for those experiences which played a primary and predisposing role in terms of the sadomasochistic fixation on the preoedipal mother, and of the eventual adaptive failure at puberty. The transactional mean- ing of the delinquent behavior is not without consequence for thera- peutic technique; however, this problem cannot be elaborated in the context of this paper.

Nancy was an only child, born two years after marriage. She was wanted by her mother who desired to have many children. The hus- band intended to wait ten years; his wife, unable to bear this delay, applied for a foster child but was turned down in her request. Soon after she became pregnant.

Nancy was breast fed for six months; at four months the infant started to bite the nipple, causing the mother considerable pain. Despite the mother's protestations the doctor insisted that the mother continue to nurse; two months later when nursing had become an ordeal she was permitted to take the baby off the breast. For two months mother and child were engaged in a battle over sucking and biting, over offering and withholding the nipple. A lasting effect of this period can be recognized in Nancy's persistent refusal to drink milk. Thumb sucking started at the age of three months; it was forcibly suppressed by the use of gloves. We can assume that the infant obtained insufficient stimulation and gratification from nursing at an early age. The child started to talk at about one year and walked well at sixteen months.

Some events in the life of this child are of special interest. When Nancy entered kindergarten she vomited daily before school; this symptom disappeared after several weeks of enforced attendance. The teacher then noticed that the child ignored her presence in a way that suggested defective hearing. Tests, however, proved this assumption to be incorrect. When Nancy started the first grade she had temper tantrums in school and would try to run away. Her mother waylaid her and returned her forcibly to the classroom; after a few weeks her running away ceased for good. From this time on her conduct in school was a constant cause for complaints. All through her latency years Nancy was "stubborn, quick-tempered, a grumbler and a complainer." Nancy slept in the parental bedroom until the age of eight. At that time she was given a room of her own. She then started to have nightmares and would come to her parents' room. No disciplinary action kept her from disturbing her parent's sleep; when Nancy refused to return to her room, the mother made her sit up during one night on a chair in her parents' bedroom. After this ordeal the child surrendered, stayed in her own room and did not complain any longer about having nightmares. Nancy knew very few children and played with them but rarely; she preferred to stay in the company of her mother. She had "imaginary companions" all through her early childhood and very likely during her latency years; in her early adolescence she still used to talk to herself in bed and forbade the mother to listen in. The mother was just as curious about her daughter's private life as Nancy was about hers. With reference to Nancy's lack of friends the mother remarked: "Nancy wants too much love."

Two complementary factors in the early mother-child interaction seem to have predisposed Nancy and her mother to a lasting ambivalent attachment. The mother expected to have babies in order to gratify her own infantile needs, while Nancy—perhaps endowed with an unusually strong oral drive—made demands on the mother she in turn was not capable of fulfilling. This battle over self-interests which were not reciprocally tolerated was destined to continue without letup and without settlement up to Nancy's puberty. Her sub-

missiveness to the mother's cruel discipline, her surrender of symptoms at the cost of masochistic gratification reveal the progressive
integration of a sadomasochistic object relationship which precluded
any successful individuation to develop; to the contrary, it resulted
in the child's close, symbiotic entanglement with the archaic mother.

Nancy's attempts at separation in early childhood and puberty
are apparent in her creation of "imaginary companions" and in her
attachment to the mother-girl friend at the age of thirteen. These
attempts at liberation were unsuccessful; pseudo heterosexuality was
the only avenue open to this impulse-driven girl in order to gratify
her oral greed, to take revenge on the "selfish" mother, and to protect herself against homosexuality. Having brought back Nancy's
delinquent behavior to the predisposing antecedents residing in the
second (sadistic) oral phase, the circle seems to be closed.

A typical personality configuration which led to delinquency in
puberty was the subject of this genetic inquiry. The preceding theoretical discussion had alluded to other configurations which, however, were not illustrated by clinical material. The case of Nancy
should be considered representative only of one type of female delinquency which permits the particular delineation as outlined in
this paper.

BIBLIOGRAPHY

Aichhorn, A. (1935), *Wayward Youth*. New York: Viking Press.
—— (1949), Some Remarks on the Psychic Structure and Social Care of a Certain Type
   of Female Juvenile Delinquent. *This Annual*, III/IV.
Brunswick, R. M. (1940), The Preoedipal Phase of Libido Development. *Psa. Quart.*, IX.
Deutsch, H. (1944), *The Psychology of Women*. New York: Grune & Stratton.
Eissler, R. S. (1949), Riots. Observations in a Home for Delinquent Girls. *This Annual*,
   III/IV.
Eissler, K. R., ed. (1949), *Searchlights on Delinquency*. New York: International Uni-
   versities Press.
Fenichel, O. (1939), Trophy and Triumph. *Collected Papers*, II. New York: W. W.
   Norton, 1954.
Freud, S. (1932), *New Introductory Lectures on Psycho-Analysis*. London: Hogarth
   Press, 1933.
Friedlander, K. (1947), *The Psycho-Analytical Approach to Juvenile Delinquency*. New
   York: International Universities Press.
Glover, E. (1956), Psycho-Analysis and Criminology: A Political Survey. *Int. J. Psa.*,
   XXXVII.
Johnson, A. M. & Szurek, S. A. (1952), The Genesis of Antisocial Acting Out in Chil-
   dren and Adults. *Psa. Quart.*, XXI.
Kaufman, I. & Makkay, E. S. (1956), Treatment of the Adolescent Delinquent. In: *Case
   Studies in Childhood Emotional Disabilities*, II. New York: American Ortho-
   psychiatric Association.

Neauks, J. C. & Winokur, G. (1957), The Hot-Rod Driver. *Bull. Menninger Clin.*, XXI.
Schmideberg, M. (1956), Delinquent Acts as Perversions and Fetishes. *Int. J. Psa.*, XXXVII.
Szurek, S. A. (1954), Concerning the Sexual Disorders of Parents and Their Children. *J. Nerv. & Ment. Dis.*, CXX.
—— & Johnson, A. M., Falstein, E. (1942), Collaborative Psychiatric Therapy of Parent-Child Problems. *Am. J. Orthopsychiat.*, XII.

TREATMENT OF UNDER-FIVES BY
WAY OF THEIR PARENTS

ERNA FURMAN (Cleveland)[1]

Work with young children by way of their parents has been used widely both for prophylactic and therapeutic purposes. One of the basic premises for such work is the unique relationship between the mother and her under-five, an interaction characterized by an unusual mutual unconscious closeness. For this and other reasons the mother is in the position of understanding and influencing her child during his first five years to an extent which will never be possible for her again. The under-five is particularly sensitive to his mother's feelings and attitudes. His relationship with her often brings to the fore aspects of his mother's personality which are not so readily affected by her other relationships. With the onset of latency the child's personality structure changes and his relationship with his mother loses these earlier striking qualities. The methods employed in working with mothers and young children are all based on the concept of the early mother-child relationship. Yet they vary considerably in different centers, and even from worker to worker, according to their interpretation of this concept and according to the aims of their work.

Roughly speaking there are three main approaches: (1) To advise the mother directly as to educational methods, to suggest specific ways of handling certain situations, e.g., feeding, toileting, and to give her intellectual understanding of the child's emotional needs in his different developmental phases. This approach presupposes that the mother is emotionally capable of absorbing and utilizing such knowledge to the benefit of the child and without causing an

[1] From the Department of Psychiatry, University Hospitals, Western Reserve Medical School, Cleveland, Ohio.

Presented at the special meeting celebrating the 35th Anniversary of the Youth Guidance Center, Worcester, Mass., on September 20, 1957.

untoward upheaval in her own personality. (2) To treat the mother
—by psychoanalysis, psychotherapy, or various social work techniques—in order to bring about changes in her own personality.
This will in turn enable her to alter her attitude to her young child
and effect changes in his behavior without direct educational advice.
The approach assumes that the mother's relationship with her child
is primarily shaped by deep-rooted unconscious factors and that the
mother can, and will, change her actual handling of her child only
after she has gained insight into her own early conflicts. (3) The
third approach is more difficult to describe. It aims at keeping the
focus of the work centered on the child. In the process of enabling
the mother to understand her child emotionally and to help him
effectively with his difficulties, one uses direct advice at times. At
other times one uses the child's material, and the mother's unconscious closeness to it, in order to give her some insight into herself
as a mother and into the nature of her interaction with her child.
One here expects that a mother of relative emotional health can
utilize given advice effectively in some areas. Moreover, one presupposes that her uniquely close bond with her young child makes
a mother capable of recognizing many of his unconscious feelings,
thoughts, defenses, and of using them with insight to help him. This
can be achieved only if the work is conducted in such a manner and
at such a pace as to make it possible for the individual mother to
profit from her instinctual closeness to her child without unduly
mobilizing her deeply unconscious conflicts—otherwise one would
threaten the structure of her adult personality and interfere with her
ability to respond to her child's immediate needs. It is this last approach which has been taught at the Hampstead Childtherapy Course
in London and which has been applied and elaborated under Dr. A.
Katan's direction at the Cleveland center. I am most grateful to
Dr. Katan for her assistance with this work throughout the past years
as well as for her discussion with me of this particular report.

Here I should like to present some aspects of this work as it is
practiced in conjunction with University Hospitals Nursery School.
Some years ago Mrs. J. Benkendorf, Mrs. A. Rolnick and I pooled
our experiences with mother-guidance work and jotted down our
thoughts about it. I have received their kind permission to include
many of their ideas here. Unfortunately the scope of this report does

not permit a detailed discussion of technique, essential though this would be to a fuller understanding of the work.

At University Hospitals Nursery School mother guidance consists of weekly fifty-minute interviews which are usually continued throughout the child's one to two years' stay. Our work with mothers is adapted to its special setting. It differs in many respects from similar work practiced in child guidance clinics and outpatient departments. Some of its features are advantageous to the work, while others create certain difficulties.

The nursery school is of invaluable help to the therapist. By observing the child there directly herself, and by obtaining the detailed reports from the director and teachers, the therapist gains a much fuller picture of the child's personality. One is also in a much better position to judge the positive or negative effects on the child of the work with his mother and to gauge its possibilities and limitations.

The nursery is most helpful in another way too. It assures understanding education of the child outside his home. The close contact between parents, teachers and therapist makes it possible for the teachers to adapt their handling of the child to his needs at any given time. The nursery supports the mother's efforts by making the child aware of his problems and, in appropriate situations, by reminding him of some interpretations which his mother has already discussed with him at home.

Incidentally the child's mere stay at the nursery is often welcomed by the parents because it relieves them for a stretch of time of his trying behavior. For this and other reasons connected with nursery attendance, mothers tend to be more willing to continue with the mother-guidance work through difficult stages, whereas in an outpatient setting they may at such times become so resistant as to interrupt the consultations.

Yet the nursery school also brings its own problems with it. While in some cases mothers are happy to find that relative strangers are, or are not, able to deal with their child apparently more effectively, others resent it greatly and it increases their hostility to the therapist. The same is true of all the additional information on the child which the school brings to the mother's notice or which the therapist presents to her. Some mothers can objectively be interested and appreciate getting a fuller picture of the child; with others it is just such new aspects of their child's personality which upset them to such a degree that they are unable to tolerate the knowledge and incapable of working with the therapist on the related problems. In a child-guidance setting mothers come to work on those difficulties of their child which acutely concern them. They are satisfied with the outcome if such manifestations are relieved. At our nursery the mother often finds herself confronted with problems, and is expected to work on matters, which she did not regard as pathological at all and which in fact she sometimes could not bear to see changed; e.g., this frequently occurs in cases where the mother would like to help her child with some fears or eating disturbance but cannot observe or acknowledge his underlying aggression or passive character formation.

By continuing the work with the mother over a long period of time and by attempting to get her cooperation in helping her child with all aspects of his disturbance, one important factor of mother guidance becomes greatly intensified and burdened, namely the mother's relationship with the therapist and the transference contained in it. Jacobs (1949) stressed in her article "Methods Used in the Education of Mothers" that the working relationship with the mother is least complicated when the consultations continue over a short period of time so that the positive transference is uppermost and helps the mother to identify with the therapist in her understanding of the child. In our work resistances arising from the transference, from the material and from reality, are very prominent. It has been one of our main technical interests to learn about them and to find ways and means of coping with them.

In evaluating and studying these implications of mother guidance, we receive great practical and psychological help from the fact that we do not have to make mother-guidance work. Our facilities are such that each child can receive individual psychoanalytic treatment if necessary—either during his stay at the nursery or in his latency years if that seems more advisable—and each mother who wishes and requires psychiatric help for herself can be referred for analysis or psychotherapy to the adult clinic. At any time during the mother guidance we may change our goals to fit the individual case, e.g., mother guidance may be used as a preparation for child analysis.

Often we are quite contented with achieving such a limited goal from the point of view of mother guidance. The main value of such cases lies in the fact that they, more than the apparently easy and successful ones, help us to pinpoint facets in a mother, or child, or in the nature of their relationship which cannot be dealt with through mother guidance. The selection of cases from the point of view of the mother and child is of utmost importance. We are constantly trying to recognize better and to learn more about which cases can or cannot be helped through this form of work and why.

Jacobs (1949) suggests that from the point of view of the child the most suitable cases for mother guidance are mothers of very young children with incipient developmental disturbances, e.g., feeding or sleep problems during the first two years of life, training difficulties as they arise in the latter part of the second year, and some early fears. Jacobs' suggestion can be amply confirmed by our experiences. The children attending our nursery do not fall into this group, but they invariably have one or more younger siblings whose problems the mothers discuss as part of their work with the therapist. It is with these siblings that the best results are often achieved. It is difficult for us to know whether many children in the three- to five-year age group may not be equally ideal cases, for the children at University Hospitals Nursery School are in a sense preselected. They are referred by pediatricians or agencies because their work with the parents or child failed, or the children come because they could not adjust at one or more previous nurseries. Others come almost directly from the medical or surgical wards of the hospital having undergone extensive physical treatments. These children therefore tend to be more severely disturbed and their difficulties are of longer standing. Also their parents often come to us with the feelings they entertained toward the previous people they worked with or at least with the intensified feelings which their child's rather long-standing problem aroused in them. Such selection, however, is purely the outcome of practical circumstances. It does not bear on the theoretical principles on which we try to base our work.

In general it is easier to assess a suitable case from the child's point of view. The mother consciously wants to give full information about him and our direct observation of him at the nursery helps to complete the picture. The selection of the child is based on the criteria outlined by Anna Freud in her paper "Diagnosis and Assessment of Early Childhood Difficulties" (1954). We accept for mother guidance primarily children whose conflicts lie between themselves and their environment, or those whose disturbance is only partly internalized. Among the latter we try to make sure that their inner conflict is of recent origin and not rigidly defended. Further, their instinctual and ego development, as well as the nature of their object relationships, should be relatively adequate for their age level and still show progression.

Betty, on whom I shall report at some length, was considered suitable for mother guidance. Her case may also serve to illustrate briefly some aspects of our work. Betty and Bobby were twins who entered the nursery shortly before they were three years old. Mrs. J. Benkendorf worked with their mother during the first year and a half of their stay at the nursery. I then continued to work throughout the following year and their period of adjustment at the kindergarten. Mrs. Benkendorf has cooperated with me in describing Betty and our respective work with her mother. Tempting though it seemed, we have largely omitted discussing the mother's personality, the technique used by the therapists as well as Bobby's disturbance and his interesting interaction with his twin sister.

Although Betty was a pretty girl, she presented the picture of a whiny unhappy child, babyish in appearance and behavior. Whenever she felt in the least frustrated, she resorted to vigorous thumb sucking. At such times she withdrew and seemed tired and listless. Betty had not yet attained bladder and bowel control. She had been a colicky baby for the first seven months and consequently had been carried and held a great deal. Her persistent demand to be picked up still characterized her relationship to both parents and was also aimed at preventing her twin brother Bobby from gaining parental attention. Betty's relationship to Bobby was quite submissive. Due to his better coordination and more advanced development of skills Bobby directed all of his sister's activities and often even acted for her. Bobby needed this arrangement in order to feel adequate; to Betty it proved her inferiority. As a playmate to others Betty was unsatisfactory. She lacked initiative, had no ideas to contribute, just offered herself as she was used to in her relationship with Bobby.

Betty's wetting and soiling was the first topic of the mother-guidance work. Whereas Bobby had been reliably clean for some time, Betty did not actively resist the mother's attempts at training but did not comply by performing. Once when placed on the toilet Betty said, "I am sticking in my penis." The mother realized herself that Betty had much feeling about being a girl and she wondered "how to make the situation more acceptable to Betty." In response to mother's verbal sympathy for her unhappiness Betty made a bowel movement in the toilet, saying, "Look at my broken beeny, Bobby keeps his in his tushi." She also wished to check the bowel movements of all the family members to establish their difference and informed the mother that Bobby and father had a penis outside, whereas she and the mother had theirs inside. After discussion with the therapist the mother was able to talk with Betty about sex differences and to interpret her confusion between bowel movements and genitals. Betty responded by having all her bowel movements in the toilet. For the first time she could have a daily bowel movement and, to her delight, became dry by day and night. Although Betty's conflict no longer interfered with her mastery of bladder and bowel functions, her intense envy of boys continued to disturb her relationships and impeded the progress of her ego activities and sublimations.

Betty now became overtly jealous of her brother, saying that she too "will look like Bobby one day, right now." Much to his distress, she criticized his appearance whenever undressed. So far Betty felt quite unconcerned about sucking her thumb and lately masturbated whenever she felt like it. The latter was clearly related to her penis envy. She called masturbating "making a beeny"—her term for a bowel movement. One day on finding herself excluded from the company of Bobby and a visiting boy friend, she was seen rubbing herself and said, "All little boys have a penis, I am only a little girl." In addition to helping Betty with the feelings which caused this behavior, the mother was advised to suggest to Betty that she touch herself in private.

The thumb sucking proved to be of a more complicated nature. Betty clung to it tenaciously. On close observation it could be seen that Betty used her thumb to avoid expressing unpleasant feelings, particularly anger. While sucking she was like a baby who could not talk; besides, the thumb in her mouth prevented all angry words from emerging. With much skill and understanding the mother gradually helped Betty to express her anger verbally. This was especially difficult as most of Betty's aggression was directed against her mother. Betty revealed her anger first in connection with her interest in babies and their origin. She blamed her mother openly for making her into a girl and told her that she herself had babies in her tummy, but they were two girls. It was particularly hard for Betty to be a twin and yet be different at the same time.

Betty's relationship to her father was not a happy one at the time. Her babyish behavior disappointed him as it lacked all the qualities he admired in Bobby. In order to gain the father's favor Betty would have to be able to enter into competition with Bobby and emerge as the victor. Even at the nursery, however, Betty was reluctant to try new activities since there were bound to be some children in the group who had already mastered them successfully. It helped Betty to be told both at home and at school that little girls could be as quick and skillful as boys in most areas.

As Betty became more contented with herself as a girl and learned to cope better with her anger toward her mother she made great strides. She turned into a happier independent child, developing new skills and social accomplishments and showing a surprising amount of imagination and humor. One also began to see signs of a new relationship toward her father. She who had always been the last ready in the mornings, started to get up early to keep her father company and prepared breakfast for him herself. She liked to learn to cook. Once when her mother asked her to leave the kitchen because she was in the way, Betty said, "But mommy, how will I ever learn to be a mommy if you don't let me work in the kitchen?"

About the age of four years, however, the impact of her oedipal feelings, coupled with the problem of being a twin, overwhelmed her. This was marked by a recurrence of her earlier difficulties and defenses. Unable to express her anger to her mother verbally, she reverted to being tired, listless, and regressed in speech and activities. She attempted to get her father's loving attention by again getting him to treat her like a helpless baby. Her inability to compete effectively with her mother extended into all areas; e.g., she professed to like being the loser in all games. Both she and Bobby resumed their old exclusive relationship in which Bobby domineered and Betty acted as a passive follower. Yet the type of family games they played revealed a new motive for their clinging to each other. Whenever interrupted in their play Betty claimed innocently, "Bobby said we should play that"; and Bobby similarly used Betty's partnership to halve his guilt. The mother showed Betty that she had again become a follower because she feared to choose the role of mother in games. When Bobby openly showed his affection for his mother, Betty did not dare be angry with her because she feared that her brother might really usurp her place with mother. It took a long time before the mother could persuade Betty that she would not lose her mother's love even if Bobby was so nice to her while Betty abandoned her in anger.

Betty's overt masturbation also increased again during this phase. She did not use it as a form of consolation, however; instead she masturbated provocatively to attract her mother's attention. When the mother pointed this out to her, Betty told her her fantasy: "I think I am a big mommy and go to the store to get a beautiful red dress. It fits just perfectly and then I come home and cook the dinner." The mother appreciated Betty's verbal account and re-

assured her about her guilt. Gradually Betty was helped to accept
her conflicting feelings. She expressed herself in words instead of
behavior and asserted herself in constructive activities. When the
mother had to be hospitalized unexpectedly for a week, Betty blos-
somed out as a little housewife and later relinquished her new role
only reluctantly, making sure that mother should get all the required
bed rest.

Just before their fifth birthday both twins had to undergo a
tonsillectomy and adenoidectomy because of impaired hearing. After
her first long discussion about this with mother, Betty reacted with
reversal of affect, saying, "And can I put on my party dress to go
into the hospital?" Yet she took in all the steps of the procedure as
the mother outlined them to her and questioned everything in detail.
Whereas Bobby's fearful fantasies emerged prior to the operation,
Betty's reaction set in afterwards. Although she recovered well physically, she regressed to being tired, helpless and very irritable with her
mother. When the mother asked her what made her so angry and
suggested that she thought there still was something wrong with her,
Betty told her mother how very mean she had been to send her to
the hospital because "it wasn't at all the way you said, mommy; now
they took it away and I won't ever be a mommy and have babies."
Betty's fantasy of having a penis-baby inside had been reactivated and
had to be worked through again. About the same time leaving the
nursery brought out Betty's apprehension about growing up. On the
one hand she enjoyed her visit to the kindergarten and chose to be in
a class without Bobby, on the other hand she stated that she was
too tired to attend the nursery and had trouble leaving her mother
in the mornings. Betty could be openly sad about leaving the nursery
and planned many visits to keep up her contacts. She adjusted well
at the public school and has begun to enter the latency period.

As to her progress I quote from her mother's recent letter: "Betty
is the verbalizer of the family. In addition to voicing her feelings and
fears, she has developed quite a facility in the use of words and is
curious about everything. She made great strides at school. In fact,
her teacher considered her to be the most mature child in her class
and made her representative to the student council. She makes
friends well and also found a little boy in school whom she insisted
was her boy friend. At least now she doesn't have to pine for men
who are already married, although she assures her daddy he is still
her favorite and shows it in a very affectionate way."

In conclusion a word about the mother. It is evident that Betty's
mother is an unusually understanding, capable and insightful parent.
In relation to Betty she was aware of feeling badly for having made
her a girl. This she called her "original sin" and Betty of course was
sensitive to this attitude in her mother. The only time when the

mother's feelings momentarily interfered with her ability to help her children was after their operation. She called the therapist in panic blaming her that nobody had told her they would be in pain. It was pointed out that the twins had been prepared for just that and the therapist asked the mother whether she could not recall this from her own tonsillectomy. The mother then remembered that indeed no one had prepared *her* at that time and that she had suffered from severe hemorrhages. She was greatly relieved and able to manage again. At all other times the mother coped extremely well with the difficult task of helping twins of the opposite sex over their acute developmental difficulties at the same time.

The case of Betty was used here mainly to exemplify the type of problems in a child which may be treated through the mother. I should now like to turn to the selection from the point of view of the mother, a problem which is of equal importance. To select suitable cases from the point of view of the mother is considerably more difficult. Dr. A. Katan finds that the initial psychiatric interview is not always a reliable indicator because it does not necessarily reveal those aspects of the mother's personality which will prove of greatest importance in her ability to work on her child's problem. Mothers who appear insightful and generally balanced may have difficulties in just the area in which their child too has trouble, others seem unaware of their child's feelings and incapable as educators, yet a very minor personality shift in the initial stages of their mother-guidance work makes it possible for them to cooperate effectively. Frequently it is possible to assess a mother's capacities only after a period of working with her.

John's mother illustrates this. She was an extremely well-dressed, intelligent but aloof young woman when John, aged four, entered the nursery school. Though highly intelligent, he was withdrawn, depressed and incapable of any creative activity. His mother had left his constant wetting and soiling unattended for so long that he suffered from large bleeding sores all over his buttocks which made it impossible for him to sit or run. The mother also had not trained or weaned two younger siblings. While she read novels, the three children would incessantly scream, fight and seriously hurt one another. John's mother described all this without affect and seemed incapable of actively stepping in or making any effective demand on her children. During the first few months of mother guidance she could verbally express her great hostility toward her children. She stated that she had never wanted even one child and knew it would be "bedlam" if she did. She blamed her husband for inflicting this calamity on her and then absenting himself on frequent business trips. After these outbursts she changed remarkably and became one of the most understanding and effective mothers. She was able to help the two younger children herself—they are now both in public school—and she has cooperated very well with John's analysis.

Some types of unsuitable mothers can be excluded fairly readily at the start. Such are psychotics or borderline cases, and extremely infantile personalities who usually simply wish to hand their child over to a person in authority. Into this group often also belong mothers who maintain allround sadomasochistic relationships (in contrast to mothers who have a sadomasochistic interplay only with one child), and mothers who do not themselves see the need for help for their child but come at somebody else's behest.

In contrast to these mothers with over-all disturbances or attitudes, it is much harder to assess particular personality traits in mothers who appear generally balanced. Certain traits have been found to interfere greatly with a mother's ability to profit from mother guidance. When a mother and child use prominently the same defense mechanisms or suffer from identical symptoms, or when the child has a symptom which his mother used to suffer from in her childhood, e.g., soiling or bed wetting, the mother's capacity to help her child is invariably so impaired that assistance through mother guidance is not worth attempting. Then there are mothers for whom the child or his difficulties have an important but pathological unconscious meaning; e.g., the child represents part of the mother's person or he stands for the partner in one of her early object relationships. In such cases the unconscious tendency counteracts the mother's conscious efforts too strongly to enable her to alter her attitude.

Some mothers need to maintain their child's problem for a different reason, namely, they are too narcissistic to be able to face their own guilt which would overwhelm them if the child improved. Mrs. M. Flumerfelt worked with one such case and has kindly allowed me to use this aspect of it as an example.

Debby was a bright pretty girl of four years who suffered from severe temper outbursts and tried her parents with unmanageably difficult behavior. Her mother could cooperate rather well as long as the problems persisted. As soon as Debby improved her mother became extremely hostile to the therapist and to the teachers and went out of her way to bring about new upheavals or to re-create the previous difficulties. She reacted similarly with an angry and punitive attitude to Debby when strangers in the park commented what a nice little girl she was. It turned out that this mother could deny her guilt as long as her child was irrevocably problematic. The mere fact that Debby had some pleasant qualities and could get better confirmed to this mother her feeling that she had caused all the troubles.

Further, there were several mothers who cooperated apparently very well, but one found in time that they merely imitated the therapist and were incapable of carrying on what they had learned once the contact with the therapist was interrupted. Earlier indications of such an attitude vary. Sometimes one could detect an extreme dependency on the therapist, sometimes such mothers had to over-stress their superficial imitation of the worker by adopting her manner of speech, hair style or buy similar clothes.

The different types of maternal traits which I have listed here at random are among the more typical. With all of them mother guidance does not prove effective and, unfortunately, all of them are difficult to detect at the outset and can be assessed in the individual constellation of a mother's personality only after working with her for some time. There surely is a much longer list of unsuitable cases which is beyond the scope of this paper.

Although I have dwelt on the topic of "unsuitable" mothers at some length, I should like to stress in conclusion that, in our experience, there is a large percentage of mothers of under-fives who are very well able to cooperate with the method of mother guidance which I have tried to outline. These mothers derive great satisfaction from learning to help their children themselves and from the improved relationship with their young child which they are able to establish on the basis of their deeper understanding.

BIBLIOGRAPHY

Burlingham, D. T. (1951), Present Trends in Handling the Mother-Child Relationship During the Therapeutic Process. *This Annual*, VI.
Coleman, R. W.; Kris, E.; Provence, S. (1953), The Study of Early Variations of Parental Attitudes. *This Annual*, VIII.

Freud, A. (1954), Diagnosis and Assessment of Early Childhood Difficulties. Paper read
   in Philadelphia (unpublished).
Fries, M. E. (1946), The Child's Ego Development and the Training of Adults in His
   Environment. *This Annual*, II.
Jacobs, L. (1949), Methods Used in the Education of Mothers. A Contribution to the
   Handling and Treatment of Developmental Difficulties in Children Under Five
   Years of Age. *This Annual*, III/IV.
Thomas, R. & Ruben, M. (1947), Home Training of Instincts and Emotions. *Health
   Educ. J.* (London).

SOME ASPECTS OF PSYCHOANALYTIC TECHNIQUE IN ADOLESCENCE[1]

ELISABETH R. GELEERD, M.D. (New York)

Since a complete discussion of psychoanalytic technique in adolescence is beyond the scope of a panel discussion, only a few isolated problems can be considered here. It seems profitable in any discussion on adolescence to determine which period of adolescence is referred to. Biologically, adolescence is estimated to run roughly from age twelve in girls and age thirteen in boys to age eighteen in both sexes. But there are considerable differences in personality structure between an early adolescent, schematically, from twelve to fourteen, the adolescent from fourteen to sixteen, or the late adolescent. It is obvious that the treatment procedure has to take these differences into account. In the three periods the adolescent is biologically as well as psychologically a very different human being. The adolescent reacts quite differently to his treatment in each of these periods, and thus the approach in the treatment must vary accordingly.

All analysts will agree that the treatment of the late latency and the early, almost preadolescent, child is one of the hardest tasks to undertake. This is the period in the life of the early teen-ager in which the group identification is intense, and the attachment to parental figures has been pushed altogether into the background. In this period the repression of the oedipal conflict has become most successful. At the same time preadolescent regression[2] has set in, so that many of the learned reaction formations seem to fall

[1] Contribution to the Panel on Adolescence, held at the Annual Meeting of the American Psychoanalytic Association in Chicago on May 10, 1957.
[2] It is a matter of discussion whether one is dealing here with a partial regression or just an increase in id energies.

263

apart. The boys look sloppy and they have numerous conflicts with the adult environment and parent substitutes about washing hands, taking baths, haircuts, etc. They are defiant and provocative in their behavior, and among themselves conversation centers around destruction, physical prowess and dirty stories. The girls show an increased interest in clothes; they use quantities of lipstick and powder and talk constantly about boys. The interest in boys and in clothes is not a satisfaction of their real feminine needs but reflects their competitiveness and penis envy. The application of powder and lipstick is a reaction formation against anal satisfaction, as well as a substitute for it. The girls also have many conflicts with the adult environment, about messy rooms and closets, or schoolwork. They make increased demands on the mother for material possessions and become more violent in their reproaches and criticism of her. In both sexes the defiance and provocativeness reflect an increase in sadomasochistic tendencies.

Due to the adolescent's rejection of parental figures, analysts are rejected with the same ease as all other adults. Treatment is more easily accepted by youngsters whose neuroses cause disturbances that are accompanied by suffering which cannot be denied, such as sleeping disturbances, nightmares, phobias, obsessions, compulsions, learning disturbances, etc. But even these patients may, after a short initial period of cooperation in treatment, deny their difficulties and want to drop out. Youngsters who are of the acting-out type reject psychological help more vehemently.

Long periods of introduction to treatment, consisting generally of playing competitive games hour after hour, and the support of cooperative parents, are necessary to initiate and sustain the opening phase of treatment.

Generally speaking, the treatment procedure for this age group does not differ very much from the approach in the latency period. Nevertheless my own experience and that of colleagues with whom I have discussed the matter would indicate that with this age group the emphasis is predominantly on problems of daily life. The amount of analytic work that can be achieved does not seem appreciably less than in the latency period, but in my cases there appeared to be a general poverty of material from which to draw conclusions, and little communication of fantasy life.

Example: A twelve-year-old boy was brought to treatment because of a management problem in school. He used obscene language freely, yet was considered a sissy by the other boys. He avoided competitive sports. In treatment he spent most of his sessions playing chess. From his concern with the various pieces and his comment about the moves, it was possible to get an understanding of his feelings about the plight of the pawns—"the little guys"—and their dependency on the King and Queen. Gradually it was possible to discuss with him his fears of getting hurt and his inadequate way of dealing with these fears. After a while he brought information about his relationship to his friends and his younger brother. He gained insight into the devices he used whenever he felt threatened. He dreamed sporadically. The manifest content of the dreams reflected his homosexual problems, but the associations were so scanty that they could seldom be interpreted.

The second period of treatment in adolescence is roughly from age fourteen to sixteen. At this time adolescence seems to be at its peak. Due to gonadal development and the resulting increased hormonal output, great changes take place in the body. As a result there is a marked development in the secondary characteristics. In the psyche, the increased libido disturbs the equilibrium between id, ego and superego. The ego reacts with an arsenal of defense mechanisms, old and new. But the breakthroughs of the id show the incompetence of the ego and superego to cope with this onslaught. The greater preoccupations with the self can be regarded as an attempt of the ego to master the increased id drives as well as a sign of the bewilderment of the ego. It results in the many narcissistic trends characteristic of the adolescent. There is no better description of what happens in this period than Anna Freud's book on *The Ego and the Mechanisms of Defense* (1936).

The handling of the adolescent patient in this stage of adolescence is very different from that in the earlier phase. Variations in technique in adolescent analysis are just as specific as in child analysis, and I believe they can be differentiated from psychotherapy both in child analysis and in analysis of adolescents. They should only be introduced after deliberate and careful evaluation of ego, id and superego, although most of the time these actions and interventions are the result more of a preconscious than of a conscious reasoning on the part of the analyst.

Anna Freud once said: "One cannot analyze in adolescence. It is like running next to an express train." I believe her statement to refer to the middle period of adolescence. However, it does not mean that one cannot take an adolescent who is in trouble into analysis. But the analyst should be aware that the analytic work at this age is somehow different from that with either adults or children, although in procedure and productions it comes closer to work with adults.

The unconscious fantasies are more readily available than in the analysis of a child in the latency period or at any other time in later life, with the exception of borderline states. Because of this availability the fantasies can more easily be interpreted. Thus the analysis seems to move faster. However, owing to the fact that shifts do occur more rapidly, giving the impression that one is dealing with a much greater fluidity of material, the analyst will have to guard against creating chaotic situations.

Example: A sixteen-year-old boy came to treatment because of unhappiness and depression. After a few months of analysis he brought, through dreams and associations, his incestuous love for his mother and his death wishes toward his father. His unhappiness and depression could be analyzed as a direct result of his oedipus complex. In the case of an adult this would have taken a year or more of analytic work. In the case of an adult also, the expectation would be that during the months following the interpretation, the analytic sessions would be occupied mainly with confirmations and ramifications of the fantasy. Instead, however, the material shifted immediately to the boy's castration anxiety. He remembered that when he was a little boy his father had threatened him with a knife for some misbehavior. In his case, I had the impression that immediate interpretation of his castration anxiety would have brought about a chaotic situation. I therefore steered the analysis to a discussion of his daily problems as he presented them. It was clear to me that the working-through process, which takes so many months or more, was minimal if not nonexistent at this stage of the boy's development.

Perhaps the period of adolescence might be compared to an active volcanic process. Continuous eruptions take place from within and keep the earth crust from solidifying. If we liken the ego to the earth crust for a moment, we might say that working through can only be achieved when there is a solid crust—an intact, solidified ego—and use the term "working through" for the insight into the various ramifications of unconscious fantasies in the ego, id and superego as manifested in all aspects of affects and behavior. Since during adolescence ego and superego are in a state of continuous upheaval due to the eruptions from the id, there is never a period of sufficient acquiescence for the contemplation of old ways of behavior. Too many new ones, often only temporary, arise. One might say that for working through, a period of relative stability is essential. This is hardly possible in adolescence.

It seems a platitude to state that every adolescent who comes to us for consultation must be carefully examined so far as maturity, sublimation, strength of defense, regressive tendencies and object relations are concerned. Since adolescence is physiologically a troubled state, a certain amount of disturbance has to be regarded as normal. Personally I would feel great concern for the adolescent who causes no trouble and feels no disturbance. It seems, from my work with adolescents, that evaluation of the capacity for object relationship has always been one of the most important considerations. It is a known fact that the adolescent, due to the revival of the oedipal complex, has to ward off both parents. In the case of the boy, the mother is too much of a threat, and the father too great a rival; and in the girl the opposite is the case.

It is true that the late latency child also has to reject the parental figures, but I believe that although the manifest behavior may seem similar in the adolescent, the dynamics are different. The latency child had to repress his feelings for the parental figures because the sexual love spelled castration and loss of love. In adolescence, due to the increased libido, the oedipal figures are recathected. But now they have to be rejected because, due to the genital nature of the relation, the incestuous threat is a real one. We are no longer dealing with the casual cold tolerance of the late latency youngster, but instead there is intensive rejection because of the too great attraction. Needless to add that unconsciously determined seductive actions and gestures by the parents are greatly disturbing to the adolescent.

The superego is built up through identification with the parental figures of the oedipal period and is the solution after renunciation of the sexual relationship to them. Due to the recathexis of the oedipal figures in adolescence, they have to be warded off with increased vigor. In some cases during adolescence the superego, which was built up through identification with the parents, is also re-sexualized. As a result the superego demands have to be regarded with suspicion and parental values have to be discarded and rejected. In addition, there is the maturational factor that at this age the human being has to strive to become independent from his parental figures in order to find the road to adulthood, and this again makes the acceptance of guidance from parents most difficult. Hence the continuously shifting values of the adolescent.

But in contrast to the late latency child's rejection of parental figures, the adolescent is constantly seeking for parental substitutes, driven as he is by the libido. This need for parental substitutes is seen quite evidently in the adolescent's love for and attachment to teachers, camp directors, or figures further removed such as actors, musicians, etc. The sexual components most of the time are clearly discernible in the so-called "crushes."

In this time of psychological and social self-finding, we know that adolescents try out many ways. As one of my patients once remarked to me: "I always find myself in agreement with the last speaker." Thus, to the adolescent, the adult is a person who is greatly needed from the point of view of the ego to learn from and to identify with, and from the point of view of the superego, for guidance. Also, because of the increase in libido which threatens, the adolescent looks for support from parent substitutes. For all these reasons it is very much easier for the analyst to establish contact with the adolescent than with the pre- or early adolescent youngster. With some understanding and skill it is easy to befriend the adolescent and gain his confidence. In some cases there is a quick change for the better soon after treatment has been started. This is due more to the establishment of a positive relationship with the therapist than to insight gained in treatment.

It is self-evident that the adolescent does not develop a transference neurosis like the adult patient. Like the younger child, he develops transference reactions which coexist with the relationship to the analyst as a need-satisfying object. To interpret this latter part of the relationship to the adolescent would undo the treatment aim of the analysis. However, as in all analytic work, negative feelings should be interpreted and if possible analyzed dynamically and genetically. Transference reactions proper should of course be handled as in all analyses. Detailed discussion of techniques for handling transference manifestations in adolescence is beyond the scope of this paper.

In the third period of adolescence, the turmoil gradually subsides and the psychoanalytic work gains more and more resemblance to work with the adult patient. Needless to say there are overlappings and at times the analyst will find his role shifting from the technique with adults to that necessary with the adolescent.

What are the variations in technique that have to be applied in analysis of adolescents?

Why do we call it analysis and not psychotherapy, just as we make a distinction in work with children between psychotherapy and child analysis?

In all psychoanalytic approaches, the analyst has to take into consideration the present status and the level of development of the ego and superego and the strength of the id. I want to refer to a paper which Dr. Loewenstein gave at the New York Society in February 1957 in which he discussed variations within the technique of psychoanalysis of adults. I believe that in child and adolescent analysis the variations are specific. Anna Freud (1927), in her book on the technique of child analysis, made the point that the analysis of children has to be very different from the analysis of adults because of the immaturity of the child's ego and because of his dependency on the environment. A child cannot exist alone and the fear of loss of love is a real one. Therefore, although we have to make the child more independent from his parents, this independence will always be a relative one and only as much as is warranted at the child's age. Also, the child has only just begun to develop the superego. He thus needs his parents and other adults to teach him what is right and what is wrong and to guide him, so that in the long run he can make his own set of values and build a conscience. But as we can so interestingly see in the latency child, sometimes he knows what is right or wrong and acts accordingly, but at other times he needs direction from parents and educators as to the right course of action. The analyst who enters the life of the child knows that, besides the analytic functions of interpretation and freeing the ego from too much invasion by the id and clearing the way for sublimation and maturation, he will also have the role of another adult in the child's life who is expected at times to give direction and to support the superego development. At other times the analyst is regarded as another parental figure which the ego needs to relate to and identify with. In the same book (1927) Anna Freud discussed how in order to achieve therapeutic work she first of all needs a cooperative environment, an environment which does not undo the analytic work, and secondly, she described her technique for making the child dependent upon her. Since then certain aspects of preparation for child analysis have undergone some changes. It is true that we still need the dependency of the child upon us; he must like us and accept us when resistance is too great. We have to build up a relationship so that he will want to come to sessions in spite of the resistance. Since we know the role which analysis of defenses plays in child analysis, a playful making aware of certain ways of behavior can partially take the place of the laborious technique which Anna Freud described originally to get the child's cooperation.

In child analysis we have to appraise carefully the state of the ego, id and superego and their interrelation. The same is true in analysis of the adolescent, although here we are dealing with a different constellation. The adolescent is definitely in need of an adult friend, one whom he can trust, one whom he can relate to, one to turn to in his many crises. Very often he needs the adult just as a sounding board for the various ways of life that he is trying out in order to find the one that will be most fitting to him as an adult. He also needs the analyst as a superego figure. Since he has to reject his parental figures, it is essential for him to find a relationship in which he can have sufficient trust and confidence to accept teaching of what is right and what is wrong. Many of my patients have come with questions: "What do you think of such and such a person?" or ". . . of such and such an event?" be it movie actors, politicians, philosophical problems, etc. My first response to this is always the analytic one, throwing the question back to the adolescent: "What do you think?" In the case of adult analysis we would leave it at that and we would analyze the adult's attitude,

tracing its beginning in order to get to a dynamic and genetic understanding of the question. With the adolescent, in addition to the
attempt to do this, I must add: "But you know, there are other
points of view, other people may look at it this way or that way,"
and present the adolescent with possibilities of variations in action
and opinion in the hope that he will not only have analyzed his
point of view and incorporated mine, but that he will also have
gotten some idea of how different people think and act. In this way
he may become more tolerant of the actions of others; moreover,
he can make a conscious choice of his own that will fit his needs
and tastes. When compared with the standard techniques of adult
analysis, some of the procedures in the analysis of children and adolescents may look like psychotherapy. However, in both child and
adolescent analysis such procedures have to be used, because at
those ages the ego is not like the ego of the adult, and therefore
analysis cannot and should not be conducted along classical lines.
Modifications directed at these differences have to be introduced.
Thus, evaluation of the state of maturity of the ego is the continuous line of approach. The modifications in many instances will need
to be analyzed at a later date.

In adult analysis every association of the patient has to be
analyzed to ourselves in order to determine whether we are dealing
with an ego production, be it defense or observation of the self
or others, or a superego or an id production. Then, of course, we
have to determine whether the situation we are dealing with is a
transference phenomenon. The analyst as a person tries to be as
neutral as possible.

In child analysis the situation is different. As you know, it is
not only what the child says but also what he does and how he
plays that have to be evaluated. But in this relationship the analyst
is also a human being, an adult person in the child's life. He therefore has to react somehow to the child. The child analyst will try
to hold back as much of himself as he can, but he cannot maintain
neutrality as in adult analysis. He has to chat with the child and
draw him out in such a way that without being aware of it he
becomes confidential. He has to enter into the child's games and
act like a playmate. At times, though, he will have to step in actively
and forbid the child certain actions, but in a mild and acceptable

way. And with every step he takes which from the point of view of adult analysis would mean a gving up of the analytic role, the child analyst has to make clear to himself what his intervention means in the analysis or to the total development of the child. And at a later date, or sometimes in the same hour, he may have to analyze this.

Example: A boy of eleven was brought to analysis because of excessive daydreaming. He was described by the parents as too feminine in his tastes and preoccupations. He had hardly any contact with the boys in his class and never participated in sports. He spent a great deal of his time in his room talking to himself or drawing pictures of engines and ghosts. In the analysis also he used to draw a great deal. I complimented him on his ability to draw so well and expressed admiration for the keen sense of observation. I wanted to achieve with this that the boy would continue to draw and bring more and more details about his preoccupations. It was obvious, from other material, that this was not a heterosexual interest, but that in his development the boy had taken the road of identification with the woman. I knew that his parents criticized his drawing in seclusion. I was also aware that I was seducing him into a greater preoccupation with his homosexuality. Some time later in the analysis the boy berated me to his mother. "She smells," he said, and refused to go to his sessions. When the mother was persuaded to bring him, he began to break all my pencils and throw papers about the room. He said that he did not want to come any more. I then told him that he was becoming disturbed about his increasing preoccupation with drawing, because I let him do it so much and talk about it to me. He felt he was drawn into doing things of which his parents did not approve and that he would become more sissyish. And since I made him show an interest in it, it seemed to him as if I had a bad influence on him. This drawing of the pictures apparently also meant something dirty. Here I had a chance to analyze his projection and could bring his feelings of dirtiness about his symptoms back to the patient. However, there is no doubt that the projection was in part produced by my behavior. In an adult analysis one would have interpreted the patient's need to be admired by the analyst and analyzed this at the proper time. The material of the analysis will make it clear whether the patient projects or wants to seduce the analyst or both.

How is it with the adolescent? I now have in mind the adolescent of fourteen to seventeen years who lies on the couch and more or less "free associates." With the adolescent also, one will have to get more information about his preoccupation. Let us take the example of an inhibited adolescent who secretly draws many pictures of women in one form or another. In this case, too, the analyst might ask him to show his drawings and might praise them—not, however, as a matter of principle but by making some honest remark about the care or minuteness or interest of the drawings. But never (unless dealing with a very sick youngster) will the analyst give the amount of narcissistic gratification he gives to the younger patient—be it child or early adolescent. Furthermore, with the adolescent, the analyst in order to get additional information has to assume an attitude of more than neutral interest, but not to the degree where it might become too seductive. The ego of the adolescent is already so threatened by the increased id drives that a very little overeagerness on the analyst's part may be too overwhelming. As a result the adolescent will either withdraw to the point of interrupting treatment to prevent a panic reaction, or the panic may actually occur.

Example: One of my patients showed me a love poem and then said in an embarrassed way: "Oh, but you know it is nothing. I really don't like to write poetry." On further questioning, she said, "It makes me nervous." This led to a discussion of nervousness in other situations, for instance, when she went to dances. She spoke of the embarrassment she felt in the company of boys. She never knew how to conduct herself when they wanted to kiss her. This in turn brought further associations and dreams indicating her guilt about sexuality, especially about masturbation.

Here analysis of the adolescent is identical with that of the adult except that analysis is frequently not sufficient in the case of the adolescent. In addition to the analysis of the guilt about sexuality, the adolescent will need some frank discussion of the topic. The adolescent has many questions; each question needs to be analyzed as in adult analysis. But in addition the adolescent needs explanation and encouragement to accept sexuality or aggression. Here the analyst becomes a parental figure, but one who states his opinions without moralistic judgments. And after analysis of the guilt one has again to go into the problem of, e.g., how to deal with boys at dances. The analyst can then explain that people have different reactions toward sex; there are some girls who seem to feel entirely free about kissing; then there are boys and girls who only kiss when they really like somebody, etc. I offer various points of view, trying not to censor and giving the adolescent a wide variety of choice. But these discussions have as many pitfalls as in child analysis, and at all points the analyst should be aware of the projections and denials which the patient will so easily make use of. The defenses are not only resistance; they are a direct result of the need of the ego to cope with the id and the superego. Never should the analyst be too seductive and force material about sex too early and too fast. Adolescents never fail to show, either in a dream or through resistance, that even the mildest discussion of sex is felt as a seduction, even by those who are overtly quite active with the other sex.

How do these attitudes and procedures vary from those which are psychotherapeutic and, in my opinion, not strictly analytic?

Let us go back to the example of the eleven-year-old who was preoccupied with drawing engines and ghosts. In this case I pursued a course of interest in the boy's preoccupation with his symptom, running the risk of increasing its severity for the time being and aggravating his neurotic behavior by bringing as much of it as possible into consciousness.

The psychotherapeutic, but not necessarily nondynamic, form of therapy would have been to assist the boy in finding his way to masculine pursuits. At the same time, in interviews with the mother, I would guide her that she learn to emphasize these with the child and decrease the possibility of indulgence in feminine activities. In analysis, it is only after the feminine identification has been understood and worked through that the analyst would go on to discuss with the child the fun or importance of masculine pursuits.

With the adolescent girl, the psychotherapeutic procedure would have been to discuss her feelings about boys, the various possible ways of behavior in their company, and to assist her to find her way toward them. In addition, the mother might be given help in working out her own problems with her daughter.

In analysis of the adolescent, just as in analysis of adult patients, the analyst will avoid contact with the family unless there are emergency situations. Emergency situations may occur more frequently with the adolescent than with the adult. He is dependent on his family, emotionally as well as financially, and when it seems that the analysis is in jeopardy through the behavior of the adult, a conference is indicated. But in his dealings with the family the analyst has to keep in mind that his role is *not necessarily* one of trying to change their attitudes. It is true that such changes might lead to behavioral changes for the better in the adolescent; but at the same time the symptoms would lessen and there would be less or no chance of analyzing them. The correctness or incorrectness of this procedure is open to discussion, since it can easily be argued that adolescence is not the optimum time for analysis anyway. But if one wants to analyze as much as possible, so that the changes which occur are due not only to changes in ego and conscious superego attitudes, but also encompass changes in the id and unconscious ego and superego, then a course of nondirection of the family and a prolonged period of overt, more disturbed behavior in the patient seems to be the choice. In the latter course it is a question of showing greater tolerance toward the symptoms and overt "abnormalities" of the adolescent and of not attempting too quick a change, so that when a change does occur, it is based on analytic insight.

One might say that in contrast to adult analysis, the person of the analyst plays a greater role. In adult analysis it is the conception that through interpretation and working through, energies become available to the ego which make maturational changes possible. In the case of the adolescent the analyst's personal relationship plays a greater role since the analyst consciously and deliberately offers himself as a person to relate to, keeping in mind of course at all times that this should be done, as in child analysis, with an ultimate of restraint and neutrality. I do not want to go here into the pitfalls of the analyst who is too seductive or for unconscious reasons competes with other parental figures.

As stated before, the adolescent searches desperately for a parental figure. And some adolescents need more of the analyst than the shadowy figure sitting behind them as they lie on the couch. In such cases I have the patient face me as he lies on the couch.

Example: One of my adolescent patients gave me the clue to this. She was lying on the couch and I was sitting behind her. She spent many sessions lying on her stomach. And though we could analyze this as a need to look at my face for approval and disapproval, there seemed to be more in it than that. This was a girl whose mother was a productive, able person, active in academic life, but who made rigorous demands on herself and others, but especially on her daughter. When this aspect of the patient's relationship with her mother was analyzed, she just could not believe it when I agreed with her that her mother really was demanding too much. She then turned to look at my face to make sure that my facial expression did not belie my words. And it dawned on me then that some adolescents need more personal contact with the analyst to establish a better contact with reality.

Also, as mentioned before, the adolescent needs the analyst as a friend who accepts him and helps him to find his values. It seems to me that some adolescents need more than "the voice with interpretations," as in the case of the adult patient, but less than in the case of the child when the analyst has to be playmate and parent substitute as well as analyst.

As to the analysis of the defenses in adolescence, here again we have a special situation. The adolescent resorts to many and varied defense mechanisms, many of which shift and are temporary and will not last through adult life. They are necessary because of the attempts to cope with the onslaught from the id. To analyze them at this time will only surrender the adolescent to his id. Thus, whether a defense should be analyzed at a given time or not is a matter of careful consideration. However, the defenses of projection and denial should always be interpreted. These defenses lead to faulty interpretations of reality and I believe that in all situations, whether in child, adolescent, or adult analysis, the analyst has to be the representative of reality to the patient. This is the attitude of the analyst with which all patients have to identify. Suppression of affects is another mechanism which the analyst cannot leave alone since it leads to an impoverishment of the personality. Reaction formations may be discussed and analyzed if the analytic material is related to it. But again, this is a matter for careful consideration. If it is an existing symptom which has led to neurotic difficulties from early childhood on, it will need analysis. If, however, it is the first attempt of the adolescent to cope with his aggressive drives in a more adequate way and if it occurs as a result of analytic work, it should be watched; only if it goes too far, as so frequently happens in adolescence, it will need careful analysis. This is in contrast to adult analysis, when analysis proper often suffices to find adequate avenues of channeling. Moreover, many an adult in analysis can derive great therapeutic benefit from being shown the positive values of defenses and of their pathogenic deviations. In analysis of the adolescent the analyst has to show the patient the positive value of the reaction formations and only assist in undoing the compulsive nature of the defenses.

The following more detailed account demonstrates some of the issues raised in this paper.

A physically mature thirteen-year-old girl was sent for analysis after a failure in school. She and her roommate had developed a crush for a girl in the senior class. They had tried in all sorts of ways to gain her friendship, but she had not responded. Finally they destroyed some of her art work as a means of getting her attention. After that the patient suggested that she and her roommate run away together and go out West disguised as boys, wearing blue jeans. At this point the school asked the parents to remove the patient and she was sent for treatment. Her disturbed behavior had begun shortly after the onset of the menarche. All during childhood she had felt isolated and had been somewhat apart from the group, but not noticeably so.

In the first period of her analysis she was only interested in the treatment as a means of helping her to be reinstated in the school, so that she might get back to her girl friend and the senior girl. To that extent she was cooperative.

She entered a new school where she immediately became involved with a classmate to whom she confided her longing for the two girls in the other school. She spent hours with this new girl friend, causing quite a disruption in the latter's family life. At the same time she became attached to a young teacher, who, for reasons of her own, responded to the patient. Everything centered around "help." The analyst had to "help" the patient get back to her old friends; so had the new friends. Finally she wanted the new girl to run away with her, wearing blue jeans, either to go out West or to visit her former friends. (It transpired here that, in a period of separation between her parents when she was four years old, the mother had taken her out West to a ranch.) The girl friend refused and her parents at that point forbade her to continue the relationship with the patient. This aroused fantasies of "helping" the girl friend by saving her from her family.

There was no way in the analysis to show her that these activities were unrealistic and might express emotions other than those she was aware of. However in order to get help in her struggle with what she felt to be an unundersetanding environment, she was willing to come to her sessions. It was obvious too that she craved the relationship with me, although at the same time she had to ward me off because of underlying conflicts with a mother figure.

This initial period of the analysis was typical for the treatment phase of an early adolescent. It was an attempt to establish contact with her and, apart from some historical information, mainly consisted in discussing her daily behavior.

In the meantime, however, she grew older, and it may be open to discussion whether the changes which now occurred in the character of the analysis were a result of the analytic work or a reflection of adolescent development. Probably both factors played a role. The patient came to lean more heavily on me for "help," although she continued to divide her confidence between me and the beloved teacher. However, the love she had for the teacher did not have the intensity of a crush. It was possible to show her that she was repeating a childhood pattern of dividing her love between her nurse and her mother. The nurse had actually given her more warmth and affection than the mother, who seemed to have been erratic and mainly concerned about her daughter's physical health. The patient's behavior as a whole had quieted down considerably, although there was seldom a dull moment with her. She stood up for all who were down-trodden and showed an interest in social problems beyond her age. But in characteristic adolescent fashion, she had no concern for anyone in her immediate environment unless they were very poor or helpless. She now fell in love with a boy who always dressed in Western clothes; he did not return her affection. Thus she needed "help" from us all to win the boy; advice from me and active cooperation from her friends, the older one and the contemporary. Help also was needed whenever situations arose in which she could not have her own way. It was fascinating to watch how at those moments she set about managing everyone and everything.

After about a year of analytic work she was well enough settled in her analysis to tolerate lying on the couch, and at some point we came to a discussion of her masturbation practices and fantasies. She had always believed she was the only one who had such problems, and the frank discussion of them helped to reduce her shyness with boys. She recalled sexual activities with a playmate throughout early childhood. He had died when the patient was five years old. She had been a "peeper" when she was about six. There had been a few isolated sexual games in latency. Her daydream throughout the latency period had been to take a group of children out West.

In the early daydreams the group had been a mixed one, but later on there were only boys.

Since she was the kind of person who liked to "manage" situations, being in analysis soon made her feel too dependent. It was not possible at this point to discuss the fear of the transference relationship as the fear of homosexuality and the masochistic fantasies related to it. Thus we reached a mutual decision, initiated by the patient, to interrupt treatment. It was made very clear, however, that she could come back at any time.

After about six months she returned. In the meantime her parents had unfortunately entered her in a new school, where she had become involved in a repetition of the two previous situations. She was again deeply attached to an older girl, fantasying about her and wanting to be near her, and at the same time appealing for help to a classmate. There was some homosexual contact with the younger girl on one occasion.

This crush was the last one. The episode, more than anything else, convinced the patient of the repetitiveness of her crushes and the need for further analysis. By now she was almost sixteen. Henceforth there were many involvements with boys. The first object of her love was a boy from a broken home with many conflicts who, due to a different background, felt very much an outsider. The patient spent all her free time with him, inciting him to rebel against his parents. She was ready to elope with him to save him from his unhappy family situation. Fortunately she had confided in me during this episode and was able to be stopped in time. She could not understand why the boy's parents were angry with her.

When it was all over she could see how she had identified with the boy and how her attempt to save him had been a displacement of her own relationship to her parents. She recalled her unhappiness over her parent's separation and over their discord when they subsequently lived together again.

From now on she was frantically involved with boys. She was most seductive and the instigator of the relationships. She was able to understand her penis envy through the relationships with these boys. Gradually oedipal fantasies could also be connected with them, and many of her dreams dealt with the fear of being found out by her mother. Her hostility to her mother was quite conscious. It was her love for her mother that could not be analyzed.

In contrast to the earlier period, there was now a wealth of analytic material. Many dreams were reported, but although she gave many associations, it was usually impossible to make interpretations. And on the occasions when I was able to interpret an incestuous fantasy—for example, her incestuous love for her father and hatred of her mother—few corroborative data were brought to

sustain the interpretation. In this period of her analysis the transference relationship could not be interpreted to her. She needed
me as a real mother figure, although from time to time it was
possible to interpret her hostility toward me. She would listen to
my explanations, whereas anything her mother tried to say was not
accepted. In this period too she brought very little historical material. The patient welcomed the insight she acquired in the analysis.
It made her less bewildered about her acting out. It was obvious,
however, that she also needed my interpretations as a token of love
and as a reassurance that she was being "helped."

Thus we struggled through the patient's adolescence. From time
to time her mother came to see me; such visits were necessary for her
reassurance and continued cooperation.

In a period of relative quiescence she again decided to stop
treatment, but continued to see me once in a while or for a few
months at a time.

Nevertheless I considered this period of analytic help of great
importance. It stopped the crushes and the too great involvement
with girls. It curtailed some of her acting out since she could partially assimilate the interpretations. In addition, she could readily
utilize the insight she had received over the years after the turbulent
phase of adolescence was ended.

In the initial period of an adult analysis emphasis is generally
on analysis of the defenses and the behavior of the patient, and the
concomitant fantasies can only gradually be understood. In contrast,
the pressure of the unconscious fantasies is so strong in adolescence
that they influence affective life and behavior to a much greater
degree. Hence the increased acting out and the need for many
defenses. With adults, therefore, the analytic work may tend to
increase the acting out, whereas with adolescents analysis tends to
decrease it. This explains why often in analytic work with adolescents some improvement may occur relatively quickly.

When the patient was eighteen she returned to analysis. She had
been able to finish high school and had entered college. Her first
dream in this period of analysis was a frank homosexual one about
her new sister-in-law who had the same name as I. This led finally
to an understanding of her homosexuality, which could now be
linked up with her relationship to me as well as to her mother.
The positive and negative transference feelings could now be analyzed, and now too I gradually obtained an account of what had
actually happened when she was first referred for treatment. It was

her classmate who first had developed a crush on the senior girl. On one occasion the older girl had beaten up the younger one. The beating incident had established the patient's involvement. It took its significance from a beating the patient had received from her father in early childhood. At the same time the younger girl had assumed a maternal role toward the patient, who had a habit of dramatizing her menstrual periods or any slight pain. The pain represented her fear of being castrated.

On one level the senior girl stood for the patient's father and represented her masochistic attachment to him. On another level she was a mother substitute whom the patient wanted to love as a man. The sadomasochistic positive and negative oedipal fantasy was condensed in this acting out. The saving and being saved and the identification with both girls in the various roles also took its significance from the fantasy. From the material now brought it became clear that the patient's mother was a seductive woman who had always aroused her daughter, though she had never frankly seduced her. And it was from the mother and the fantasies about her that the patient had to be saved.

The driving force behind her seductive behavior to men was her castrative fantasies toward them which satisfied her desire for revenge on her father. He indeed had deserted her and her mother when the patient was four years old. She also wanted to humiliate men, since she had felt humiliated by the father when he had beaten her at the age of three. At the same time the humiliation was a source of masochistic satisfaction.

The source of her intense guilt toward men was also revealed. When she was three years old her father had broken his arm coming down a slide with the patient in his arms, and she had blamed herself for the incident. Shortly afterwards the boy playmate had died. In turn then, men had to be saved from her.

Gradually her seductive behavior toward men and boys changed and she went through an ascetic phase in the analysis. She became interested in studying and there was a marked improvement in her college work. She majored in psychology of delinquents, a sublimation of the fantasy of helping and saving.

Another form of the patient's acting out—her involvement with poorer or socially inferior people—could now be analyzed. They represented sexuality and warmth. This was determined on the one hand by the coldness and snobbishness of her parents and on the other by her observations of the primal scene; at the age of four she had discovered her nurse with a man; but it was also from this nurse that she had received real warmth. Furthermore, while out West from the age of four to six, during the period of her parents' separation, she had observed her mother's involvement with a cowboy. Here was the origin of the patient's fantasy of going out West. During the latency period, all the above experiences had been condensed into the fantasy about going out West with a group of boys and girls wearing blue jeans. The patient was the leader of the gang. This represented her identification with men; to be a cowboy—her mother's lover. But it also represented being strong and powerful, someone who could manage everything, and thereby warded off masochistic fantasies and satisfied fantasies of having a penis. All these fantasies had been acted out with increased intensity during adolescence, but only some of them could be reached by interpretation. The frank discussion of masturbation in the analysis had enabled the patient to overcome her shyness toward boys. She had had innumerable dreams which showed concern about being found out and an idea that sexual activities were something practiced only by poor people and Jews and Negroes. But only after adolescence could the masturbation fantasy be linked up with her sadomasochism and intense guilt feelings. The reassurance and the discussion earlier in treatment, though beneficial, had never reached the unconscious guilt.

Shortly after terminating the analysis she married and has maintained a satisfactory adjustment. She is active in community problems, specifically those concerning minority groups and delinquency.

In general, one might formulate that analysis of adolescents differs from that of adult patients in six ways:

1. In adolescence, a greater effort has to be made to increase the tolerance of the ego to pathogenic conflicts.

2. A greater amount of help in learning to test reality is necessary in adolescence.

3. The analyst fulfills the need of a parent substitute, although in a reserved, restrained and most neutral way.

4. A consistent and systematic analysis of all defense mechanisms is not possible, and in some instances is contraindicated.

5. The working-through process is only possible to a limited degree.

6. The handling of the transference is different in adolescence.

I have tried here to give a bird's-eye view of some problems of analytic technique. I am convinced that in such a short paper many oversimplifications have been made. But I hope to have been able to present some of my views on the analysis of adolescents.

BIBLIOGRAPHY

Bernfeld, S. (1923), Über eine typische Form der männlichen Pubertät. *Imago*, IX.

Deutsch, H. (1944), *The Psychology of Women*. New York: Grune & Stratton.

Freud, A. (1927), *Psycho-Analytical Treatment of Children*. London: Imago Publ. Co.

—— (1936), *The Ego and the Mechanisms of Defense*. New York: International Universities Press, 1946.

Gitelson, M. (1948), Character Synthesis. The Psychotherapeutic Problem of Adolescence. *Am. J. Orthopsychiat.*, XVIII.

Jones, E. (1922), Some Problems of Adolescence. *Brit. J. Psychol.*, XIII.

Katan-Angel, A. (1937), The Role of "Displacement" in Agoraphobia. *Int. J. Psa.*, XXXII, 1951.

MOTILITY IN THE THERAPY OF CHILDREN
AND ADULTS

BELA MITTELMANN, M.D. (New York)[1]

In this paper, the various aspects of the theme of motility will be discussed as they appear in the course of psychological therapy, along with the technical devices by which the motor theme can be woven into the fabric of the treatment.

The observational material and constructions and the survey of the literature will be done within the framework of the following formulations presented by the author in two previously published papers on motility (1954, 1955): (a) There is a motor urge (or drive), and satisfaction of this urge is attended by pleasure. (b) Motility is an important means of mastery, integration, and reality testing. These statements are true throughout life, but particularly so during the second year of life and for several years thereafter as a result of the rapid evolution of postural, locomotor, and manipulative skills. Among the characteristic psychological features of this period are increase in self-assertion and independence alternating with continued dependence on the environment, increase in aggression, fear of motor retribution, motor (imitative) identification, the readiness to translate impulses into activity, predominance of motor language in communication with the environment, and certain affectomotor expressive patterns, e.g., flapping of the hands during joy. Skeletal motility is closely connected with nearly every other physiological and psychological striving, such as orality, genitality, evaluation of the self, aggression, dependent longings, and interpersonal relations in general. In the course of normal development, motility, both as an urge and as a means of mastery, undergoes certain more or less regular vicissitudes. These vicissitudes may be determined by pain-

[1] From the Department of Psychiatry, Albert Einstein Medical College, Yeshiva University, Bronx, N. Y.

ful or anxiety-arousing experiences and to environmental interference and disapproval. Fear of loss of motor control and of falling
from a height becomes evident after the child learns to climb upstairs at about one year of age and seems more or less universal.
Hurt or fright as an outcome of a mishap resulting from a vigorous
activity may lead to temporary cessation of a newly acquired motor
function. Restriction of motility—for example, when the child is
held while being diapered—usually results, at about one year of age,
in a mixture of rage, anxiety, and struggle to escape. Disapproval
by the environment is aroused either by the motor activity alone or
because of the other impulses—e.g., genital or oral—associated with
it. The motor function may develop certain signs or undergo certain
changes as a result of such intervention and disapproval. To ward off
external and internal dangers such as fear, anxiety or guilt, there
may be motor compromise formation, i.e., incomplete (or incipient
symbolic) action: the child moves his hands toward the object without touching it; reaction formation: he holds his hands behind his
back instead of reaching; doing and undoing: he picks up the object
and immediately replaces it. There may further be increase or
diminution of motility of a tonic or clonic nature. Increase in activity
may represent unconscious flight from or fight against the impulse
or guilt or against externally perceived danger. It may also represent a substitutive motor satisfaction and be employed, e.g., in place
of the forbidden genital activity. Motor pathology may be the result
of pathogenic effects striking the individual in the motor function
directly or in other areas of physiological and psychological functioning—e.g., rejection, genital trauma, etc. Similarly, factors attacking the motor function directly may produce the main symptom in
other spheres of function—e.g., punishment for motor activity may
result in nail-biting via oral aggression turned toward the self.

The fear of motor retribution is an important element in the
precursor of the superego. The child handles objects because of his
motor and manipulative urges, to which aggression gets added later.
This is clearly seen, for example, in the child's handling of animals.
He grasps the cat's fur and then shakes it with the hand slashing
characteristic of joy reactions. The animal objects and gradually the
child handles it with intentional aggression. A similar development
takes place toward human beings with added motivation, e.g., of

sibling rivalry. In the next developmental step the child's fear is that
the more powerful parental figure will visit on him the same motor
aggression as he intended or actually visited on the sibling. This
fear may be displaced onto a large inanimate object, but charac-
teristically one manipulated by human beings, for example, auto-
mobiles. Here is a brief clinical illustration:

A child displayed considerable motor aggression toward his sister,
a year younger, for which he was frequently censored by his parents.
At the age of two and a half years he had his first reported dream (a
dream with anxiety): "Bump-bump," his term for cars colliding. His
behavior toward his sister gradually became gentler and ultimately
showed very few traces of sibling rivalry. When he started treatment
for a persistent nocturnal enuresis at the age of five and a half (his
sister was already dry for a year and a half), his initial repetitive
game consisted of violent crashing of cars, thus expressing both his
unconscious motor aggression and his fear of motor retribution.
Of course, a motor interpretation does not imply the absence of
sexual determinants as well.

"Passive" motility, that is, the desire to be moved or to be
inactive and relax, is a normal pleasure component of motility, but,
contrary to active motility, it has no function of mastery and integration except as in setting the stage for thinking. It may become
intensified, however, in pathology as a defense against danger or as a
substitute gratification in place of active satisfaction.

The motor experiences of early years are usually completely forgotten and do not appear as memories in the course of therapy.
They have to be observed directly. Exceptionally, motor memories
are preserved from this period. Tolstoy writes (Mead, 1954):

Here are my first recollections: . . . I am tied. I want to free
my hands but I cannot do it, and I am crying, weeping, and my
cry is unpleasant to me, but I cannot stop. Somebody is staying
upon me [sic in translation]. And it is all half-darkness. But I
remember that they are two. My crying affects them. They worry
because I am crying, but they don't unbind me as I want them
to, and I cry louder. It seems to them it is necessary, and I want
to prove it to them, and I break out crying, which is repugnant
to me but irrepressible. I feel the injustice and cruelty, not of
the people, because they are sorry for me, but of fate, and I pity
myself. I don't know and will never learn what it was, whether
I was swaddled when I was sucking and drew out my hand or

was swaddled when I was more than a year old, in order not to let me scratch a rash; whether I collected in one memory many sensations, as one does in a dream.

One may remember at this point Tolstoy's ideas, as expressed in his writings and activities, on humaneness in general, freedom and the liberation of serfs in particular. They are suggestive of the notion that motor experiences as well as the impact of object relations on motility may contribute significantly to character formation. (See also Greenacre, 1944; Gorer, 1949.)

SURVEY OF THE LITERATURE

We shall start the survey of literature with the consideration of general conceptual formulations in relation to motility. In the *Three Contributions,* Freud (1905) considers active and passive motility as one of the sources of sexuality. He writes: "Children feel a need for a large amount of active muscular exercise and derive extraordinary pleasure from satisfying it" (p. 202). Sometimes motility in analytic parlance is referred to as one of the "component instincts." Sadger (1912) speaks of "muscle erotism," Abraham (1913) of "pleasure in movement." Some of Freud's (1905) remarks refer to the close tie between motility and aggression: "One of the roots of the sadistic instinct would seem to lie in the encouragement of sexual excitation by muscular activity" (p. 203). In another place (1915) he says that aggression seems particularly closely tied to the musculature. (See also Hartmann, Kris, and Loewenstein, 1949.) In *The Ego and the Id,* Freud (1923) says that the ego controls the access of impulses to conscious motility, thus assigning motility, in another respect, to the ego. We may say in terms of analytic theory that the analyst may consider either the id or the ego aspects of motility. This is in harmony with my emphasis that motility is both an urge and a form of mastery and integration throughout life and dominantly so at about the second year of life. In terms of prevalent analytic theory one may speak of that period as the motor phase of ego and libido organization. Apart from mastery and integration, "ego aspect" of motility may refer to the presence or absence and degree of impulse control or to the use of impulse or action as defense or protection against another impulse and anxiety or guilt

(W. Reich, 1933, 1942; A. Freud, 1936; Kris, 1951). An Understanding of these various aspects of motility can of course be very important in elucidating the behavior of both children and adults.

We shall now turn to the survey of formulations relating to pathology of motility. In connection with hysterical paralysis as one of the "defense-neuropsychoses" Freud (1896) said that the "symptoms arise through the psychical mechanism of (unconscious) defense, that is, through an attempt to repress an intolerable idea which was in painful opposition to the patient's ego" (p. 155). One could translate this into later terminology by saying that the symptoms are the result of the conflict of sexual and aggressive impulses on the one hand and the resultant anxiety and guilt on the other. The solution may represent a cessation of function through inhibition (e.g., flaccid paralysis) or through excess function (e.g., hysterical spasm) or through partial and symbolic action (e.g., hysterical tic). To this we may add that the motor nature of the symptomatology may be determined by one or several of the following possible points: the forbidden impulse is primarily motoric in nature; the muscle involved is an integral, indispensable part of the tabooed function; the motor function concerned was involved in a conflict or impaired during the motor period of developmental organization.

In discussing active and passive motility as one of the sources of sexuality, Freud (1905) mentions the observation that in many individuals the first sexual excitement occurs while wrestling as children and adds later: "In many people the infantile connection between romping and sexual excitation is among the determinants of the direction subsequently taken by their sexual instinct" (p. 203). Abraham (1913) observed in several cases of "street phobia" a strong pleasure in movement (e.g., walking) when anxiety was not present, and enjoyment of dancing when alone in the room at home, and a tendency to definite rhythm when unobserved while walking across the room. One of his patients stated quite spontaneously that this rhythm reminded him of sexual rhythms. Abraham concluded that choice of "locomotor anxiety" (i.e., agoraphobia) was based on a (probably constitutionally) excessive development of the pleasure in movement (with subsequent guilt?). To Abraham's formulation I would like to add a remark on the object aspect of the dynamics of phobia. The protective adult of the infant has two derivatives for the phobic patient: the home and the individual whose presence is required to spare him an anxiety attack. The venturing forth within a limited circumference and the anxiousness to return to the place of safety are similar. Thus we may say that the motor aspects of phobic behavior show features of regression to the behavior of the anxious, overdependent infant (Mittelmann, 1954).

In a later writing, Freud (1926) states that if the skilled function of walking acquires the meaning of trampling on mother earth— i.e., if this ego function acquires qualities of aggression and eroticism —the patient develops astasia-abasia.

The last few formulations dealt with symptoms as directly and simply related to conflict over instinctual impulses. The next two authors present formulations that relate certain symptoms to the vulnerability of the organism. Ferenczi (1921) assumed that the tic patients are incapable of enduring an ordinary stimulus without motor defense. The tic may represent a flight from the external stimulus or an active defense against it, or the patient may be defending himself against his own person, e.g., in the scratching tic. Both the incapability of tolerating stimuli and the need for motor response are the expression of narcissism, i.e., an overvaluation of, an excessive libidinal attachment to, and a preoccupation with oneself and one's own organs. One may add that this overattachment would result in or might be produced by an excessive fear of damage to the organs or to the self. Secondarily, Ferenczi assumes, the tic may represent a masturbatory equivalent. The chronic, therapeutically difficult tic which Ferenczi[2] discusses should be differentiated from the hysterical type of tic (Gerard, 1946).

According to Kardiner (1932, 1947), in traumatic neurosis the traumatic event represents a situation with which the victim is unable to cope. As a result, activities involved in successful adaptation to the external environment become blocked in their usual outlets. As a further result, earlier forms of adaptation and mastery are revived in the form of regressive motility and readiness for rage reactions. This is seen, for example, in patients in whom all locomotion stops and, in the process of recovery, first crawling returns.

In the remaining survey we shall deal with formulations relating to intricate phenomena of instinctual conflict and impulse control

2 See also Mahler (1944).

along with some observational and technical material. According
to Fenichel (1945), hysterical paralysis, whether spastic or flaccid, is
both an insurance against action and a distorted substitute for it.
In a general way, a pathogenic defense always implies the blocking
of certain movements; thus, the struggle of the defense reflects itself
in functional disturbances of the voluntary muscular system. A
patient in psychoanalysis, who can no longer avoid seeing that an
interpretation is correct but nevertheless tries to, frequently shows
a cramping of his entire muscular system or of certain parts of it.
It is as if he wanted to counterpoise an external muscular pressure
to the internal pressure of repressed impulses seeking an outlet in
motility. The muscular expression of a conflict may be hypertonic,
hypotonic or "dystonic," i.e., alternation of hypo- and hypertonia.
Apart from the general defense, dystonic motility may be the expression of anal and genital tendencies as well as that of rage and
anxiety. The spasm of the anal sphincter may be extended to the
whole body musculature. A continuous misuse of the muscles for
"neurotic spasms" frequently results in fatigue which is most outspoken in cases of inhibited aggressiveness. It may also result in
pain in the muscles. In some somatically predisposed personalities,
the dystonia may result in nonspecific alterations in the tissues of
the joints.

Freud (1920b) observed "accidental" symptomatic acts: "They
merge, without any definite line of demarcation into the gestures and
movements which we regard as expressions of the emotions. To this
class of accidental performances belong all those apparently pur-
poseless acts which we carry out as though in play with clothing,
parts of the body, objects within reach. . . . All such performances
have meaning and are genuine mental acts" (p. 55). To this I would
like to add the following remark: symptomatic acts occurring in a
conflict situation show, on a small scale, regression to the motor
phase of development in the tendency to carry impulse into action.

Felix Deutsch (1952) made extensive and systematic observations
of patients' behavior on the analytic couch. For this purpose he included in the initial instructions the statement that the primary rule
included association to bodily sensations and movements, and that
the patient may move or turn on his side or his stomach when he
wished, but was expected to express accompanying feelings and

thoughts in words. He found that there was a characteristic frequency and quality to the movements of individual patients which changed with the phase of the analysis. The movement and posture of the patient had characteristic motivational background and could be connected with genetic situations. Thus one of his patients raised and lowered his head slightly on the couch several times, each time before he started to talk about his mother. Crossing of the legs usually represented compromise between sexual excitement and defense against it. Bending the legs at the knees represented an unconscious desire to expose the perineal region to the therapist. The quality and quantity of the movements usually change with shifts of emphasis on one or another parent. One side of the body, the left, was mainly the "mother" side, the right side the "father" side. Deutsch found that calling the patient's attention to these movements and interpreting them causes a change in the patient's posture and movement and for this reason considers it best not to do so for a long period in the analysis. Sometimes, however, he found it advantageous to direct free association to the posture, e.g., when resistance unduly delayed progress, particularly with patients who did not move at all. Ultimately in all analyses Deutsch utilizes these postures and movements for interpretation extensively. However, he does not give concrete illustrations for his interpretive approach and the patient's reactions to it.

The most extensive use of psychomotor constellations in the dynamic constructions has been made by Wilhelm Reich (1933, 1942). He assumes that all neurotic patients present alterations in their motility, particularly in the form of hypertonicity, though at times also of hypotonicity, and that this altered motility is part and parcel of the neurotic process. Both the impulse and the defense against it are expressed in the contracted state of the muscle and both are traceable to infantile experiences and represent also a current method of coping with neurotic conflicts. As an illustration, the rigid mouth expression of an adult patient served unconsciously to prevent clonic movements of the mouth in crying and in rage. Besides these two affects, the impulse to suck was also being warded off. This constellation arose in the patient's childhood. He had a bullying brother whom he hated but toward whom he was excessively kind in order to have the love of his mother. As noticeable in this example, the rigidity of the muscles, while containing also the warded-off impulse, according to Reich, serves predominantly the purpose of defense in the same manner as the patient's habitual modes of behavior, i.e., his character. The above patient consistently displayed an emotional detachment. Reich thus equates character armor with muscle armor. One function that becomes regularly affected in childhood is that of breathing. To suppress sensations in the abdomen produced by anxiety, rage or sexual excitement, the diaphragm contracts as do the abdominal muscles and those of the pelvic floor. Because of the contraction of the diaphragm, there is a continuous state of partial inspiration, the patient being practically unable to carry out a complete expiration; but the muscles of the jaw, neck, chest, and extremities are also affected. He accents the patient's tendency to hold the pelvis backward as one of the major reasons for blocking adequate sexual function. Various different character neuroses have their respective motor status and behavior. The hysterical type is characterized by fluid, flirtatious, sexually provocative motility; the obsessional type, by generally rigid musculature as part of the need for control.

Two articles will now be added to this survey, which show the grave pathology which may ensue in response to severe physical and psychological restriction of motility. In both instances, the traumata were widespread and recurrent, involving many aspects of psychic life, but the motor trauma was certainly a prominent one.

Levy (1938, 1944) posits a motor drive in the same sense that there is an oral drive. Serious frustration or interference through space restriction or restraint can lead to repetitive movement, e.g., of a tic-like variety, both in animals and in infants, or to more generalized active and aggressive behavior disorders. He observed the child of two artists, who was confined in the bedroom from the age of two and who was not allowed to touch anything in the studio. Beginning at about that period he developed aggressive, destructive behavior. When seen at the age of four years, eight months, he attacked the therapist, threw things out of the window and tried to set fire to the playroom.

Greenacre (1944) describes a twenty-year-old girl who failed in her first year in college. The mother stated that the girl was bright but extraordinarily slow throughout her life. In the hospital as a baby she had nursed well; but at home the mother, who was depressed, labored for an hour and a half to get the infant to take the breast. From eighteen months to two years, she wore braces on her legs and aluminum mitts on her hands. The mother had been insistent upon the braces because she thought the child's legs were a little bowed and not properly developed. The baby hated the braces and would bang them against her crib. The child was "unbelievably stubborn." At nine, she would stand on the street corner looking skyward for a time before crossing the street. This seemed to have been a negativistic response to the mother's anxious admonitions to look in both directions before crossing. On one occasion, the child broke the stems of all the geraniums her mother had bought and on another occasion broke five panes out of sixteen of a newly bought antique sideboard. In adolescence the girl's posture was bad in spite of postural exercises and dancing classes. The mother seemed to be in a chronic psychosis which she covered up, driven by terror of her husband's abandonment of her. The author describes the patient's condition as "an angry ambulant catatonia." Treatment soon became a hopeless task because of detailed restrictive measures applied to the girl's visiting the psychiatrist. To avoid detection "and disgrace," she was to walk upstairs rather than to ride in the elevator in order to avoid the elevator operator, must never leave her name with the secretary when she telephoned the psychiatrist, and must pay the fee in cash so the psychiatrist's name would not appear on checks seen by the bank. The author comments that at first the girl lived in an almost complete physical strait-jacket, "consisting of a series of metal braces, and then an expanding psychic strait-jacket. . . . She was practically a synthetic person, [with] not only the external strings of control but the opposing forces within. . . . The major part of her energy was used in a series of blind attempts to separate herself" from the mother (p. 206).

In the subsequent discussion of the motor theme in the clinical setting, the quoted authors' formulations will be utilized along with proper emphasis on other phenomena mentioned in the early part of this paper, namely, self-assertion along with dependence on the environment, motor aggression, fear of motor retribution, (motor) imitative identification, the readiness to translate impulses into activity, predominance of motor language in communicating with the environment, certain affectomotor expressive patterns, and motivational closeness of skeletal motility to nearly every other physiological and psychological striving. Two additional factors should be emphasized. The qualities just described have a period of maximum intensity starting with the second year of life but still show considerable intensity up to the tenth year of life, even into late adolescence to a lesser degree. As repeatedly mentioned, they may reappear in a regressively intensified manner in danger and conflict situations. The second comment refers to the complexity of motivational systems. The infant is to a considerable degree motorically helpless and, therefore, depends on the parent for his needs. In addition, the child derives very important pleasures from motor contact and motor play with the parents. While these experiences are normal, the feeling of dependency increases if the child becomes afraid of abandonment as a result of traumatic experiences. The fear of abandonment in turn may arise or become intensified as a result of fear of retribution for the child's hostility or engaging in forbidden acts. The fear of abandonment, of retribution and of genital injury, and inhibition of motility may then contribute to the feeling of motor helplessness and thus lead back circularly to the increase of dependent needs. In the following, therefore, the motivational aspects of motor phenomena will be considered highly complex with one or another aspect dominating at a given time.

The Motor Theme in the Course of Treatment

It can be said in general that the motor topics appear in the course of therapy in two forms: (a) observable motor manifestations, including drawings, of the patient during the therapeutic hour, and (b) introspective data which include motor memories, dreams and fantasies. Technically the motor theme can in general be considered in three ways: (a) constructions that the therapist makes to himself on the basis of motor data but which he does not communicate to the patient, (b) interpretations, (c) motor experiences on the part of the patient which may in themselves have therapeutic implications.

Motor Theme in the Treatment of Infants

In infants, during the first two years of life, one can rely mainly on direct observation along with some scanty verbal statements and one's knowledge of the situation as imparted by the parents. Treatment can consist of careful handling of the child and limited manipulation of the situation.

It has been mentioned earlier that a painful or frightening experience may lead to a temporary cessation of a newly acquired function.

A ten-month-old active infant, an excellent crawler, turned over the baby carriage as a result of energetic shaking. The carriage's falling on him may have hurt him temporarily but it left no bruises. He was certainly frightened. Following this he stopped all locomotion for about two weeks.

A month and a half later, in the course of energetic crawling, for the first time he climbed up some stairs rapidly. At the fifth step he lost his balance and was about to fall but was caught by his father. The child was, of course, frightened and cried. Following this, he either avoided the stairs or, if brought to them, was reluctant to climb. The next day, with steady encouragement from the father standing at the foot of the stairs and the mother at the head, he finally made the climb, pausing and looking around after each step.

Anxiety and caution undoubtedly play a role in such phenomena. However, the cessation of function seems to be deep-seated and automatic, at least in some instances. This was certainly the case when the crawling stopped for two weeks. This type of mechanism may be the prototype of conversion hysteria, that is, of hysterical paralysis. This assumption is even more convincing in the next observation.[3]

While being swung around playfully by his arms by his father, an eighteen-month-old boy began to cry. His left arm then hung down limp as if paralyzed. He wanted to be lifted onto his father's shoulders and carried home. He moved his arm freely and adequately within an hour. Three months later, at twenty-one months of age, while his father playfully held him by his arms, he slumped down and, when lifted to his feet, cried, ran to his mother and said,

3 I am indebted to Dr. Lothar Gidro-Frank for the following observation.

"Daddy hurt me." He put a diaper around his left arm, similar to the sling that he had worn for about an hour on the previous occasion. The limpness of his left arm lasted all evening and was still present the next morning. Then he was shown a picture book and, as the pages were being turned, he started to turn them. In about ten minutes' time he used his arm freely.

It should be remarked in connection with this observation that motor play represents an important form of contact between parent and child. With the father, this contact usually has a rougher quality than with the mother and merges early into enjoyed aggression. It is interesting that on the first occasion, when hurt, the child turned to the father for help, on the second occasion he turned to the mother and complained about the father. At this point he was more attached to the mother and was in mild rivalry with the father. He must have taken the hurt as a form of motor retribution for the rivalry, the appearance of fear of motor retribution being characteristic of the motor phase of development. We shall return to the significance of the motor aspects of parent-child relationships in connection with some of the children and adults to be described later.

The next observation[4] is particularly impressive because alteration of the motor situation led not only to suspension of the recently acquired function but also to widespread neurotic symptomatology. All manifestations proved reversible with the correction of the motor situation but some showed a lag.

A nineteen-month-old girl who was in the "I do it myself" phase had busied herself with learning to walk for a few weeks prior to the parents' moving to their summer home. There was no change in her relationship with significant adult figures, but two older siblings went to camp. All those who took care of the child, the mother and the maid as well as the father, were present. The house to which they moved, however, was not only new to the child, but it had a floor so uneven that whenever she tried to continue her motor exercises, as she had done with vigor and pleasure in the past, she felt frustrated with every new step. She fell. She could not balance. These interferences with locomotion in turn set off a sequence of problems in the following order. She became anxious

[4] I am indebted to Dr. Peter Neubauer for this observation.

when the mother merely stepped into the next room, she stopped eating, and she developed sleeping disturbances.

The parents were perplexed by these changes until the child was taken to visit a friend who is a psychoanalyst (Dr. Leo A. Spiegel) and who located the cause of the problem. In his house the child found a perfectly even floor and soon resumed her locomotion with pleasure. As soon as she was able to move around freely her appetite came back and soon she ran and ate! It is interesting to note that it took about three or four days for her separation anxiety, and about two weeks for her sleeping disturbances to disappear.

Rhythmic "autoerotic" movements, e.g., rocking, within limits are normal in infants. Excessive and sustained activity of this type is seen particularly in institutional infants with lack of variety of stimulation, limitation of motility, and inadequate object relations (Mittelmann, 1954). The proper therapeutic procedure is adequate emotional care and freedom of movement.

The Motor Theme in the Treatment of Children

Play therapy is of course permeated by movement in general and action in particular. This is in harmony with the intensity of the motor urge, the readiness to carry impulse into action, to master problems through action, and, particularly, the tendency to communicate through motility—more or less up to about the tenth year of age.

Without systematic approach to technical innovations needed in the treatment of children, Freud made two significant contributions to the interpretation of their actions, which can be considered precursors of play therapy. When little Hans playfully butted his father's abdomen with his head, Freud (1909) interpreted it as an act of aggression. Watching a child play with a spool, making it disappear and reappear, Freud (1920a) interpreted it as an attempt on the child's part to turn the passive experience of separation from the mother into an active one and in that way master his anxiety. It may be remarked in passing that the child may attempt in five different motor ways—all of which may be of significance in evaluating his behavior—to master his anxiety: he may refrain from action, cling to the protective adult, escape from the danger situation, attack, handle the situation with exaggerated courage, or turn a passive experience into an active one. Hug-Helmuth (1921) used to

visit children in their homes and watch them play as part of the
therapeutic procedures. The regular use of play in the therapeutic
situation was developed by Melanie Klein (1932) through the
systematic introduction of appropriate toys into the treatment situation, which since then has become the standard procedure. It may
be added that the child naturally does not always use the toys and
not always symbolically; but they encourage or induce a readiness
in the child to express himself in the therapist's presence through
activity and thus create an atmosphere that facilitates verbal communication also.

The motor manifestations of the child in the play session may
reveal (a) motivational forces—i.e., impulses which may be of essentially motor or of tender, aggressive or sexual, etc., nature; these
impulses and attitudes may manifest themselves directly or through
compromise movements or defensive actions; (b) immediate affective
responses or compensatory actions—e.g., against anxiety, anger or
guilt—and thus represent "expressive" movements. In either case
(1) the motility can be "regressive," that is, show reappearance of
earlier types of patterns, for example, flapping of the hands or
crawling or "hitching." (2) These can be regularly recurrent motor
play patterns essentially in harmony with the child's maturational
stage. As such they can be within the estimated normal range of
intensity or of the restricted, inhibited or, on the contrary, the
excessively overactive type often combined with destructiveness.
Moreover, it is important whether these activities are directed toward
animate or inanimate objects or represent movement for movement's
sake like jumping around.

In addition to raising the question or interpreting why the child
does what he does, too vigorous or destructive behavior may require
verbal interdiction. In some situations children, with vehement
impulses carried into action and out of control, feel threatened by
their own impulses and by the anticipated consequences of their
actions and welcome appropriate controls which they themselves
cannot supply. If, in excited situations, interpretation, verbal interdiction and attempt at substitute activity are unsuccessful, some
therapists advocate actual temporary physical restraint by the therapist in a gentle but firm manner. Other therapists consider it preferable to interrupt the session. How much and what type of activity

the therapist allows depends in part on his own views and also on his own endurance.

In what follows, some not uncommon forms of play behavior will be described together with an examination of their motivational aspects and therapeutic utilization. The discussion will be rather schematic, as meaning and technique vary with the individual child and situation.

The Game of Hide-and-Go-Seek. The child usually plays this repetitively, asking the therapist to cover his face while the child hides behind some furniture or the drapes. At a signal from him, the therapist is supposed to find him, but only after looking for him for some time. Such scenes represent a threefold reversal of the anxious child's searching for his parent: in the game *he* is being looked for, the parent does the looking and the game is initiated by the child. It is an elaboration of the theme of turning a passive situation into an active one via the transference. The play may also represent a game of teasing or finding the hidden penis by the little girl who wants to possess one. The aim should be for the therapist to alert himself to the feeling of abandonment or other trends on the part of the child and, in case of increase in this play, he may inquire from the parent or, tentatively, from the child whether some relevant event has taken place. At times the game acquires additional features. The child may utilize the occasion of being found for a great deal of bodily contact or, instead of hiding behind the drapes or the furniture, he may slide under the couch, squeezing himself into a fairly narrow and almost totally dark place. On being "found" the child may ask the therapist to move or lift the furniture to enable him to get out. Such behavior has a masochistic quality. It further may contain the fantasy of being rescued by the therapist and it forces him into activity while the child is passive. Squeezing in under the couch may also be an enactment of the fantasy of supporting a heavy weight and of being subjected to sexual activity by the adult. If the physical contact is excessive on being "found," the therapist may raise the question of why the child does it and later, more as a comment in connection with the incident than as an interpretation, remark that the child feels lonely. The masochistic squeezing behavior has to wait for interpretation a long time and eventually it may be more effective to bring the topic in at an

appropriate juncture rather than interpreting the play behavior
directly.

Engaging in Some Recurrent Gymnastic Activity. The child may
jump from the play table or a chair with pride and pleasure, asking
for the therapist's praise and gradually increasing the height or
distance. This kind of activity, like the hide-and-seek, may acquire
additional functions. The child may ask the therapist to catch him
as he jumps or play wheelbarrow with him, the therapist holding
up his legs while the child walks on his hands. At still other times,
the child may cling to the therapist's shoulder and neck and ask him
to whirl him around. Other children may jump rope or turn cart-
wheels in the play session.

Such motor activities have common features with varying accents.
It has been mentioned earlier that during the motor phase of development the child derives considerable self-esteem and pride from
adequate motor accomplishment. Secondly, motor activity is one of
the most important bonds with the parent. Such repetitive behavior as described above is apt to be engaged in by children with
a shaky self-esteem from a variety of sources and, if the game includes
a great deal of bodily contact, by children with a feeling of loneliness.
Thus the motivational features are (a) pride in accomplishment
and, through that, raising self-esteem and self-image; (b) interpersonal contact via motor activity; (c) an exhibitionistic and seductive sexual element patterned on the relationship with the parents,
particularly with the father. The raising of the self-esteem via
accomplishment is strongest in the jumping. The interpersonal contact is about equal in the wheelbarrow and whirling. The exhibitionistic and seductive aspects are strongest in the wheelbarrow. In
all three there is strong motor pleasure. All of these appear, of
course, in a transference relationship. If such energetic motor activity
is combined with tomboyish behavior on the part of a girl, it indicates a desire to be the equal of boys and to possess the penis.
These activities or requests for them, at least for a long time, are
best used mainly for the purpose of constructions in the therapist's
mind and also as an index to the nature of the child's transference.
When and how much bodily contact and exhibitionistic, seductive
elements should be permitted is usually considered a difficult and
delicate problem. Avoidance is not always easy, because the child

does not see the seductive and exhibitionistic aspects. He is apt to be perplexed by or ignore verbal comments and take interdiction as a rejection and threat of abandonment.

Some children exhibit awkward motility in their younger years. It may be difficult to know whether this awkward and unskillful motility in a maturational period is essentially an anatomical-physiological process or is due to psychological reasons or a combination of both. The psychological element may be insecurity due to fear of abandonment; or the impairment of motility may be due to the attempt to prevent forbidden impulses from being carried into action; or the rigidity of movement may be caused by excessive, almost perverse genitalization of motor pleasure, e.g., walking with stiff legs as part of foot fetishism. Clumsy motility, whether psychogenic or maturational, in turn may increase the child's readiness for anxiety (Bender, 1940). Such awkward motility then contributes significantly to the child's lowered self-esteem which receives other contributions from feelings of being rejected and abandoned by the parents, guilt in connection with aggression and sexual activity, and in relation to the contempt of other children. The repetitive attempt at superior gymnastic performance in the play session may then represent a general and transference attempt to remedy this distressing clumsy motility and its unconscious consequences. As a remedial measure the child may want to excel in some aesthetic motor performance at school, e.g., dancing. This would remedy the feeling of inadequacy and the feeling of being rejected and looked down upon by the other children. However, the child may not be an exceptional dancer. This attempt at remedy then leads to new pain. The therapist then can comment with sympathy how badly the other children must make the patient feel when they ridicule her dancing but that the child must think very poorly of herself and that is why she so desperately wants to be one of the best dancers.

A child with similar needs may exhibit, both in the play session at times and in play with mates, an exaggeratedly affected motility. This may be the expression again of an exaggerated need for aesthetic behavior along with seductiveness aiming at remedying the rejection and scorn of the playmates. It can be pointed out to the child, however, that in practice such behavior actually aggravates the children's unfavorable reaction, strengthened by the child's over-dependent and self-effacing behavior.

The phenomena described may occur in the same child.

An eight-year-old girl, with symptoms of nightmares, fear of being alone, submissive behavior with other children and aggressive disobedience at home, manifested all the phenomena described, playing hide-and-go-seek with the therapist with masochistic motor elements, engaging in jumping off the play table, and periodically affected seductive motility in the play session and in the company of children. She also showed occasional regressive affectomotor patterns such as handflapping, rocking, and tossing her body around like a disturbed infant and, in circumscribed situations, tic-like head tossing and head turning. The discussion of these phenomena will follow.

The parents of this girl were divorced, and her mother had re-married. She lived with her father but visited her mother about once a week. She had been left alone a great deal in the past, and her father still threatened to do so as a disciplinary measure. She displayed very considerable fear of abandonment. She had a close and seductive relationship with her father, with constant bodily contact of a semigymnastic nature.

Affectomotor Patterns of a Regressive Type. Regressive affecto-motor patterns may be, for example, the child jumping up and down and shaking his hands several times, hour after hour. Or it may be transient: the child may get annoyed or sexually excited and flap his hands like a one-year-old infant, toss his whole body around or rock or bounce up and down. Immediate interpretation in the transient type is usually justified and its target is the con-stellation that evokes the affectomotor pattern, such as annoyance, excessive readiness to feel hurt or sexual excitement, along with the comment that the child behaves like a baby because he gets so upset or because he would like to get pleasure like a baby. In the repetitive type, interpretation is best postponed for a long time and then, apart from the babyish aspect, a complex affective and motiva-tional interrelation has to be elucidated recurrently. These may be: the child is usually excited and enjoys this excitement; he wants to increase his enjoyment by babyish jumping around; he obtains sexual excitement and expresses sexual excitement in this manner because he considers other forms, either masturbation or perversion, forbidden.

"Strongly marked affectomotor and vigorous rhythmic autoerotic patterns during pleasurable excitement in infancy may facilitate the development of perversion in two ways: (a) the infant executes rhythmic movements with resultant genital excitement, e.g., while fondling the adult's feet; (b) his interest in the adult's feet, and his identifying them with his own, is maintained at a high level because of the kinesthetic sensations during those movements" (Mittelmann, 1954).

Transient Ticlike Movements. Tic may be of two types: one, the *maladie des tics,* is close to compulsion neurosis and schizophrenia, often with involvement of the respiratory and phonative systems, very chronic, with a strong element of defense against threat to the body and self-preoccupation (narcissism) (Ferenczi, 1921; Mahler, 1944). It is very difficult to treat successfully. The other is the hysterical type of tic (Gerard, 1946), usually more limited in extent and well accessible to therapy. All chronic tics, like all psychosomatic disorders, are heavily overdetermined. The kind of tic discussed here is transient and occurs only in well-circumscribed constellations. Its dynamics and handling will be described here briefly in connection with the ticlike movements of the eight-year-old girl referred to above.

One day in the office the child executed two kinds of repetitive movements with her head and neck. One was a slow sideways movement of about ninety degrees to the right with rapid movement back to the midline. The other was a short sideways movement to the right as if she were tossing her hair out of her eyes. After about five minutes both types of movement stopped. Such movements occurred in the child only when she was brought to the office by the mother (as against the nursemaid or the father), and after a night spent at the mother's and stepfather's home. It had several determinants. At home the child slept in the same room with her father. When she stayed with her mother, she slept in a room by herself. She has always displayed sexual curiosity toward her stepfather who was indulgent when she only asked questions but who threw a wet towel at her and roughly ordered her out of the bathroom when she fingered the towel draped around his waist. The ticlike movements represented motor conflict solutions of the types which first appear in the motor phase of development. They were incomplete action:

looking only with the eyes and head instead of turning the whole body and involuntarily, without control, having renounced responsibility for the act; doing and undoing: turning the head and looking and then looking away, motivated by the desire to see the stepfather's genitals and the primal scene; a partial substitution of motor pleasure for sexual—seeing pleasure also takes place. The second determinant of the movements was fear of the stepfather. She looks around defensively, fearing that the stepfather might hit her. The short, hair-tossing movement partly meant getting the hair out of the eyes "to see." In part it was an expression of the fear of the stepfather. Both types of movement, particularly the ticlike movement, apart from the motor pleasure, also represented looking away from the stepfather whom she did not want to see, i.e., was rejecting.

Such transient, circumscribed ticlike movements, particularly if they occur well along in the treatment, are easily accessible to interpretive comment. The child accepted the therapist's suggestion that the tic was connected with the mentioned disturbances in her relationship with her stepfather. The discussion also led to further clarification of various aspects of her relationship with him.

Diminished Intensity of Movement and Activity. This can be either a transient or a chronic form of behavior. The transient form is usually due to some disappointment. After a while, the therapist, particularly if he has received some suggestive information from the parent, may say sympathetically that the child must be disappointed in this or that event. The chronic form may be due to shyness and anxiety or to masked depression or to schizoid withdrawal. Most important in the handling of it is a sympathetic patience over a long period and friendly, cooperative gestures on the part of the therapist to engage the child in some kind of activity. When the child begins to emerge from the subdued behavior, the direct discussion of the behavior can commence.

Overactive and Hyperkinetic Behavior. The transient form can be due to excess joy or anger or sexual excitement which the child tries to keep under control. In the transient form, the therapist can usually go to the question of motivation. The chronic form, often with a strong destructive admixture, is, as is generally known, one of the most complex problems and therapeutically stubborn. Often it is on an organic basis. It can be a late reaction to early restraint of motility instituted because of somatic or psychosomatic illness. The hyperactivity then may arise during the third year of life, as

in the case of a child with megacolon congenitum who was repeatedly operated on and spent most of his first three years of life
in bed. After he was allowed to go about, he developed hyperkinesis.
One of the most important attitudes on the part of the therapist in
situations like that is tolerant patience. While the treatment frequently fails, in many instances the child proves accessible.

The child just mentioned, who came for treatment in the sixth
year of his life, was at first hyperactive and destructive, running
around the room and playing very rough, attacking games with
the therapist. After several weeks, however, he started to ask the
therapist to do some of the things to him that he was doing to the
therapist—for example, "shoot" him. Then he asked the therapist to
sit down with him in a large box which he called the jail. As the
therapist sat down with him, for the first time the child looked at
him affectionately. He then asked the therapist to sit down on the
(covered) toilet seat, sat down next to him, and again looked at
him affectionately. Such episodes interrupted the hyperkinetic and
aggressive play. The hyperkinetic, aggressive behavior represented
in part a reaction and rebellion against the motor limitation in the
early years of life imposed in the hospital and at home and also a
rebellion against the mother's still-continued accent on physics and
enemas.

Next a case will be described to show the extensive effects of a
major motor trauma and to illustrate in detail how motor material
may be utilized interpretively in the progress of the treatment.

A child with infantile eczema and history of motor restraint.
This child was briefly presented, together with some of his drawings,
in a previous paper (Mittelmann, 1954) to illustrate some aspects
of the psychodynamics of motility. Here new material will be given,
with an accent on the crucial role played in the treatment by the
interpretive use of motor themes.

An eight-year-old boy suffered from infantile eczema, nightmares,
aggressive behavior and general restlessness in school and at home.
His eczema started when he was five months old. During his third
year, his hands were tied to the crib to prevent scratching, first
for several weeks in the hospital and later at home, by his mother,
for several months.

He drew the human figure at first without upper extremities,
manifesting a profound impairment of his body image. We may
add to this the construction that the tying down not only impaired
his body image as regards his upper extremities but also resulted

in the fear of abandonment, fear of starvation, fear of being attacked, and later an intensification of fear of genital injury, all while totally immobilized and in retribution for reactive rage. It may be remarked that restraint is more apt to be seriously traumatic if it is applied after the child has learned locomotion, in other words, during the motor phase of developmental organization— particularly if it is not followed by improvement in the eczema, as in this child.

The child's struggle against the impairment of his self-image and fear of immobilization was manifest in the two most frequently recurrent activities of the play sessions: drawing extensive, highly mobile and vehement battles between cowboys and Indians and playing baseball. A bat was fashioned by rolling up a sheet of stiff drawing paper and a ball by tying a piece into a knot, and he would pitch and bat in the playroom, running from "base" to "base." This game must have been played over a hundred times. In the course of excitement, particularly if the score was close, he would start slashing with the "bat" in the air or at a chair, thus showing a regressive affectomotor pattern fused with incomplete aggressive action. We may say that the child wanted to prove his intactness through motor performance superior to that of the therapist and that he expected to be cured by obtaining this motor ability from him as a gift.

The child said that he remembered his hands' being tied to the crib by the doctors and by his mother, and the evidence that he did remember was fairly convincing. The mother stated that recurrently since the actual event the child had made remarks about it to his brother, one and a half years younger, and to the mother herself. Thus several years before he had told his mother, "If you hadn't tied my hands down you would have gotten farther with me." Further, in the second hour, the child, talking freely, said, "When I was one year old, my hands were tied to the bed, and I went like this," he swung his arms forward and upward, "and threw off all the bandages, and they never dared put the bandages on again." This shows the tie-up between the child's fear of restraints and his fantasies, which in general had a self-magnifying character and usually contained a strong motor element, at times with a genital coloring as in the next fantasy: He said, "I have a white stallion in a corral. I ride him 'most every day. I can jump on his back while he's running without touching him with my hands." Once when he felt that his teacher was mistreating him or some other children, he said that he shot a man-sized arrow from his house to the school to frighten her.

In spite of a warm, friendly relationship with the therapist and great eagerness to come for treatment, for quite a period the child would not allow any questions as to the actuality of the fantasied stories he related, although, of course, he perfectly well knew that they had not happened. He protested equally against any suggestion that he was afraid of anything. Such an attitude of denial is not uncommon in children, but this child showed it to a greater degree than most. The first interpretation that he accepted and that could make a break in this defensive and compensatory position was to the following effect: "Your hands were once tied to the crib and you never want them to do it again, so you keep moving around and you keep fighting." When the child agreed with this, the formula was gradually extended to his stories. He was told that he had to make up the stories to show how strong he was so that he would not be tied down again. At first he objected mildly, then allowed the remark, and when he related the next fantasied story he responded to the therapist's questioning comment with a transient smile. In the course of months, the formula was gradually extended to include his feelings of helplessness and of threat in other areas.

An incident occurring at about this time in the treatment will now be added, showing that the child's motor behavior may give a confirmation of the interpretation given. This motor behavior may represent, in addition, a constructive development in the child's therapy. The mother reported the following remark from the child: "The doctor wants to find out whether I am an active child and then he will send me to someone else." When the therapist quoted the remark back to him, the child asked with a somewhat anxious facial expression, "Aren't you going to send me away?" The therapist replied, "No, I won't send you away. I will treat you and try to help you," and then added, "I guess you want to be very active to make up for the trouble you had because your hands were tied down; and sometimes you get excited because you want to be very active and you're afraid that I don't like it and I will send you away." The child listened to this with a pleased facial expression and said, "That's right. I want to do things," and then proceeded to give to his activity a direction which had not occurred in the sessions before. He got up on the low play table and jumped off a few times with obvious pleasure and feeling of accomplishment. Then he put a chair on top of the table and jumped from that. He raised the platform still higher and then said playfully, "I got wings also, so I can jump very well." He took a towel, put it around his shoulders and jumped with great enjoyment mingled with some anxiety. In this manner, he proceeded not only to confirm in motor language the interpretation, but also to master his anxiety through playful, semireal fantasy instead of through such grandiose stories as jumping on the back of a running stallion. Following this incident the grandiose fantasies stopped.

The child's fear that he would be sent away by the therapist because of overactivity illustrates the role of motility in the circular sequence of reactions between anxiety and aggression. Thus, if he felt the teacher was mistreating him, he engaged in violent fantasies of killing her. This resulted in the fear of counterattack which in turn maintained his anxiety. The resultant overactivity led to punishment, this in turn aroused his anxiety which in turn resulted in defensive and compensatory overactivity.

In the account so far given the motor problem and its working through were relatively simple, although with wide ramifications and crucial therapeutic effect. A more intricate aspect of the motor theme will be touched on here briefly, which was taken up very cautiously and much later, in the second year of the treatment.

Once the child remarked, with vehemence and anxiety, "If they took me to the hospital and if the doctors put me to sleep and operated on me and took away all my sores [he called his eczema "sores"] even if they took it away from my back, I would scratch it back again." The child was not psychotic, but the remark is a premonition that under certain circumstances he could develop in that direction. He needed the eczema because (1) it was "his" and he did not want to lose it passively, because it was a symbol of his being master in his own house; and (2) scratching meant for him freedom of movement and, therefore, self-determination. Thus the possession of the eczema and the relief of itching represented to him the relief of all other needs on his own, a guarantee against being overwhelmed, against starvation, against abandonment, and against genital injury. This is the kind of orientation that in some adults leads to a psychotic reaction when a psychosomatic disorder is suddenly removed, e.g., by hypnosis. The theme was doubly significant. First this anxiety and its paradoxical mastery maintained the child's readiness to scratch and thus renew the eczema; secondly the whole nature of thinking involved had an autistic quality and represented a psychotic potential. The topic aroused anxiety because the child's first reaction to interpretive efforts was the fear that the therapist was joining the camp of the enemy doctors. But cautiously, bit by bit, this fear could be analyzed and the topic worked through. The motor anxiety was fused among others with two main topics: the mistrust of the mother who had "allowed the doctors and nurses" to tie the child's hands and then continued to do so herself and, on that pattern, mistrust of the whole world; secondly fear of genital injury, of castration. At about the age of five, when he masturbated, his eczema became localized mainly in the genital region. His nurse, according to information obtained from the mother, told him that his penis would fall off if he did not stop. The material illustrates strikingly that castration fear, like any other fear, has different qualities depending on its other components and antecedents, and these differences should be determined with therapeutic advantage. In this child these fears were cutaneous and passive motor.

The accent in this presentation was on the motor theme but, needless to say, the child's other internal and external problems— separation and divorce of the parents—were dealt with in the treatment.

Another paradoxical orientation was revealed in the child's recurrent nightmares at one point in the treatment when he was temporarily placed in a boarding school by the family, while he also continued treatment. He dreamed that an ugly woman with iron claws, patterned on the housemother, killed children and then scratched them back to life. In these dreams the child was identifying with the aggressor (scratching), but also in them cessation of motion equals death, scratching equals life.

He made steady progress in his treatment with the customary fluctuations in his symptomatology. During the third year of treatment, his mother, in spite of her own psychotherapy, developed a schizophrenic psychosis. The child was placed in a boarding school, but his contact with the therapist continued. His father remarried six months later a warm, motherly woman, and the patient and his brother went to live with them. The treatment was terminated in another year.

A motor trauma (restraint) played a significant role in the history and structure of this child's neurosis. He expressed many pertinent transference reactions and constructive new developments through motility. Other past and current traumatic situations, before and after the main motor trauma, were dealt with, but there is little doubt that attention to the motor aspects contributed considerably to the success of the treatment. The first significant interpretation which the child accepted and which broke through his defenses was based on the motor trauma. A more intricate and potentially psychotic motor theme was cautiously worked out in a later phase of the treatment. The restraint occurring during the motor phase of developmental organization impaired his body image and resulted in fears of starvation, abandonment, of being overwhelmed and castrated—all this while immobilized and helpless in retribution for reactive rage.

Motor Themes in the Treatment of Adults

In the adult, the following further developments take place in motor phenomena and organization: (1) Closer tie-up takes place between genitality and motility during puberty. (2) There is a further evolution of motor control both as regards skill and as regards keeping impulses from being carried into action. (3) The motor urge manifests itself more periodically than in childhood or even adolescence. For this reason, in neurotic adult patients—except when special devices are used for the purpose—objective motor manifestations are rarer than in children, but there may be a wealth of introspective motor material (history, memories, dreams).

In some patients motor dreams can be impressive. An adult dreamed the night before his initial interview that he was carrying in his arms a limp figure, his own self, into a restaurant where he had to make this figure sit up and feed it, otherwise it would be dead. Here postural control and being fed are equated with survival. This same patient dreamed at significant turning points in his analysis that a man had trouble walking up a long flight of stairs. On one occasion this man was on crutches because his legs were paralyzed, fell, and the patient rushed to his aid. The dream illustrates, on the pattern of the great task of the child's learning to walk upstairs, the consistent equating of incapacity and helplessness with motor paralysis as well as the idea of help obtained from a supporting figure, including the analyst, in terms of motor help.

The observable motor manifestations will be presented in connection with two cases. The motor data are utilized therapeutically for interpretation.

A patient with tremor of the hands, some awkwardness, and motor anxieties in childhood and motor rivalry with the father. One of the symptoms of a medical student who entered analysis was tremor of the hands appearing when he had to perform some fine motor action in the presence of others with "controlled violence," for example, puncturing a vein. His other symptoms were explosive temper and some marginal compulsive symptoms, e.g., not undertaking anything new on Fridays. The patient mentioned his tremor early in the analysis but only passingly. It gradually turned out that nearly every one of his significant problems contributed to and, in reverse, were dynamically colored by this symptom. The problems were defended against and their investigation limited by his avoidance of situations which elicited the tremor. The implication was, "If I have no tremor I have no problems."

The patient's first memory was that of walking, at about the age of two, up subway stairs with pleasure and pride, while his father held his hand. It has been mentioned several times in this paper that motor accomplishment is an important source of pride in infancy and parental help in it an important sign of love and support.

We will come back later to the reason for the strong affective accent on this memory. At the age of three and a half, while playing roughly with his ten-month-old sister's crib, he knocked it over and she fell out. She later developed a long hooked nose, and the patient was blamed by his parents for having caused it. It has been mentioned earlier in the paper that in the motor phase of development lively motility easily merges into aggression. The kind of blame mentioned here has a tendency to attach the same kind of guilt to motility in general as is apt to get attached to aggression. The guilt, by projection, increases the hostility toward objects of the motility as it did in the case of this patient toward his sister. At about the age of four, the patient noticed that his father had a tremor, for example, when he poured cocktails, and that one of his father's fingers was amputated. Both of these observations led to impairment of the self-image via imitative motor identification, and intensified his fear of motor retribution and castration.

The patient had motor problems beginning at least at the age of four and up through his late adolescence. He avoided crossing plank bridges for fear of falling and, if the necessity arose, either avoided going with his playmates or met them at the agreed-upon place under some excuse and took a detour. He was afraid of diving, but forced himself to do so in late puberty to show girls how "manly" he was.

When the patient was about seven years old, most of his father's rivalry with him took place in the field of motor activity. The patient had difficulty catching balls, and the father made a special point of playing catch with him. The mother preferred the patient to the sister and even to the father. When they came home after playing, the father made a special point of boasting of his own excellence and of telling the mother that the patient had not performed particularly well. This humiliated and vexed the patient. The patient's first indication of something like a coarse tremor occurred while he was playing catch with boys. In his excitement, reaching out while running, his arms were shaking coarsely. On the pattern discussed in the children's section, the patient's poor motor skill and motor anxieties as a child were probably determined by both maturational and psychogenic factors, the latter comprising his conflict over his aggression toward his sister and his rivalry with his father. He also had refractive errors of the eyes although at the time he required no glasses. In any case, these motor problems increased the threat to his self-image and his vulnerability. The accent on his first motor memory—walking up subway stairs with·pride—was an attempt to restore his preoedipal, supportive, self-esteem-building relationship with his father.

The tendency to coarse tremor increased after the patient started to masturbate. The finer tremor started after he became a medical student when he had to puncture veins, perform spinal taps or prick fingers to obtain blood.

The patient had wide, flowing gestures, and his hands constantly accompanied his speech, regardless of whether he lay on the couch or sat up. This represented the maintenance of the regressive tendency for motor communication with the environment, motivated by his fear of not being adequately understood and appreciated. Genetically allied to this was another symptom of the patient, namely, the tendency to action in temper outbursts. For instance, if a car passed his "unfairly" on the road, he would get angry and would even drive beyond his turn-off to corner the other car and scold the driver. He thus carried impulse into action along with an overevaluation of motor reality, as if he had not won out over his father unless he actually beat him at the ball game.

The various motor themes were recurrently touched upon in the course of the treatment. When the concentrated and sustained analysis of the tremor finally took place—one of the most revealing periods of the treatment—the following meanings of the tremor (which could be classified partly as a conversion, partly as an anxiety symptom) became evident. It had a primitive, regressive element, inasmuch as in young children a somewhat atactic coarse type of tremor is not uncommon and infants regularly show tremor while crying. Dynamically it represented motor aggression toward his sister, rivalry and aggression toward his father, the attempt to establish his self-esteem and to surpass his father, identification with the weaknesses of his father (tremor), guilt over his sexual activity, fear of retribution for aggression, and guilt, exposure and disgrace. The tremor and the attendant feelings about it were integrally connected with current reactions. For example, after the patient's explosions with his wife or with other people, his tremor increased, the tremor itself being a symbol of his vulnerability and of the various activities about which he felt guilty. This in turn made him more sensitive and more defensive, and ready for future explosions. His fear of failure and his need to perform excellently, rooted partly in his past motor fears and motor awkwardness, increased both his need to perform well before his professors as well as his fear of failure. This again became symbolized in his tremor and the presence of his tremor in turn confirmed his feeling of vulnerability and inadequacy. It further expressed a conflict about wanting and not wanting to act, being brought about by a tension of both agonist and antagonist muscles.

In the patient just described, the traumatic motor situation consisted mainly in rivalry with the father. One may call this the oedipal type of motor constellation. Here another type of constellation will be described in which anxiety on the part of women, particularly the mother, leads to limitation of motility and acts as an anxiety-inducing, self-depreciating agent along with either rebellion over the restriction or a submissive, compliant behavior. The restriction and the submissiveness may be accented by the mother's perfectionistic and compulsive requirement that the child always be neat.

A patient with anxious maternal limitation of motility in childhood and with infantile affectomotor patterns. According to the memory of a thirty-year-old patient, his freedom of movement was restricted by his mother as far back as he could remember, beginning at least at the age of two and a half and lasting to the middle of his elementary-school years. The mother was afraid that he would hurt himself while crossing the street or when he climbed and constantly cautioned him, would not allow him to roller skate or ride a bicycle. In addition, she expected him always to be neat and not soil his clothes, particularly if they went visiting. This manner of handling formed one of the most important sources of the patient's anxieties, his image of vulnerability of himself along with feelings of rebellion, guilt, and fear of retribution and abandonment. At a somewhat later period of development, this restriction and vulnerability were present apart from other sources in the area of genital function as well. Both the locomotor and the genital anxiety is expressed in the patient's dream that follows, along with probably more primitive motor and infantile experiences. This dream occurred not long after the patient's wife gave birth to their first child.

"I am visiting the hospital and my baby has a deformity, a very heavy third leg, like a piano stool. Somebody points out to me that the baby has another kind of deformity, namely, some anomaly at the junction between the toes and the leg, and he would not be able to walk. I reply that it isn't that kind of deformity and the baby will be able to walk."

Apart from the motor, genital, and transference aspects (the man who points out the deformity to the patient), the dream expresses the patient's inordinate optimism, which originated from the patient's utilizing his dependence on his mother and his submissiveness to cover up his anxieties and his rebellion. This optimism was one of the defensive and restitutive elements that had to be broken through in the analysis, particularly in the beginning and recurrently later. Interestingly, it also had a motor concomitant. When the patient would get enthusiastically excited about something he would gesticulate with both hands symmetrically in a manner resembling the hand-waving of young children. After a while this connection was pointed out to the patient, but the gesture kept recurring until the patient's naive optimism disappeared.

Motility in the Treatment of Schizophrenics

Motor symptoms in schizophrenia are apt to be dramatic both in children and in adults, particularly with catatonic features in the latter. Schizophrenic motility is a complex problem and many elements in it may be of a maturational nature in children (Bender, 1940) and of primary pathophysiological nature in adults. The interweaving of primitive regressive elements with fantasy elaborations and symbolic action is illustrated by an eight-year-old child. In one of his favorite fantasies he was a bird waving his arms as if they were wings. The more archaic element in this fantasy probably was the tendency to hand-flapping of normal one-year-olds (Mittelmann, 1954), which is frequently found in older schizophrenic children. Schizophrenics of early adulthood often behave in a general motor manner characteristic of some children in the play sessions. They get up, walk around, lie down on the couch, walk around again. Three brief illustrations will be given of the utilization of motor material in the treatment of schizophrenics.

New Motor Phenomena in Borderline Patients. The sudden appearance of dramatic postures or gestures in a borderline patient who is otherwise not given to dramatic behavior should be considered indicative of a threatening open psychotic break, which with adequate therapeutic measures may be averted.

A twenty-five-year-old woman with predominant symptoms of anxiety and obsessional thoughts but with some borderline manifestations was jilted by her boy friend. In the next hour she stood in the corner of the office, facing away from the analyst with her head bowed. She said that the situation was too painful to face and talk about. When after kind urging she sat down, her expression was distant and her face immobile. With a combination of urgent reassurance by the therapist and a discussion of her reaction to the event, it was possible to pull her out of this psychological state.

Affective and Expressive Motility in Schizophrenics. A twenty-one-year-old schizophrenic was catatonic at periods in that he was mute, also undressed himself, and engaged in stereotyped gestures. At other periods he was communicative but defensive. He revealed then a little of his fantasies, which were of a religious and grandiose nature, but argued in the main that he was well and ought to be allowed to leave the hospital. At such periods three types of motor phenomena occurred. He suddenly felt weak all over and had to lie down on the bed. Or he started to walk around the room and asked the interviewer to come with him out on the balcony or into the corridor. These two phenomena occurred in a similar constellation, namely when in the course of the discussion the interviewer stood his ground that the patient was not well and that he ought not leave the hospital. The patient's reaction to this could be constructed as one of feeling cornered, disappointed, and thwarted. His reaction was then further either one of helplessness when he suddenly felt weak all over, or a dramatization of the idea of escape from the situation. In the first instance also the aggression felt toward the interviewer became directed toward himself; in the second it manifested itself in an impulsive increase of his motor urge. These motor phenomena could be taken as good indications of the patient's reactions and could be utilized within limits in communicating with him. The same patient at times engaged in motor communication with the interviewer when he was disinclined to express a verbal agreement. In discussing the patient's disinclination to accept his need for help the interviewer quoted a talmudic saying to the effect that if one walks on the street convinced that one is sober but three people say that one is drunk, one ought to go home and lie down. The patient grinned and lay down on the bed.

Symbolic Motility in Contacting Inaccessible Psychotics. Motility plays a large role in most of the established psychotherapies of uncommunicative schizophrenics. Frieda Fromm-Reichmann (1943) recommends that at times in treating mute, verbally unresponsive catatonics, the therapist may engage in the same motor activities as the patient—e.g., sit on the floor and make the same gestures—to make contact with the patient. Or he may sit on the desk where the patient has settled in a threatening posture to show that he is unafraid. In Rosen's technique (1953), proper selection of a gesture of the patient for questioning and comment may establish contact with an otherwise inaccessible patient. The following example illustrates such an incident.

After about five minutes of purely verbal attempts to contact a hallucinating, disconnected, twenty-seven-year-old woman patient, the patient put her hand in front of her mouth. She was then asked, "Why did you do that?" For the first time a relevant response occurred. "To prevent the bad smell from coming out." The next

question was, "Where do the bad smells come from?" The patient
answered in motor language, pointing to her anus. With this exchange, essentially coherent, relevant verbal communication was
established.

SUMMARY AND CONCLUSIONS

Skeletal motility is a significant means of pleasure seeking and of
reality testing and integration throughout life. It is one of the dominant functions in these areas, beginning with the second year of life,
for several years. This period is further characterized by increase in
self-assertion along with continuation of dependence on the environment, increase in motor aggression, imitative identification, predominantly motor communication with the environment, readiness
to translate impulses into action, and certain affectomotor (expressive) patterns. In addition to being a function in its own right,
skeletal motility is significantly connected with all other physiological and psychological needs and impulses, particularly with self-
evaluation and self-determination. Skeletal motility with its psychological concomitants has its characteristic vicissitudes. Among these
are motor anxiety—for example, fear of high places—anxiety and
rage in response to restriction, ready inhibition of new skills in
response to fear and pain and disapproval and, as a result, fear of
motor retribution and abandonment, and guilt and self-injury. Conflict solutions are: incomplete (and primitive symbolic) action, reaction formation, increase or diminution in motility, and regressive
action.

Motility is one of the significant areas of function to be systemati-
cally explored in therapy, like orality or genitality. Its disturbances
may arise either from traumata directed at the motor function directly or through the expression of other motivational conflicts in
the motor area. The utilization of motor data, comprising observable
manifestations, motor memories, and dreams, contributes to the
effectiveness of the treatment of both children and adults. While in
children as a rule the observable manifestations predominate, in most
adults the predominantly verbal communication and interpretation
of these data are effective. With some patients, their motor behavior,
gestures, symptoms, motor elements in dreams and fantasies, and
motor memories need to be interpreted and carefully worked through

for full therapeutic effectiveness of the analysis. In disturbed schizophrenics the interpretive utilization of symbolic action is indispensable.

The most frequent situations to be dealt with in therapy are: (1) restriction of freedom of motility; (2) awkward motility. Restriction of freedom of motility in infancy may be based on external conditions or considerations of health and may have massive psychological consequences. Restriction in childhood, particularly in boys, may be a result of rivalry with or fear of parents, particularly the father, or may result from (mostly) the mother's anxiety over possible injury to the child. In either case the resultant disturbance may have a strong genital element (castration). Awkward motility usually is a consequence of a mixture of congenital and psychological factors and results in a disturbance of self-evaluation. Motor traumata may have a crucial significance in the development of neurosis and psychosis.

BIBLIOGRAPHY

Abraham, K. (1913), A Constitutional Basis of Locomotor Anxiety. *Selected Papers on Psycho-Analysis*. London: Hogarth Press, 1927.

Bally, G. (1945), *Vom Ursprung und von den Grenzen der Freiheit*. Basel: Schwabe.

Bender, L. (1940), The Psychology of Children Suffering from Organic Disturbances of the Cerebellum. *Am. J. Orthopsychiat.*, X.

Breuer, J., and Freud, S. (1895), *Studies in Hysteria*. New York and Washington: Nervous & Mental Disease Publishing Co., 1936.

Buxbaum, E. (1954), Technique of Child Therapy: A Critical Evaluation. *This Annual*, X.

Deutsch, F. (1952), Analytic Posturology. *Psa. Quart.*, XXI.

Eissler, K. R. (1943), Limitations to the Psychotherapy of Schizophrenia. *Psychiatry*, VI.

Erikson, E. H. (1940), Studies in the Interpretation of Play: Clinical Observation of Play Disruption in Young Children. *Gen. Psychol. Mon.*, XXII.

—— (1950), *Childhood and Society*. New York: Norton.

Fenichel, O. (1939), *Problems of Psychoanalytic Technique*. New York: Psychoanalytic Quarterly, Inc.

—— (1945), *The Psychoanalytic Theory of Neurosis*. New York: Norton.

Ferenczi, S. (1913), A Transitory Symptom: The Position During Treatment. *Further Contributions to the Theory and Technique of Psycho-Analysis*. London: Hogarth Press, 1950.

—— (1914a), Embarrassed Hands. *Further Contributions to the Theory and Technique of Psycho-Analysis*. London: Hogarth Press, 1950.

—— (1914b), Rubbing the Eyes as a Substitute for Onanism. *Further Contributions to the Theory and Technique of Psycho-Analysis*. London: Hogarth Press, 1950.

—— (1914c), Sensations of Giddiness at the End of the Psycho-Analytic Session. *Further Contributions to the Theory and Technique of Psycho-Analysis*. London: Hogarth Press, 1950.

—— (1919a), The Phenomena of Hysterical Materialization. *Further Contributions to the Theory and Technique of Psycho-Analysis*. London: Hogarth Press, 1950.

—— (1919b), Thinking and Muscle Innervation. *Further Contributions to the Theory and Technique of Psycho-Analysis.* London: Hogarth Press, 1950.

—— (1921), Psychoanalytic Observations on Tic. *Further Contributions to the Theory and Technique of Psycho-Analysis.* London: Hogarth Press, 1950.

Freud, A. (1936), *The Ego and the Mechanisms of Defence.* New York: International Universities Press, 1946.

—— and Burlingham, D. T. (1944), *Infants Without Families.* New York: International Universities Press.

Freud, S. (1896), Further Remarks on the Defence Neuro-Psychoses. *Collected Papers,* I. London: Hogarth Press, 1946.

—— (1905), Three Essays on the Theory of Sexuality. *Standard Edition,* VII. London: Hogarth Press, 1953.

—— (1909), Analysis of a Phobia in a Five-Year-Old Boy. *Standard Edition,* X. London: Hogarth Press, 1955.

—— (1915), Instincts and Their Vicissitudes. *Collected Papers,* IV. London: Hogarth Press, 1925.

—— (1920a), Beyond the Pleasure Principle. *Standard Edition,* XVIII. London: Hogarth Press, 1955.

—— (1920b), *A General Introduction to Psychoanalysis.* New York. Liveright, 1935.

—— (1923), *The Ego and the Id.* London: Hogarth Press, 1927.

—— (1926), *The Problem of Anxiety.* New York: Norton, 1936.

Fries, M. E., and Woolf, P. J. (1953), Some Hypotheses on the Role of the Congenital Activity Type in Personality Development. *This Annual,* VIII.

Fromm-Reichmann, F. (1943), Psychoanalytic Psychotherapy with Psychotics. *Psychiatry,* VI.

Gerard, M. W. (1946), The Psychogenic Tic in Ego Development. *This Annual,* II.

Gorer, G. (1949), *The People of Great Russia.* London: Cresset Press.

Gostinsky, E. (1951), A Clinical Contribution to the Analysis of Gestures. *Int. J. Psa.* XXXII.

Greenacre, P. (1944), Infant Reactions to Restraint: Problems in the Fate of Infantile Aggression. *Am. J. Orthopsychiat.,* XIV.

Hartmann, H.; Kris, E.; Loewenstein, R. M. (1949), Notes on the Theory of Aggression. *This Annual,* III/IV.

Homburger-Erikson, E. (1937), Configurations in Play—Clinical Notes. *Psa. Quart.,* VI.

Hug-Hellmuth, H. v. (1921), Zur Technik der Kinderanalyse. *Int. Ztschr. Psa.,* VII.

Jacobson, E. (1929), *Progressive Relaxation.* Chicago: University of Chicago Press.

Kardiner, A. (1932), *The Bio-Analysis of the Epileptic Reaction.* Albany, N. Y.: Psychoanalytic Quarterly Press.

—— and Spiegel, H. (1947), *War Stress and Neurotic Illness.* New York: Paul B. Hoeber.

Klein, M. (1932), *The Psycho-Analysis of Children.* London: Hogarth Press.

Kraus, H. (1949), *Principles and Practice of Therapeutic Exercises.* Springfield, Ill.: Chas. C. Thomas.

Kris, E. (1951), Ego Psychology and Interpretation in Psychoanalytic Therapy. *Psa. Quart.,* XX.

Levy, D. M. (1938), On Instinct-Satiation: An Experiment on Pecking Behavior of Chickens. *J. Gen. Psychol.,* XVIII.

—— (1944), On the Problem of Movement Restraint: Tics, Stereotyped Movements, Hyperactivity. *Am. J. Orthopsychiat.,* XIV.

Mahler, M. S. (1944), Tics and Impulsions in Children: A Study of Motility. *Psa. Quart.,* XIII.

Mead, M. (1954), The Swaddling Hypothesis: Its Reception. *Am. Anthropol.,* LVI.

Mittelmann, B. (1945), Analysis of Patients with Acute Symptoms. *Psa. Rev.,* XXXII.

—— (1954), Motility in Infants, Children, and Adults: Patterning and Psychodynamics. *This Annual,* IX.

—— (1955), Motor Patterns and Genital Behavior: Fetishism. *This Annual,* X.

Peller, L. E. (1954), Libidinal Phases, Ego Development, and Play. *This Annual,* IX.
Piaget, J. (1951), *Play, Dreams and Imitation in Childhood.* New York: Norton.
Reich, W. (1933), *Character-Analysis.* New York: Orgone Institute Press, 1949.
—— (1942), *The Function of the Orgasm.* New York: Orgone Institute Press.
Rosen, J. N. (1953), *Selected Papers.* New York: Grune & Stratton.
Sadger, I. (1912), Haut-, Schleimhaut,- und Muskelerotik. *Jahrb. Psa. & psychopathol. Forsch.,* III.
Waelder, R. (1932), The Psychoanalytic Theory of Play. *Psa. Quart.,* II.

A NEUROSIS IN ADOLESCENCE[1]

NATHAN N. ROOT, M.D. (New York)

This communication concerns a girl who became ill with an anxiety hysteria and masochistic depressive character neurosis, which was triggered by her marriage at the age of seventeen years. The data from this case are presented because they may be of interest and because few detailed accounts of analytic case material from the period of adolescence have been reported (whether obtained directly in work with adolescent patients or indirectly from work with adults).

Freud (1932) wrote: "Pathology, as you know, has always assisted us, by isolation and exaggeration, in making recognizable things which would normally remain hidden." In the present instance, the unfortunate fact of her mother's death caused this patient to experience an adolescence that is not typical. But the loss of her mother caused the analytic process to light up most sharply the need for this patient to do the work of mourning, a need which she unconsciously kept trying to deny. It then became an easy step from this case to picture the maturational progress during adolescence, which is one of detachment from infantile libidinal positions, as proceeding alongside the path of a mourning process.

The patient began to suffer from neurotic symptoms when she was seventeen, and had been married one month to a fellow student at college. She started analysis nearly two years later, at nineteen. By this time, she was suffering keenly. She complained mainly of recurring feelings of "sickness" and nausea. She also had constant feelings of fatigue, depression, and general anxiety. In addition, she exhibited marked inhibition, indecision, and a sense of inadequacy. Indeed, she exhibited her suffering. She underscored her shortcomings, obviously and in many subtle ways. Her demeanor was timid,

[1] Contribution to the Panel on Adolescence held at the Annual Meeting of the American Psychoanalytic Association in Chicago on May 10, 1957.

shy, hesitant. Her look was a subdued, gentle but anxious cry for help. Despite being tall and good-looking, she gave the impression of a naive little girl trying to be grownup, almost as if in her mother's clothes.

Consciously associated with the onset of the illness were two episodes. The one was a first visit to her husband's family two months after marriage. Because the father-in-law was a bigoted, harsh old man, and not well, it was understood among the family that the fact of a religious difference would be withheld from him. The patient agreed but felt ashamed and guilty toward him. She had a severe attack of nausea with vomiting at this time.

The other episode occurred several weeks later back at college. She was working at a press which "got stuck." She became "very shaky" without any conscious reason (an anxiety attack). She was assigned another task, but soon had to quit and in the privacy of the ladies' room had an outburst of uncontrollable weeping.

The use of terms like feeling "sick" and feeling "good" or "bad" served to allow expression of urges and affects disguised by the non-specificity of generalization and condensation. Generalization and condensation gave important aid to the patient's denial and repression of both superego reactions and also id forces. By focusing on the total immersion into a nonspecific emotional state, the patient could avoid dealing with important components and connections. The term "sickness" she could not clarify. She used it in the way hospital patients often complain of "having the misery" (like malaise).

It was learned that the patient had repressed the fact that each menses was accompanied by her main symptoms ("sickness," nausea, fatigue, depression, and anxiety), though they were not limited to the time of the menses. Repression here was aided by distraction in that the patient's attention fixed on the one difference, namely, that menstruation was also accompanied by abdominal cramps, often of severe degree.

The lifting of repression revealed several important facts about the onset of the neurosis. During the visit to her in-laws, the patient awoke one morning with the severe nausea already mentioned and the simultaneous utterly dismaying conviction: "My God, I'm pregnant!" A month before this, and one month after her wedding, she had had her first noticeable bout of nausea, less severe in degree, accompanied by a less convincing thought of being pregnant. Even during the relatively happy courtship period, she had some mild nausea, attributed by her to sinusitis. Also repressed were her reactions to learning that her husband had, about half a year earlier, impregnated a girl at college, resulting in an abortion. It was two months after the patient first knew of this that they became engaged. The wedding was three months later. Moreover, as soon as she had set the date, she became worried that she could not have children because of an operation when she was eleven years old. She felt compelled to consult her physician, who reassured her that she had had only one ovary removed, that it had been a benign cyst, and that she should have no difficulty in having children.

One unrepressed event occurred in the prodromal period of the neurosis. During her first intercourse she bled a good deal, alarming her husband. She was surprised because she had been certain that she had no hymen after all her active bicycling and horseback riding. Her husband insisted on consulting a doctor. When the doctor said that nothing was wrong, the patient felt a strong sense of relief even though she had been unaware of any prior anxiety.

Thus it is clear that the patient had a strong desire to have a child, which became increasingly urgent, especially when she was married. She had long been aware of her intense wish for children, but in the future, when the practical details could be arranged. She was not conscious of the powerful urgency of her wish for the child right now, at this moment as it were, nor of the hungry demand she felt toward her husband. She was also unaware of her great fear of pregnancy. The wish was expressed unconsciously by the signs which meant pregnancy for the patient, namely, feeling sick and nauseated. To feel very sick and nauseated meant to be very much pregnant.

At the same time, getting sick and nauseated also meant menstruating to the patient. She usually spoke of the menses as "getting sick." She noticed her first menstrual bleeding at the age of ten and a half years, soon after rough-housing with her father. She was so convinced of having suffered an injury that she was surprised and annoyed when her father calmly told her that it was menstruation. Then she became excited and felt like talking about it, but no one else was at home but her father, and she felt quite frustrated. She began to suffer with every period the symptoms already mentioned. In addition, she

developed between-period cramps, until oöphorectomy at eleven relieved her of this symptom. In the analysis she associated to every
menses with thoughts and feelings of losing and insufficiency. After
her surgery, she believed that her menstrual life and the number of
children she could have had been cut in half. In her opinion, each
ovary had a limited number of possible babies. Thus each menses
reduced the number by one. In short, each menstrual period was
for the patient an aborted pregnancy which was experienced physically in the symptoms of "sickness" and nausea, and emotionally as
frustration, anxiety and sadness. Concomitant aggressive feelings
were denied, repressed, displaced, or turned against the self.

To understand the multideterminants of the symptomatology, it
is necessary to review her earlier life history. Less than two months
before the onset of menstruation, the patient suffered her greatest
tragedy. Her mother was instantaneously killed in an auto accident.
Her father, who was driving, received only mild injuries. The fault
was proved in court to be that of the other driver, a woman, who
paid damages to all three members of the family—the patient, a
brother two years older, and her father. At the time of the accident,
the patient was awakened by the noise of many people in the house
during the night. The two children were told their mother was in
the hospital because of an accident. It was a time of fear, suspicion,
disbelief and many fantasies. The truth came out in the open the
following day. It was easy for the mood of doubt and disbelief to
continue, which aided her propensity for denial. Her mourning over
the loss of her mother was incomplete, and in a repressed form was
soon intertwined with the sense of loss associated with the menses.
When she yearned to talk about the onset of menstruation only a
few weeks later, she thought only of the family maid who had her
day off. The patient had felt even closer to a previous maid, who left
the family in the patient's eighth year. Their tearful parting was
easily recalled with much emotion and weeping. She could also shed
tears for an orphaned beggar girl. In the analysis, she could not at
first comprehend, even intellectually, that she missed her mother.
Dreams and fantasies of a pleasant mood were remembered, of re-
union with her mother, and of her mother's being in a sanitarium,
and also frightening ones of seeing her with the gory signs of head
and face injuries.

The patient had had much experience of missing her mother who had all along continued her work as a teacher and had done much home tutoring. The child was mostly in the care of an indulgent maid. The mother was the mainstay of the family income. She was ambitious, conscientious, and usually worried about the patient in connection with illness and behaving well. It was a family joke that whenever mother was given something she liked, she would cry. She used active measures to combat illness: sticking the finger down the throat to induce vomiting, and giving enemas. The patient could remember that when she complained of feeling sick during ages four to six, her mother would urge her to induce vomiting or to have an enema. Father was used as an example to show how easy it was. The patient recalled the pain of enemas, the struggle over trying to vomit, and her intense hate of these experiences, especially of "getting sick" (meaning vomiting). Sickness and badness were equated and were to be exorcised by means of the forcible penetration. The patient recalled how her mother, or both mother and father, were angered by her refusal to comply because of her fear of these procedures.

The patient felt that both parents preferred her brother. He always seemed happier and stronger than she. He would dominate the conversation in every group. When she was three years, during auto trips, she felt enviously resentful of him because he could wear boys' clothes, which had such great advantage for urinating among the bushes. The use of the concept that clothes make the man to deny the difference between the sexes, took the form later at the age of six, of asking her mother how girls and boys could be differentiated at birth since the ways to distinguish them at a later date could not be applied at birth, namely, the hair style and the clothes. In another respect, too, the patient felt she lost out. Her brother wet the bed. At the age of four she knew this fact. Several times she awoke with the urge to urinate. She awakened her mother to inform her of the intent and asked to be accompanied. Her aim was competitive exhibitionism, but she soon gave up these efforts because her mother became angry. During latency, the patient had fantasies of watching from outside the window a happy family around the dining table.

It was difficult for the patient to experience, and to gain insight into, her aggressive feelings toward her mother. The same was true of her strong positive attachment. The first statement about her mother in the analysis was that she "was a wonderful woman." This was spoken with a special emphasis but with emotional isolation. There were memories of happy times together, often during summers, but these were also associated with some fears, such as of a storm or lightning striking a tree. One of the more vivid memories involved much giggling about their simultaneous urge to urinate and difficulty in getting to a toilet in time. She enjoyed getting into her parents' bed in the morning. On the day of her mother's death, she had implored her mother not to go out. Later she became furious at a neighbor boy's teasing and threatened him with retaliation from her mother. When a prize was established in her mother's honor, she tried hard to win it and her failure to do so was a keen disappointment.

After her mother's death, she took over mother's place at the table and the responsibility of running the home. She felt guilty about taking pride in this. For a short time, she continued to get into her father's bed on Sunday mornings, until one day she had the thought she might become pregnant. She began to have fears of robbers breaking into the house, especially when she was alone. She would leave her door open at night to facilitate speedier help from her father and brother. The oedipal significance is obvious. Taking over mother's place also had the meaning of preserving it for mother. On two occasions she had wanted her father to marry again and had been on good terms with both women. But she made the proviso in her own mind that she would continue in her mother's place at the table. However, her father did not remarry until after the patient had married.

The repressed hostile feelings toward mother could be expressed toward both father and brother. With the latter, she could hit out verbally and physically. She was inclined to scold and nag him. She often felt a motherly big sister attitude for him, but she also felt frustrated that he could tease and hurt her while she could never tease and hurt him. She often resented that he did little of the work in the house. Her anger would well up, especially when father and brother were enjoying a chat in the other room while she did the dishes.

The patient felt that she could never please her father and "so gave up." When her school grades were three A's, B, and C, he complained about the C. In high school she became interested in psychiatric social work. He wanted her to study medicine. When dinner was twenty minutes late, he would become angry. He complained that she did not try hard enough to excel in some one activity. When she was fifteen, her father brought up the subject of boarding school. She experienced his suggestion as a deep hurt and rejection. In this connection, it should be mentioned that she unconsciously experienced her mother's death as being abandoned. When feeling hurt and angry with her father, she would withdraw in tears, often running off to an older woman relative or friend. After the boarding school episode, she decided to leave home for college as soon as possible. Moreover, her brother was expecting soon to be called up for military service, another abandonment for her.

She had of course not completely given up her desire to please her father. Displacing her mother as mistress of the home increased her guilt, which had become excessive even before. At five she had been very afraid of her father. Whenever she heard him talk angrily, she guiltily worried what had she done wrong. She anticipated being hit with his razor strop with which she had been threatened by both father and mother. Her masochistic wishes were present early in life and appeared projected onto all three members of her family. Masochism was fostered by the demands to give up her stomach contents, her feces, and all sexual pleasures. Her way of pleasing father was like that she used with her mother; she exhibited her sacrifice and suffering. On such occasions her mother showed more concern for the patient, as she did at times of illness. Her father too liked to tease. He would lean over as if falling upon her, which he performed so realistically that she could not control her fear that he was actually falling over onto her.

Moreover, despite having turned her positive feelings at one time more toward one than toward the other, the patient always placed her mother first as the more lovable, admirable, and estimable of the two. She believed that everyone would always immediately like and respect her mother, whereas her father had at least a few detractors. She felt that her mother was the more reliable in satisfying her wish to be protected and fought for. Her brother too had demonstrated such willingness more than her father. One day when she had just turned twelve, while on her bicycle, a boy chased her home, caught up with her and "pawed" her before she could reach safety inside. She felt panicky and deeply humiliated. It was her brother (disappointingly not her father) who ran out to avenge her. This incident occurred on the day of the unveiling of her mother's tombstone. There was now no one to protect her against father's and brother's teasing.

Outside the home, there were more pleasant relations. She did well scholastically. Although sensitive to criticism and shy, she had several close friends and one kindly mother treated her as part of the family. She also had a boy friend, against whom one girl friend warned her at the outset, telling her that he was considered fickle. He went into military service before she entered college. When she started her relationship with her husband, she felt guilty toward the former boy friend, procrastinating over informing him of this friendship until the time of her wedding. At fifteen, she heard from her friend's mother, for the first time, that a woman experienced pleasure in sexual contact, the emphasis in this discussion being on kissing and caressing. The patient was deeply impressed with the idea that sex could be "nice." She had heard from her own mother about the facts of sex, but there had been no hint that it involved any pleasure. She had, moreover, no conscious memory of masturbation.

The satisfactions obtained in contacts away from home were overshadowed by her disappointment and frustration in the home situation. She had taken to heart her father's declaration after mother's death that now "we three must go on together." She accepted conscientiously what she felt to be the drudgery of household chores, and often sacrificed outside activities. She felt that her efforts were unappreciated, and her resentment grew. This state of affairs fitted quite well into her masochistic fantasy life.

From this sketch of the patient's past, we now turn our attention to the precipitation and elucidation of the neurosis. Here our interest will center mainly on the patient's object choice, object relations, and aims. It is not my purpose to discuss the process of the analysis, but rather to derive from it a psychological picture of the patient's adolescence. Suffice it to say that the analysis became mainly a struggle against the patient's excessive guilt, passivity, and masochism, which characterized her way of relating to persons and situations. These characteristics, in turn, derived a large measure of their strength from incompletely warded off aggression and sadism.

When the patient went off to college at sixteen, she was in a state of expectant urgency. She wanted so much to get away from home quickly that she rushed through high school with the necessary minimum college requirements, but without getting her diploma. She longed for love, admiration, acceptance, happiness and also for defiant retaliation. She was in a hurry to grow up, fall in love, marry and have a happy family. Within nine months she was married.

The patient herself could not have expressed her plans with such definiteness. It was her way to act with little awareness of a dominant urge, of the experience of gratification, or the accompanying sense of guilt. The motivating force was apparently experienced mostly on a preconscious level. Her conscious emotional reactions were blurred and vague, with the superego exerting its mastery. Thus her symptoms of "sickness" and nausea were the suffering of guilt and shame, coloring thickly sexual excitement and physical sensations displaced from the genital. She could not at first achieve an orgasm, but a few months after marriage she had what she described as "little orgasms coming too quickly."

Her husband became aware of the aggravation of symptoms by sexual contact. The patient denied the connection. Her ego ideal of a modern progressive young liberal could not tolerate fears of sex or of pregnancy. In addition to the guilt-derived anxiety over sexuality per se, there were other anxieties, such as the perfectionistic fear of failure, especially in a new situation, and fear of exhibitionism. Another main source of anxiety was the result of her concept of the sadistic male sexual role. After marriage she began to have frank rape fantasies as well as a resurgence of the earlier fantasies of physical assault. She also had unconscious fantasies that the male excreted a poisonous revolting urinary mess into the female and that the penis, like a fetus, caused inner damage, as a devouring cancer did. Her own unconscious sadism was more difficult to reach. But one time during intercourse, in the period of her analysis, she had a conscious fantasy that her vagina could snap off her husband's penis. She immediately "tightened up" and intercourse became painful.

An additional source of anxiety was the fear of being overwhelmed by the instincts. This was revealed in her increasing fear of loss of control, with its concomitant spreading inhibition, as well as in her state of emotional urgency and low tolerance for frustration. Anna Freud (1936) described the repudiation of instinct as a defense against the strength of instincts in puberty and adolescence. Jacobson (1957) has recently investigated the use of denial against internal as well as external reality, including id and superego forces. The data in the present case seem more understandable on the basis of the latter formulation. It may be admissible, then, to speak of denial of instinct as a mechanism within the individual. One meets with such denial quite frequently in the area of psychological theory.

Nevertheless, our patient had been able to feel in love, to feel loved, to attempt to have sexual gratification, and to continue functioning well at school and socially. After marriage, her defenses broke down, and she became increasingly inhibited in all areas. By the time she began analysis, she had quit college because of inability to concentrate. She had decided it would be best to find a job, but proscrastinated even as to the kind of job. She felt sick enough to spend much time in bed. Sexual intercourse was avoided for months at a time. She gave up her interests for the most part, and with much effort tried to devote herself to her chores. She was ashamed that she could not refrain from frequently nagging her husband for little things. They teased one another. There were quarrels and sullen withdrawals. The patient became aware that she felt like provoking him and could not control the urge. He generally acceded to her wishes. He gave up making sexual advances but responded to hers. He left most decisions to her. His lack of ambition was a deeply felt disappointment to her.

The patient had known early in her relationship with her husband that he had had an unhappy childhood. His mother too had died, after a chronic illness, when he was ten years old. He was considered a bitter person, especially at a first meeting. Her goal had been to get him over his bitterness. When she expressed this to her father, he said that "it would take a lot out of her." The patient

identified with her husband and planned to give him what she
wanted herself, namely sacrificial devotion. To make a sacrifice also
opened the way to assume again the masochistic role of her relations
with father and brother. She felt similarly burdened by his dependence and her taking responsibilities, and similarly unappreciated. He could have sexual gratification, whereas she had to suffer
physically and emotionally with her symptoms. As with father and
brother, the teasing, provoking, and fighting were ways of dis-
charging sexual tension. In both situations, she exhibited her suffering with the dual motivation of asking for love in the form of
sympathy and protection, and of making an accusation while pro-
testing her own innocence of any aggression. Her neurotic symptoms
embodied these motives as well as the urges to get and present the
love gift of a baby from mother as well as father, and pregenital
urges welded together in the urge to castrate, carried along within
the outer garment of the masochistic submission to castration.

It was especially difficult for this patient to relinquish her
incestuous oedipal goals and objects. Her major attachment was
to mother, and the patterns of dealing with her (mainly as a phallic
mother) were applied in her heterosexual object relations. The
masochistic role had first been played with mother, who had insisted
on submission to forcible penetration and had demanded the sacrifice of body contents and of instinctual gratification. To sacrifice,
to be hurt, to suffer, to be ill—these were the means to obtain a
worrisome mother's care and devotion and also the means to provoke her indirectly. Since mother could tolerate little aggression,
father and even more the brother became its recipients. There was
thus a fusion of objects, the loss of any one of which involved loss
of all three. This was fostered by the concept of the three remaining
members carrying on together after mother's death.

Holding onto mother via father and brother assisted the maintenance of denial of mother's death. Denial was directed mainly at
the emotional reactions to the trauma. But there was also a denial
of the event itself in an unconscious isolated corner of the ego.
Denial and repression put off the pain and work of conscious mourning, which became even more painful when the trauma of mother's
death was followed soon after by the trauma of menstrual onset.
But these defenses allowed regressive reactivation of infantile am-

bivalence and destructive aggression toward the mother. The patient could not tolerate aggression towards mother on account of her excessive guilt and separation anxiety. Moreover, she had not been able to give up the destructive goal of her aggression. Even to experience sexual pleasure was too aggressive an act toward mother. The work of mourning involved dealing with even greater quantities of aggression resulting from loss of the mother and also from earlier feelings of deprivation, such as her sense of castration, penis envy and defeat in the rivalry with her brother.

Marriage, of course, thrust reality upon the patient and caused too great a strain on her denial defense. Breaking the bond with father and brother, with the unconscious meaning of also losing mother, soon made the experience of marriage one of suffering a greater and greater sense of loss. Relief came to the patient only after she could accomplish the task of mourning her mother's death, and also the loss of giving up her oedipal and preoedipal goals and objects. Her symptoms and the character of her relations with her husband were also unsuccessful attempts at denial that her marriage required giving up childhood.

The study of this analytic material suggested the following thoughts:

1. The work of mourning, which was underscored in this instance, is an important psychological task in the period of adolescence. The infantile parental attachments must now really be given up on the way to adult maturity.

2. The mechanism of denial of both inner and outer reality may readily be called upon during the instinctual storms of adolescence, with the resultant damaging effect upon the maturational development of the ego.

3. During the course of analysis of adults, even when no special feature (such as the death of the mother in this case) highlights the period of adolescence, which then may appear relatively quiescent, a careful study of this period should nonetheless be undertaken lest valuable information be lost.

During the analysis, even after the patient had begun to be conscious of both grief and remorse over her mother's death, she often displaced her sadness onto something else or felt sad for someone else. The working through of the mourning reaction required much repetition. Greenacre (1956) stressed the importance of repetition in the working-through process, comparing it to the repetitive aspect of the work of mourning as described by Freud (1917). Fenichel (1945) and Lewin (1950) credited Sandor Rado with comparing the working-through process to the work of mourning. Annie Reich (1950) described the giving up of the analyst at the end of an analysis as similar to a mourning reaction. Anny Katan (1951) considered the shift of libidinal cathexis in the adolescent from the incestuous to the nonincestuous object as a one-way displacement, which she terms "removal." In our patient, such a shifting of cathexis was intimately bound up with the real loss of the mother at a time when the latter was still much needed. In this situation one would expect painful grief when a cathexis shift is attempted. So it was with our patient. When well along in her analysis, she spoke of grieving as "letting mother die."

But then every adolescent must make a real psychical renunciation and suffer the "loss" of childhood and its aims and objects. He must do this much more completely than in the more infantile earlier struggle with the oedipus complex. Freud (1905) described the adolescent "detachment from parental authority" as "one of the most significant, but also one of the most painful, psychical achievements." I think that the achievement must be hampered if the mourning reactions are evaded.

Berta Bornstein has observed depressive reactions in children, in the latter part of latency or prepuberty, upon their becoming aware of parental imperfections.[2] Those who refuse to let the parents off the pedestal may develop delinquent tendencies. She considers as a kind of mourning reaction the instances when patients reproach the analyst for depriving them of their fantasies. I observed rather violent grief of this kind in one patient. An adult patient (who could be considered as a case of "prolonged adolescence") often showed a negative therapeutic reaction, which would first be manifested by aggression as well as aggravation of suffering, and then by the appearance of depressive features. The sequence indicated that the feelings of depression were both denied and expressed via the negative therapeutic reaction, which regularly occurred when

[2] Personal communication.

his infantile attachments to his parents were shaken.

Turning briefly to the mechanism of denial, the term "denial of instinct" used above requires an amendment. What is actually denied is a perception, or a perceptual concept, which may be conscious or preconscious, relating to an external or internal source.[3] Denial is quite common and is often taken for granted, as in the kind of reassurances which adults often give children, namely, "Everything will be all right"; or, "There's nothing to be afraid of." The elucidation of a simple piece of denial may stir a patient's interest in analytic work. But denial often becomes involved with other mechanisms in complicated ways (Jacobson, 1957). Denial plays a relatively more important role in states of actual or relative "weakness" of the ego. A kind of vicious cycle occurs, in that the maintenance of denial requires ego splitting, which causes further interference in ego functioning. The effect is more disastrous during a period of great lability and growth of the ego, as in adolescence. Our patient demonstrated the progressively spreading interference with functioning in all areas. It is therefore important thoroughly to work through all aspects of denial.

Denial played a part in another way in this patient's life. In combination with other factors, it led to her early marriage. Her state of "urgency" at the time of starting college was mentioned. This was, of course, a state involving anxiety. Helene Deutsch (1944) pointed out that as sexual fulfillment comes nearer, it is felt as a greater danger. Moreover, in the new situation, her need for an object was stimulated even more. She had to deny her loneliness and missing her family. Associated to these feelings and aggravating them were the infantile ties, especially the attachment to her mother. The strength of the heterosexual urge is not to be minimized here. Narcissistic needs as well as exhibitionistic urges, to be gratified by possession of a boy friend, also added to the emotional urgency. In addition, the homosexual mother attachment had to be warded off. All these forces led to impulsive action and a kind of acting out, which represented attempts both to gratify the maturing libidinal urges and to deny the infantile.

It is hoped that this report will increase interest in the study

---

[3] See Freud (1925), Anna Freud (1936), Lewin (1950), and most recently Jacobson (1957).

of the psychology of adolescence and that further study may sub-
stantiate some of the thoughts expressed.

BIBLIOGRAPHY

Deutsch, H. (1944), *The Psychology of Women*. New York: Grune & Stratton.

Fenichel, O. (1945), *The Psychoanalytic Theory of Neurosis*. New York: W. W. Norton
& Co.

Freud, A. (1936), *The Ego and the Mechanisms of Defense*. New York: International
Universities Press, 1946.

Freud, S. (1905), Three Essays on Sexuality. *Standard Edition*, VII. London: Hogarth
Press, 1953.

—— (1917), Mourning and Melancholia. *Collected Papers*, IV. London: Hogarth Press,
1946.

—— (1925), Negation. *Int. J. Psa.*, VI.

—— (1932), *New Introductory Lectures on Psychoanalysis*. New York: W. W. Norton
& Co.

Greenacre, P. (1956), Re-evaluation of the Process of Working Through. *Int. J. Psa.*,
XXXVII.

Jacobson, E. (1957), Denial and Repression. *J. Am. Psa. Assn.*, V.

Katan, A. (1951), The Role of "Displacement" in Agoraphobia. *Int. J. Psa.*, XXXII.

Lewin, B. D. (1950), *The Psychoanalysis of Elation*. New York: W. W. Norton & Co.

Reich, A. (1950), On the Termination of Analysis. *Int. J. Psa.*, XXXI.

DELINQUENCY, A DEFENSE AGAINST LOSS OF OBJECTS AND REALITY[1]

MARGARETE RUBEN (Los Angeles)

The following report and discussion of the analysis of a delinquent boy in his latency should be of interest for two reasons: (1) The etiological factors in the patient's delinquency are clearly revealed in his anamnesis. (2) There is a relative paucity of published material gained in child analysis from delinquents in their latency. This abbreviated clinical paper presents primarily those facts which have an immediate bearing on the subject of the patient's delinquency.

One of the crucial stages in the child's development is the beginning of the latency period. The outcome of the resolution of the oedipus complex has far-reaching consequences in regard to character development, intellectual maturity and social adaptation. The most important result of the decline of the oedipal phase is the establishment and consolidation of the superego by a process of internalization and desexualization. The balance between superego and id depends upon the strength of the mediating agent—the ego. If a relatively well-developed ego can influence either side and prevent disastrous inner psychic battles, the child's judging mind is open for further identificatory processes and desexualized object relationships. If, however, one of the driving agents—the superego or the instinctual impulses—dominates in the child's struggle, a psychic equilibrium will not be achieved. In cases in which the superego is unusually rigid, it has lost its character as a protector and its functions as regulator for instinctual demands. Then the superego's severity may be understood in terms of the child's own aggressive disposition and the preference for parental prohibitions instead of an established identification with former love objects. In spite of its

[1] Presented at the Midwinter Meetings of the American Psychoanalytic Association, New York, 1956.

rigidity this poorly integrated superego will show little strength at times of heightened instinctual needs.

The following case report of a boy in his latency illustrates the pathological outcome of a struggle between a rigid, unstable super-ego and id impulses. It led to the symptom formation of delinquency. In her paper "Certain Types and Stages of Social Maladjustment" Anna Freud (1948) describes a type of delinquent which is familiar to us under the broader term of psychopaths. Their disorders differ from other delinquent behavior problems in so far as they are not based on the early stunting of object love "but on conflicts which belong to the normal realm of the child's emotional attachments."

CASE REPORT

Diagnostic Study

Ten-year-old Jackie was an adopted child, conceived in a short-lived love affair between a working-class girl and a student of technology who never learned that he had impregnated the girl. Jackie was brought to the analyst for a diagnostic interview. His long-standing, increasingly frequent delinquent acts had recently brought him into contact with the police. His parents reported that he had received a severe warning from them that repetition of his delinquent acts would result in his having to appear in court. They consisted in persistent stealing (mainly money), and began at home when he was about six years old. (According to the parents, his first theft occurred when he was three to four years of age. He took his mother's diamond ring and buried it under the dead autumn leaves in the yard where it was found by the gardener.) With the beginning of school life his real thievery started. He victimized every adult with whom he had contact. He also engaged in shoplifting, taking mostly objects of lesser value, and embarked on a career of vandalism which included throwing stones or milk bottles at passing cars, damaging property in office buildings, etc.

The most recent and very frightening experience for his parents occurred when Jackie committed burglary, stealing a gun.

The parents' reaction to the delinquent acts was one of extreme indignation. It was mainly the increasing frequency of Jackie's stealing and his insistent lying and denying of guilt which led the father to intensified and severe punishment until finally he took recourse to his leather belt, in desperation strapping the boy severely, but without results. While the father appeared thoroughly shaken by the misdeeds of his son, the mother had gradually become fed up with his behavior. She would have preferred to send him to a boarding school rather than have him receive therapy. She had become weary of the incessant unreasonable demands her son made on her.

Jackie's Personality

Jackie was a slender, blue-eyed, blond, good-looking boy, with very broad and sensual lips. He was a charmer, especially popular with adults, conquering their hearts immediately. Three previous therapists whom the parents had consulted in various interviews succumbed to his charm, considering his delinquency as an innocent juvenile behavior disorder. They predicted he would grow out of it naturally, because he had such a well-rounded personality, was very bright, an "A" student in school, and good at sports. Shortly after leaving the testing psychologist, the parents received a phone call from her, reporting that Jackie had stolen her wallet, containing twenty dollars and all her important credentials. (To quote the parents: "We were flabbergasted!" He must have done this right under her eyes! He had kept the psychologist's money and thrown the wallet into the unlighted incinerator.)

While the parents emphasized the various aspects of his delinquency and emphatically denied the potential existence of other disturbances, it turned out that Jackie has also been sleepwalking from early childhood on.

In surprising contrast to the indignant attitude of the parents, Jackie gave the impression of a subdued, embarrassed little boy, who wondered what the fuss was all about. He sat in his chair, denying stubbornly all accusations of the current delinquent acts. When alone with the therapist he gave himself away by telling his favorite story, about Lassie, the dog who always went home to her master, regardless of how far she had been sent away. This sad story was in sharp contrast with the boasting remark a few minutes later when Jackie maintained that he just liked *adventures of his own* and therefore he did not want to become a Boy Scout as his father had been. He had been a Cub Scout for a short time, but feeling unwanted by the group, had dropped out.

Jackie's Home Environment

Jackie grew up in an average liberal Jewish milieu, in an atmosphere of so-called "progressive education." His father, who preferred his adopted son to his natural daughter, was an impulsive, warm-hearted person whose preoccupation with and interest in this boy was a means of escape from his emotionally sterile married life; it also served to perpetuate a continuation of an unconscious affectionate relationship with his younger brother, a gay blade in his youth, whom he had always admired for his daring attitude toward life. At the time of Jackie's adoption the father suffered from asthma attacks.

Jackie's mother was a withdrawn person, without friends, who expressed her anxiety by burying herself in studies. His sister Martha, six years older, was always a remarkably "good" child, and an "A" student in school.

When Jackie was three to four years old his mother often read to him from a book entitled "The Chosen Baby." At that time he was also told that he had been adopted and this fact was discussed with him in great detail.

Jackie's History

Jackie was adopted when he was two weeks old, and immediately became a feeding problem. He suffered from pylorospasms which his father described as follows: "There was Jackie lying on his bed with an angelic face during feeding time—when suddenly a jet of milk came out of his mouth, without whimpering or crying, as if it was something as natural as taking in the milk." To avoid any commotion, Jackie was kept as quiet and as little touched as possible. On the other hand, he was on a "continuous demand schedule," because he could take milk only in small amounts. Even after solid foods had been introduced, this feeding method continued until he was eighteen months old. He was never encouraged to eat more than the little he wanted, but he ate often. He never sucked his thumb.

While his speech development was slow, his motor development showed no retardation. He spoke only a little and unclearly when he was two, but was already walking in his crib at seven months. When he was one year old and fell while trying to walk, he was so shocked that for the next year he insisted on holding his mother's hand, not daring to walk alone.

Jackie's mother remembered no difficulties in toilet training, but Jackie claimed during his analysis that he kept his feces in a jar in his early days because he did not want to part with them.

After Jackie's second birthday, his parents moved to California. The mother's father joined the family and lived with them for a few years.

Immediately after the family had settled down in the new environment, two-year-old Jackie fell in love with the mother's colored day help. He sat waiting on the steps in front of the house for hours before she was expected. When she arrived, he picked up his mother's hat to encourage her to leave and do her shopping. According to both parents, the maid, who remained with the family for a year, showed exceptional warmth and understanding for Jackie, by making him "do things," letting him share her activities, like hanging up laundry in the yard, etc. When Jackie was three years old, she left, and the family moved to another home, where a series of unsuitable domestic helpers provided Jackie with an unfavorable environment. In the course of the next few years the family moved three times.

It was during this unfortunate time, soon after the maid's departure, at the age of three years and two months, that Jackie took his mother's diamond ring from the kitchen shelf while she was doing the dishes and buried it under the autumn leaves.

In the years before school started, Jackie was always clinging to his mother, was shy and anxious. He also tried to attach himself to the grandfather, because the parents took many trips. During one of these times he became so withdrawn that a relative remarked that she had never seen such a lonesome child before. He even stopped eating two days prior to the parents' return. To spare the "worried little worrier," as Jackie was called in those days, unnecessary anxiety, he had been lured at the age of four years and eight months under false pretenses to the hospital for tonsillectomy, a betrayal to which he never became reconciled.

Whereas Jackie had difficulties in nursery school because he hated taking naps (on account of his masturbatory anxieties), he adapted himself with ease to kindergarten. However, he promptly stole the teacher's *keyring*, with an attached whistle. This episode marked the beginning of his thievery. Gradually these "stealing rampages"—as Jackie himself defined them once in his analytic session—increased to daily occurrences as the years went on.

Otherwise, Jackie developed into a successful youngster. He became the best baseball player of his class and an excellent swimmer and diver.

Jackie always succeeded in getting caught in his delinquent acts; therefore I made the tentative diagnosis that he was "a criminal from a sense of guilt" (Freud, 1915), combined with hysterical somnambulism. The danger that the patient's behavior disorder might turn into serious criminal activities led to a recommendation of analytic treatment five times weekly.

Jackie's First Analysis

Jackie's first analysis did not differ in content and in its emphasis on the defense mechanisms of repression and denial from any other analysis of a child with neurotic symptom formation. When after fourteen months of work, Jackie had become symptom-free, his parents were satisfied with the results and decided to stop the analysis in spite of the analyst's warning, who felt she had not yet understood the core of the patient's delinquency.

The analyst's prediction was justified. Although the analysis showed therapeutic results, it did not carry Jackie through the hazards of an unexpected trauma in the immediate future. A second analysis had to be undertaken which brought the deeper motivation of the patient's conflict to the surface.

Jackie's Second Analysis

After eight months of well-being Jackie's mother reported that his sister Martha, now eighteen years old, had a psychotic breakdown after several unsatisfactory love affairs. She had given up her studies and was about to run away to South America to marry a young waiter whom she had once met on a trip with her parents. Our patient reacted to this event with a stormy repetition of his delinquency.

Jackie started his second analysis in a mood of hopeless despondency, desperate stealing, tangles of lies, and nightly sleepwalking. When he entered the consulting room for the first time he shouted excitedly: "It has all to do with Martha!" He expressed the hope that she would find her boy friend in South America married and be forced to come home; but the worst of all would be that very likely she could not find her way back, because she was so terribly helpless; so desperately helpless, in spite of her always having had good grades in school.

How correct Jackie was in his assumption that his relapse into illness was intimately linked with his relationship to his sister was realized when Martha's therapist called to report that she had confessed to him the seduction of her brother when he was three years old, an event which Jackie dated correctly in his analysis to the age of five. The actual facts of the unfortunate traumatic experience consisted in the children's practice of fellatio and cunnilingus at times when the parents were out of the house and had left eleven-year-old Martha as a sitter. Jackie reacted to these guilt-laden, but short-lived events by adopting blackmail tactics. To silence him his sister had to give him two cents each time he asked for it, and to fulfill any demands he made on her. However, the damage done to him was greater than both offenders could have known. Revengeful killing fantasies, a wealth of sadomasochistic images and thoughts and a deep thrust into femininity, accompanied with highly sexualized castration anxiety, must have overwhelmed Jackie's psychic household at the time of the seduction. This was now reactivated by his sister's sudden illness and inundated the patient's conscious thought processes completely for quite a time.

After Jackie's first session marked by desperation and worry in regard to his helpless sister, he underwent a fast and complete swing of mood overnight. On the next day he was elated and determined to find himself a girl with whom he wanted to go steady. He asked me: "Have you girl patients also? What are they looking for when they want a boy friend?" He spent weeks in fighting hypochondriacal fantasies of early death, rescue fantasies by sacrificing himself, and the search for a girl friend, all accompanied by continuous stealing adventures. Once when he discovered that I treated a girl patient about the same age as his sister—a time at which he also felt very uncertain about his new girl friend's love for him—he stole $100 from a newsstand. Justifiably suspected, he stubbornly denied the theft for twenty-four hours before he was willing to show his pleading and exasperated mother the hiding place. He had stuffed the money into a paper bag and had thrown it into a corner of a driveway in the neighborhood, where it had remained unnoticed and thus could be returned to the owner.

During those first weeks Jackie was either emotionally not ready to bring into the analysis the seduction trauma which must have reached preconscious levels through the new events, or he had lost the sense of its reality in his state of complete psychological upheaval. After a month of "helpless and hopeless" acting out he asked the analyst for a "sexy story," which gave me the opportunity to confront the patient with the seduction trauma in the form of a story (Ekstein, 1957). Then the patient was able to verbalize his innumerable incestuous fantasies of having been married to his sister, being castrated and changed into a girl by her, and above all, his hate and contempt and deep mistrust of damaged, inferior women. The following excerpts from the analysis will illustrate these facts:

His sexualized castration anxiety found its expression when one day he told the analyst excitedly about an expected sitter, whom he wanted to seduce in the same way as he had been trying to seduce his sister continuously by sitting after his bath in a dark corner of the living room, with an open fly. At night he would not put on pajamas, hoping—and sometimes being convinced—that Martha would rip his blanket off, grab his penis, and tear it off. The next morning he would look again and again whether his organ had really been torn off, or whether he had only imagined it.

In another session he expressed his *feminine identification* with his sister by bringing a little suitcase with a hand mirror, hair oil, brush, comb, and a towel to beautify himself for fifty minutes. He told the analyst that he frequently undertook these beautifying procedures in the bathroom at home, wearing his sister's brassiers as well (which she hangs in the bathroom to dry).

In spite of the relief Jackie experienced from working through the seduction trauma, he continued and even increased his compulsive stealing. The parents became disappointed in the analysis. They began to make plans to send him to a military boarding school because his grades also had deteriorated rapidly after he fell ill again.

A Change in Technique

At this point the analyst succeeded in persuading the parents
that they should postpone their decision to terminate the analysis,
and instead wait to see the results of a changed therapeutic technique. They were advised to vent their disappointment openly at his
failure to benefit from treatment; further they should go ahead and
punish him as they desired, by depriving him of his allowance, of
TV, and of his expected Christmas presents, and above all to con-
fine him to his home after school hours. The only exception to this
should be the permission to attend Scout meetings, which the patient
now desired as ardently as he had rejected them earlier. The analyst
assumed that this newly developed ambition to become a Boy Scout
might disclose repressed material. Furthermore, it was hoped that
the changed atmosphere would precipitate a stronger relationship to
the analyst. This did in fact occur when the patient snuggled himself
into a symbiotic relationship with her. The parent's outspoken
rejecting attitude did not alarm Jackie at all, thus showing the
shallowness of his libidinal ties.

The Boy Scout Situation Becomes the Platform for the
Patient's Inner "Psychosexual Drama"

Jackie's unconscious need for a symbiotic relationship clashed
painfully with his ego-directed passionate desire to become a Boy
Scout. The preconscious motivations for Jackie's sudden interest in
the Scout movement were twofold. It offered him the opportunity
to be together with people of his own sex who were by far less dangerous to him than representatives of the female sex, whose frightening unreliability he had experienced once more through his sister's
breakdown. Secondly, he hoped for a more intimate relationship
with his father, whose disappointment in his son's disinterest in the
Scout movement had always stood between the two.

But Jackie's unconscious need for a common activity with his
father had different and deeper reasons than the wish for a tightening
of his erotic bonds. It was the situation per se, the shared activity
itself—"doing things together"—at which he aimed unconsciously.
This was fully recognized by the analyst after she had advised the
father to stop participating in the son's new Scout activities, where-

upon Jackie collapsed completely, and was unable to attend evening
Scout meetings or to join in the week-end trips. He vainly attempted
to deny his anxieties and developed new transitory symptoms such as
enuresis, asthma, and a blinking tic. As this parameter technique
had channeled his anxiety into an analyzable conflict situation, the
patient revealed a wealth of pregenital fantasies which could be interpreted. A few examples will be given here.

His first attempt to join the Boy Scouts on a week-end trip failed
at the very moment when the troop was about to leave. He burst
into tears and asked his father to take him home. Deeply ashamed
about it, he reported in the session, "I felt like the dying woman
about whom the counselor had spoken to my daddy before; but I
heard another boy speaking of initiation of newcomers and I knew
I could not stand that." As such times of failure, when the world
around him seemed to have the meaning of death and castration, he
fell into deep depressions, missed school for a few days, and remained
in bed pretending to have a headache. Although the analyst was
tempted to look at the fears he expressed merely as defenses against
homosexual desires and castration anxieties, Jackie's reasoning was
of a different nature. He argued: "If you lose your way even in
school surroundings sometimes—such a confined space—and you
can't find your way back, then how terrible it would be in a camp!"
Or: "I know when one gets lost and can't find the way back, one
should sit by the road and wait for the searchers. I did it and was
praised for it when I was in my first camp"—a summer camp from
which he was sent home (at the age of five), too homesick to stay.
The mere thought of being away from home and losing parental
protection in the Scout situation established again in the patient a
traumatic situation of being abandoned "helpless, hopeless and
alone"—a repetition of his former anxieties also projected onto his
sister at the beginning of his second analysis.

When Jackie began partially to understand that being away from
home stood for being abandoned, he started to participate in week-
end trips. However, he was only able to do it by consistently stealing
money or shoplifting. The high value he attached to the stolen
objects showed his displaced need for human ties which he was as
yet incapable of establishing and for which he substituted inanimate
objects. In order to take part in the program he had to steal the best

compass available to secure his orientation, or a special Scout knife or a certain lantern. Before going on a trip he practiced "sleeping in a tent" at home rationalizing that it was a hot night. But actually he was afraid of leaving the tent in the night to urinate, because he might wet the Scoutmaster in the dark, or a bear might come and bite off his penis.

In one session, when Jackie memorized the Scout Code with its high moral precepts, which includes the rejection of masturbation, he accused the analyst of immoral views because her opinion differed. Then it came to the open that Jackie's intense desire to become a Boy Scout was motivated by the hope that with this new code he could successfully master his masturbatory activities, which he had resumed after his sister's breakdown. They frightened him because of their compulsive and lengthy character as well as their failure to relieve tension. These activities consisted of manipulation of the penis with bobby pins and were not accompanied by fantasies. These were instead enacted in his delinquent behavior. The struggle against masturbation led to a new outbreak and increase of delinquent behavior, as an attempt to avoid masturbation as well as a substitute for it.

After a year's help of analytic interpretations he was able to become a Life Scout, earning one more merit badge than his father. He showed only narcissistic, exhibitionistic pride in wearing his beautiful uniform, covered with awards. During his Scout activities, he never related to others, was not interested in forming a friendship with any of his companions, and showed no appreciation for the beauty of nature. Instead, the food he would take on these trips was of great importance to him, as well as the exciting rituals which have their place in the Scout ceremonies. But apart from the narcissistic and exhibitionistic satisfactions Jackie received from this achievement (which exactly paralleled the pattern of his school accomplishments, since he was the fifth best scholar in school), a certain inner learning process had taken place in this analytic period as well. The patient had gained understanding of the discrepancy between his own nebulous self-image, his hitherto projected and denied instinctual desires, and the reality in which he lived. Moreover, the analyst's interpretive attitude toward his thievery established a relationship of "doing constructive things together" which enabled the patient to change his symbiotic attitude to the analyst into an object relationship.

The Unconscious Motivation for Jackie's Need for Symbiotic Object Ties

The leitmotif in Jackie's analysis was the fear of being left alone and abandoned. His need for a "helping hand" continued to be shown in other analytic material as well. It was the discussion of the film *Rebel Without Cause* which demonstrated the fixation point of the patient's preoedipal object relationship. He was so aroused by this film that he stole a woman's bag in the movie theater, in order to have money immediately to buy the original book. Jackie had identified in this film with the friendly but weak rich boy who had been brought up by the colored maid and had been neglected by his socially preoccupied parents. When the analyst criticized the hero as a leaf in the wind, without any backbone, Jackie replied: "But when he was with women or his girl friend he could stand up straight and behave manly." The same underlying longing for an early infantile symbiotic object relationship was expressed in the following day-dream before a week-end trip with his parents.

"First I had a masculine fantasy. I was a boy going out in the dark with a pistol filled with shots, but I stopped this thought immediately because I then had a feminine fantasy. I hoped I would meet a girl of rich parents at the resort and we would do everything together, every hour of the day. We would be occupied with a lot of eating, changing clothes, and sports, and in the afternoon before dinner I would sit up in bed for a rest and drink a bottle of coke. She would have to sit at my bedside and watch me drinking. She would have to be with me every second." (The mother reported Jackie ate voraciously and continuously on their trip.)

The patient's early infantile object relationship explained his dependence on inanimate objects and what they stood for. Their meaning will now be discussed more fully.

Jackie's Unconscious Dependence on Inanimate Objects

Jackie never came to treatment without some kind of object to manipulate. At times of oral longings, he would lie on the couch, sucking pills out of a toy bottle and not relating to the analyst. At other times of heightened anxiety he would spend many sessions shooting caps, unable to verbalize any thought. In times of resistance he would bring school work or even his family's shoes, along with his shoe polish box, and polish shoes silently, pretending to be too busy to talk. When his incestuous love relationship with his sister came to the surface, he would bring his own recording machine and records with the most revealing love songs, but no verbalization followed. When he struggled with his voyeurism, he brought his (crude) pornographic photos with him and left them secretly but intentionally in the consulting room. Jackie spent endless sessions with his magic tricks. He had acquired an amount of magic devices which could have qualified him for any magic show.

Jackie's use of and dependence on inanimate objects is best illustrated by the two following sessions. Jackie came to an analytic hour and immediately and unreasonably asked for a *blue* typewriter ribbon because he wanted to type out something. He refused a black one. Though he was offered money to buy a blue one after the session, he could not stand the frustration; nor did he want to analyze the urgency for a *blue* ribbon; instead he threw himself on the couch in fury and fell asleep, a defense to which he resorted repeatedly at times of overwhelming anger. Over the phone the mother confirmd the analyst's suspicion that Martha's favorite color was blue and that she liked to wear blue hair ribbons.

The next day the analyst showed Jackie his increased anxiety about an imminent camping trip and his renewed desire to be his sister, who was spared the frightening activities. Only then did he reveal his anxiety and secretly planned retreat from this trip.

The Turning Point in Jackie's Analysis at a Time of Open Hostility and Loss of Reality

When Jackie stole something, the choice of the object was determined less by its symbolic significance but rather by what Jackie expected this object would do for him. For instance, to him a stolen chemistry set seemed to combine all the desirable qualities usually displayed by human beings. When I interpreted this to him, his response was an outburst of angry, resentful reproaches against his mother who never wanted him to be happy. At that time Jackie brought a cartoon to the session. The first picture in the sequence represented a man reading and being amused by a book. In the second picture he tries to induce his wife to read the book. She refuses and continues to knit rapidly. This reaction precipitates a fight which results in the woman killing her husband with her knitting needles. Thereupon she picks up the book, starts reading, and is vastly entertained. (Jackie's mother was an ardent and excellent knitter.)

The following incident marked a turning point in Jackie's analysis. After two years of treatment, Jackie's parents "dared" to make a two-week trip because of his improved condition. He reacted favorably and refrained from performing delinquent acts during their absence. However, at the end of his session, two days before his parents' return, he declared that he would that night steal a gun from a locked cabinet at school in order to kill people—whoever might come along. To the analyst's inquiry about the reason for so dangerous a plan, he shrugged his shoulders and said: "Because I want to kill, and then my parents will hear about it and come home sooner." He repeatedly told me that he would call that night at ten o'clock to tell me all about the crime. Shortly after ten o'clock, Jackie phoned. He reported that he had stolen the gun; however, for the first time in his life, he suddenly became aware that he—"I"—should not kill, and return the gun. This was an inner injunction. At the following session, Jackie threw himself on the couch and exclaimed proudly in a state of radiant excitement: "I think I am getting soft. I also did not cheat in Latin this morning at school, although I could have done it easily, *because I wanted to see what I could do myself.*"

Although this acting out was a condensation of many unconscious drives and emerging recollections, only one aspect was analyzed. The interpretation was made that he had to steal in order to hold on to objects in the outside world. He even needed to manipulate dangerous weapons in order to be able to differentiate between his inner hostile omnipotent fantasies and outside dangers. He did not trust his ability to control his hostile feelings in regard to people he loved; therefore he turned to objects and played make-believe with them, as a means of warding off and simultaneously expressing his hostile feelings. The most crucial aspect of this episode, however, was that he experienced from within himself the command not to steal or kill.

It was only at this point that I could fully understand one of the first hours of Jackie's first analysis. At that time he had related the following daydream: "I thought my parents would have a car accident and die. Then I would move to my uncle's (father's brother) and cousin who has a beebee gun. I would not live with my sister. But," Jackie immediately assured me, "if my parents should really die, I would commit suicide because I would miss their speech and faces so much." It is this remark which reveals his fixation to primitive conceptions of objects. Speech and face—part objects—are not yet fully fused into a whole.

The interpretation of Jackie's compulsive need to test reality with inanimate objects was of decisive therapeutic value for him. He declared, "That session helped me more than many or most of the others." He also related differently to his parents. His mother reported that "Jackie was pleasantly excited on our return, but one could feel he was calm underneath." Jackie changed in his relationship to the analyst as well. He had never stolen from me before, but a few weeks later, he stole an expensive pen. When I inquired whether he had stolen my nice pen because he was mad at me, he answered, smiling sheepishly, "On the contrary." It was a repetition of his first theft in infancy and his first "stolen love" object in the analysis, which was the beginning of a genuine transference relationship indicative for classical treatment (Eissler, 1950).

But Jackie's urge to steal a gun not only had the purpose of reality testing; something more was involved in this primitive infantile drama. By calling me over the phone he had identified with his mother, who often called me at night to report, a way of communication which Jackie so far had accepted with narcissistic satisfaction. By saying, "I shall tell you everything tomorrow," he was acting like his mother and taking over responsibility for himself in identification with her. Thus he renewed his early infantile attempts for individuation.

DISCUSSION

Technique and Diagnostic Evaluation

In this "preparatory phase" (Eissler, 1950) the planned attachment to the omnipotent therapist led to a surprisingly good "blessed object relationship" in which the patient and analyst "were doing things together." The analyst became a quasi-symbiotic partner with whom he could gratify his ego needs. The increasing emergence of

the patient's hostile magic world in the treatment expressed itself
temporarily in an uncooperative, haughty and contemptuous attitude
to the analyst, and even in refusal of contact. But the analysis succeeded in carrying the patient successfully through time of intrapsychic stress. The patient's predominant method of communicating
his conflict was by "acting out" (Ekstein and Friedman, 1957). This
device served the function of "necessary distance representation"
(Ekstein and Wright, 1952) and was an expression of the patient's
regressed preverbal form of communication "to call the helper."

The compulsive and periodic character of Jackie's thievery has
stopped and he is symptom-free. He declared that only on rare occasions did he feel tempted to steal. Jackie's delinquency can be considered to be a repetition of a preoedipal trauma condensed into an
acted-out masturbation fantasy.

*Jackie's Preoedipal Traumata and the Genesis of the Delinquent
Symptom Formation in the Light of His Early Object Relationship and His Libido Development*

Jackie's psychosexual development and early object relationships
had an unfortunate beginning already in the first weeks, as the intake
of food was not a matter of libidinal pleasure, nor an instinct satisfaction which leads normally to integrative processes and to the
establishment of strong object ties. Instead, feeding became an arti-
ficial, hazardous process. He was deprived of motherly warmth and
closeness so much needed in babyhood. The combination of "emotional malnutrition" (A. Freud, 1949) and a precarious biological disposition was bound to become dangerous for Jackie's maturational
growth. He was master of his own feeding regulations as to time,
frequency, and quantity. His passive sovereign performances continued far into his second year of life, thus prolonging his omnipotent narcissistic drives. The first learning process for necessary frus-
trations was retarded and, as it turned out in later life, never fully
completed.

His mother only dutifully discharged her obligations of motherhood and divided her attention in Jackie's infancy between his feeding problem and her husband's asthmatic attacks.

In spite of all the hazards Jackie experienced in the oral stage of
his infancy, he successfully completed his bowel training and became

a happy toddler in whom the process of individuation took place. Jackie disengaged himself from the symbiotic attachment to his mother, to whom he had not yet real object ties, by turning away from her to the warm and understanding colored maid. In these formative years, separation anxiety is a child's basic fear. Jackie, who belongs to the "active congenital activity type" (Fries and Woolf, 1953), took the initiative in fighting this anxiety actively, by encouraging his mother to leave him and do her shopping. He was rewarded for this achievement with a year of blessed object relationship with the maid and a time of stimulating activities, until he experienced the sudden trauma of abandonment by her. Jackie's mother did not remember any reactions on his part to the unexpected loss, but the analytic material brought out his identification with the anxious and helpless boy in the movie *Rebel Without Cause*. He and Jackie felt neglected by their parents and were attached to a colored maid; both turned into wayward youths.

The following screen memory throws more light on the chequered event of Jackie's early object loss. Jackie was supposed to write an autobiography for school. He started it in his session by writing jokingly, "Jackie the Thief." Jackie started to become a thief when he was five years old because his parents had sent away his not yet fully housebroken dog, the only real love he ever had—an actual event in Jackie's life. This screen memory was a condensation of Jackie's contradictory feelings in his previously described traumatic experience at a time when he might not have been fully housebroken himself. His guilt feelings led him to the presumption that the maid's disappearance was the consequence of his own failure in cleanliness training. Simultaneously, he was afraid he would be sent away by his parents if he should regress to earlier stages. His story in the very first analytic interview about Lassie, the dog who always came back to her master, represented the living danger in Jackie's unconscious mind of being left alone or sent away, as the maid had been—an anxiety strongly intensified by the fact that he had been adopted.

An even more profound manifestation of the painfulness of this early trauma was Jackie's hostile "crime" a few months later when he grabbed his mother's diamond ring and let it disappear in the garden. From the report about this event one could recognize that the parents were challenged with a meaningful but peculiar action of their son, and in turn exaggerated the theft far more than the situation called for. Their agitated reaction overwhelmed Jackie with attention, excitement, confusing threats of punishment, in addition to the parents' verbalized suspicion of having adopted a "born" delinquent.

The Meaning of the Stolen Ring

In his paper "Transitional Objects and Transitional Phenomena" Winnicott (1953) states: *"Pseudologia and thieving* can be described in terms of an individual's unconscious urge to bridge a gap in continuity of experience in respect of a transitional object." He also draws attention to the importance of the infant's first toys which serve the purpose of making healthy experiences in regard to the infant's own self and "other than me" objects. In relation to the transitional object the infant passes from magical, omnipotent control to control by manipulation and to reality testing. If the passing of this stage has been a normal one, no residues of these experiences will remain, and the object becomes gradually decathected. However, direct observations and clinical material (Stevenson, 1955) have proved that in time of stress, older children fall back on a transitional object by cathecting an object again with all those qualities which belong to the conception of an infant's psychic world.

In Jackie's case we can claim that the "theft" of his mother's ring represented a regression and a clinging to a transitional object. Its planned manipulation was hoped to be a help in surviving and overcoming the shock of abandonment by the maid. It also was an attempt magically to incorporate mother's love via an inanimate object. One may assume that Jackie, left to himself while his mother was doing the dishes, not welcome to participate in her activities, had regressed to an earlier stage of part-object relationship. He must have endowed this glittering object with illusions of his mother's magic power and love. Viewed from the aspect of reality testing, one can say that he used the ring to do actively what he had experienced passively: he made it disappear and "die," as the loved maid had disappeared and passed out of his life. Above all, his lack of participation in the family's search for the ring betrays his identification with the sadistic "robbing" mother who had deprived him of the possession of his first love, as she had taken him away from his original parents, and had thus instigated his revengeful hostility.

We can conclude from the anamnesis that Jackie's failure in stealing mother's ring (for purposes of integration) propelled him into deeper regression because it was at that developmental stage—some time after habit training had been concluded—that he again regressed to a narcissistic appreciation of his feces and kept them secretly in a jar. He was once more faced with the decision between a "narcissistic or an object-loving attitude" (Freud, 1916) to his environment, but he relapsed into a symbiotic relationship to his mother.

The traumatic event of early object loss and his failure to bridge painful experiences with new and better ones seemed to have had undue influence on the patient's development. However, dream material and screen memories indicated that the event coincided with the patient's early observation of the primal scene, witnessed through a keyhole, which added to his emotional perplexity. The parents' nightly activities and their punishing reactions to the ring episode became an added trauma to the object loss. During the following years additional unfavorable experiences—the unexpected tonsillectomy and above all the seduction by his sister—further contributed to the impoverishment of the patient's maturational growth. He developed in the years from three to six into a lonesome child and ended up at the height of his oedipal longings as a neurotic, phobic child. He could not attend nursery school because he had to avoid nap hours on account of his masturbation anxieties. We may assume that the manipulation with a bobby pin—which resembles a clothes pin—may have been the last vestige of a telescoped pregenital fantasy of happier times spent with the colored maid.

The boy's shaky psychic equilibrium became completely upset a second time through the seduction trauma. The frightening evidence of his sister's presumed castration seemed to have accomplished the dangerous split between physical masturbatory restrictions (Anna Freud, 1949) and the overflow of sexual excitement into delinquent acts.

We may gain an even better understanding of the patient's pathological development if we bear in mind his libidinal position at the time he experienced the traumata. Ruth Mack Brunswick

(1940) stresses the importance of the first great pair of antitheses, active-passive, in the child's first period of life. We can assume that the libidinal pleasure the boy derived after his second birthday consisted in newly acquired autonomous activities. He treated his mother—in identification with her doings—like a child, when he provided her with a hat when she had to leave the house. In Ruth Mack Brunswick's words, he had completed "the arduous task of changing his own attitude to the original love object, the mother," although previously he had a prolonged passive attachment to her. The sudden end of his exciting participation in the maid's work must have considerably shaken his newly gained active libidinal position. However, it was sufficiently well established to continue his identificatory actions by taking the mother's ring and letting it disappear as the mother had let the maid disappear, thus turning the passively endured loss into identificatory active actions. Jackie's growing interest in activities which extended to the doings of his parents at nighttime led him to primal scene observations through the keyhole of the parents' bedroom door. (The teacher's stolen keyring finds its place in this connection.)

The understanding of parental coitus of a three- to four-year-old child is based on actual physical experience the child has had at the hands of the mother which is "the original passive desire of the child to be masturbated by the mother" (Ruth Mack Brunswick, 1940).

We may assume that the patient's active primal scene observations again stimulated earlier passive sexual desires. They originate in a regression to a level at which his libidinal interest remained predominantly passive narcissistic. His sense of object relationship remained undeveloped far into latency. His father had to serve as a maternal protector instead of becoming a masculine identification figure. The patient's apparently senseless thievery represented an activity designed to provoke punishment which in turn led to the unconsciously desired passivity.

One of the predominant characteristics of acting-out psychopaths is their restlessness and hyperactivity; hence one could ask whether their struggle between activity and passivity is still an unsolved problem and whether their pathology similarly indicates preoedipal traumata as in the case of our patient.

BIBLIOGRAPHY

Bornstein, B. (1951), On Latency. *This Annual*, VI.

Brunswick, R. M. (1940), The Preoedipal Phase of the Libido Development. *Psa. Quart.*, IX.

Eissler, K. R. (1949), Some Problems of Delinquency. In: *Searchlights on Delinquency*. New York: International Universities Press.

—— (1950), Ego-Psychological Implications of the Psychoanalytic Treatment of Delinquents. *This Annual*, V.

Ekstein, R. & Friedman, S. W. (1957), The Function of Acting Out, Play Action, and Play Acting in the Psychotherapeutic Process. *J. Am. Psa. Assn.*, V.

—— and Wright, D. (1952), The Space Child. *Bull. Menninger Clin.*, XVI.

Freud, A. (1949), Certain Types and Stages of Social Maladjustment. In: *Searchlights on Delinquency*. New York: International Universities Press.

—— (1951), Observations on Child Development. *This Annual*, VI.

Freud, S. (1915), Some Character Types Met with in Psychoanalytic Work. *Collected Papers*, IV. London: Hogarth Press, 1925.

—— (1916), On the Transformation of Instincts with Special Reference to Anal Erotism. *Collected Papers*, II. London: Hogarth Press, 1924.

Fries, M. E. & Woolf, P. J. (1953), Some Hypotheses on the Role of the Congenital Activity Type in Personality Development. *This Annual*, VIII.

Stevenson, O. (1954), The First Treasured Possession. *This Annual*, IX.

Winnicott, D. W. (1953), Transitional Objects and Transitional Phenomena. *Int. J. Psa.*, XXXIV.

Woolf, M. (1949), The Child's Moral Development. In: *Searchlights on Delinquency*. New York: International Universities Press.

ON CHANGES IN IDENTIFICATION FROM MACHINE TO CRIPPLE

LISBETH J. SACHS, M.D. (New York)[1]

CASE REPORT

Robert, aged five years and three months, was brought for treatment by his mother because of serious behavior difficulties, insomnia and night terrors which followed a tonsillectomy at the age of three years and eight months. After the operation Robert was, according to the mother, "like in a state of shock, lying in bed for days, still with a blank expression on his face"; he did not respond even to painful stimuli such as pinching or shaking by his mother. Robert himself described the tonsillectomy as follows: "Then the elevator doors closed and I cried and cried and cried. Then the operation was over. Then a few days ago [he meant "after"] I got all blind; then my grandmother carried me in her arms all the time and then I could see again." He ate poorly and whined a great deal. After he developed insomnia and night terrors, he insisted that his mother sleep with him. He was hyperactive and restless, had unprovoked outbursts of rage and destructiveness, alternating with withdrawn behavior in which he did not seem to hear what was said to him. He never played with other children. The immediate reason for seeking treatment was Robert's repeated threats to throw himself down a flight of stairs and to jump out of the window. Once he was found on a window sill ready to jump. He repeatedly played with bobby pins in electric outlets despite warnings, punishments, and burns on both hands.

Robert comes from a broken home. His father left after many quarrels and trial separations, when the child was one year old. One year later, the mother established a common-law relationship with an actor. Robert considers this man his father, and his feelings for

[1] Chief Psychiatrist, Children's and Adolescents' Services, Kings County Hospital Center, Brooklyn. Assistant Professor of Psychiatry, New York State University, College of Medicine.

I would like to express my thanks to Dr. Stanley Lesser for many valuable suggestions.

him are quite positive. Robert's mother has had a long history of mental disturbance, with many years of treatment by agencies and psychiatrists. She has been diagnosed as a schizophrenic. Her relationship to her own mother has been a very hostile one since early childhood; yet she lived for over two years in her mother's home after the child's birth. Robert was often the cause of violent quarrels between the two women. While the grandmother believed in a strict regime for the child, the mother was lackadaisical to the point of neglect. She had never wanted the child.

When treatment began, on a once-a-week basis, Robert was a husky-looking youngster whose outstanding feature was a completely bland, expressionless face. He did not look at me. He moved slowly and heavily, with an awkward gait.

At the beginning of the first session, he followed me into the playroom, and in a dragging, monotonous voice asked whether I had another gun, pointing to the one he carried. When he saw a gun in the toy chest, he hastily buried it in his pocket. He then took an airplane and pretended that it was flying high through the air, while making loud, roaring, weird noises. Every flight ended with a plane crash against the toy chest, and all these crashes were greeted by screams, indicating that a catastrophe had happened. "Five people are killed, all are dead," was all he said, without displaying any affect. Then he took a doll and swung it through the air, as he had done with the plane, crashed it against the toy chest and said monotonously, "Dead, just killed." Thereupon he swiftly pulled the gun out of his pocket, aimed it at me, and played at shooting me, again producing weird sounds and screaming innumerable times, "Killed" and "Dead."

This first session was typical of many that followed. He always asked for a second gun at the beginning of every session. In addition to the shooting and dying game, Robert also played at being a plane, a space ship, or just a machine, and frequently combined both. The space ship would collide with a planet, or the door would open in mid-air. Each time Robert would demonstrate his dying by trembling and shaking, holding his breath until his face was bluish red. Then he would throw himself on the floor, his eyes closed and his whole body shaking convulsively. This "dying" was repeated innumerable times in every session and was part of the plane game as well as the shooting game. He made loud, weird noises of machines roaring, planes crashing, and guns shooting while drawing "machines" on the walls.

He spoke little during these games, and when he did speak usually uttered disconnected words, and some neologisms. At times actual word salad was noted. Once he walked out of the office and pointed a gun at a little boy sitting in the hall. "You are in jail.

Go through the window in the jail, in the jail." He returned to the office, revolving the desk chair, getting more and more excited, turning the chair with the left hand, holding the gun in the right hand, screaming, shooting an imaginary person on the desk chair, and suddenly throwing the gun away. Then with a panicky expression, he asked: "What happened? What happened? I shot him, I shot him, machine engine, God of machine engine, space patrol engine, machine power protector, engine power, machine power, power machine engine, moon and captain fister, engine power, patty rocket door, engine captain, machine rocket power engine, space control engine, pecker engine, rocket doll patty engine." After a pause, he remarked, "That's right, more machine." On this, as on many other occasions, rage was followed by panic; as if he were afraid of retaliation for his aggression.

At times, after aiming the gun at me, he suggested that I close my eyes to indicate death, but in general he seemed to pay very little attention to me. Often he ordered me to sit as far away from him as possible, or to look out of the window. Once when I suggested that he was afraid of me, he looked straight into my eyes and, with a worried, serious expression, he said, "Yes, I am . . . . You will kill me, Doctor."

After three months of treatment he dictated a letter: "This letter has God in it, please it says God in life, no prisoner has gone to be dead unless they are dead, God in life. If dolls are broken in half or electronic man, God of life is a lady of prisoners, a man is a man of prisoners and he says God of life."

At that time Robert also walked over to a little boy in the hall and pummeled him without the slightest provocation. When the little boy struck back, Robert pushed him to the floor and hit his head hard against the stone floor. Robert airily said to me, "Forget about it, I sent him out into space. He is in space now, all dead."

This letter as well as this incident showed that the child was regressing; though no gross changes for the worse were observed either in the day nursery or by the mother, he presented a more chaotic picture during the sessions. It was unclear whether he seemed more disturbed because his disconnected thoughts were being expressed or whether he actually was falling apart. I felt that my passive attitude might have encouraged the child's pathological behavior. Therefore I decided to structure the treatment situation more definitely.

In the next session I placed several toys on the table: a baby bottle with a nipple, baby clothes and a rattle. As usual, Robert walked into the playroom, shot at me several times, took crayons and drew machines on the wall. Uttering senseless words and weird sounds, he proceeded to play at being a machine. Then, noticing the baby bottle on the table, he walked over reluctantly, looked first at the bottle, then in a questioning, unsure way, at me, and I encouraged him to play with the bottle. When he still hesitated, though he obviously was quite interested, I suggested that we play baby. With a shy smile that I had never seen before, he silently grasped the bottle, climbed into my lap, nestled in my arms, and with closed eyes sucked the nipple vigorously. He stayed in my arms for several minutes while I spoke soothingly to him; then with a deep sigh of relief, he busied himself with the baby clothes. He put the baby sweater around his neck as if it were a bib and climbed back into my lap, closing his eyes and nestling against me. This time he made sucking movements and noises with his mouth without using the bottle. Robert went home from this session with a smile on his face.

At the beginning of the next session he walked into the office energetically, made me sit down and immediately climbed into my lap and played baby. This game was repeated for several months at the beginning of each session, but without props. He merely lay in my arms for awhile. Now, with the introduction of playing baby, the types of games which he played and his attitude toward me changed markedly. His incoherent talk decreased and in a few months disappeared. Machine games with motor noises and dying, though he still played them, took up less and less of our time and finally were abandoned, only to appear again during a period of stress.

A new activity appeared: he drew a switch in the form of a stick, with one or two balls at the ends. He drew them on the wall near me, explaining, "So you can get to them, Doctor." I would use these switches to turn off Robert's weird machine noises and screaming as well as his word salad accompanying the space ship games. Robert always reacted to my turning off the switches with mock anger; sometimes he heaved a sigh of relief, but he always stopped his solitary playing, came over to me and engaged me in a different type of game. At times he actually reminded me: "Doctor, Doctor, you have the controls," whereupon I would turn the switches drawn on the wall so that we could start a new kind of game.

Now many new games appeared, all of them involving me to a much greater extent. In one of them, he played with a small doll called a "Lady, President of a Jail." She tried to climb into a glass jar. Upon reaching the rim, she lost her balance, and Robert asked me to help the doll. This game was repeated with different dolls, but each time Robert asked me to save the dolls from falling into the jar. Thereupon I told the dolls that I would not permit their getting injured. I patted their heads and reassured them. Robert looked at me fascinated and said, "Don't do that." Then he changed

his mind. "Oh yes, please, please do it." Then he shot me with his
gun, but this time did not let me die as before: he rescued me. Then
he asked me to shoot him, but he, too, wished to be rescued. He
seemed happy and excited playing this game, screaming, "You saved
me, you saved me, and I saved you and I saved my mother." He
spoke of wanting to put his head into the small glass jar. "I will
be in there all alone, lonesome, and you will save me." I assured him
that I would help him with his loneliness. He looked at me seriously, nodded his head, and said vigorously, "Good, good, good."

In the next session he made a little boy doll fall into the glass
jar and then observed that now the boy had become a superman.
I protested, "He is just a lonely little boy who wants to be helped
and protected." Robert looked at me in amazement, and said again,
"Good, good." He went on to other games and became engrossed
in a toy cash register. Robert played storekeeper, while I was either
a little boy or the mother. The storekeeper sold or gave away things
lavishly to the boy; he overwhelmed him with toys and food. But
the mother received nothing. "The store is empty, I haven't got
nothing," he would say. Speaking to the little boy customer, he
would shout in anger, "Your mother can't have any cake. She gets
too fat. No meat. She gets too fat. No candy. She gets too fat. No
mother." In subsequent sessions Robert vented more resentment
against his mother: "You should be ashamed of yourself not to make
breakfast for your little boy." He would sneer and spit, then turn
away in disgust.

He also played sheriff and robber, sheriff and outlaw, or just
good man and bad man. He and I alternated in these roles.

I began to prepare the patient for my absence during vacation.
We built an airplane of tinker toys to take me to my destination.
First Robert suggested that he would be the pilot and so could stay
with me. I pointed out that they would miss him in nursery school.
"O.K. so I stay here on the ground, but I keep in touch with you by
radio." As the airplane took off he reassured me, through an
imagined radio from the ground, that I would have a good flight,
because he had checked the engines. Then the plane returned, and
I descended from it to greet the ground crew, including Robert.
He beamed at me, shook my hand, and asked whether I had had a
good time. Then he suddenly collapsed and lay stretched out on the
floor, making convulsive movements and playing dead. This vacation
game was repeated many times, always ending the same way. For
some time it was not entirely clear to me why he had chosen this
finale. At first he was unwilling to talk about it, but then he said
reluctantly, "Maybe it is not real dying. Maybe I am not dead.
Maybe just the bad man is dead. The good man can live." When
he repeated this vacation game after this discussion, he got up after

falling to the floor and laid the imaginary dead man on his arms. Bent over from the burden of the corpse, he walked slowly to the door and threw the body into the hall. After a swift kick at the imaginary corpse, he closed the door carefully and with a deep sigh of relief remarked, "He is gone. The bad man is gone. Thank God." The idea of the bad man became clearer when, after I returned from my vacation, he dictated the following letter to me: "Little Betty is my friend, and Mac and Jerry and Michael. Sometimes he beats me up and I tell the teacher. Give my regards, not to the teacher, just to you, Doctor. You know what you should write. Robert killed the bad man for a reason, so the bad man should not kill Dr. Sachs. Just for a reason, just for a reason. Because he could choke and kill you and stab a knife in you. I don't want to die, I want to live, to live. To live my life all over again, I want to live because I love my Doctor and because she loves me. Help me to get the bad man. Turn the gas on and bake him. He is cooking. He is all ready, put spaghetti on him and ketchup and sugar. Eat him up, ooooh, ooooh, it tastes good. A good lunch, we ate the bad man up, I am too full, too full now. Now I throw him up (he gags). Ugh! Ugh!, I throw him up, he is all gone, the bad man is gone."

In a later session Robert discovered the sink in the office and began to play with water. He derived a great deal of enjoyment from splashing it against the wall, and managed to make a few drops hit me. Whenever the water splattered me, he smiled as if it was all a big mistake, but then repeated it. The water play became wilder and wilder, he became more and more excited and made little gurgling sounds. The game culminated with Robert's opening his zipper and excitedly declaring his intent to urinate into the drain. Restrained from this, he went on to more excited splashing of the walls and me.

One day he asked me whether he could dance for me. He went into a wild wiggle and shake, dancing until he became exhausted and soaked with perspiration. "I hope so very much you liked it," he said afterward, adding, "For you I would do anything."

There was more playing of sheriff and bad man, but now I was more often the assistant sheriff, and both of us went out to look for the bad man. Usually we were successful and the outlaw was put in jail, the therapist often acting as lady jailer. Toward fall I became the sheriff's wife, who cared for the house while the sheriff went out to catch the bad man all by himself.

About this time Robert suggested presenting a puppet show to me. First two men appeared, a Dr. Livingston, with whom Robert identified himself, and a Dr. Patton. The two fought. Dr. Livingston was victorious and broke Dr. Patton's leg. Robert then called for the ambulance to have the now legless Dr. Patton removed to a hospital.

Next a lady came on the scene. Dr. Livingston danced happily, and when he saw the lady he hugged her and kissed her and slapped her buttocks. Then a boy appeared who pushed Dr. Livingston away and took the lady for himself. Dr. Livingston disappeared, and the boy bowed in front of the imaginary audience and thanked them for the imagined applause. Robert now identified with the boy and called him by his own name. It seemed that in this puppet scene Robert re-enacted his family story. His real father had lost out to his stepfather, and in the finale of the play Robert expressed his wish to push the stepfather out and have his mother for himself. Robert seemed very pleased with the performance, called it "my theater" and asked to be praised.

Many changes took place in Robert's behavior and attitudes during the first year of therapy. The slow, detached, withdrawn little boy with an expressionless face had developed into a demanding, willful and readily smiling child. He now wanted my undivided attention: "Now I don't want you to look out of the window. Pay attention to what I say. Hear me. It is my 'pointment.' I want to stay here day and night, a hundred thousand hours, that is forever."

After one year of treatment, Robert entered a public school. The day nursery which he had previously attended reported that he had improved considerably, that his solitary impersonation of machines had been absent for many weeks at a time, and that he had begun to seek children to play with. The mother also reported marked improvement. She stated that he was much easier to manage, and that he slept through the night without night terrors. Several times he had come home from playing in the evening, whistling happily.

In his new school, he was assigned to a class taught by an elderly woman who believed in strict discipline. One day because he had talked out of turn and had not done his work properly, this teacher called him a sissy, and sent him home. That afternoon, on his way to the therapy session, he cried continually, and worried about disappointing the therapist. He looked withdrawn, and at once drew machines and airships on the wall, again making weird noises. He also played dying again. He had not done this for many months, and knowing nothing of the crisis at school, I questioned him without success. Instead of answering my questions, he said to me in an angry voice, "Don't you understand? I told you where the switches are. You are in control. Use them." I finally perceived his intent and used the controls to stop Robert. He then called his parents in from the waiting hall and asked them to tell me of the events at school. "I can't tell you," he said, "I am ashamed. You are not going to like me any more," and he sobbed bitterly. I tried to comfort him and reassured him that I liked him regardless of what had happened and promised to arrange a transfer to another class with a more understanding teacher. Robert, as in earlier times, climbed into my lap, nestled in my arms, closed his eyes and listened to me. Then he got up and with a deep sigh walked off with his parents. In the following weeks Robert exhibited definite regressive features. He did not mix with the children of the new class to which he had been transferred but spent much time in solitary machine games at school as well as at home. However, he did not revert to night terrors, incoherence or word salad, or suicidal threats.

After several weeks Robert quieted down. Then another crisis arose. Robert was in the fifteenth month of treatment when the real father's lawyer suddenly notified the mother that a divorce could be arranged immediately if she would go out of the state for the divorce proceedings. The mother left hurriedly, happy at the prospect of a divorce and hoping to marry her lover. She left Robert with this man, who promised to take good care of the child, which he could do because he was unemployed. Unfortunately for Robert, he obtained employment just after his mother left town, and the child had to be boarded out with various relatives. This upset the child greatly. When his mother returned after she had been granted the divorce, she found Robert very difficult to manage. The school authorities also felt that he was too difficult and initiated steps to suspend him. There was much turmoil in the home after the mother's return. She had expected her common-law husband to marry her now that she was free, but he refused and threatened to break all ties if pressured into marriage. At one time they actually separated at his insistence, whereupon mother and child moved out of town to her parents for a week.

In therapy sessions at this time Robert again engaged in much solitary play, accompanied by shouting. There was, however, one important difference: he did not play at being a machine, as in earlier times, but at being a cripple, either Captain Hook or Mr. Pegleg or both. He always gave the impression of being very helpless and of suffering greatly from his handicaps. He would moan and groan and shout loudly or curse and sneer at his imaginary enemies. In order to look like Captain Hook, he insisted on wearing long-sleeved shirts. He would pull his left hand up so that it was completely covered by the shirt and hold a shower curtain hook in his hand, thus giving the impression of having a hook instead of a hand. When he played Mr. Pegleg, he pulled his left foot up into his trousers, jumping on his right leg only or walking with a severe limp.

The child was completely absorbed in playing these characters and could not be made to give them up, either by the teacher or by the parents. But there was much more contact between the patient and me during treatment sessions than in the earlier episodes of playing machine. Often while playing he would call for help: "Dr. Sachs, come help me, poor Pegleg. The enemies are all over me." He would throw himself on the floor and rise only after I had pushed the imaginary enemies away.

I suggested to the patient that his mother's going out of town and his stepfather's threat to leave home had frightened him and made him feel helpless and crippled. He was also told that by crippling himself he punished himself for his anger at them and at the same time prevented himself from attacking them.

For reasons beyond the scope of this report, I attempted to persuade the common-law husband not to break up the family unit. Eventually they were reconciled and married.

For about three months, Robert spent practically all his waking time playing at being crippled, then gradually he quieted down. Improvement was noted at home and in school, and the principal spontaneously stopped the suspension proceedings at the Board of Education. Instead of playing cripple, he now engaged in games such as hide and seek with me.

At the end of the second year of treatment he graduated from the first grade. The family went to the country for the summer and he was placed in a day camp nearby. His stay at the camp was successful. His mother reported that there had been no solitary play at being a machine or cripple, that at all times he had participated in the various group activities, and that he had enjoyed camp life. He learned how to swim and received an award for being the second best camper in his group of more than twenty children.

In the third year of treatment new stresses arose. Robert's mother left rather unexpectedly for a week-end visit to her husband out of town. Robert appeared irritable, and at the end of the session he begged, "Please give me a 'special' today" (meaning an additional session). "Just today because you love me." When I explained why this was not feasible, he threw himself on the floor in anger, refusing to leave. I pointed out that he was angry at his mother for leaving him, and afraid that she would not return. To the first he nodded vehemently, almost banging his head against the floor; to the second he shook his head just as vehemently, then got up and left for home. The mother reported that for a few days he was very demanding and short-tempered, but he no longer showed the severe regressive features previously noted in similar situations.

Shortly thereafter Robert suffered another disappointment. His best friend, Joe, with whom he had been playing regularly for the past six or seven months, had taken a quarter from him. Robert called him a cheat, and upon his denial, a liar. After this episode, Joe's parents did not permit him to play with Robert. The child was heartbroken. For several days he refused to go into the street to play, and when his mother finally persuaded him to do so, he put an eye patch on his left eye before leaving the house. He also decorated himself with a gun and sheriff badge and called himself "the sheriff who got wounded." The next day the eye patch was forgotten, and a few days later Robert came home radiant with a new friend, Gilbert. Proudly he described Gilbert as the best student in the class and his best friend. He has played with Gilbert since.

A few months later he came limping into the office: "Hi doc, I'm sorry to tell you but I got a metal leg today." There he really tricked me. I suggested that we both should try to find the reasons for the anger that made him play cripple again. With a giggle he replied, "I just wanted to see if you would get real sad when I told you that again."

Now after thirty-four months, Robert appears very different from the boy who started treatment. He does not show any bizarre symptomatology, he has acquired social graces and developed a good sense of humor. While during the first part of treatment he was completely unable to concentrate on learning, he now is a good student in the brightest class, bringing home "100's" and "A's." But most important, his relationship to his mother has changed radically. He now expresses his love for her readily and frequently. He has erected within himself a stable image of her. This is borne out by the fact that he is able to separate from her, and wait for her return without retreating into a world of fantasy.

DISCUSSION

The child's identification with a machine and the subsequent emergence of the cripple is of interest. The identification with a machine and some of the bizarre symptomatology are undoubtedly related to the traumatic experience of the tonsillectomy. However, though many attempts were made to relate the material to the operation, the child even now is not ready to discuss it.

The child not only played at being a machine, but also drew a machine when asked to draw a person (Fig. 1), thus showing a primitive type of identification. We assume that this identification with a machine is a projection of his own aggression and constitutes an attempt to control it by immobilizing himself (catatonic-like state postoperatively, death game). He gives up other ego functions and concentrates all energies on controlling aggression. His anger against people (especially his mother whom he makes responsible for separation and operation and probably for long-standing neglect and discord in the family) is overwhelming. He turns away from them.

Even language is no longer used for communication. Neologisms and word salad result. "I used to make up words," he once stated, giving examples. When asked what a particular word meant he answered, "No meaning, I made them out of real words. I made them sound funny, that's all."

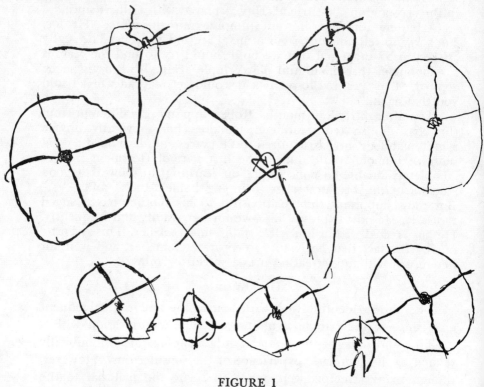

FIGURE 1
Machine stage (beginning of first year of treatment)

The problem of identification with machines has been considered by several authors. Rank and Macnaughton (1950) described a child's identification with an egg beater and propeller. Ekstein's (1954) patient invented a "time machine" and later "a dimension-trans-former" which the author considers to be projections of the child's power as well as an attempt to gain distance from his drives. Bornstein's (1949) phobic boy invented the "remembering and projecting machine." H. Sachs (1933) agrees with Tausk (1933) who states: "The machines produced by man are unconscious projections of man's bodily structure." In the case of Natalie A. the machine was "a human body, indeed the patient's own form."

The emergence of the cripple in this material is striking. The cripple appears after separations from mother, during the school crisis, and the loss of a friend. Separation is thus experienced (and the reaction to it expressed) as body destruction or body damage, probably related to the real experience of the tonsillectomy where separation was followed by operation. The identification with these dangerous-looking cripples also bears witness to the extent of his aggression. However, it is still he who becomes the recipient of it.

The changes in identification were clearly expressed in his drawings. As treatment progressed, Robert drew a machine with such human features as eyes (Fig. 2).[2] Gradually the drawings began

FIGURE 2

Beginning of the human, embryo-like figure; switches developing into eyes (middle of first year of treatment)

2 Interestingly enough, these eyes were circles connected with a line, and looked very much like the switches he used for controls. Seeing and not seeing are thus

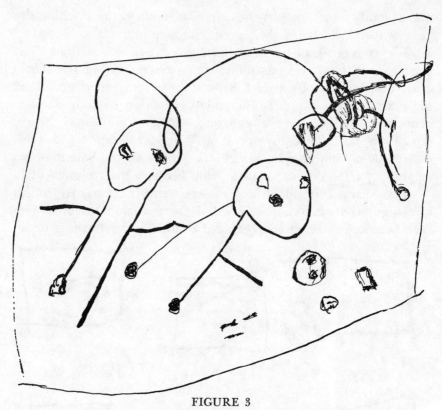

FIGURE 3

The process of human birth; baby in upper right-hand corner showing
much anxiety (middle of first year of treatment)

to resemble human beings, though they looked more like embryos
than boys of his own age, as would be expected from a healthy child
(Fig. 3). Later he was able to draw people, quite sophisticated, with
a considerable amount of detail, but these figures were crippled.
They were either peg-legged or hook-armed (Fig. 4). (These body-
damaged human figures were drawn during the time his mother left
town to obtain a divorce and during the upheaval at home that
ensued.) These figures had to protect themselves from destruction
with guns and sheriff badges, but they nevertheless looked dangerous. They could be expected to lash out and destroy.

---

intimately linked to primitive processes of having and not having contact with the
object. After the tonsillectomy, he becomes blind. The first control switches are connected with the eyes. After losing his friend, he puts a patch on his eyes.

During the treatment the child begins to cope with his murderous impulses by a self-division into a "good man" and a "bad man." At times he projects the badness onto the therapist. First he put the controls over the bad self into the hands of the therapist. Then, as

FIGURE 4

Identification with cripples (beginning of second year of treatment)

therapy continued, he took over himself. He became a sheriff, carried handcuffs and put them on the bad man. He killed the bad man and threw him out of the room.[3] In his drawings he depicted the bad man or criminal being caught; that is, made harmless by the good man or sheriff.

[3] It is of interest that the "death of the bad man" is expressed in oral terms: he is first eaten up and then "thrown up." In the earlier storekeeper games, Robert had refused food to the mother, as he had felt starved by her. Unfortunately nothing is known about Robert's early feeding experiences beyond the fact that he was seriously neglected.

At the end of the second year of treatment, his drawings depicted happy events (Fig. 5), such as his seventh birthday, with a comic twist—a cat in human clothes standing upright and presenting him with a birthday cake and seven candles. There was a whole series

FIGURE 5
Safe and happy as part of the family unit (middle of second year of treatment)

of drawings, vividly depicting his activities and life at summer camp. He drew brightly colored pictures with sunshine and flowers, with mother and son walking hand in hand (Fig. 6).

Of interest is a drawing at the time of his seventh birthday in which five burglars are about to steal sacks of gold, while three sheriffs are watching and preventing the looting (Fig. 7). Destruc-

FIGURE 6

Mother and son walking hand in hand (end of second year of treatment)

tiveness apparently is well under control here. K. Machover, in a personal communication, felt that oedipal material is touched upon here for the first time in his drawings. The burglars are trying to steal (mother's) treasures while the authority (father) prevents them from doing so. After having symbolically obtained a good mother, he begins to deal with his oedipal wishes. Identification with the father is apparent in this drawing, as well as in others. Gradually his drawings become less original, more conforming, more conventional.

The identification with the machine coincides with his playing dead and the concomitant convulsions and devitalization of his body, a feature that appears again at the time of the therapist's planned vacation. His catatonic-like state after the tonsillectomy, described by the patient as blindness, his withdrawal and suicidal threats, his lack of affect at the beginning of treatment may have

FIGURE 7

The "Holdup" (end of second year of treatment)

a similar symbolic meaning as his dying games during therapy sessions. It seems that the dying was introduced by the child for the purpose of preventing himself from acting out his murderous impulses directed against others (especially his mother) and himself.

The child's wiggle and dance, then, could be interpreted as "a revitalization, a primitive overcathexis of his body, his gestural rebirth, an orgastic and ecstatic episode."[4] The child can now permit himself to be alive again. He ends the dance scene by inquiring

4 Suggestion of Dr. Margaret S. Mahler.

FIGURE 8
This drawing from real life shows his identification with the father
(end of third year of treatment)

whether the therapist is pleased, and then he adds, "For you I would do anything." This feeling is similar to that expressed in his letter: "I want to live, to live, to live my life all over again. I want to live because I love my doctor and she loves me." He apparently realizes that he is not doomed to feel merely destructive and murderous impulses. He can permit himself to feel, because he has the capacity for positive emotions, for love, and this love will be reciprocated. He hopes that with the help of the therapist he can keep his homicidal and suicidal impulses under control. "You saved me, I saved you and I saved my mother." Parent, therapist and the child have been "saved" from his destruction.

A few words about the technique used in the treatment of this case are in order. In this case the approach employed with neurotic children not only met with failure but presented the possibility of damage to the child, similar to the effect that intense, uncovering

FIGURE 9
Boy and girl rabbit kissing; peer problems are appearing
(end of third year of treatment)

treatment would have on a psychotic adult. Therefore, after about three months of this treatment, I assumed a much more active role, at the same time being more permissive and indulgent than one would be toward neurotic patients. I allowed the patient to nestle in my lap and suck a baby bottle; I pushed him in a baby carriage, and frequently reassured him. On the other hand, I made him aware of reality whenever he seemed to lose his grip on it. "This is make-believe" was an expression frequently used by me and later adopted by the patient. I acted as an auxiliary ego; e.g., by using "controls" to stop his regressive behavior and withdrawal. His fears, anxieties and aggression, as expressed in his rages, and his fantasies of omnipotence were interpreted to him again and again.

There was another important difference in approach. I gave actual suggestions and advice in regard to changing the school as well as in the family crisis. This is quite different from what I would have done in treating a neurotic child or one with a behavior disturbance.

While this boy improved satisfactorily during the thirty-four months of treatment, a prediction as to his future course cannot be ventured. True enough, he was able to overcome newly arising stresses, such as the school crisis, the collapse of his friendship, and the separations from his mother, with decreasing difficulties and less and less regression. Nevertheless, the fact that the psychotic process developed at such an early period in his life does not permit too much optimism.

Bornstein, B. (1949), The Analysis of a Phobic Child. *This Annual,* III/IV.

Ekstein, R. (1954), The Space Child's Time Machine. Round Table: Childhood Schizophrenia. *Am. J. Orthopsychiat.,* XXIV.

Rank, B. & Macnaughton, D. (1950), A Clinical Contribution to Early Ego Development. *This Annual,* V.

Sachs, H. (1933), The Delay of the Machine Age. *Psa. Quart.,* II.

Sechehaye, M. A. (1956), The Transference and Symbolic Realization. *Int. J. Psa.,* XXXVII.

Tausk, V. (1933), On the Origin of the "Influencing Machine" in Schizophrenia. *Psa. Quart.,* II.

APPLIED PSYCHOANALYSIS

ON "SEEING THE SALAMANDER"

ROBERT PLANK, LL.D., M.S.W. (Cleveland)[1]

I

One of the few specific childhood memories that Benvenuto Cellini (1500-1571) relates in his autobiography is this:

> When I was about five years old, my father happened to be in our basement . . . where a good fire of oaken logs was burning. He had a viola in his hand and was playing and singing all alone by the fire. It was very cold. As he gazed into the fire, he chanced to see in the middle of the hottest flames a little creature like a lizard which was sporting about in the strongest flame. He instantly perceived what it was, had my sister and me called, pointed it out to us children and gave me a violent box on the ear which immediately made me cry. He comforted me kindly. "Sonny," he said, "I did not hit you for any wrong you did, my darling, but only to make you remember that this lizard which you saw in the fire is a salamander, a creature which has never been seen by anyone else of whom we have a true report." And so he kissed me and gave me some pennies.

What did Giovanni Cellini and his children see? Obviously not a specimen of the real animal which is now called salamander— or of any real animal, for that matter. What they thought they saw was a being of much nobler lineage than the lowly amphibian: a creature well known to fable and myth, though a total stranger to zoology.

Giovanni Cellini projected. The similar projections that we encounter today are usually solicited and attenuated. A Rorschach subject may well see a salamander in Card VIII, but will say that the blot "looks like" salamanders. Giovanni Cellini, however, created

[1] The author wants to acknowledge his gratitude to the friends and scholars, too numerous to be listed, who helped him to collect and evaluate abstruse material and devious thoughts.

his own Rorschach situation; and he believed that what he saw was there.

His children, actuated by that suggestibility that makes the *folie à deux* possible, willingly saw the salamander, too. He impressed the incident on his son Benvenuto by slapping him and giving him money—a method reported to have been traditional in some European cultures when an adult wanted to make sure that a child would not forget a memorable event. He may not have needed to do so— Benvenuto may have retained the memory because of its intrinsic significance. In any case, he included it in his autobiography, and so it has become a symbol which other writers (e.g., Dumas, 1852) have referred and alluded to three and four centuries after it happened. Among them is Mark Twain who in his autobiography says:

> I used to remember my brother Henry walking into a fire outdoors when he was a week old. It was remarkable in me to remember a thing like that, and it was still more remarkable that I should cling to the delusion, for thirty years, that I *did* remember it—for of course it never happened: he would not have been able to walk at that age. If I had stopped to reflect, I should not have burdened my memory with that impossible rubbish so long. It is believed by many people that an impression deposited in a child's memory within the first two years of its life cannot remain there five years, but that is an error. The incident of Benvenuto Cellini's salamander must be accepted as authentic and trustworthy . . . [Clemens, 1925].

Did Mark Twain notice the strange inconsistency of accepting Cellini's recollection while rejecting his own? He wrote that part of his autobiography in 1897/98 in Vienna. It is a pity, perhaps, that he did not take a walk of a few blocks to see a certain doctor who could have explained to him something about screen memories. A comment on wit and its relation to the unconscious would also have been in order, for Mark Twain goes on:

> I am grown old and my memory is not as active as it used to be. When I was younger I could remember anything, whether it had happened or not; but my faculties are decaying now, and soon I shall be so I cannot remember any but the things that never happened. It is sad to go to pieces like this, but we all have to do it.

A more obscure allusion is found in the report that W. B. Yeats (1922) gives of a séance led by a man named Mathers:

> He gave me a cardboard symbol and I closed my eyes. Sight came slowly, there was not that sudden miracle as if the darkness had been cut with a knife, for that miracle is mostly a woman's privilege, but there rose before me mental images that I could not control: a desert and black Titan raising himself up by his two hands from the middle of a heap of ancient ruins. Mathers explained that I had seen a being of the order of Salamanders because he had shown me their symbol.

Two books on Yeats (Menon, 1942; Jeffares, 1949) quote this, but do not attempt to interpret it. Though presumably intelligible to the initiated, the meaning of "salamander" here has become esoteric.

The most interesting reference to Cellini's salamander experience, and one that is as clear as light, is that made by Sir Osbert Sitwell (1944):

> I was about five years old . . . It was a Saturday afternoon in June, the first real exquisite day of summer that year, and I was doing some of my first lessons; but so much did I long to be in the golden air outside . . . I resolved to make a dash for freedom. Accordingly, I hurled my copy of *Reading Without Tears* down upon the floor and ran out of the room, a screaming Swiss governess in pursuit . . . I hid under the billiard table . . . Extricated with some difficulty, I was carried upstairs by my father . . . and in the course of the journey I kicked him very hard in the belly . . . fearful scenes ensued. I felt disgraced and humiliated forever . . . My mother had been out at the time but, when she returned . . . she rescued me, restored my self-respect, told Davis [the nurse] to give me tea, and, though it was by now rather late for my usual promenade, for it was about six, sent me out alone with Davis.
>
> . . . skillfully eluding Davis, I ran to the edge of the precipitous cliff and stood there looking straight in the face of the evening sun. The light bathed the whole world in its amber and golden rays, seeming to link up every object and every living thing, catching them in its warm diaphanous net, so that I felt myself at one with my surroundings, part of this same boundless immensity of sea and sky and, even, of the detailed precision of the landscape, part of the general creation, divided from it by no barriers made by man or devil . . . as I watched, I lost myself. . . . All this must have endured only an instant, for presently—

but time had ceased to exist—I heard Davis calling. The eye of the sun was lower now. The clouds began to take on a deeper and more rosy hue, and it was time for me to return home; but this strange peace, of which poetry is born, had for the first time descended on me and henceforth a new light quivered above the world and over the people in it.

Like Cellini before me, I had seen the salamander; I had seen it, not in a fire within a house, but in the flames that lit the eye of the sun.

What is it that makes "seeing the salamander"—in the sense that Sitwell has given to the expression—so different from other experiences?

It is a brief, fleeting glimpse. It is not related—on the face of it—to the happenings that the person perceives and reacts to in ordinary living. The event itself is typically not of marked actual importance to the person who experiences it. It does not affect everyday happenings; they go on just as though the salamander had never been seen. The event may, as far as its actual content goes, be most trivial, hardly noticeable; yet its emotional significance is the very opposite of banal.

What makes it especially strange is the fact that these events happen without preparation or visible causal connection. The "salamander" appears uncalled: there is nothing, apparently, that the individual has done, or could have done, to conjure him or even to merit his sight. "Seeing the salamander" thus appears as a glimpse of another world, as a gift of the gods.

The special constellation has been superbly formulated by C. S. Lewis (1955) who relates three "episodes" that together formed the "central story" of his life. Yet what were they? One was "a memory of a memory," and the other two were "glimpses." They happened to him "at the age of six, seven and eight." Evidently recognizing the meagerness of his factual report, he goes on as follows:

I will only underline the quality common to the three experiences: it is that of an unsatisfied desire which is itself more desirable than any other satisfaction. I call it Joy, which is here a technical term and must be sharply distinguished both from Happiness and from Pleasure. Joy (in my sense) has indeed one characteristic, and only one, in common with them; the fact that anyone who has experienced it will want it again. Apart from that, and considered only in its quality, it might almost equally well be called a particular kind of unhappiness or grief, but then it is a kind we want. I doubt whether anyone who has tasted it would ever, if both were in his power, exchange it for all the pleasures in the world. But then Joy is never in our power and pleasure often is.

It would be foolish to argue with the persons who have had such experiences about their importance for them: the very nature of these events places them beyond the reach of effective interpersonal communication. They are *par excellence* the stuff that autobiographies are made of. Obviously, they cannot be observed; we can learn about them through introspection or from the freely given accounts of those who have had them.

II

We cannot expect such narrations to make easy and easily convincing reading. Since these experiences are—by definition as it were—outside of all ordinary frames of reference, they are bound to be hard to describe.

This characteristic has long been noted with regard to certain experiences which may be considered as similar to the salamander experience (though it is true that we shall still have to show the similarity). William James, in his standard work (1902) lists "ineffability" as the first characteristic of "mystical states." Bertram D. Lewin, in a much more recent book (1950), comments critically on the "allegation of inarticulateness or of difficulty in putting the experience into words" which he found a " 'manifest element' in many descriptions of the ecstatic state."

Those who have nevertheless tried to describe the allegedly undescribable were eminent writers, hence masters of the word; but at this point they seem indeed to stumble and to grope for the right term. So Spitteler, who decides for *"Wonne"*—here rendered as "bliss," also translatable as "rapture"—which comes very close to the word "joy" in the specific meaning in which C. S. Lewis uses it.

Then I fell ill, and *Tante Gotte* [godmother] nursed me: so faithful she was, so devoted, so gentle, that she won my heart.

When I was almost well again, I experienced a blissful moment.
I had slept and was still dozing. Before I was quite awake, somebody stepped to my bed . . . and when I opened my eyes to
learn what may be coming, the face of *Tante Gotte* smiled toward
me while at the same time the calm, mild, sun-drenched afternoon light touched me . . .

At this opening of my eyes, with that glance into a friend's face
on which the beautiful day played, a wondrous feeling streamed
through me which I do not know how to call by any name but
bliss. What, when you think it through, does "bliss" mean? I
open my dictionary and read: "Bliss: pasture of the soul." Quite
right, pasture of the soul it is, but in harmony with the physical
happiness as it is composed of feeling of health, vitality after
gladdening sleep, greeting by the colorful daylight. Daylight and
color seem to be essential for bliss to emerge, at least in my
experience. I have later experienced the feeling of bliss several
times more, and it always happened on awakening from a light
sleep in daytime; most perfectly when the friend's face greeted
me through a curtain of color [Spitteler, 1920].

Spitteler's novel *Imago* (1922)—the one from which psychoanalysis took the name of one of its concepts and two of its journals—centers around a related state in an adult:

. . . jointly experienced hours whose content, as far as events
are concerned, was nought—but of eternal poetic value (for
myself, I call these hours *Parusie*) . . .

. . . He who has not felt the breath of *Parusie*.

. . . the immortal picture of *Parusie* . . .

The German word *Parusie* is about as rare as its English counterpart *parousia* which means "coming or event; specifically the second
coming of Christ" (Webster, 1951). The corresponding Greek word
occurs in the New Testament. When Spitteler decided to use it in
a significantly different sense, he may have been familiar with it
through his studies of theology. He had been destined to become a
minister but lost his faith.

He, the unbeliever, tried to determine the conditions under
which the phenomenon of *Wonne* is capable of occurring. Other
autobiographers—as far as they were not too "surprised by joy" to

ask any such questions at all—found a more facile answer; or at least a direction.

> . . . It must be understood that to me God *is* the experienceable quality in the universe . . .
>
> I must have been between five and six when this experience happened to me. It was a summer morning and the child that I was had walked down through the orchard alone and come out on the brow of a sloping hill where there was grass and a wind blowing and one tall tree reaching into infinite immensities of blueness. Quite suddenly, after a moment of quietness there, earth and sky and tree and wind-blown grass and the child in the midst of them came alive together with a pulsing light of consciousness. There was a wild foxglove at the child's feet and a bee dozing about it, and to this day I can recall the swift, inclusive awareness of each for the whole—I in them and they in me, and all of us enclosed in a warm lucent bubble of livingness. I remember the child looking everywhere for the source of this happy wonder, and at last she questioned—"God?" because it was the only awesome word she knew. Deep inside, like the murmurous swinging of a bell, she heard the answer, "God, God."
>
> How long this ineffable moment lasted I never knew. It broke like a bubble at the sudden singing of a bird, and the wind blew and the world was the same again—only never *quite* the same [Austin, 1931].

III

Having now achieved at least a preliminary definition of the "salamander phenomenon," we can turn to some questions that this material naturally poses. How widespread is the phenomenon, and how "normal" is it? In what individuals does it occur, and what does its occurrence indicate in terms of their personality make-up? What attitude to it can psychoanalysis take?

How rare is the salamander phenomenon? If we infer its frequency from the frequency of reports of it, we have to say that it is extremely rare. However, this inference—which is so freely applied in so much psychological and sociological research—will not do here: for it is an inherent quality of the phenomenon that it balks at being reported. It is therefore entirely possible that it occurs many times more often than it has been described.

The question of how often and in which types of individuals it is found can thus be broken down into two questions, relating to (a) the persons who report it, and (b) those who experience it but do not report it. Number (a) is undoubtedly exceedingly small.

The observation that even masters of literary expression grope for words when they face this task makes it quite clear that only persons of unusual boldness and ability in this field will even make the attempt: only poets (the word here taken to include imaginative prose writers) will do it.

To express feelings which because of their quality or intensity cannot be expressed by others who likewise experience them, has of old been considered the mark which—as a blessing or as a curse— distinguishes the poet. Thus Goethe lets his Tasso say:

When man in his torment falls silent,
A god has given me to say what I suffer.

This may well be applied to feelings which differ in their coloring but not in their intensity from "torment." The number of those (b) who have been "surprised" by seeing the salamander and who have fallen silent may be much larger than those who say what they suffer (or what unearthly joy they feel), but it is assuredly still small. The phenomenon is rare; we do not know how rare.

Our horizon would at once tremendously expand if we should make bold to draw certain mystic and religious experiences into our purview which are not marked by the manifest appearance of a salamander. The sudden vision of the heavens opening up; or of a god or an angel appearing; the dialogue with a deity; the infinitely satisfying flash of the feeling of being one with the universe; the lifting of the curtain which seems to have shut out a more beautiful and at the same time more real world behind the one we have known; the splendid moment in which space has vanished and time has stood still—all these experiences (here clumsily described because their very nature forbids lucid description) of which reports have come down to us from mystics and visionaries of all ages and all religious denominations: these mystic experiences show some kinship with the salamander phenomenon though they seem to differ from it fundamentally in that they are not marked by that incoherence, seeming triviality, and utter lack of consequence which is so peculiar to "seeing the salamander."

This difference may be more apparent than real. Since the difficulty of describing the salamander phenomenon resides in the absence of a frame of reference, the availability of a serviceable frame of reference into which the phenomenon can be pressed with but slight deformation will be irresistibly tempting. The religious person who as a matter of creed has always theoretically admitted the possibility of a miracle possesses that frame. He may lead himself to believe that he has been the recipient of a miraculous perception when he has actually gone through a fleeting stage of emotion. He may persuade himself that he has seen a god when he has actually seen a salamander.

The following report of an experience which Father Jean-Joseph Surin, a French Jesuit of the seventeenth century, had at the age of about thirteen, may serve as an illustration:

> One day, as he was attending Vespers, his heart found itself suddenly flooded with a heavenly joy that obliged him to sit down as his body could not support it. He had a supernatural light which revealed to him in an ineffable manner the grandeurs of the essence of God. All divine attributes were manifested to him . . . [Bremond, 1926].

What, one might ask, would Surin have made of this if he had not been the adherent of a religion that believes in the existence of God?

The few reports of seeing the salamander which we have may thus be but the residue of a far larger number—most of which, however, have been changed into reports of religious visions and mystic experiences before they ever became reports outside of their originators' minds. This is such a strong possibility that one even might turn matters around and ask how any such experience escapes this elaboration, how any reports of sightings of the salamander have survived without being distorted into visions of other worlds or mystic unions.

The answer is probably that the elaboration failed where the person who experienced the phenomenon either had broken the religious frame of reference or else had his experience at an age when this frame was not yet developed. This may in part account for the preference shown by the reported salamanders for the age level of about five.

To digress for a moment: the distinct quality of these experiences of being felt as something completely out of the context of ordinary life makes it understandable that mystics and their advocates have thought up an explanation for them by postulating a real "other world," however philosophically untenable or even ridiculous such an attempt may seem to us. Their related quality of occurring un-prepared and unwilled, of coming as a pure gift—the quality that Lewis brought out so well in the title of his book, SURPRISED *by Joy,* places those in a doubtful light who experiment with methods of forcing the unforceable to take place.

Oriental religions have developed elaborate disciplines to achieve just this. In the West, such efforts have been more haphazard and individual. Some have found the difficulties less great than expected, but the limitations also very real:

> There is scarcely any time in my adult life in which it cannot be summoned; with more effort at some time than at others. It is furthest from me when I am most absorbed in the emotional reactions of personal existence, but never entirely out of reach. Often it seems to float like a bubble inside me, and in moments of abstraction and relaxation, without my volition, it encloses me with ineffable warmth and light [Austin, 1931].

These seem still to be the most prized moments. Where the "volition" is assisted by such relatively trite devices as the ingestion of drugs, one might rightfully be even more skeptical about the value of the results. This—along with the insistence on the literal reality of the "other world"—is the fundamental weakness of such works as the pertinent books by Huxley (1954, 1956). Even if drugs could bring about experiences which in every other respect are similar to "seeing the salamander," the one essential element of "surprise" would still be lacking, unless it sprang from another source.[2]

The view advocated here is to consider mystic experiences (and some religious visions which cannot perhaps, properly speaking, be classified as mystic) as a subspecies of the salamander phenomenon—

---

[2] Cf. the recent vogue of renewed interest in hallucinogenic mushrooms.

albeit a much more common and infinitely more famous type than the unadulterated variety. This is in contrast to the more conventional way of looking at this experience which would rather consider it the other way around and would at best concede the existence of the salamander phenomenon as a subspecies of the mystical experience.

Greenacre (1956) is of course quite right in most cases—actually in *all* cases except just those in which the salamander phenomenon occurs in its pure form—when she notes that "even in the manifest content in all instances there was a religious atmosphere." The question, however, is whether this atmosphere was the matrix of the experience or merely its rationalization.

The answer presented here has one inestimable advantage: it frees us from a most awkward dilemma which no other concept has been able to escape.

What we are otherwise caught between when we try to evaluate a report of a mystic experience or religious vision are the Scylla of conceding the literal truth of the vision and the Charybdis of discounting the whole episode as a hallucination. The former is usually quite unacceptable, and the latter is neither always fair nor usually correct. The difference between the hallucination of the psychotic and the salamander phenomenon is basic, as is the contrast between the meaning of isolation in the one case and the other case. The one who sees the salamander may crave for similar experiences— which may not be vouchsafed to him; the psychotic may yearn to get rid of his, but will be condemned to repeat them. The psychotic fears to be expelled from the world, and forever; the one who sees the salamander feels lifted out of it, for one glorious instant. The psychotic's feeling of remoteness is neither fleeting nor pleasurable; the transient experience of having seen the salamander is held as an imperishable treasure.

> The experience so initiated has been the one abiding reality of my life . . . I can recall, even as a child, leaving the companions of my play to bask in it, as one might abandon the shade to walk in the sun [Austin, 1931].

> The reader who finds these three episodes of no interest need read this book no further, for in a sense the central story of my life is about nothing else [Lewis, 1955].

It is quite inevitable that he who has "seen the salamander" should feel singled out, nobilitated, raised and exalted above other men. The lack of a proper frame of reference into which the experience can be placed is changed into its special virtue. The seeming deficiency that it cannot be communicated thus carries its own reward. The uniqueness of the experience becomes the most powerful ego support.

It is at the same time perceived as ego-alien, as something that has come upon the self from elsewhere. It is understood by the individual as a transaction between himself and an outside power (which cannot be perceived, which may not exist) rather than as a transaction between himself and another individual. This places it outside of the jurisdiction of a psychiatry that conceives of itself as a science of interpersonal relations.

IV

If we try to go farther, we are apt to find ourselves treading the soft ground of speculation; placed in the position of the alchemist who attempts to conquer nature with motley weapons: a stone from here, an herb from there—disparate items of material that later research may show to have no bearing on each other or on the problem at hand. If we want to try this, we can proceed somewhat as follows.

The individual who has "seen the salamander" is driven to postulate an outside power, however impersonally conceptualized. In the same degree in which he uses the experience to exalt himself, he is compelled also to exalt that power. This explains why his feeling is apt to be tinged with awe (which in some religious experiences may be sharpened into terror)—Austin's *awesome* word, Lewis's uncertainty whether "Joy" isn't really a kind of unhappiness or grief.

This leads toward the field so splendidly covered by Greenacre in her study of the feeling of awe in childhood (1956), and there is also a connection between the feeling of awe and the pride in the possession of the phallus, which can be illustrated in an indirect way. German thinking of the last hundred years has devoted an inordinate amount of energy to the elaboration of differences between Germans and Jews. On a folklore level, the crucial distinction has usually been thought to be that Jews are, or used to be, circumcised—a practice not popular among German gentiles. On a higher level of sublimation, the decisive difference has been sought in such alleged characteristics of the Jews as sneering, arrogance, being jaded, disrespectful, coldly intellectual. The sharply anti-Semitic and very influential philosopher Schopenhauer put it most concisely in a much quoted passage in which he speaks of

> the well-known faults which are inseparable from the national character of the Jews: most outstanding among these is a marvelous absence of everything that is expressed by the word *verecundia;* though this is a defect which is more useful in the world than perhaps any positive quality.

Schopenhauer here exhibits the same compulsion to grope for the right expression that we have noticed in several reports of the salamander phenomenon. He resorts to inserting, in his German text, a Latin word: *verecundia*—which in this context means *awe.*

The capability of feeling awe appears here as an honor denied to those who have suffered vicarious castration. The connection is not as far-fetched as it may seem. Otto Weininger for instance, author of a philosophical book on sex which was a sensation in its day (1903), based his attacks on Judaism largely on Schopenhauer and made much of the Jews' alleged lack of *verecundia.* He also stated that Jewish men were less potent than "Aryan" men. Unfortunately he did not say how, in those pre-Kinsey days, he found that out. If perchance there should be any truth in the assertion of a connection between sexual vigor and the ability to feel awe, it would follow that a triumphant assertion of the possession of the phallus may be a force that helps to bring about the salamander phenomenon, with its undercurrent of awe.

We have stressed that the "salamander" will "descend" entirely uncalled and "surprising," but we must not be misled into believing that this, though subjectively a fact, is necessarily more than outward appearance. The observation that the individual who has the experience derives such enormous gratification from it leads to the suspicion that, even though unbeknownst to himself, he has engineered it that way. He escapes into seeing the salamander from a conflict situation with which he could not cope on the terms set for it. He calls allies from another world and escapes by lifting himself on to a higher plane. The salamander experience is a clarion call which proclaims that one period has been brought to a victorious close and another period may commence. The significance of this for the psychoanalytic study of the child lies in the assumption that in the most classical cases this would be a special form of the transition from the oedipal phase to latency.

V

Let us now try to return from speculation to firmer ground.

We have formulated the hypothesis that the salamander phenomenon is phallic—meaning that it acts like the proverbial "light from above" to show the individual who is mired in conflict that he has a way out, and upward, by asserting a valuable possession (which may be his phallus). If there is truth in this, then we can through it elucidate a very peculiar and otherwise scarcely understandable feature of the salamander phenomenon: namely, that light and fire play such a role in it, even though it is by no means primarily a visual experience.

Our examples make this role clear, and the connection has been noted in the literature:

> Preter-natural light and color are common to all visionary experiences. And along with light and color there goes, in every case, a recognition of heightened significance [Huxley, 1956].

Freud (1932) pointed out the symbolic significance of fire:

> Primitive man could not but regard fire as something analogous to the passion of love—or, as we should say, a symbol of the libido . . . There can be no doubt about the mythological significance of flames as a phallus . . . The male sexual organ has two functions . . . It is the channel for the evacuation of urine, and it performs the sexual act . . . The two acts are incompatible—as incompatible as fire and water.

Autobiographical literature offers testimony to the validity of this connection. So the British artist Gill (1941) apropos masturbation:

But how shall I ever forget the strange, inexplicable rapture of my first experience? What marvellous thing was this that suddenly transformed a mere water tap into a pillar of fire—and water into an elixir of life?

Myth and folklore know of creatures which partake of this particular duality, which combine in themselves the two incompatible elements of fire and water. Several come to mind. Freud (1932) has pointed out that the *hydra* of Lerna which succumbed to Hercules, though a water snake according to its name, owed this quality to the reversal which occurs in dreams and really represented a firebrand. But the outstanding pertinent fantasy formation is none other than the salamander.

The oldest reference to this mythical creature that we have (apart from a passage of doubtful authenticity in Aristotle) is found in a book by Theophrastus (372-287 B. C.). He recommends the use of vinegar or a mixture of vinegar and egg white to extinguish fires (an interesting idea considering Freud's hypothesis that urine was the first fire extinguisher) and goes on thus:

> If the power of cold is added to such a fluid, this cooperates toward the extinction of fire, and this property is said to be found in the salamander; for this creature is cold by its nature, and the fluid flowing out of its body is sticky and at the same time contains such a juice that it penetrates forward. This is shown by water and fruits which, when touched by it, become injurious, and usually have a deadly effect. The animal's slowness of motion is also of assistance; for the longer it tarries in the fire, the more it will contribute toward its extinction. However, it cannot extinguish a fire of any dimensions, but only one commensurate with its nature and physical ability; and a fire in which it did not dwell long enough will soon light up again [Laufer, 1915].

Though the association which this might evoke in the reader is obvious, it still reads somewhat like a description of the real animal. Pliny even undertakes to describe the creature's physical appearance, though he also extolls its fire-extinguishing capabilities and speaks of its poisonous character as though it were an atomic bomb: by defiling food and wells, the salamander "is able to destroy whole nations at once, unless they take the proper precautions against it." Incidentally, the belief that salamanders are poisonous—

which they are not—is reported still to be widespread in the Southern United States (Strecker, 1925; 1926) and to persist for instance in the Azores (Jünger, 1948).

The reversal which transformed the salamander from a cold slimy animal that is inimical to fire into one that *lives in fire* is credited to that great innovator, St. Augustine. The middle ages followed his hallowed example. Shakespeare still does so when he lets Falstaff refer to Bardolph's alcoholic nose as "that salamander of yours" (*Henry IV*, Part I, Act III, Sc. 3). The troubadour Pierre de Cols d'Aorlec, to mention one of many,

> speaks of the erotic fire burning in his heart as so pleasing to him that it is the more desirable to him the more it burns him, like the salamander which is happy in fire and blaze [Laufer, 1915],

—or, we might add, like Lewis's "Joy."

Asbestos was mined in the Middle East throughout this period and was occasionally exported both to Europe and to China. Recipients were tremendously impressed with its fire resistance. Seeing that it was fibrous, they were inclined to believe that it was the hair of a fire-resisting animal. It came to be called "salamander hair" and the salamander was thought to be fur-bearing and to look like a marten; or asbestos might be the feather of a fire-resisting bird, and so Arabic writers identified the salamander with the phoenix. But what might the phoenix be?

> Probably the earliest significance of the phoenix was that of the revivified penis after its state of flaccidity, rather than that of the sun setting in the evening glow and then rising again [Freud, 1932].

It was Marco Polo whose report marked the beginning of the end of these speculations. For he related the sobering fact that in Central Asia he had been shown an asbestos mine. Thus realizing that asbestos was neither fur nor feather but a mineral, he ushered in an era of skepticism in which Giovanni Cellini would feel constrained to say that a salamander had never been seen by anyone of whom we have a true report. It still took a century until the name was applied to an existing genus—possibly abetted by observing salamanders emerging from hibernation in logs which were thrown into the fire (Wallin, 1956). The animal which extinguishes fires, or else lives in them, slumped into oblivion.

The first reference in English literature that we have in which the word salamander is used in the modern sense is of 1611 (Murray, 1914). The circle was closed.

If Giovanni Cellini had not heard of the salamander, what might he have seen in the flames? There are surprisingly few reports of what people see in fire (Plank, 1957). Two such narratives, remarkable by their content and their similarity, have been preserved from antiquity, both referring to mothers of Roman kings.

> It is said that one day the virgin Ocrisia, a slave-woman of Queen Tabaquil . . . was offering as usual cakes and libations of wine on the royal hearth, when a flame in the shape of the male member shot out from the fire . . . Ocrisia conceived by the god or spirit of the fire, and in due time brought forth Servius Tullius . . . [Frazer, 1894].

"God or spirit of the fire"—it is interesting to note in passing that the Renaissance physician Paracelsus attributed elemental spirits to the four elements; he thought that the salamander sloughs off his old skin in the fire (Pachter, 1951) and his spirits of the fire are called salamanders, though he preferred *"Vulcani"* (Sigerist, 1941). Goethe used this in the scene in which Faust forces Mephistopheles to shed his disguise as a poodle.

The other example is that of Rea Silvia (*Enciclopedia Italiana*, Vol. 28). As Plutarch tells the story, her father saw a phallus rising in the flames of his fireplace; an oracle explained this as presaging that this phallus would mate with a virgin who would bring forth a man of marvelous valor and luck. Rea Silvia was impregnated by Mars and became the mother of Romulus and hence the origin of the grandeur that was Rome.

VI

Clearly, a cultural factor is involved in the differences between these widely scattered reports. An unbroken line of development (called progress by some) runs from the semimythical figures of the ancient Romans who saw the phallus in the flames and were convinced that it was there because they saw it, to Giovanni Cellini who saw a salamander instead but still held the same conviction, and on to us disenchanted moderns who may see this or that but are not inclined to believe what we see. When we consider the attributes of the legendary salamander, though, we can understand it as more than a coincidence that it was this fantasy animal rather than any other which replaced the original vision, and that Cellini's salamander has maintained its strength as a symbol against the onslaughts of rationality which have surged up for centuries.

It was no coincidence either that Mark Twain associated Cellini's salamander to a recollection which does not have anything manifestly to do with it: though he does not stress it and probably was unaware of the meaning, his brother did not merely walk, but walked into a a fire—the same element in which the salamanders live.

It is not too bold to say in the light of all this that there is evidence (though it must also be stressed that this evidence is indirect and tenuous) to explain the salamander phenomenon as being of phallic significance. This is not, however, its most important aspect.

As scientists we desire to understand what we observe; but we must not equate understanding of a phenomenon with limited knowledge of the conditions under which it may occur. We must at the very least distinguish the necessary and the sufficient conditions. Michelangelo would not have painted his immortal mural if the Sistine Chapel had not offered its magnificent wall. This is quite true, but it does not get us very far toward understanding the *Last Judgment*. When Spitteler noted special conditions of light and time as prerequisites of the phenomenon of bliss, he did not mean to *explain* bliss.

It is possible to take the stand that it is not especially necessary to understand the dynamics of the salamander phenomenon. What is incumbent upon us is rather to recognize it when we find it, and to treat it with the respect it deserves. After all, it does not happen every day that in digging underneath the frequently pretty surface of personality we come upon something that is beautiful and admirable.

Newton is reported to have said a short time before his death:

I do not know what I may appear to the world; but to myself I seem to have been only like a boy playing on the sea-shore, and diverting myself in now and then finding a smoother pebble or a prettier shell than ordinary, whilst the great ocean of truth lay all undiscovered before me [Brewster, 1855].

Our salamander is that prettier shell, it is that smoother pebble; and it is a product of that ocean. Newton did not feel such baubles were beneath him; but the attitudes that seem more widely practiced are either to ignore the salamander phenomenon, or to feel frankly bewildered by it, or to confuse it with pathology. I am reminded of a patient who in the first interview related as one of the things that puzzled him about himself that from time to time—especially when he was alone, perhaps reading a book, perhaps watching the sunset—he had a brief sensation which he felt unable to describe; all that he could say was that it was like an immense roar, but distinctly inaudible. Though in the formal record of the interview this came under the heading of "complaints," this patient (whose opinion of himself probably outstripped his real gifts) seemed quite pleased with himself for having these experiences. The next step was to give him an electroencephalogram—a prudent measure, no doubt, but the electroencephalogram was normal, and the inaudible roar remained as mystifying as before.

The Minnesota Multiphasic Personality Inventory (MMPI), a rather popular psychological test, consists of sentences which the subject sorts into "true" and "false." It contains a statement (H 12), "I have had very peculiar and strange experiences." The manual provides that an affirmative answer raises the individual's schizophrenia score (Hathaway, 1943).

The psychologist who goes by this will undoubtedly catch some schizophrenics; he will scarcely see a salamander.

BIBLIOGRAPHY

Austin, M. (1931), *Experiences Facing Death*. Indianapolis: Bobbs-Merrill.
Bremond, H. (1926), *Histoire Littéraire du Sentiment Religieux en France*. Paris: Blond & Gay.
Brewster, Sir D. (1855), *Memoirs of the Life, Writings, and Discoveries of Sir Isaac Newton*. Edinburgh: Thomas Constable & Co.
Cellini, B. *Vita di Benvenuto Cellini*. Firenze: G. C. Sansoni, 1901.
—— *The Autobiography of Benvenuto Cellini*. Garden City, N. Y.: Garden City Publishing Co., 1927.
Clemens, S. (1925), *Mark Twain's Autobiography*. New York: P. F. Collier.
Dumas, A. (1852), *The Road to Monte Christo*. New York: Chas. Scribner's Sons, 1956.
Frazer, Sir J. (1894), *The Golden Bough*, II. London: Macmillan & Co., 3rd ed., 1911.

Freud, S. (1932), Acquisition of Power over Fire. *Collected Papers,* V. London: Hogarth Press, 1950.

Gill, E. (1941), *Autobiography.* New York: Devin-Adair Co.

Greenacre, P. (1956), Experiences of Awe in Childhood. *This Annual,* XI.

Hathaway, S. R. et al. (1943), *Manual for the Minnesota Multiphasic Personality Inventory.* New York: The Psychological Corp.

Huxley, A. (1954), *The Doors of Perception.* New York: Harper.

—— (1956), *Heaven and Hell.* New York: Harper.

James, W. (1902), *Varieties of Religious Experience.* New York: Longmans, Green & Co., 1928.

Jeffares, A. N. (1949), *W. B. Yeats: Man and Poet.* New Haven: Yale University Press.

Jünger, E. (1948), *Atlantische Fahrt.* Zürich: Verlag der Arche.

Laufer, B. (1915), Asbestos and Salamander: An Essay in Chinese and Hellenistic Folklore. *Extrait du T'oung-pao,* XVI.

Lewin, B. D. (1950), *The Psychoanalysis of Elation.* New York: W. W. Norton.

Lewis, C. S. (1955), *Surprised by Joy.* New York: Harcourt Brace.

Menon, V. K. N. (1942), *The Development of William Butler Yeats.* Edinburgh: Oliver & Boyd.

Murray, Sir J. A. H., ed. (1914), *A New English Dictionary.* Oxford: Clarendon Press.

Pachter, H. M. (1951), *Magic into Science: The Story of Paracelsus.* New York: Henry Shuman.

Plank, R. (1957), Spontaneous Projection of Meaningful Form. *J. Projective Techniques,* XXI.

Pliny the Elder. *The Natural History of Pliny,* tr. John Bostock. London: Henry G. Bohn, 1855.

Schopenhauer, A. (1850), *Parerga und Paralipomena,* 2nd Part, Ch. IX. Leipzig: Insel-Verlag (no date).

Sigerist, H. E., ed. (1941), *Four Treatises of Theophrastus von Hohenheim, Called Paracelsus.* Baltimore: Johns Hopkins Press.

Sitwell, Sir O. (1944), *Left Hand, Right Hand!* Boston: Little, Brown & Co.

Spitteler, C. (1920), *Meine frühesten Erlebnisse.* Jena: E. Diederichs.

—— (1922), *Imago.* Jena: E. Diederichs.

Strecker, J. K. (1925), *Reptiles of the South and Southwest in Folk-Lore.* Publications of the Texas Folk-Lore Society, IV.

—— (1926), *Reptile Myths in Northwestern Louisiana.* Publications of the Texas Folk-Lore Society, V.

Wallin, H. E. (1956), The Red Eft. *The Emerald Necklace* (Cleveland Metropolitan Park System) 5, No. 7.

Webster's New International Dictionary (1951), 2nd ed. Springfield, Mass.: Merriam Co.

Weininger, O. (1903), *Geschlecht und Charakter.* Vienna & Leipzig: Wilhelm Braumüller, 26th ed., 1925.

Yeats, W. B. (1922), *Autobiographies: The Trembling of the Veil: Four Years: 1887-1891.* London: Macmillan & Co., 1955.

THE CHILDHOOD AND LEGACY
OF STANISLAVSKI[1]

PHILIP WEISSMAN, M.D. (New York)

The name Stanislavski is to the art of acting what Shakespeare is to the art of playwriting. In the broadest outline, from the beginning of this century, Stanislavski was the guiding genius of the Moscow Art Theater until the 1930's when·he was forced into semiretirement by a heart ailment. He died in 1938 at the age of seventy-five. The Moscow Art Theater has been described as "perhaps the greatest acting unit the world has ever known." For forty years Stanislavski was not only its co-director and guiding force, but also one of its chief actors.

John Gielgud, in an introduction to one of Stanislavski's three books, *An Actor Prepares* (1936), has aptly stated, "He is Olympian, a specialist in every department of the theatre, who cares so passionately for his art that he wishes to bequeath something from his great store of experience and knowledge to anyone who cares to read what he has set down." Stanislavski's most celebrated achievement is the development of a theory and system of dramatic acting and teaching referred to as the Stanislavski Method. This theory, briefly stated, emphasizes that it is essential for the actor to enter the lives of the characters he portrays, their emotions and personality, as thoroughly as possible.

The psychoanalyst, interested in creative imagination, turns to the life history of a person and, in Stanislavski's case, finds that many positive factors contributed to the development of his great talent and genius. Stanislavski's childhood suggests that the notion an artist must suffer to create is wrong. One should rather say that an artist

[1] This paper is part of a longer study on several outstanding creative personalities in modern drama, in which their lives or their works or both are psychoanalytically studied from the viewpoint of creative imagination (1957).

will suffer only if creativity is hindered by environmental or developmental factors. Art and neuroses are not synonymous; a study of the artist's life need not be a study of pathography; favorable developmental and environmental factors may further the fuller discharge of creative capacity.

This does not imply that an artist's life evolves without conflict. Frequently his personal conflicts are intimately interwoven in his creations. But it is also possible for the artist to adopt (and adapt), by identification, another's tragedy which he need not have experienced himself. Kris (1952) pointed out that, e.g., Prince Hal's conflict went far beyond any personal experience of Shakespeare's.

There is every indication that in our attempt to advance in the study of creative imagination and artistic talent, we must leave the safety and security of the exclusive preoccupation with an individual's pathological conflicts. We must investigate how the artist functions in spite of his conflicts, reactive to his conflicts, and utilizing his conflicts. We must therefore turn to the period when conflicts begin to develop: to the artist's early childhood.

I. CHILDHOOD

Konstantin Stanislavski was born in 1863. From his biography (1924) I quote the following description of his parents and family life. "They were home-loving people. My mother spent all her time in the nursery, devoting herself completely to her children—and there were ten of us. My father, until his marriage, slept in the same bed with his father, who was famous for his old-fashioned patriarchal method of life. After his marriage, my father passed to his conjugal couch, where he slept to the end of his days, and where he died. My parents loved each other when they were young and when they were old. They loved their children and tried to keep them as near themselves as they could."

This description of his family life certainly portrays a background of reasonably sound maternal care and parental accord. Perhaps most fundamental and crucial in all these factors was the nature of the early maternal relationship. Greenacre (1957) is of the opinion that the infancy of the future gifted person or genius is characterized by an early and marked sensitivity to sensory stimulation from the primary object (the mother's breast). She states, "We might conceive that the potentially gifted infant would react to the mother's breast with an intensity of the impression of warmth, smell, moisture, the feel of the texture of the skin and the vision of the roundness of the form, according to the time and nature of the experience." We would then suppose that it is most fortunate when an optimally endowed infant has the loving and nurturing care of the mother. This particular combination may produce one type of genius who as a child is readily recognized as a prodigy, then shows subsequent fulfillment (young genius), and a final maturing, developing, uninterrupted creative expression throughout his life. This would certainly be true of Stanislavski's life.

This is not to be understood as a statement to the effect that a good nurturing mother, or being a favorite child, creates a talent or genius. Nor is it intended to indicate that a poor mother can destroy a potential talent. Perhaps we are saying no more than this: the early and full functioning of a creative talent can be enhanced by such an optimal relationship. Greenacre makes the point that fortunate is the potentially gifted person who has a suitable father with whom to identify. I would add that it might even be a better fortune for the gifted one to have a mother with whom the earliest object relationship is optimal.

Stanislavski's mother had been deserted by her own mother and left with her father whose second wife became a good stepmother to her. Perhaps her own early experience motivated her to become a good mother. The fact that Stanislavski's father slept with his own father until he married suggests that Stanislavski's father may also have experienced the loss of a mother either through death, divorce or illness which may have accentuated his development as a home-loving, family-devoted man and father.

Having a wealthy father is frequently found to be a disadvantage to a son. The father's wealth and success, by representing paternal potency to the son, often threaten the maintainence of the resolution of the oedipus conflict in adult life. Moreover, parental wealth frequently robs both the child and the parent of realistic preparations for the child's independent future. Stanislavski's father was a rich man, the owner of a mercantile firm that was a hundred years old. The generation of his parents was in the first stage of a cultural revolution—the creation of the Russian intelligentsia which was completed in Stanislavski's generation. His parents had already crossed the threshold of culture. In spite of the lack of higher education in the tradition of the aristocracy, they were privately educated and "made much of culture their own. In the transition, the educated, cultured but impoverished aristocracy hesitatingly mixed with wealthy merchants who became the conscious creators of the new life. Numberless schools, hospitals, asylums, nurseries, learned societies, museums and art institutions were founded by their money, their initiative and even their creative effort. They made money in order to spend it on social and artistic institutions."

In his autobiography, Stanislavski (1924) then tells us about the ideals that his parents' generation of merchants created for his own generation. "We, the children of the great fathers and creators of Russian life, tried to inherit from them the difficult art of being able to be rich. To know how to spend money is a very great art. . . . The majority of our generation of rich people received a good education and were acquainted with world literature. We were taught many languages. We traveled very extensively and, in a word, we were plunged into the very heart of the maelstrom of culture. Having become equal in education to the nobles and aristocrats, class distinctions disappear as if of themselves."

In this state of cultural flux, to be the artistically gifted son of a cultural-minded merchant has the aura of a blessed event. To have a son who not only might perpetuate the cultural heritage as a filial duty, but who also could enrich the entrusted culture, must have been the rare fulfillment of a father's own unfulfilled aspirations and fantasies. Such a father will supply all available resources and energies at his command to stimulate a child's first expressions of talent. Conversely for the gifted child, the awareness that one's natural inclinations are rewarded by parental love reinforces the innate powerful energies.

Stanislavski's talents contributed to the happy solution of his oedipal conflicts. His dramatic play in childhood won his father's approval. Thus, his early exploits did not make him his father's rival in these areas. He rather felt that he was subservient to his father's wishes. In addition, he had his mother's admiration; she also loved the theater.

In his teens, Stanislavski undertook amateur theatrical productions in his home which he both directed and acted. His father, older brother and older sisters usually were members of his cast.[2] In the dramatic world of his home, he was the precocious patriarch from an early age. In Stanislavski's home, as in the homes of rich Russians, the custom of the domestic theater flourished. The domestic theater was often part of a wealthy man's estate. Here dramatic productions were given by a cast consisting of the members of the family and the servants. This too was part of the cultural revolution. Prior to this period these domestic theaters were found only on the estates of the nobility. This institution originated at the time of Tsar Alexander, in the latter half of the seventeenth century. He assigned an alien pastor, Gregori by name, to organize a dramatic group of young people. Performances had the character of church mysteries and were given in the palace for the nobility.

Stanislavski's home had such a theater wing, and his earliest memories relate to his first stage performance between the ages of two and three.[3] He recalls that the production consisted of executing tableaus of the four seasons of the year. In the first scene, the stage floor was covered with cotton representing snow. He was dressed in a fur hat and coat and wore a beard and was told to sit motionless on the floor. During the scene he felt embarrassed, bashful and frightened. His performance was greeted by a round of applause which he liked. After this he was again put on the stage in a different pose. A lit candle was placed in a small bundle of branches to produce the effect of fire. He was given a piece of wood and told to pretend that he was putting it into the fire. He was warned that it was only make-believe and not real, and that he was not to bring the wood close to the candle. He writes: "Why should I only make believe when I could really put the wood in the fire? And perhaps

[2] Magarshack (1951) states that Stanislavski was the second oldest of the ten children. He was two years younger than his brother Vladimir. His sister Zina was two years younger than himself; Anna the next sister was born a year later.

[3] Magarshack (1951) places the stage incident between the age five and six years. His source of information is the untranslated memoirs of Stanislavski's sister Anna. The latter states that the family had no domestic theater until Stanislavski was of the above-mentioned age. She states that she also acted in this "production" and was then two years old. It is quite possible that this is a screen memory of Stanislavski's (as well as his sister's). However, the memory would have different implications for each of them.

that was what I had to do, just because I was forbidden to do it?"

As the curtain rose, he put the wood toward the candle. He explains that it felt easy and pleasant to do this, for there was meaning to the motion. Subsequently the cotton caught fire and in the midst of great excitement he was "unceremoniously lifted from the stage and carried into the big house where I was severely scolded. In short, I had failed cruelly, and the failure was not to my taste."

There is every indication in this memory that Stanislavski already felt himself to be more the bad actor than the bad child. The impression is that he was little concerned with his misbehavior and with his having started a fire which brought upon his head the admonition of his elders. He writes: "These four impressions of the pleasure of success, of the bitterness of failure, of the discomfort of unreasonable presence on the stage, and the inner truth of reasoned presence and action on it, control me on the stage even at the present day."

It becomes quite evident that an "artistic ego" was already in operation and seemed to relegate the "personal ego" of the child to a secondary significance. Distinctions between "artistic" and "personal" ego are designated in ego terms of autonomous functions, free from conflict, and capacities for dissociation. In what follows I will show that this pattern persists throughout Stanislavski's life. His personal life was completely subjugated to his artistic life. For the moment, it is to be noted that the nucleus of a total psychic structure was being laid down in relation to the "artistic ego." His feelings of pleasure in success (self-esteem) and bitterness over failure (superego disapproval) as an actor illustrates the early formation of an artist's superego and ego ideals. His impressions of "discomfort of unreasonable presence on stage and the inner truth of reasoned presence and actions on it," bespeak of an ego which discriminatingly rejected and approved of the various artistic emanations of his instinctual drives. Other instances will be cited which illustrate that Stanislavski's acting (sublimated exhibitionism) served the role of sanctioning his aggressive drives throughout his life. We have already mentioned that via acting he dominated both his father and older brother as well as the rest of his family.

Beres (1956) refers to the dissociation of the ego in the creative person.[4] That part (autonomous) which deals with drives directed toward the creative function operates less restrictedly than the personal part of the ego. Thus via acting and directing, Stanislavski in later life was able to express his obstinate revolt against old methods of acting, as in earlier life he expressed his superiority over his older siblings and father without feelings of guilt. The stage incident at the age of two or three years appears in a chapter entitled, "Struggle with Obstinacy." He then recounts two other incidents of obstinacy directed against his father which occurred off stage. In these battles he surrendered in obedience to his father. The life of the stage became the area in which his ego constantly accepted revolutionary departures from orthodox acting. However, these innovations had to meet the high requirements of his own standards and ideals. A conformist in his personal life, he was a rebel in his life of art.

Stanislavski's artistic standards and demands upon himself are responsible for his ability to develop a theory and technique for his art. This is an extraordinary achievement since great actors are too often readily seduced by fame and success—that is, the adoration of the audience—and are disinclined to self-scrutiny. At this early performance he was sensitive to his own embarrassment and disapproval of his initial motionless performance in spite of his enjoyment of the applause. Subjugation of the person to the created character, minimal awareness of the audience and increased awareness of inner feelings are important principles in Stanislavski's theories and techniques of acting.

Throughout Stanislavski's childhood, most of his play had the quality of stage acting. During his mid-latency period, he spent Sundays organizing a circus. He had an orchestra, a ballet master and actors—his friends, his brothers and sisters. Yet his play acting also permitted the expression of a personal fantasy, as ordinary play of children would. This is clearly illustrated in the following description: "The ballet was called 'The Naiad and the Fisherman' and I did not like it. It called for the representation of love, it was necessary to kiss someone and I was ashamed. What I wanted was to kill, to save, to sentence, to pardon." But he was even more dissatisfied that this was not theater in the absence of costumes and scenery and so he switched to a marionette theater with "scenery

4 See also Glover (1943).

effects and a full line of theatrical necessities." The artistic need for real theater was greater than the personal need of an outlet for aggressive fantasies. In describing his games of war with his friends, he shows great appreciation of the beautiful costumes of the enemy Persian armies, the blowing of the hunters' horn, the imitated Persian head-dress. Again we note that play acting and stage acting serve as an outlet for his aggressive drives. In an earlier paper (1956) I attempted to differentiate normal repetitive (autonomous) play in early childhood from pregenital compulsive (non-autonomous) behavior and compulsive symptoms. The conclusions of this study have relevance to the current issues, i.e., the creative part of the ego ("artistic ego") is related to more autonomous activities.

One of the most amusing illustrations of the precedence or art over personal life is set forth in Stanislavski's autobiography in a chapter entitled, "Marriage." This is a ten-page affair in which Stanislavski discusses his theatrical undertakings in the Society of Art and Literature, the different plays that he did that season. He continues to discuss the technical acting problem of body restraint. As yet he has mentioned nothing in relation to a personal romance and the chapter is almost completed. Four paragraphs before the end he still ardently discusses his struggle with the problem of body restraint in the roles of Don Juan and Don Carlos when we come upon the following:

> It is a pity that the next role I attempted that season was, if not Spanish in verses, still so long in boots, sword, love speeches and high style. I played the part of Ferdinand in the tragedy of Schiller, "Villany and Love." Louisa was played by M. P. Perevozchikova whose stage name was Lilina, the same amateur actress who, in spite of society's opinion, came to act with us. It seems that we were in love with each other, but did not know it, but we were told of it by the public. We kissed each other too naturally and our secret was an open one to the public. In this performance I played less with technique than with intuition, but it is not hard to guess who inspired us, Appolo or Hymen. Right after the performance, there appeared willing matchmakers. In the spring at the end of the first season of the Society of Art and Literature, I was declared a bridegroom and on July 5 was married. Then we went on a honeymoon and returned in the autumn to the theatre with the news that my wife could not fulfill her

duties in the theatre during all of next year. Everybody will understand why.

The last three paragraphs of the chapter on marriage refer to the technical problem of acting and the problems of the Society. Only one more reference to his personal life appears in a single sentence. Referring back to the play *Villany and Love,* he writes, "Could we, after the marriage, as man and wife, still possess the same artistic technique and inspiration that we possessed until our engagement?"

We might measure the ratio of artistic life to personal life in the proportions of the two paragraphs of personal life in the ten-page chapter called "Marriage." Stanislavski had a gigantic romance with the world and a rather stable, affectionate, unheralded personal romance. This seems often to be the pattern in genius and highly creative talent of the more mature and stable type. His romance with the world may have played a role in his integration in the new political regime. In his autobiography, he viewed the revolution from the viewpoint that it produced a new kind of audience—the working man. His new audience interested and intrigued him and he delighted in their numbers, their characteristics and their enthusiasm. The domestic theater, staffed with actors from both rich landowners and servants had early made them equal citizens in his world of art.

Viewing this from a developmental rather than a biographical angle, we are dealing with the problem of the capacity of the potentially highly creative infant to shift and extend readily his relationship from the primary object (the mother's breast) onto the "alternate objects" in the world about that are similar to the original object. This arrangement becomes the prototype for the subsequent love affair that the creative person has with the world. Following Greenacre's hypothesis, an inordinate amount of sensitivity is required in the equipment of such a special person.

Greenacre (1957) has enumerated the basic characteristics of creative talent under four headings: (1) greater sensitivity to sensory stimulation; (2) unusual capacity for awareness of relations between various stimuli; (3) basic predisposition to an empathy of wider range than average—the empathy to extend from one's own body to external objects and a peculiar empathic animation of inanimate objects; (4) an intactness of sensorimotor equipment, allowing the building up of projective motor discharge for expressive function.

It is my impression that these four conditions must exist co-ordinately and inclusively in the individual. The absence of one or the other creates a significant gap in creative equipment which seriously reduces the creativity or removes it entirely from that class.

The following examples and illustrations of Stanislavski's childhood experiences will fall in well with the above-stated criteria.

I have already mentioned the episode of Stanislavski's first stage experience. He had exquisite, elaborate emotional responses to the acting situation, which were retained intact and integrated and connected with his work throughout his life. He writes of early memories: "If I am not to reckon my memories of my own christening, which I created after the stories of my nurse in my mind that even until now I consider myself a conscious witness to that ceremony." High sensitivity, universal awareness of interrelation of stimuli, wide empathic capacity to the nurse and his own body reactions and sensations, and the subsequent functional expressive discharge are coordinately contained in these reminiscences. He adds, "What I remember best are the emotions which I lived through in the period of my struggle with obstinacy and not so much the facts that caused them." His autobiography is studded with examples of sensitive sensory stimulation in his personal life.

Similar extraordinary responses are to be seen in his early childhood to experiences of artistic nature which he witnessed—the circus, theater, opera, ballet, etc. I quote the first paragraph of the chapter "Value of Childhood Impressions," which illustrates the above and needs no explanatory comments.

My brother and I were taken to the Italian Opera in our earliest childhood, when we were six or at most eight years old. And I am very thankful to my parents, for I have no doubt that it acted beneficially on my musical hearing, on the development of my taste, and eye which grew used to the beautiful. We had season tickets which entitled us to be present at forty or fifty performances, and we sat in the orchestra very near the stage. But as we often said at the time, the opera was merely a side line for us, and we begged our parents not to count it as part of our regular theatrical fare, especially the circus. Music made us tired. Nevertheless the impressions I received at the opera are still alive in me and are much clearer, sharper, and greater than the impressions left by the circus. I think that this is so because the strength of the impression was tremendous but was not felt consciously, being received organically and not only spiritually but physically also. I began to understand and value these impressions at their true worth only much later, in my memory. But the circus amused me in childhood, although memories of it were of no interest to me in my maturer years.

Modestly enough, Stanislavski extends his gratitude to his parents for the opportunities they provided. He remains unaware of the unusual sensory integrative and expressive equipment with which he was endowed and which he brought to these experiences. He approximates this when he speaks of his organic impressions. I think that the study of Stanislavski's creative imagination may add a striking feature to the prerequisites already postulated for the characteristics of creative genius or highly creative talent; that is, the lifelong durability of sensory experiences, perhaps even from infancy, and their lifelong potential transformability into creative expression. Recently a biographical sketch of Picasso showed the same quality in Picasso: the lifelong retention of early sensory impressions and their creative expression.

In 1910, Stanislavski was traveling in Italy. While walking in the streets of Rome with a friend, they heard someone sing in a nearby house. Stanislavski expressed the opinion that it was the voice of the baritone Cotogni. Further inquiry established that he was correct. He had heard Cotogni sing only once when he was seven years old—forty years earlier.

This and similar incidents bear testimony to his extraordinary sensitivity to all forms of sensory stimuli—sound, spoken or musical; colors, design, movement, texture, etc. All this was evident in childhood in his theatrical productions. He was director, stage manager, scenic and costume designer and musical director. In his mature years all the various theatrical specialties were under his direct supervision. He was considered a master in every department.

Any consideration of the life of a genius must touch upon the inescapable enigma of heredity, though no study of creative genius from the viewpoint of genetics has yet established evidence for or against hereditary predisposition. I would only mention that one aspect of Stanislavski's life known to me could be considered from the hereditary viewpoint, namely that his mother was the daughter of the famous French actress Varley.

II. LEGACY

Kris (1952) showed that many artists create and actually shape their lives according to a legendary image. A similar conscious or unconscious tendency is to be found in the attitude of his biographer. In spite of this, the writer, painter, sculptor or composer, by the nature of his art, leaves a true record of his talents in his creative works. This is obviously not the case in the performing arts, if we exclude cinema and recordings and its siblings, radio and television. Thus, for a dramatic performing artist to leave a true representation of his actual creations becomes almost impossible. Legendary evaluations are the natural result in this field of endeavor. The absence of a permanent record operates in two directions. In the field of valuation it tends to exaggerate favorably the works of the artist. It is similar to the state of mourning in which the lost object becomes exaggeratedly loved after death. Secondly, in the realm of perpetuation, acting tends to be a lost art. That is, if it is not carried on by capable disciples from one generation to another, it is likely to disappear. Examples of this are to be found in all fields of performance, such as dancing, singing, as well as acting.

Stanislavski's insight into the legendary cloak of celebrated people, including his own self, is well illustrated in the book *Stanislavski Directs* (1954) written by a famous disciple, Gorchakov. When Gorchakov was twenty-six years old he began to work with Stanislavski as an apprentice in the renowned Third Studio in 1924. Since 1939, the year after Stanislavski's death, Gorchakov has been in charge of stage direction at the State Institute of Theatrical Art in Moscow. As a young man, Gorchakov asked Stanislavski the question, "What is a director?" Stanislavski understood this oft-asked question correctly to mean that the young man wanted to know whether he had the qualities to become a director. A short while before, the young man had accompanied Stanislavski to the house of Isadora Duncan, the famous dancer, to bid her farewell as she was about to depart for France. Stanislavski then asked Gorchakov what impressions he had had of the meeting between Duncan and himself. In response to the brief answer that he had only been aware of being in the presence of two famous people, Stanislavski commented, "You noticed the most essential element—we were playing at being two world celebrities—but you did not understand for whom we were acting. You didn't notice a short man who was sitting in the corner of the room? This man is Duncan's secretary who was taking notes on all he saw and heard. He is going to write a book on her life. She was playing a role and so was I. Do you remember that we spoke French? How did you think our French was?" In response to Gorchakov's comment that he thought it was good French, Stanislavski continued, "We spoke very poor French, pretending it was exceptionally good. When we were in the hall she shook my hand so hard I still feel it. Did you notice this? I think she likes me and I like her very much. You could have observed this too. You saw only the result of our acting but you did not see what we were acting and why."

This incident, reported by an outsider, is of considerable value in determining the authenticity of the autobiographical data. A famous person who in a sense can self-analyze or make conscious the tendency of his own and other famous people to alter their true image into a legendary one is more likely to present us with biographical data which are less distorted than is usual. It is a further tribute to his inborn sensitivity that he was constantly aware of everything he was experiencing, both from within and without.

The measure of Stanislavski's creative genius as actor and director confronts us with the above-mentioned difficulties relative to the performing arts. In this respect we can only accept the statement of drama critics, highly recognized theatrical authorities and audiences who saw his works and attested universally to his greatness. He was actively engaged in his professional career for fifty years, the last forty years with the Moscow Art Theater which he co-founded and co-directed with Nemirovich-Danchenko. In this organization he introduced the repertory system. He overcame the natural handicaps of his art form and left a significant and unique legacy in recorded form via his writings on the theories and technique of acting.

We will examine these theories and techniques, since their application deals predominantly with the utilization of psychological principles and mechanisms. His system has psychodynamic validity.

Stanislavski's new concept of the art of acting is an integral part of the historical alteration in all fields of arts and sciences—that is, a concept which places more importance upon the individual and less on nature. In the field of literature this is referred to as the romantic movement in which art expresses emotions and is no longer the reflection of nature (Abrams, 1953). Before Stanislavski, acting lagged behind its fellow arts and was mainly representational. In representational acting, living the part is merely preparatory to what is intended by the actor. His ambition is to perfect the part, then to memorize it and to reproduce it constantly. In Stanislavski's concept of creative acting, it is essential that the actor live the part every moment he plays it and each time he does so.

Stanislavski does not totally discredit representational acting. The following excerpt expresses the nature of both art forms, the differences between them and their final aesthetic values. Beginning with representationalism, he writes: "This type of art is less profound than beautiful. It is more immediately effective than truly powerful; in it the form is more interesting than its content. It acts more on your sense of sound and sight than on your soul. Consequently it is more likely to delight than to move you— Your astonishment rather than your faith is aroused— But delicate and deep human feelings are not subject to such technique— Nevertheless, representing the part since it follows our process in part must be acknowledged to be creative art."

Another passage from Stanislavski's book, *An Actor Prepares* (1936), gives us the true aims of his art form. "Our experience has led to a firm belief that only one kind of art, soaked as it is in the living experience of human beings, can artistically reproduce the impalpable shadings and depths of life. Only such art can completely absorb the spectator and make him both understand also inwardly experience the happenings on the stage, enriching his inner life and living impressions which will not fade with time."

Stanislavski conceives of creative acting as an art which communicates from the unconscious of the actor to the unconscious of the spectator.

Now that we know what Stanislavski demands from his actors, we will examine how he induces them to do this. Briefly, he wants the actor to identify as completely as possible with the created character.

The actor must live the part and "Fit his own human qualities to the life of this other person and thus create the inner life of a human spirit."

There is no question that the conscious identification with another, be it a real person or created character, elicits in the actor some of the characteristics of the "person" with whom he has identified. There is a parallel to the daily work of the analyst. In Freud's writings on technique, he suggests that the analyst listen to the analysand's associations with free-floating attention. In this process he partially identifies with his patient, and thus gains understanding of the patient's unconscious. Here the artist and the analyst part. The aim of the analyst is to lay bare the unconscious wishes and fears. The aim of the actor is to express unconscious contents in an artistic form.

Stanislavski's system has often been misused by dramatic directors and teachers for the purpose of clinical self-analysis and clinical analysis of their pupils. This coincidental abuse of the technique does not detract from its validity as a plausible means for promoting creative artistic and unconscious expression in its proper application.

Grotjahn (1957) states, "The work of the scientist is concerned with the transformation of objective truth into knowledge. The work of the analyst stands between the work of the artist and the scientist. Like the artist he is concerned with inner truth; like the scientist he limits himself to understanding and interpretation. Unlike the artist, he creates not by giving form but by giving insight and knowledge."

Fenichel (1946) takes up the question of identification in the personality of the potential actor. He suggests that actors often lack a distinctive personality, ego development, and are "Rather a bundle of identification possibilities." Actors are correspondingly inhibited in their object relationships—and objects are used for identification rather than relations and are sources of narcissistic gratification.

I found this to be so in the case of a professional actor who came for analysis with complaints of feeling depersonalized and "not quite knowing who and what I am." In his earliest development he was rather severely restricted by his mother from putting stray objects (dirt, lollypops, toys, etc.) into his mouth. He was permitted to play with dirty objects (mud, dirt, etc.). His subsequent attitude toward school learning was that he became part of the knowledge and would master it by creating from it an enactable role. It was totally foreign and incomprehensible to him to hear other people talk of "taking in" or digesting knowledge. The early relationship to animate and inanimate objects seemed to hinder the development of his ego's permanent borders and he constantly longed for new objects to identify with. Being in a state of identification produced a state of temporary ego stability and, when he was acting dramatic roles, his feelings of depersonalization decreased. This patient was an enthusiastic follower of the Stanislavski system.

Ego psychology of creative expression confirms one other major component in Stanislavski's theory and technique of creative acting. The actor should develop a controlled, responsive and prepared vocal and physical apparatus. This requires extensive training of the actor's voice and body movements. The intensity of this preparation has led to the erroneous view that the Stanislavski method is a rigid system in which improvisation is not permitted. Stanislavski writes, "In order to express a most delicate and largely subconscious life, it is necessary to have control of an unusually responsive, excellently prepared voice and physical apparatus. This apparatus must be ready instantly and exactly to reproduce most delicate and all but intangible feelings with great sensitiveness and directness. That is why an actor of our type is obliged to work so much more than others, both on his inner equipment which creates the life of the past, and also on his outer physical apparatus, which should reproduce the results of the creative work of his emotion with precision."

According to psychoanalytic ego psychology, the ego, in the state of artistic creativity, is well organized and integrated, and functions optimally in arranging unconscious derivatives into artistic forms. Partial regression has the limited purposes of permitting unconscious expression to enter consciousness. Kris (1952) has illustrated this in poetry, where stringencies are as essential as ambiguities to the total creative expression.

Stanislavski's demands for well-developed vocal and physical apparatus would be in the service of having a well-integrated ego participate in the creative expression.

Psychoanalysis has often stressed the relation between acting and various types of exhibitionism. A familiar experience is that of the actor—the "ham," for instance—who is predominantly interested in showing himself to the audiences. In this case, the performance is a form of sexualized exhibitionism. In Stanislavski's concept of creative acting, such performances would come under the heading of exploitation of the given art form. In his system, the actor exhibits and utilizes the body to express "delicate and deep human feelings." Psychoanalysis would consider this as a thoroughgoing sublimation of exhibitionism (in both aim and object); it would also evaluate this form of exhibitionistic body functioning as an autonomous function of the ego. His specific theories and technique of acting are outgrowths and extensions of his specific type of resolution in childhood of exhibitionistic and aggressive conflicts via acting and directing.

In Stanislavski's acting, no actual performance can avoid containing some representational aspects along with the major creative expressions. "Side by side, we see moments of living a part, representing the part, mechanical acting and exploitation. That is why it is necessary for actors to recognize the boundaries of art." Analysis would contend that any instinctual drive, such as the exhibitionistic drive, is partly enacted sexually and partly sublimated. Again it is a matter of degree whether a given exhibitionistic act is neurotic, perverted or sublimated.

Stanislavski left us his theory and technique in his three books, *My Life in Art* (1924), *An Actor Prepares* (1936), and *Building a Character* (1949). Perhaps the most significant and vital part of his legacy is a large international group of disciples and followers—creators in their own right—who perpetuate Stanislavski's system in the theater, dramatic schools, and experimental workshops. In England, the United States and Israel, there are the most enthusiastic students and practitioners of his system. The Moscow Art Theater of today still preserves and perpetuates the teachings and traditions of Stanislavski. Completing this, a number of significant playwrights accept the Stanislavski method as the exclusive route to the true interpretation of their own creations.

Inherent in Stanislavski's nature was a strong sense of paternalism. Gorchakov (1954) writes that Stanislavski paid the members of the Third Studio (a part of the Moscow Art Theater) a surprise visit when its famous director, Vakhtangov, became gravely ill and Stanislavski felt that this group would be seriously upset by this event. In this same book an incident is related in which Gorchakov had to seek help from Stanislavski to meet the financial crisis of the Third Studio. He quotes Stanislavski as follows:

> You did not write me for advice or permission for your tour either. Now you are asking for our help like spoiled children.—We all have children.—I have a son and a daughter (he looked at us sternly, but suddenly softened, we looked so desperate) and they too are the children of the Moscow Art Theatre. I am very excited now and might say unnecessary things but it is because I love the theatre and I am very uneasy about the fate of our new art. The theatre is not only a director and an acting company with well-produced plays; it is the entire ensemble of the theatre—director, administrator, and wardrobe mistress included. Only in this way can the new theatre develop and bring its culture to the audience.

To comprehend the nature and scope of Stanislavski's legacy to the world of theater, we must appreciate the origins of his paternalism and the origins of his generous nature. There is every indication that the optimal opportunities of his early life became the bequeathing character of his maturity. A recapitulation and re-examination of his childhood shapes the key to the vault of his legacy. In the forefront stands the fortunate infantile foundation of his sound ego development due to the optimal nurturing relationship with his mother. To be well taken care of, nurtured and loved in infancy is the precursor and prelude to the future return of these gifts to the outer world from which these bounties had originated.

As the roots of a "giving to" and "loving of the world" nature lie in the quality of the relationship to the mother, so equally does the paternalism lie in the nature of the relationship with the father. Stanislavski's father felt his son's boundless artistic expression to be a fulfillment to the father. In childhood the life of theater (which seemed to encompass almost all of life), Stanislavski was more often than not director to his father and older siblings. The intensity of his childhood sensitivity to theater, merged with the intense love of theater in the Stanislavski household, were the forerunners of a life in which his personal love, his art, his children, and his disciples were fused into an inseparable oneness over which he reigned and administered with the qualities of a loving mother and a mature father.

In "the love affair with the world" that every creative person or genius may have, his personal life and development are crucial to the final outcome. If the creative person has the capacity and conditions emotionally to develop to the stature of a parent in his romance with the world, we are assured that a more permanent and sizable legacy will be left. This legacy is often missing when the creative talent is embodied in an artist who is but a child in love with the (parental) world, rather than an artist who like Stanislavski could grow to be a parent loving his world.

BIBLIOGRAPHY

Abrams, M. H. (1953), *The Mirror and the Lamp*. New York: Oxford Universities Press.

Beres, D. (1956), The Contribution of Psychoanalysis to the Biography of the Artist. Presented at the Midwinter Meeting of the American Psychoanalytic Association, December.

Fenichel, O. (1946), On Acting, *Psa. Quart.*, XV.

Gielgud, J. (1936), Introduction to C. Stanislavski, *An Actor Prepares*. New York: Theatre Arts.

Gorchakov, N. M. (1954), *Stanislavski Directs*. New York: Funk & Wagnall.

Glover, E. (1943), The Concept of Dissociation. *Int. J. Psa.*, XXIV.

Greenacre, P. (1957), The Childhood of the Artist: Libidinal Phase Development and Giftedness, *This Volume*, pp. 47-72.

Grotjahn, M. (1957), *Beyond Laughter*. New York: Blakiston.

Kris, E. (1952), *Psychoanalytic Explorations in Art*. New York: International Universities Press.

Magarshack, D. (1951), *Stanislasky: A Life*. New York: Chanticleer Press.

Stanislavski, C. (1924), *My Life in Art*. New York: Little Brown.

—— (1936), *An Actor Prepares*. New York: Theatre Arts.

—— (1949), *Building a Character*. New York: Theatre Arts.

Weissman, P. (1956), On Pregenital Compulsive Phenomena and the Repetition Compulsion. *J. Am. Psa. Assoc.*, IV.

—— (1957), Conscious and Unconscious Autobiographical Dramas of Eugene O'Neill. *J. Am. Psa. Assoc.*, V.

CONTENTS OF PREVIOUS VOLUMES

VOLUME III/IV, 1949

VOLUME V, 1950

VOLUME VIII, 1953

VOLUME IX, 1954

VOLUME X, 1955

VOLUME XI, 1956